Knowledge Management, Organisational Learning and Sustainability in Tourism

This book explores the link between environmental knowledge management and the sustainability challenges being faced by organisations, individuals, and society. Comprising both theoretical and empirical chapters, the volume describes how knowledge management and organisational learning can help achieve a sustainable tourism sector.

Environmental knowledge has become one of the most important resources for organisations in the current competitive environment. Organisations need to turn their knowledge into agile structures to respond to the challenges resulting from current and future environmental challenges, and from increased competitiveness and social changes. It is therefore important for business decision-making processes to be based on environmental knowledge instead of relying on unconfirmed, often biased information. In this vein, reliable knowledge structures and a framework become an imperative for sustainable development. Development of these innovations shall be addressed through systematic mechanisms such as integration of sustainability and environmental issues, attention to technological innovation, improved absorptive capacity, targeting social challenges as well as investment in human resource development.

The book will be of great value to students and researchers of social sciences with a focus on tourism, human geography, marketing, knowledge management, and environmental studies. The chapters in this book were originally published as a special issue of *Journal of Sustainable Tourism*.

Aurora Martínez-Martínez is Associate Professor in the Department of Business Administration at the Universidad Politécnica de Cartagena, Spain. Originally a CFO, she joined academia after completing her Ph.D. She is a member of the International Association for Knowledge Management (IAKM). Her research is focused on knowledge management, organisational learning, and sustainability.

Juan-Gabriel Cegarra-Navarro is Full Professor at the Technical University of Cartagena, Spain. He also serves as an Associate Editor and Regional Editorial for several flagship journals, including *Knowledge and Process Management* and *Journal of Knowledge Management*. His research interests include knowledge management, technology transfer, innovation, and technology management.

Alexeis Garcia-Perez is Professor of Digital Business and Society at Aston University, Visiting Research Scholar at Georgetown University and Visiting Professor at Coventry University. Alexeis leads research on the challenges related to digital transformation and serves as an advisor for a number of UK and international bodies.

Knowledge Management, Organisational Learning and Sustainability in Tourism

Edited by
Aurora Martínez-Martínez,
Juan-Gabriel Cegarra-Navarro
and Alexeis Garcia-Perez

LONDON AND NEW YORK

First published 2024
by Routledge
4 Park Square, Milton Park, Abingdon, Oxon OX14 4RN

and by Routledge
605 Third Avenue, New York, NY 10158

Routledge is an imprint of the Taylor & Francis Group, an informa business

© 2024 Taylor & Francis

All rights reserved. No part of this book may be reprinted or reproduced or utilised in any form or by any electronic, mechanical, or other means, now known or hereafter invented, including photocopying and recording, or in any information storage or retrieval system, without permission in writing from the publishers.

Trademark notice: Product or corporate names may be trademarks or registered trademarks, and are used only for identification and explanation without intent to infringe.

British Library Cataloguing in Publication Data
A catalogue record for this book is available from the British Library

ISBN13: 978-1-032-62648-2 (hbk)
ISBN13: 978-1-032-62649-9 (pbk)
ISBN13: 978-1-032-62651-2 (ebk)

DOI: 10.4324/9781032626512

Typeset in Myriad Pro
by Newgen Publishing UK

Publisher's Note
The publisher accepts responsibility for any inconsistencies that may have arisen during the conversion of this book from journal articles to book chapters, namely the inclusion of journal terminology.

Disclaimer
Every effort has been made to contact copyright holders for their permission to reprint material in this book. The publishers would be grateful to hear from any copyright holder who is not here acknowledged and will undertake to rectify any errors or omissions in future editions of this book.

Contents

Citation Information vii
Notes on Contributors ix

1 Sustainability knowledge management and organisational learning in tourism: current approaches and areas for future development 1
   Aurora Martínez-Martínez, Juan-Gabriel Cegarra-Navarro and Alexeis Garcia-Perez

2 Corporate social responsibility and strategic knowledge management as mediators between sustainable intangible capital and hotel performance 14
   Patrocinio Carmen Zaragoza-Sáez, Enrique Claver-Cortés, Bartolomé Marco-Lajara and Mercedes Úbeda-García

3 Developing sustainable business models: local knowledge acquisition and tourism lifestyle entrepreneurship 37
   Álvaro Dias, Graça Miranda Silva, Mafalda Patuleia and Maria Rosario González-Rodríguez

4 Greening hotels: does motivating hotel employees promote in-role green performance? The role of culture 57
   Nhat Tan Pham, Charbel Jose Chiappetta Jabbour, Tan Vo-Thanh, Toan Luu Duc Huynh and Clarice Santos

5 Building dynamic capabilities in tourism organisations for disaster management: enablers and barriers 77
   Yawei Jiang, Brent W. Ritchie and Martie-Louise Verreynne

6 A safe space for local knowledge sharing in sustainable tourism: an organisational justice perspective 103
   Raymond Rastegar and Lisa Ruhanen

7 Conceptualising trust as a mediator of pro-environmental tacit knowledge transfer in small and medium sized tourism enterprises 120
   Conor McTiernan, James Musgrave and Chris Cooper

8 Systems thinking to facilitate "double loop" learning in tourism industry: a COVID-19 response strategy 138
   Ayham A. M. Jaaron, Duong Thuy Pham and Marielyn Espiridion Cogonon

9 Responses to vignettes as a methodology to reveal hoteliers' sustainability practices, knowledge and competencies 157
   Cláudia Martins Pantuffi, Janette Brunstein and Mark Edward Walvoord

   Index 176

Citation Information

The chapters in this book were originally published in the *Journal of Sustainable Tourism,* volume 31, issue 4 (2023). When citing this material, please use the original page numbering for each article, as follows:

Chapter 1
Sustainability knowledge management and organisational learning in tourism: current approaches and areas for future development
Aurora Martínez-Martínez, Juan-Gabriel Cegarra-Navarro and Alexeis Garcia-Perez
Journal of Sustainable Tourism, volume 31, issue 4 (2023), pp. 895–907

Chapter 2
Corporate social responsibility and strategic knowledge management as mediators between sustainable intangible capital and hotel performance
Patrocinio Carmen Zaragoza-Sáez, Enrique Claver-Cortés, Bartolomé Marco-Lajara and Mercedes Úbeda-García
Journal of Sustainable Tourism, volume 31, issue 4 (2023), pp. 908–930

Chapter 3
Developing sustainable business models: local knowledge acquisition and tourism lifestyle entrepreneurship
Álvaro Dias, Graça Miranda Silva, Mafalda Patuleia and Maria Rosario González-Rodríguez
Journal of Sustainable Tourism, volume 31, issue 4 (2023), pp. 931–950

Chapter 4
Greening hotels: does motivating hotel employees promote in-role green performance? The role of culture
Nhat Tan Pham, Charbel Jose Chiappetta Jabbour, Tan Vo-Thanh, Toan Luu Duc Huynh and Clarice Santos
Journal of Sustainable Tourism, volume 31, issue 4 (2023), pp. 951–970

Chapter 5
Building dynamic capabilities in tourism organisations for disaster management: enablers and barriers
Yawei Jiang, Brent W. Ritchie and Martie-Louise Verreynne
Journal of Sustainable Tourism, volume 31, issue 4 (2023), pp. 971–996

Chapter 6
A safe space for local knowledge sharing in sustainable tourism: an organisational justice perspective
Raymond Rastegar and Lisa Ruhanen
Journal of Sustainable Tourism, volume 31, issue 4 (2023), pp. 997–1013

Chapter 7
Conceptualising trust as a mediator of pro-environmental tacit knowledge transfer in small and medium sized tourism enterprises
Conor McTiernan, James Musgrave and Chris Cooper
Journal of Sustainable Tourism, volume 31, issue 4 (2023), pp. 1014–1031

Chapter 8
Systems thinking to facilitate "double loop" learning in tourism industry: a COVID-19 response strategy
Ayham A. M. Jaaron, Duong Thuy Pham and Marielyn Espiridion Cogonon
Journal of Sustainable Tourism, volume 31, issue 4 (2023), pp. 1032–1050

Chapter 9
Responses to vignettes as a methodology to reveal hoteliers' sustainability practices, knowledge and competencies
Cláudia Martins Pantuffi, Janette Brunstein and Mark Edward Walvoord
Journal of Sustainable Tourism, volume 31, issue 4 (2023), pp. 1051–1069

For any permission-related enquiries please visit:
www.tandfonline.com/page/help/permissions

Notes on Contributors

Janette Brunstein is Provost for Undergraduate Education, a researcher, and professor of the Stricto Sensu Post Graduation Program in Business Administration from Universidade Presbiteriana Mackenzie, Portugal. Her work is focused on education, learning, and the development of competencies for sustainability in the academic and organisational environments. During the last ten years, she has been coordinating projects within the national scope, supported by the Brazilian Government, which aim to insert the theme of sustainability into Business Administration courses.

Juan-Gabriel Cegarra-Navarro is Full Professor at the Technical University of Cartagena, Spain. He also serves as Associate Editor and Regional Editorial for several flagship journals, including *Knowledge and Process Management* and *Journal of Knowledge Management*. His research interests include knowledge management, technology transfer, innovation, and technology management.

Charbel Jose Chiappetta Jabbour is Global Chair Professor at Lincoln International Business School (UK). Previously, he was a Full Professor at Montpellier Business School (France). He worked for the University of Stirling, UNESP-Sao Paulo State University, and USP-University of Sao Paulo. He is Associated Editor of the prestigious *Journal of Cleaner Production*.

Enrique Claver-Cortés is Professor of Business Administration and Strategic Management at the University of Alicante, Spain. His doctoral dissertation focused on corporate social responsibility, but his primary areas of research cover tourism management and strategic management. He is also a member of the Tourism Research Institute at the University of Alicante. He has taken part in various public projects highlighting, amongst many others, the European project 'Next Tourism Generation Alliance', the competitive project for the creation of the Tourist Observatory of the Valencian Community (Spain), and other private projects. He is the Head of the Department of Management at the University of Alicante.

Marielyn Espiridion Cogonon is a senior student at Thai Nguyen University of Economics and Business Administration (T UEBA) – Thai Nguyen University, Vietnam. She is recipient of the full scholarship from T UEBA in 2019. Her research interests are focused on systems-thinking methodologies in service departments and has greatly contributed to the development of literature review of systems-thinking principles in this article.

Chris Cooper is Professor in the School of Events, Tourism and Hospitality Management. Chris has more than 30 years' experience in tourism and has worked as a researcher and teacher in every region of the world. He has worked at the Universities of Surrey and Bournemouth and established the School of Tourism at the University of Queensland in Australia as the Foundation Chair of Tourism. In 2009 he became Dean and Pro Vice Chancellor at Oxford Brookes University. Chris was

Co-Founder of *Progress in Tourism, Hospitality and Recreation Research*, and the *International Journal of Tourism Research* and is now the Co-Editor of Current *Issues in Tourism*. He is a member of the editorial board for leading tourism, hospitality, and leisure journals and has authored a number of leading text and research books in tourism. He is the co-series editor of the influential Channel View book series '*Aspects of Tourism*'.

Álvaro Dias is Professor of Strategy and Entrepreneurship at Universidade Lusofona and ISCTE-IUL, both in Lisbon, Portugal and a tourism researcher at Universidad de Sevilla, Spain. He has over 26 years of teaching experience. He has had several visiting positions in different countries and institutions including Brazil, Angola, Spain, Poland, and Finland. He regularly teaches in English, Portuguese, and Spanish at undergraduate, master, and doctorate levels, as well as in executive programs.

Alexeis Garcia-Perez is Professor of Digital Business and Society at Aston University, Visiting Research Scholar at Georgetown University and Visiting Professor at Coventry University. Alexeis leads research on the challenges related to digital transformation and serves as an advisor for a number of UK and international bodies.

María Rosario González-Rodríguez is Associate Professor at the University of Seville, Spain. Her research interest on tourism focuses mainly on cultural tourism and authenticity, efficiency and competitiveness in hotel industry and intermediation sector, customer satisfaction, market segmentation analysis in tourism and its strategies of promotion and advertisement, measurement, and analysis of the tourism impact on the economy and society, among other topics. She is currently on the editorial board of *Advances in Hospitality and Tourism Research* (AHTR) and *Electronic Journal of Applied Statistical Analysis* (EJASA), and is a guest Professor at different European, Latin and Indian Universities.

Toan Luu Duc Huynh is a Ph.D. scholar at WHU – Otto Beisheim School of Management, Germany. He has published his research in *Energy Economics*, *Journal of Environmental Management*, among others.

Ayham A. M. Jaaron is Senior Lecturer in Business and Management at the Department of Management and Entrepreneurship of De Montfort University, UK. Before this, he was an Associate Professor at the Industrial Engineering Department of An-Najah National University in Palestine 2010–2019. His research is focused on systems thinking design for service operations design, green manufacturing, green logistics and supply chain management, green human resources management, and sustainability management.

Yawei Jiang is a Ph.D. candidate in the Business School of University of Queensland, Australia. Her research interests include strategic management in tourism crisis and disasters, organisational recovery, resilience in managing environmental uncertainties, and risk communication strategies for tourism destinations.

Bartolomé Marco-Lajara is Professor at the University of Alicante, Spain. His research interests are strategic management and tourism management. He is a member of the Tourism Research Institute at the University of Alicante since its foundation and the main researcher of the European project 'Next Tourism Generation Alliance' and of the public competitive project for the creation of the Tourist Observatory of the Valencian Community (Spain). He has taken part in others public and private projects, such as the development of the strategic plan of the Alicante province for the period 2010–2020. He is the Assistant Dean of the Economics Faculty at the University of Alicante.

Aurora Martínez-Martínez is Associate Professor in the Department of Business Administration at the Universidad Politécnica de Cartagena, Spain. Originally a CFO, she joined academia after completing her Ph.D. She is a member of the International Association for Knowledge Management (IAKM). Her research is focused on knowledge management, organisational learning, and sustainability.

Cláudia Martins Pantuffi holds a doctoral degree in Administration from Mackenzie University, Brazil; holds a master's degree in Psychology from São Marcos University; and is a specialist in Human Resources' consulting and Psychopedagogy. She has worked in Human Resources at National and Multinational organisations. Currently, she teaches subjects related to people management, organisational behaviour, people development, and training in the courses of: Hospitality (Bachelor), Business Administration (Bachelor) and Technology in Human Resources at Senac São Paulo University Centre.

Conor McTiernan is Lecturer in the Department of Tourism at Letterkenny Institute of Technology, Ireland. His research interests are in the role of trust in knowledge transfer within inter-organisational networks. He is establishing a strong publication background in assessing the impact of organisational culture and innovation system structure on knowledge transfer between collaborating organisations. More specifically, in examining if the absence or presence of trust between partners has a mediating impact.

James Musgrave is Head of the UK Centre for Events Management in the School of Events, Tourism and Hospitality Management, Leeds Beckett University, UK. James has extensive experience in education and training across several sectors such as events, manufacturing, and hospitality. His areas of interest are in corporate social responsibility, pro-environmental behaviour change, strategy and consumer insights. James has provided training and education across the world including USA, China, and India and continues to be invited to talk on areas related to Sustainable Events Management. He was Director of Networking for EuroCHRIE – 2018 and 2019. He is co-author of various textbooks, contributor to many book chapters and regularly provides reviews for journals.

Mafalda Patuleia has a Ph.D. in Tourism from the Faculty of Economics of the University of Algarve, Spain. She is the Head of Tourism Department of the Lusofona Group and Dean of the Higher Institute of New Professions (INP), where she also teaches, among other subjects, Tourism Studies and Sociology of Leisure and Tourism. She is President of the Technical and Scientific Council of INP. She also teaches at various national and foreign universities and writes in several newspapers related to tourism.

Duong Thuy Pham is Lecturer at Thai Nguyen University of Economics and Business Administration – Thai Nguyen University, Vietnam. She has also been recognised as an international scholar who has worked as a consultant/speaker/jury in the Department of Leisure and Recreation Management, College of Management, Asia University, Taichung, Taiwan since 2019. Her research interests are focused on the areas of hospitality management, leisure and recreation management, corporate social responsibility (CSR), entrepreneurship, mass customised services, operational management, and systems thinking principles applied for service innovations.

Nhat Tan Pham is Lecturer at International University – Vietnam National University HCMC, Vietnam. His research interests are human resource management (HRM), sustainable HRM, Digital HRM, and sustainable tourism. He has published his research in *Tourism Management*, *International Journal of Hospitality Management*, *Journal of Environmental Management*, *Safety Science*, among others.

Raymond Rastegar is Lecturer and Researcher in Tourism at the UQ Business School, University of Queensland, Australia. His research focuses on sustainable tourism development in developing countries with specific interest in local community livelihood, participation, empowerment, and environmental conservation. Recent research projects have investigated the impacts of tourism at the local level and delivered new insights into the tourism phenomenon to advocate a more just and sustainable tourism future.

Brent W. Ritchie is Associate Dean (Research) in the Faculty of Business, Economics and Law and a professor at the University of Queensland, Australia. His research interests are associated with tourism risk management. His work on organisations explores risk attitudes and response strategies to effectively respond and recover from crises and disasters.

Lisa Ruhanen is Professor and the Director of Education at University of Queensland Business School, Australia. She has been involved in almost 30 academic and consultancy research projects in Australia and overseas. Her research areas include sustainable tourism destination policy and planning, climate change, and Indigenous tourism.

Clarice Santos is Lecturer in organisational behaviour at the Middlesex University, UK. Her research interests are the work–life interface, organisational policies, cross-cultural studies, etc. She has published her research in *Employee Relations*, *Asia Pacific Journal of Human Resources*, among others.

Graça Miranda Silva is Assistant Professor in the Lisbon School of Economics & Management (ISEG) at Universidade de Lisboa, Portugal. She earned her Ph.D. in Industrial Engineering, majoring in Quality Management, from Faculdade de Ciencias e Tecnologia (FCT-UNL). Her research primarily focuses on quality management (e.g., TQM), innovation management (e.g., radical and incremental innovation, product and process innovation), and sustainability (e.g., green supply chain management, social and environmental practices). Her research has appeared in *International Journal of Operations & Production Management*, *Business Strategy and the Environment*, *Industrial Marketing Management*, *Journal of Business Research*, and *Journal of International Marketing* among others.

Mercedes Úbeda-García is Professor at the University of Alicante, Spain. She is a member of the Tourism Research Institute in this University. Her research interests are in the areas of organisational design, human resource management, knowledge management, and tourism management. She has taken part in several public projects highlighting the European project 'Next Tourism Generation Alliance', the competitive project for the creation of the Tourist Observatory of the Valencian Community (Spain), and other private projects. She is the author of several books, book chapters and international articles related to teaching methodology, human resource management, and strategy. She is the Head of the Official Master in Tourism at University of Alicante.

Martie-Louise Verreynne is Associate DVC Research and Innovation and Professor of Innovation at RMIT University, Australia. Her research in innovation and resilience focuses on how firms leverage capabilities and networks to gain a competitive edge.

Tan Vo-Thanh is Associate Professor at Excelia Business School, France. His recent research has been published in *Information & Management*, *Journal of Business Research*, *International Journal of Hospitality Management*, *Journal of Sustainable Tourism*, *Journal of Environmental Management*, among others.

Mark Edward Walvoord is Assistant Director of the Student Transformative Learning Record in the Center for Excellence in Transformative Teaching and Learning at the University of Central Oklahoma, USA; and an instructor of Biology at the University of Oklahoma. Since 2002 he has worked in higher education in biology education, student services, and faculty development. Mark's publications and presentations cover zoology, biology lab teaching, peer learning and tutoring, educational technologies, and transformative learning. He serves as president of the Oklahoma Compost and Sustainability Association and is on the boards of directors for three other non-profits: Partners for Madagascar, Association for Biology Laboratory Education, and Joiners, Inc.

Patrocinio Carmen Zaragoza-Sáez is Senior Lecturer at the University of Alicante, Spain. Her research interests are focused on knowledge management, intellectual capital, international management, and tourism management. She has taken part in several public projects highlighting the European project 'Next Tourism Generation Alliance' and the competitive project for the creation of a Blue Print Book for the Tourism in the Valencian Community (Spain).

Sustainability knowledge management and organisational learning in tourism: current approaches and areas for future development

Aurora Martínez-Martínez ⓘ, Juan-Gabriel Cegarra-Navarro and Alexeis Garcia-Perez

ABSTRACT
Tourism is one of the major drivers of socio-economic growth. For tourism organisations to remain competitive, they must be able to adapt to the current dynamic scenario where the sector operates. Organisational learning strategies can provide the sector with the knowledge required to transform tourism research and intellectual property into capabilities for the industry and stimulate tourism models with a minimal effect on the environment. Knowledge management involves managing tacit and explicit information in a way that ensures it is available where and when needed. From a knowledge management perspective, environmental learning refers to the processes of acquiring, distributing and using knowledge of the natural environment, involving the processes of socialisation, externalisation, combination and internalisation of knowledge and its central aim is to improve performance. This article describes how knowledge management and organisational learning can help to achieve a sustainable tourism sector. Sustainability in this context is understood as efforts to progress simultaneously in environmental, societal and economic development. The article argues that the principles of sustainable tourism lead to both improved strategies and avenues for future research, provided they are informed and supported by learning and knowledge management; value co-creation; co-operation and trust-building; corporate social responsibility and pro-environmental behaviour.

Introduction

Over the past years, scholars and practitioners from all sectors have increasingly viewed knowledge as one of the key resources for organisations to succeed in the current socioeconomic environment (Akhavan et al., 2016). Knowledge management (KM) has evolved significantly as a discipline, and its relevance for organisations has increased in last years (Bolisani & Bratianu, 2018). Firms from all sectors, including tourism, have learned that KM leads to organisational learning (OL), the creation of new ideas, and innovation in products, services, processes, technologies, and projects (Wang & Noe, 2010). Implementing a KM approach can support tourism organisations in their efforts to learn and address the challenges related to environmental change. KM is the key antecedent for the innovation capability of organisations (Baker & Yusof, 2017), and OL can help tourism companies become more resilient and better able to cope with uncertainties (Leta & Chan, 2021).

If one particular sector other than healthcare can be singled out as having been significantly hit by the COVID-19 pandemic, that sector was tourism. Local and national lockdowns, limited movement, and curfews, among others, reduced tourism activity to historic levels during the COVID-19 pandemic (Gössling et al., 2021; Sigala, 2020). The pandemic brought major changes to our daily lives, and countries that were by 2019 facing the challenge of tourism saturation have since had to deal with a total absence of tourists (Jones & Comfort, 2020). In this dynamic environment where the tourism sector looks for new business models to reply to the demands of customers and other stakeholders.

OL is presented as a core strategy, in line with a continuous improvement of their processes and operations (Edwards, 2022). OL can be defined as a process that develops over time, and links information to knowledge utilisation and improved performance (Boiral, 2002; Senge, 1997; Sun & Scott, 2006). A learning organisation is one that is skilled at building, developing, and transferring knowledge and changing its behaviour to indicate new knowledge and understandings (Jaaron et al., 2021). Although COVID-19 triggered to consideration of organisational learning as many organisations' core strategy, this is also partly linked to forced learning and has some negative consequences, for example, lack of culture, unknowledge how to redesign processes to adapt to COVID-19 or lack of IT resources.

As the sector recovers, it seems apparent that the demand for less crowded and more sustainable destinations will grow, as will the demand for tourism products with greater flexibility for changes and cancellations (Vanapalli et al., 2021). Hygiene measures, in both facilities and food, will also need to increase. In addition, tourists will pay more attention to issues that did not seem as important in the past, such as airlines' air filters. From the point of view of marketing, air and water quality will be key elements to be considered. The demand for adventure activities in nature and outdoors will grow. Travel and luggage insurance policies will also be valuable marketing tools. Information and communication technologies are also expected to impact the sector positively, reducing charges and increasing competition. Accommodation options will be sought with the availability of computers and printers to combine vacations with work (Sharma et al., 2021).

Based on the above analysis, it can be argued that knowledge in itself does not hold a competitive advantage unless tourism organisations are willing to not only use that knowledge but also renew it and adapt it to the different contexts where it brings value. In this vein, KM can help tourism organisations to see in current sustainability concerns a scope for opportunities rather than threats, and face sustainability challenges with optimism. Both large companies and SMEs need adaptability and an open culture to enable the capitalisation of their knowledge assets to survive and remain competitive (Jones & Comfort, 2020; Singjai et al., 2018). This way, not every impact from the COVID-19 pandemic will necessarily be harmful to the tourism sector. Opportunities will arise, and the companies that know how to adapt and change will be those that know how to make efficient use of updated knowledge. Other companies may disappear or simply endure an uncertain future. Stakeholders' expectations of new skills, knowledge, capabilities, and qualifications from the tourism sector make this an extraordinary moment for the application of KM and OL strategies and tools in order to reduce the environmental influence of the tourism industry and improve its sustainability (Jaaron et al., 2021; Sigala, 2020).

The term "sustainability" refers to balanced development between environment, society and economy (Horng et al., 2017). It is well known that natural resources are declining, and action must be taken now to reduce and reverse the degradation of the environment. In this regard, the use of environmental knowledge has attracted the interest of diverse stakeholder groups, including both organisations and society as a whole (Dumay et al., 2016). KM may help tourism companies to innovate and search for new, alternative solutions to maintain and improve the quality of sustainable services (Rogers, 2012). In doing so, KM plays an essential role in allowing business decision-making processes to be based on verified information instead of relying on unconfirmed, often biased information from a variety of sources (Barley et al., 2018; Kim & Kim, 2017). The main focus of this Editorial Letter is environmental sustainability.

With the aim of advancing the current debate on the subject, this special issue explores the potential links between KM, OL and the sustainability challenges faced by the tourism industry. The selected studies provide new insights into how sustainability opportunities can be turned into innovations by using systematic mechanisms which are based on organisation learning processes at individual, group, organisational and societal levels (Lam, 2000). The special issue seeks to advance scholarly understanding of key areas of research and practice, including integration of sustainability and environmental issues, consideration of technological innovation, improved organisational learning, targeted responses to social challenges, and investment in human resource development for sustainability in tourism (Binder, 2019; Salehzadeh et al., 2021).

Organisational learning and knowledge management

The COVID-19 pandemic has had a significant impact on environmental matters. While certain issues such as CO_2 emissions have had a lower environmental impact due to a reduction in travel, others including the use of plastic, an increased number of single-use products, or waste derived from products such as personal protective equipment have experienced a tangible increase (Kang et al., 2021). While the tourism sector is perceived as a driver of recovery for local economies, it is also a major contributor to global climate change. The current socio-economic context, defined by the COVID-19 pandemic, therefore becomes an ideal scenario for the tourism industry to learn, unlearn and relearn how to deal with the current challenges, as a mechanism to foster eco-innovations in the sector (Jaaron et al., 2021).

This special issue has been conceived to address the correlations between the sustainability challenges currently faced by organisations, individuals and society, and the domains of KM and OL (Huber, 1991). To that aim, the issue includes theoretical and empirical research that explores a range of topics of relevance for the domains of sustainability knowledge. In the context of this special issue sustainability knowledge refers to the understanding by individuals and organisations of the social, ethical and environmental issues related to sustainability (Adams & Lamont, 2003; Lee, 2010). A key resource for organisations in the current competitive environment, sustainability knowledge can be better known as the grade to which an individual or organisation has become and remains aware of and concerned with ecological and socio-cultural issues (Boiral, 2002). In the current literature, the concept is often used to refer to the stocks of data, information and knowledge resources (i.e. sustainability memories), which have been collected by using the organisational knowledge structures (Day et al., 2001) and OL processes (Aramburu et al., 2006).

Key to understanding the concept of sustainability memories are the differences between knowledge stocks and knowledge flows. At a particular point in time, the knowledge that has not yet been turned into innovation can be considered a knowledge stock (Dias et al., 2020). If, on the other hand, the knowledge has been adapted and used over a period of time, it is said to have become a knowledge flow (Roper & Hewitt-Dundas, 2015). A key area of KM research and practice is a model for knowledge stocks and knowledge flows that emphasises the imperative of absorptive capacity, knowledge transfer and knowledge exchange as a strategic management function in the tourism industry (McTiernan et al., 2021). As Dias et al., 2020 point out, knowledge spillovers that stem from those processes allow entrepreneurs in the tourism industry to discover and exploit opportunities.

The considerations above point towards the need for organisations to turn their knowledge assets into agile structures to answer to the socio-economic challenges that emerge as a result of current and future sustainability-related issues, increased business competition and continuous social changes (Jiang et al., 2021; Rogers, 2012; Vihari et al., 2019). In the presence of a framework for their exploitation, reliable organisational knowledge structures become a key driver for sustainable development (Butowski, 2019; Hall, 2019). However, their exploitation requires the deliberate integration of sustainability issues, improved absorptive capacity, aiming at social challenges, and investment in human resource development (Hair Awang et al., 2013).

It should also be noted that lack of resources can slow down companies' sustainability-oriented innovation and value creation strategies (Ma et al., 2017). This includes, for example, limited financial resources, resistance to change, lack of intellectual property rights, resistance from organisational participants, reduced internal knowledge, lack of in-house knowledge or lack of information and knowledge about technologies. Inter-organisational collaborations could help reduce the impact of the current scarcity of resources. Co-creation describes a joint effort to create value, involving firms and their stakeholders. It is an inclusive and participatory process that can result in different sets of commercial, intellectual, or collaborative values (Pantuffi et al., 2021). Co-creation of value is a process that aims to be goal-oriented and collaborative towards learning and achieving goals of common interest. Some motivations to collaborate can include the desire for an improved reputation, financial performance, social performance (Ja-Shen et al., 2017), emotional drivers (Font et al., 2021), and lack of resources or environmental knowledge (Loureiro et al., 2020).

In times of high uncertainty such as the COVID-19 pandemic, knowledge sharing strategies implemented in collaboration with stakeholders can help with both stocks and flows of knowledge in organisations from most sectors (Rupietta & Backes-Gellner, 2019). Under this framework, companies with embedded knowledge and learning structures are more flexible and able to respond to market changes quicker and more effectively than those with less dynamic structures (Jiang et al., 2021). With dynamic and rapid changes in the tourism sector, a significant volume of knowledge has become outdated and therefore needs to be replaced with new knowledge (Bossle et al., 2016). It also means that the current knowledge base of organisations will in time prove insufficient. In these circumstances, unlearning can help the tourism sector discard old and outdated knowledge structures to make way for new knowledge (Zhao & Wang, 2020). Looking towards the future, this also implies relearning new processes or services for tourism in a context of continuous improvement (Jaaron et al., 2021).

From the studies selected in this special issue, it can be inferred that OL and KM are complementary and support each other in efforts to achieve the desired sustainability goals. Easterby-Smith and Lyles (2003) defined OL with a focus on the process of acquiring and using new knowledge, whereas the focus of KM strategies would be on the the objective and subjective forms of knowledge acquired by the organisation (Alavi & Leidner, 2001). The connection between both concepts has also been based on a perception of OL as the ultimate target of KM strategies. From both perspectives, OL becomes one of the most important mechanisms through which organisations can sustainably improve the utilisation of knowledge. KM helps the business understand the needs and expectations of its stakeholders and—in the process, update their own knowledge structures in line with those requirements. Instead, OL helps develop internal training programs in tourism companies in order to overcome challenges such as limited understanding of environmental regulations or a low motivation in the workforce to engage in the implementation of sustainable strategies.

Sustainable knowledge management in tourism

Sustainability helps reinforce the capacity of organisations to generate competitive advantage while caring for the environment (Nieves & Haller, 2014; Zaragoza-Sáez et al., 2020). It is, however, a broad and complex concept that involves both 'environmental' and 'sustainable' knowledge. Despite the fact that both concepts are often used interchangeably, 'environmental' and 'sustainable' knowledge do not refer to the same processes or activities. While sustainable knowledge could be understood as knowing what is necessary to perform an activity over time without damaging the environment or the resources necessary to carry out the activity (i.e. the activity is maintained by itself), environmental knowledge is the knowledge that individuals have of themselves and of the environment that surrounds them (Myung, 2018).

The above considerations lead us to mention that while sustainable knowledge belongs to the company and is the result of (not only but mostly) KM strategies (Dayan et al., 2017), environmental knowledge belongs to the individual and is mostly the result of OL strategies. However, as the studies in this special issue suggest, both environmental and sustainable knowledge are flow variables. That is, they feed off each other and the importance of one over the other varies over time. For this reason, continuous feedback between OL and KM is required to maintain the stock and flow of environmental knowledge (Obeso et al., 2020). However, the literature supports that knowledge flows from individual to groups, to intra and inter-organisational levels and in opposite directions. Individuals' knowledge is also the source of the groups, intra and inter-organisational knowledge. Besides, many individuals learning is determined by their personal traits and behaviours, and they learn even when their companies do not necessarily appreciate or are concerned about OL strategies (Grieves, 2008) .

Sustainable knowledge management can be the result of an appropriate balance between OL and KM. While OL allows tourism workers to pose concepts and questions with a wider environmental perspective, KM allows tourism organisations to identify environmental opportunities and benefit from them. Under this framework, sustainable knowledge management is the bridge that allows managers and public administrators to link employees' environmental knowledge with the sustainable knowledge of the company. This is in broad agreement with the conclusions of authors such as Rastegar and Ruhanen (2021), who assert that knowledge sharing builds environmental knowledge of natural disasters, and plays a key role in sustainability, hence building capacity for sustainable tourism. In fact, sustainable knowledge management strategies focus on recognising the role of environmental concerns in society and the need to reorganise resources to meet environmental requirements and expectations (Po-Shin & Li-Hsing, 2009).

Environmental knowledge has also been identified as local knowledge (i.e. a body of knowledge and practices related to a specific geographical location, culture, or tradition), which can be transmitted from one group to another and evolves over time (Cuaton & Su, 2020). In the case of local stakeholders' knowledge, it has the potential to contribute to the organisational environment or the context of the destination. Further, local knowledge has been found to play a critical role in encouraging knowledge sharing across different stakeholder groups (Kim & Lee, 2013).

Based on the conclusions from research reported in this special issue, this study considers that while sustainable knowledge involves the discarding of certain existing values, behaviours and practices by members of a specific community, environmental knowledge involves learning the skills of co-operation: how to negotiate with peers, give and take, collective problem-solving (Sessa & London, 2006). Therefore, the sharing of sustainable knowledge is also important for the purposes of sustainability (Hair Awang et al., 2013; Jiang et al., 2021). A company's capability to update, integrate, and reconfigure its operations to align its current knowledge with sustainable demands, will allow it to be strategically successful.

The above considerations lead us to argue that sustainable knowledge management strategies are as important in the local contexts as they are at an international level. Local trust is essential if tourism managers are to support efforts to transfer environmental tacit knowledge across the organisation (McTiernan et al., 2021). For it to be effective, knowledge transfer requires a degree of social relationships having been previously established among knowledge actors. In a knowledge transfer process, social capital plays an important role. Internal and external collaboration between parties contributes to creating social capital and to knowledge transfer

(Jiang et al., 2021). The academic literature also refers to the perception of sustainable knowledge management as a valuable tool to examine individuals' knowledge sharing behaviours, and hence a new avenue for research in the sustainable tourism domain. The applicability of the above principles to the context of sustainable tourism and their potential for future research are also explored in the special issue.

Papers appearing in the special issue reflect developments in the field from a more traditional view of knowledge and its definition, such as strategies for value creation based on the concept of tacit knowledge as defined by Nonaka (1994). Given that tourism lifestyle entrepreneurs are often associated with a place, tacit local knowledge is likely to have a higher strategic value. Besides, tourism lifestyle entrepreneurs could be benefited from including knowledge stickiness, mainly while covering the local tacit knowledge and its sharing. Not only is local knowledge difficult to access and replicate by competitors, but it can only be accessed through impersonal interactions, often in the right location (Dias et al., 2020). To address the challenges of local knowledge conversion—as per Nonaka's SECI model, Dias et al., 2020) have proposed unique mechanisms to acquire local knowledge in the context of tourism lifestyle entrepreneurs. Socialisation can contribute to minimising or avoiding internal barriers to applied environmental knowledge, a principle that has been further explored in this special issue. In line with previous research (Dias et al., 2020; Hallak et al., 2015), the interpersonal links between tourism lifestyle entrepreneurs have been found to contribute to sustainable business models that lead to greater innovativeness and self-efficacy in the sector.

External changes, such as a change in customers' expectations regarding corporate social responsibility, could serve as a motivation for managers to seek opportunities to engage in the creation and nurturing of pro-environmental behaviours (Pham et al., 2020; Pomering & Dolnicar, 2009; Zaragoza-Sáez et al., 2020), which can be defined as "deliberate and effective actions that respond to social and individual requirements whose expected consequence is the protection of the environment" (Páramo, 2017, pp. 43). For example, in the context of hotels, it is important to motivate employees to provide suggestions for green practices that lead to environmental protection. Management could also volunteer for engagement in environmental actions and encourage stakeholders to implement green behaviours in the workplace (Pham et al., 2020). In other words, environmental knowledge, skills, and awareness facilitate pro-environmental behaviour and green practices in hotels (Juvan & Dolnicar, 2014; Myung, 2018). This dimension of sustainability in tourism has received attention in this special issue, in research that found that green practices motivate employees, drive environmental knowledge sharing and also contribute to environmental strategies of hotels.

As unexpected and unpredictable natural, health and economic crises have a direct influence on the tourism industry (Ritchie & Jiang, 2019), tourism organisations increasingly need to develop their dynamic capabilities (Winter, 2003). Dynamic capabilities provide the tourism organisation with mechanisms to strategically adapt, build or reconfigure their internal and external competencies, resources, and routines, to address rapidly changing environments, which can help tourism companies to meet future needs (Teece et al., 1997). Therefore, resources and dynamic capabilities such as culture, organisational agility (Walter, 2021), leadership or knowledge (Grant, 1996) can enable the organisation and the sector to improve their performance in a sustainable manner (Kabongo & Boiral, 2017).

The literature on the subject also contains reports that suggest that businesses, especially SMEs, barely harness the knowledge gained from past experiences into crisis preparedness practices and strategies. Tourism SMEs face limitations and barriers that prevent them from knowing and being willing to cope with change and adapt quickly to unexpected situations (Jaaron et al., 2021; Jiang et al., 2021). In uncertain times, identifying enablers and barriers has been found to be a competitive advantage for companies and the environment (Jiang et al., 2021). The COVID-19 crisis should become a mechanism for reorganizing the tourism industry and offerings through continuous learning processes (Jaaron et al., 2021; Pantuffi et al., 2021).

A synopsis of the methods of research included in the special issue

A significant contribution of this special issue is the diversity of methodologies applied to OL and KM in order to achieve different goals, with particular emphasis on the protection of the environment. The special issue addresses key KM and OL challenges and their theoretical and practical implications for sustainable tourism strategies and tools through a combination of quantitative and qualitative research methods. A range of methods are employed, including case studies, theoretical and applied approaches, as well as the use of techniques for complex modelling in social science and business research, such as PLS-SEM, in quantitative analyses. Vignettes are also applied to acquire the learning and competencies established in the perspective of the tourism organisation (Gherardi, 2012; Pantuffi et al., 2021).

Conceptual frameworks developed with qualitative methods are proposed in the special issue, to provide a conceptual basis for appreciating different principles and worldviews and promote local knowledge identification and assimilation in sustainable tourism. For example, Rastegar and Ruhanen (2021) draw upon the work of Jabareen (2008) to address multidisciplinary phenomena linked to knowledge management and sustainability. Rastegar and Ruhanen develop a broad, sector-wide approach to an increased understanding of tourism sustainability, based on principles drawn from the knowledge management domain including knowledge sharing, organisational justice, and local knowledge systems.

There is a need to better understand how administrators of small and medium-sized tourism enterprises obtain, absorb, and use pro-environmental tacit knowledge in practice (McTiernan et al., 2021). McTiernan et al. (2021) follow Jaakkola (2020) to examine the connection between pro-environmental knowledge, trust, and tacit knowledge transfer in a tourism-related context. McTiernan, Musgrave and Cooper research the relationship between critical elements such as trust, self-efficacy, social standards, the credibility of knowledge sources and social capital, approaching these as a combination of psycho-social elements, both asynchronous and context-dependent. Arguably, maintaining and fostering these antecedents will reduce resistance to the transmission of pro-environmental knowledge in developing the elements of inter-organisational knowledge transfer to manage psycho-social conditions of trust-based decisions in tourism.

Qualitative studies have attempted to understand the mediating role of sustainable intangible capital between hotel performance, corporate social responsibility, and strategic knowledge (Zaragoza-Sáez et al., 2020). Zaragoza-Sáez et al. (2020) conducted a qualitative study involving a sample of 120 respondents from Spain. In terms of the methodology of research, this study provides statistical techniques to learn how to extrapolate to other studies. Using the data from interviews with CEOs and HR Directors, Zaragoza-Sáez et al. (2020), identified relevant aspects for future research into intangible assets, such as defining corporate social responsibility from the triple (the economic, social, and environmental) bottom line.

Local knowledge acquisition and tourism lifestyle entrepreneurship could facilitate sustainable business models in tourism as environmental knowledge becomes a facilitator of tourism lifestyle entrepreneurs (Dias et al., 2020). Dias et al. (2020) in their mixed-methods study based on a sample of tourism entrepreneurs in Portugal and Spain used the variance-based SEM methods and SmartPLS to find that entrepreneurial communication has a positive effect on the innovativeness and self-efficacy of tourism lifestyle entrepreneurs (Dias et al., 2020). Value co-creation of experiences between local stakeholders and communities is seen as key to creating valuable knowledge for tourism and setting economic and non-economic goals (Dias et al., 2020). Co-creation and use of local knowledge provide services and experiences that are unique and difficult for competitors to replicate (Agrawal et al., 2015). The framework and qualitative study developed by the authors not only make a significant contribution to the extant literature on the subject but also open new avenues for research into value co-creation in other contexts.

The stakeholders' strategy to quickly respond to the impact of the Covid-19 pandemic was found to have a positive impact on other tourism stakeholders. In this editorial letter stakeholders in tourism organisations are considered anyone who is involved with a particular project, organisation or business. Jaaron et al. (2021) used case study research and Jiang et al. (2021) used 40 in-depth interviews of tourism business operators and other stakeholders to explore tourism in contexts such as the luxury cruise business in Vietnam during the peak of the Covid-19 outbreak. The findings were also presented from tourism organisations' perspectives highlighting the resources to develop dynamic capabilities. The authors found that changes made to the operation of tourism organisations during the crisis and other lessons learned from the pandemic enabled stakeholders to generate new services with improved health protocols (Gössling et al., 2021).

Finally, the application of vignettes to OL and KM is a novel research method which allows the researcher to obtain perceptions and opinions from responses or comments to stories that represent different scenarios or contexts. This method was also used as a practice-based lens that serves to study the reasoning behind sustainability decisions. In this special issue, vignettes are stories by specialists that address the research question from the perspective of social and environmental problems (Pantuffi et al., 2021).

Conclusions

The current socio-economic context presents significant challenges for the tourism sector and the tourism organisation. In addition to meeting an increase in demand as the world emerges from a pandemic, the sector will be required to balance the creation of value with a significant increase in environmental, social and economic expectations and standards. Confronted with this unique context, the tourism sector is today expected to transform its business models, taking into consideration concepts such as environmental knowledge and sustainable knowledge, which support the sustainability expectations of the new tourist. Therefore, this study contributes to the vast literature devoted to sustainability by proposing sustainable knowledge management as a tool to achieve a sustainable balance between OL and KM.

Individuals' and societies' relationships with the environment and their understanding of environmental challenges have made sustainable KM one of the most significant resources for tourism organisations. From the perspective of the papers selected for this special issue, sustainable KM takes advantage of the opportunities that the current context offers to organisations in the tourism sector, while simultaneously enabling learning processes with the aim of taking advantage of the skills and attitudes of the tourism workforce. This result is significant in the current discussion surrounding the link between OL and KM, and confirms what authors such as Fai Pun and Nathai-Balkissoon (2011) mean when they argue that boundary objects may be useful to incorporate the theories of KM and OL into organisational practice. A boundary object is a class of information that can be used in different ways by different communities (Kanwal et al., 2019). Therefore, this editorial letter provides a better understanding of 'sustainability' as a boundary object by helping focus the efforts of multiple organisations into the common, wider aim of sustainability.

The OL and KM fields can be studied through a combination of quantitative and qualitative research methods including case studies, theoretical and applied approaches, as well as the use of techniques for complex modelling in social science and business research, such as PLS-SEM, in quantitative analyses. The special issue addresses key knowledge management and organisational learning challenges and their theoretical and practical implications in sustainable tourism strategies and tools. In this special issue tourism and KM scholars can find examples of how to deal with bias problems; however, in future work in this area, we encourage researchers to follow the measured latent marker variable (MLMV) method to identify possible problems of common method variance (CMV) (Chin et al., 2013). Since endogeneity may arise when non-random samples are selected and/or some important variables are omitted in the model (Antonakis et al.,

2010), we also encourage authors to follow the recommendations of Hult et al. (2018) to test endogeneity issues.

Qualitative studies with a vignettes approach are also applied to describe the learning and competencies developed in the context of the tourism organisation (Gherardi, 2012; Pantuffi et al., 2021), which is a novel methodology when applied to KM and OL. Vignettes are used to capture the lessons learned by hotels through stories and a clear focus. Their findings are derived from the inclusion of a variety of stakeholders and represent social and environmental sustainability dilemmas, problems or disruptions which are valid in the context of other tourism institutions (Hughes & Huby, 2004; Pantuffi et al., 2021).

From the different methodologies employed in this special issue, it can be asserted that the variables that support OL, KM and the sustainability of the tourism sector are latent and complex variables, and to a large extent are only theoretical constructs created by scientists (i.e. artificial variables). This might mean that only by using different techniques is it possible to avoid bias problems and extrapolate the results to different contexts. For this reason, future studies should focus on analysing the nature of the constructs, for example, composites versus factors, for example, composites versus factors. Related to composites and factors, while PLS is an estimation approach that can operationalize latent variables as composites, covariance-based structural equation modelling usually use factors. Composites are latent variables whose indicators do not necessarily share a common cause, while a factor is a latent variable whose indicators necessarily share a common cause. PLS-PM does not fit a common factor model to the data, it rather fits a composite model. It is also important to note the similarity and parallelism between the variables studied in this special issue, for example, environmental knowledge and sustainable knowledge. Future studies from the methodological point of view should also address the discriminant validity of the constructs under investigation.

As the tourism organisation becomes concerned with ecological issues, new opportunities emerge for the tourism sector to improve its strategies and operations. This special issue has been developed to bring together the experience of knowledge management and sustainability scholars and practitioners to address these and other challenges facing the tourism sector. The articles in the special issue explore, from a variety of perspectives and in different contexts, how sustainability can rise to the stature of the socio-economic importance of tourism for countries and regions around the world.

The authors in the special issue have exposed solutions based on co-operation and trust-building mechanisms, on learning, unlearning and relearning strategies, on absorptive and desorptive capacities, on knowledge transfer and value co-creation in the management of tourism destinations. More than established solutions, these concepts become avenues for further research as tourism scholars and practitioners collaborate with those from other subjects to address sustainability challenges. It is hoped that this special issue will contribute to the current debate on how KM and OL can align with and support the way the tourism organisation works today and in the future, helping the sector meet the growing sustainability expectations of business and society.

Disclosure statement

Ministerio de Economía, Industria y Competitividad of the Spanish Government for financing the research project ECO2017-88987-R (MINECO/ FEDER;UE), cofinanced from the European Union FEDER funds.

Funding

This work was supported by Ministerio de Econom?ı a, Industria y Competitividad of the Spanish Government;Cofinanced from the European Union FEDER funds.

ORCID

Aurora Martínez-Martínez http://orcid.org/0000-0001-5579-8142

References

Adams, G., & Lamont, B. (2003). Knowledge management systems and developing sustainable competitive advantage. *Journal of Knowledge Management*, *7*(2), 142–154. https://doi.org/10.1108/13673270310477342[Mismatch]

Agrawal, A. K., Kaushik, A. K., & Rahman, Z. (2015). Co-creation of social value through integration of stakeholders. *Procedia - Social and Behavioral Sciences*, *189*, 442–448. https://doi.org/10.1016/j.sbspro.2015.03.198

Akhavan, P., Ebrahim, N. A., Fetrati, M. A., & Pezeshkan, A. (2016). Major trends in knowledge management research: A bibliometric study. *Scientometrics*, *107*(3), 1249–1264. https://doi.org/10.1007/s11192-016-1938-x

Alavi, M., & Leidner, D. E. (2001). Review: Knowledge management and knowledge management systems: Conceptual foundations and research issues. *MIS Quarterly: Management Information Systems*, *25*(1), 107–136. https://doi.org/10.2307/3250961

Antonakis, J., Bendahan, S., Jacquart, P., & Lalive, R. (2010). On making causal claims: A review and recommendations. *The Leadership Quarterly*, *21*(6), 1086–1120. https://doi.org/10.1016/j.leaqua.2010.10.010

Aramburu, N., Sáenz, J., & Rivera, O. (2006). Organizational learning, change process, and evolution of management systems. *The Learning Organization*, *13*(5), 434–454. https://doi.org/10.1108/09696470610679974

Baker, M. B., & Yusof, Z. M. (2017). A framework for knowledge sharing in ERP system usage in small and medium enterprises: A preliminary review. *International Journal of Business Information Systems*, *24*(3), 387–398. https://doi.org/10.1504/IJBIS.2017.082041

Barley, W. C., Treem, J. W., & Kuhn, T. (2018). Valuing multiple trajectories of knowledge: A critical review and agenda for knowledge management research. *Academy of Management Annals*, *12*(1), 278–317. https://doi.org/10.5465/annals.2016.0041

Binder, P. (2019). A network perspective on organizational learning research in tourism and hospitality: A systematic literature review. *International Journal of Contemporary Hospitality Management*, *31*(7), 2602–2625. https://doi.org/10.1108/IJCHM-04-2017-0240

Boiral, O. (2002). Tacit knowledge and environmental management. *Long Range Planning*, *35*(3), 291–317. https://doi.org/10.1016/S0024-6301(02)00047-X

Bolisani, E., & Bratianu, C. (2018). The emergence of knowledge management. In *Emergent knowledge strategies: Strategic thinking in knowledge management* (pp. 23–47). Springer International Publishing. https://doi.org/10.1007/978-3-319-60657-6_2

Bossle, M. B., Dutra De Barcellos, M., Vieira, L. M., & Sauvée, L. (2016). The drivers for adoption of eco-innovation. *In Journal of Cleaner Production*, *113*, 861–872. (https://doi.org/10.1016/j.jclepro.2015.11.033

Butowski, L. (2019). Tourist sustainability of destination as a measure of its development. *Current Issues in Tourism*, *22*(9), 1043–1061. https://doi.org/10.1080/13683500.2017.1351926

Chin, W. W., Thatcher, J. B., Wright, R. T., & Steel, D. (2013). Controlling for common method variance in PLS analysis: The measured latent marker variable approach. In H. Abdi, W. W. Chin, V. Esposito Vinzi, G. Russolillo, & L. Trinchera (Eds.), *Springer Proceedings in mathematics and statistics* (Vol. 56, pp. 231–239). Springer. https://doi.org/10.1007/978-1-4614-8283-3_16

Cuaton, G. P., & Su, Y. (2020). Local-indigenous knowledge on disaster risk reduction: Insights from the Mamanwa indigenous peoples in Basey, Samar after Typhoon Haiyan in the Philippines. *International Journal of Disaster Risk Reduction, 48*, 101596. https://doi.org/10.1016/j.ijdrr.2020.101596

Day, E. A., Arthur, W., & Gettman, D. (2001). Knowledge structures and the acquisition of a complex skill. *The Journal of Applied Psychology, 86*(5), 1022–1033. https://doi.org/10.1037/0021-9010.86.5.1022

Dayan, R., Heisig, P., & Matos, F. (2017). Knowledge management as a factor for the formulation and implementation of organization strategy. *Journal of Knowledge Management, 21*(2), 308–329. https://doi.org/10.1108/JKM-02-2016-0068

Dias, Á., Silva, G. M., Patuleia, M., & González-Rodríguez, M. R. (2020). Developing sustainable business models: local knowledge acquisition and tourism lifestyle entrepreneurship. *Journal of Sustainable Tourism*, 1–20. https://doi.org/10.1080/09669582.2020.1835931

Dumay, J., Bernardi, C., Guthrie, J., & Demartini, P. (2016). Integrated reporting: A structured literature review. *Accounting Forum, 40*(3), 166–185. https://doi.org/10.1016/j.accfor.2016.06.001

Easterby-Smith, M., & Lyles, M. (2003). Organizational Learning and Knowledge Management. Blackwell. https://www.wiley.com/en-us/The+Blackwell+Handbook+of+Organizational+Learning+and+Knowledge+Management-p-9780631226727

Edwards, J. S. (2022). Where knowledge management and information management meet: Research directions. *International Journal of Information Management, 63*, 102458. https://doi.org/10.1016/j.ijinfomgt.2021.102458

Fai Pun, K., & Nathai-Balkissoon, M. (2011). Integrating knowledge management into organisational learning. *The Learning Organization, 18*(3), 203–223. https://doi.org/10.1108/09696471111123261

Font, X., English, R., Gkritzali, A., & Tian, W. (. (2021). Value co-creation in sustainable tourism: A service-dominant logic approach. *Tourism Management, 82*, 104200. https://doi.org/10.1016/j.tourman.2020.104200

Gherardi, S. (2012). Organizational learning: The sociology of practice. In *Handbook of Organizational Learning and Knowledge Management* (pp. 43–65). John Wiley & Sons, Ltd. https://doi.org/10.1002/9781119207245.ch3

Gössling, S., Scott, D., & Hall, C. M. (2021). Pandemics, tourism and global change: A rapid assessment of COVID-19. *Journal of Sustainable Tourism, 29*(1), 1–20. https://doi.org/10.1080/09669582.2020.1758708

Grant, R. M. (1996). Prospering in dynamically-competitive environments: Organizational capability as knowledge integration. *Organization Science, 7*(4), 375–387. https://doi.org/10.1287/orsc.7.4.375

Grieves, J. (2008). Why we should abandon the idea of the learning organization. *The Learning Organization, 15*(6), 463–473. https://doi.org/10.1108/09696470810907374

Hair Awang, A., Yusof Hussain, M., & Abdul Malek, J. (2013). Knowledge transfer and the role of local absorptive capability at science and technology parks. *The Learning Organization, 20*(4/5), 291–307. https://doi.org/10.1108/TLO-12-2011-0059

Hall, C. M. (2019). Constructing sustainable tourism development: The 2030 agenda and the managerial ecology of sustainable tourism. *Journal of Sustainable Tourism, 27*(7), 1044–1060. https://doi.org/10.1080/09669582.2018.1560456

Hallak, R., Assaker, G., & Lee, C. (2015). Tourism entrepreneurship performance: The effects of place identity, self-efficacy, and gender. *Journal of Travel Research, 54*(1), 36–51. https://doi.org/10.1177/0047287513513170

Horng, J. S., Liu, C. H., Chou, S. F., Tsai, C. Y., & Chung, Y. C. (2017). From innovation to sustainability: Sustainability innovations of eco-friendly hotels in Taiwan. *International Journal of Hospitality Management, 63*, 44–52. https://doi.org/10.1016/j.ijhm.2017.02.005

Huber, G. P. (1991). Organizational learning: The contributing processes and the literatures. *Organization Science, 2*(1), 88–115. https://doi.org/10.1287/orsc.2.1.88

Hughes, R., & Huby, M. (2004). The construction and interpretation of vignettes in social research. *Social Work and Social Sciences Review, 11*(1), 36–51. https://doi.org/10.1921/17466105.11.1.36

Hult, G. T. M., Hair, J. F., Proksch, D., Sarstedt, M., Pinkwart, A., & Ringle, C. M. (2018). Addressing endogeneity in international marketing applications of partial least squares structural equation modeling. *Journal of International Marketing, 26*(3), 1–21. https://doi.org/10.1509/jim.17.0151

Jaakkola, E. (2020). Designing conceptual articles: Four approaches. *AMS Review, 10*(1–2), 18–26. https://doi.org/10.1007/s13162-020-00161-0

Jaaron, A. A. M., Pham, D. T., & Cogonon, M. E. (2021). Systems thinking to facilitate "double loop" learning in tourism industry: A COVID-19 response strategy. *Journal of Sustainable Tourism*, 1–19. https://doi.org/10.1080/09669582.2021.1948554

Jabareen, Y. (2008). A new conceptual framework for sustainable development. *Environment, Development and Sustainability, 10*(2), 179–192. https://doi.org/10.1007/s10668-006-9058-z

Ja-Shen, C., Don, K., Yunhsin, C. C., & Chinhui, A. (2017). Business co-creation for service innovation in the hospitality and tourism industry. *International Journal of Contemporary Hospitality Management, 29*(6), 1522–1540. https://doi.org/10.1108/IJCHM-06-2015-0308

Jiang, Y., Ritchie, B. W., & Verreynne, M.-L. (2021). Building dynamic capabilities in tourism organisations for disaster management: Enablers and barriers. *Journal of Sustainable Tourism,* 1–26. https://doi.org/10.1080/09669582.2021.1900204

Jones, P., & Comfort, D. (2020). The COVID-19 crisis and sustainability in the hospitality industry. *International Journal of Contemporary Hospitality Management, 32*(10), 3037–3050. https://doi.org/10.1108/IJCHM-04-2020-0357

Juvan, E., & Dolnicar, S. (2014). The attitude–behaviour gap in sustainable tourism. *Annals of Tourism Research, 48,* 76–95. https://doi.org/10.1016/j.annals.2014.05.012

Kabongo, J. D., & Boiral, O. (2017). Doing more with less: Building dynamic capabilities for eco-efficiency. *Business Strategy and the Environment, 26*(7), 956–971. https://doi.org/10.1002/bse.1958

Kang, J. H., Kim, E. J., Choi, J. H., Hong, H. K., Han, S. H., Choi, I. S., Kim, J., Kim, J. Y., Park, E. S., & Choe, P. G. (2021). Minimizing contamination in the use of personal protective equipment: Simulation results through tracking contamination and enhanced protocols. *American Journal of Infection Control, 49*(6), 713–720. https://doi.org/10.1016/j.ajic.2020.11.002

Kanwal, S., Baptista Nunes, M., Arif Chen Hui, M., & Madden, A. (2019). Application of boundary objects in knowledge management research: A review. *Electronic Journal of Knowledge Management, 17*(2), 100–113. https://academic-publishing.org/index.php/ejkm/article/view/1134

Kim, S. S., & Kim, Y. J. (2017). The effect of compliance knowledge and compliance support systems on information security compliance behavior. *Journal of Knowledge Management, 21*(4), 986–1010. https://doi.org/10.1108/JKM-08-2016-0353

Kim, T. T., & Lee, G. (2013). Hospitality employee knowledge-sharing behaviors in the relationship between goal orientations and service innovative behavior. *International Journal of Hospitality Management, 34*(1), 324–337. https://doi.org/10.1016/j.ijhm.2013.04.009

Lam, A. (2000). Tacit knowledge, organizational learning and societal institutions: An integrated framework. *Organization Studies, 21*(3), 487–513. https://doi.org/10.1177/0170840600213001

Lee, K. (2010). The green purchase behavior of Hong Kong young consumers: The role of peer influence, local environmental involvement, and concrete environmental knowledge. *Journal of International Consumer Marketing, 23*(1), 21–44. https://doi.org/10.1080/08961530.2011.524575

Leta, S. D., & Chan, I. C. C. (2021). Learn from the past and prepare for the future: A critical assessment of crisis management research in hospitality. *International Journal of Hospitality Management, 95,* 102915. https://doi.org/10.1016/j.ijhm.2021.102915

Loureiro, S. M. C., Romero, J., & Bilro, R. G. (2020). Stakeholder engagement in co-creation processes for innovation: A systematic literature review and case study. *Journal of Business Research, 119,* 388–409. https://doi.org/10.1016/j.jbusres.2019.09.038

Ma, S., Gu, H., Wang, Y., & Hampson, D. P. (2017). Opportunities and challenges of value co-creation. *International Journal of Contemporary Hospitality Management, 29*(12), 3023–3043. https://doi.org/10.1108/IJCHM-08-2016-0479

McTiernan, C., Musgrave, J., & Cooper, C. (2021). Conceptualising trust as a mediator of pro-environmental tacit knowledge transfer in small and medium sized tourism enterprises. *Journal of Sustainable Tourism,* 1–18. https://doi.org/10.1080/09669582.2021.1942479

Myung, E. (2018). Environmental knowledge, attitudes, and willingness to pay for environmentally friendly meetings – An exploratory study. *Journal of Hospitality and Tourism Management, 36,* 85–91. https://doi.org/10.1016/j.jhtm.2017.03.004

Nieves, J., & Haller, S. (2014). Building dynamic capabilities through knowledge resources. *Tourism Management, 40,* 224–232. https://doi.org/10.1016/j.tourman.2013.06.010

Nonaka, I. (1994). A dynamic theory of organizational knowledge creation. *Organization Science, 5*(1), 14–37. https://doi.org/10.1287/orsc.5.1.14

Obeso, M., Hernández-Linares, R., López-Fernández, M. C., & Serrano-Bedia, A. M. (2020). Knowledge management processes and organizational performance: The mediating role of organizational learning. *Journal of Knowledge Management, 24*(8), 1859–1880. https://doi.org/10.1108/JKM-10-2019-0553

Pantuffi, C. M., Brunstein, J., & Walvoord, M. E. (2021). Responses to vignettes as a methodology to reveal hoteliers' sustainability practices, knowledge and competencies. *Journal of Sustainable Tourism, 0*(0), 1–19. https://doi.org/10.1080/09669582.2021.1994981

Páramo, P. (2017). Reglas proambientales: una alternativa para disminuir la brecha entre el decir-hacer en la educación ambiental. *Suma Psicológica, 24*(1), 42–58. https://doi.org/10.1016/j.sumpsi.2016.11.001

Pham, N. T., Chiappetta Jabbour, C. J., Vo-Thanh, T., Huynh, T. L. D., & Santos, C. (2020). Greening hotels: Does motivating hotel employees promote in-role green performance? The role of culture. *Journal of Sustainable Tourism,* 1–20. https://doi.org/10.1080/09669582.2020.1863972

Pomering, A., & Dolnicar, S. (2009). Assessing the prerequisite of successful CSR implementation: Are consumers aware of CSR initiatives? *Journal of Business Ethics, 85*(S2), 285–301. https://doi.org/10.1007/s10551-008-9729-9

Po-Shin, H., & Li-Hsing, S. (2009). Effective environmental management through environmental knowledge management. *International Journal of Environmental Science & Technology*, *6*(1), 35–50. https://doi.org/10.1007/BF03326058

Rastegar, R., & Ruhanen, L. (2021). A safe space for local knowledge sharing in sustainable tourism: An organisational justice perspective. *Journal of Sustainable Tourism*, 79:1–17. https://doi.org/10.1080/09669582.2021.1929261

Ritchie, B. W., & Jiang, Y. (2019). A review of research on tourism risk, crisis and disaster management: Launching the annals of tourism research curated collection on tourism risk, crisis and disaster management. *Annals of Tourism Research*, *79*, 102812. https://doi.org/10.1016/j.annals.2019.102812

Rogers, K. S. (2012). Exploring our ecological selves within learning organizations. *The Learning Organization*, *19*(1), 28–37. https://doi.org/10.1108/09696471211190347

Roper, S., & Hewitt-Dundas, N. (2015). Knowledge stocks, knowledge flows and innovation: Evidence from matched patents and innovation panel data. *Research Policy*, *44*(7), 1327–1340. https://doi.org/10.1016/j.respol.2015.03.003

Rupietta, C., & Backes-Gellner, U. (2019). Combining knowledge stock and knowledge flow to generate superior incremental innovation performance — Evidence from Swiss manufacturing. *Journal of Business Research*, *94*, 209–222. https://doi.org/10.1016/j.jbusres.2017.04.003

Salehzadeh, R., Seddighi, M., & Ebrahimi, E. (2021). How to increase organisational learning and knowledge sharing through human resource management processes? *International Journal of Process Management and Benchmarking*, *11*(3), 309–331. https://doi.org/10.1504/IJPMB.2021.115007

Senge, P. m. (1997). The fifth discipline. *Measuring Business Excellence*, *1*(3), 46–51. https://doi.org/10.1108/eb025496

Sessa, V. I., & London, M. (2006). *Continuous learning in organizations: Individual, group, and organizational perspectives*. Lawrence Erlbaum Associates.

Sharma, A., Shin, H., Santa-María, M. J., & Nicolau, J. L. (2021). Hotels' COVID-19 innovation and performance. *Annals of Tourism Research*, *88*, 103180. https://doi.org/10.1016/j.annals.2021.103180

Sigala, M. (2020). Tourism and COVID-19: Impacts and implications for advancing and resetting industry and research. *Journal of Business Research*, *117*, 312–321. https://doi.org/10.1016/j.jbusres.2020.06.015

Singjai, K., Winata, L., & Kummer, T.-F. (2018). Green initiatives and their competitive advantage for the hotel industry in developing countries. *International Journal of Hospitality Management*, *75*, 131–143. https://doi.org/10.1016/j.ijhm.2018.03.007

Sun, P. Y. T., & Scott, J. L. (2006). Process level integration of organisational learning, learning organisation and knowledge management. *International Journal of Knowledge and Learning*, *2*(3/4), 308–319. https://doi.org/10.1504/IJKL.2006.010998

Teece, D., Gary, P., & Amy, S. (1997). Dynamic capabilities and strategic management. *Strategic Management Journal*, *18*(7), 509–533. https://doi.org/10.1002/(SICI)1097-0266(199708)18:7<509::AID-SMJ882>3.0.CO;2-Z

Vanapalli, K. R., Sharma, H. B., Ranjan, V. P., Samal, B., Bhattacharya, J., Dubey, B. K., & Goel, S. (2021). Challenges and strategies for effective plastic waste management during and post COVID-19 pandemic. *The Science of the Total Environment*, *750*, 141514. https://doi.org/10.1016/j.scitotenv.2020.141514

Vihari, N. S., Rao, M. K., & Doliya, P. (2019). Organisational learning as an innovative determinant of organisational sustainability: An evidence based approach. *International Journal of Innovation Management*, *23*(03), 1950019. https://doi.org/10.1142/S1363919619500191

Walter, A.-T. (2021). Organizational agility: ill-defined and somewhat confusing? A systematic literature review and conceptualization. *Management Review Quarterly*, *71*(2), 343–391. https://doi.org/10.1007/s11301-020-00186-6

Wang, S., & Noe, R. A. (2010). Knowledge sharing: A review and directions for future research. *Human Resource Management Review*, *20*(2), 115–131. https://doi.org/10.1016/j.hrmr.2009.10.001

Winter, S. G. (2003). Understanding dynamic capabilities. *Strategic Management Journal*, *24*(10), 991–995. https://doi.org/10.1002/smj.318

Zaragoza-Sáez, P. C., Claver-Cortés, E., Marco-Lajara, B., & Úbeda-García, M. (2020). Corporate social responsibility and strategic knowledge management as mediators between sustainable intangible capital and hotel performance. *Journal of Sustainable Tourism*, 1–23. https://doi.org/10.1080/09669582.2020.1811289

Zhao, Y., & Wang, X. (2020). Organisational unlearning, relearning and strategic flexibility: From the perspective of updating routines and knowledge. *Technology Analysis & Strategic Management*, *32*(11), 1251–1263. https://doi.org/10.1080/09537325.2020.1758656

Corporate social responsibility and strategic knowledge management as mediators between sustainable intangible capital and hotel performance

Patrocinio Carmen Zaragoza-Sáez, Enrique Claver-Cortés, Bartolomé Marco-Lajara and Mercedes Úbeda-García

ABSTRACT
Although in recent years intangible assets are considered a basic factor of production, it is necessary to show that their mere possession will not always guarantee superior performance. Accordingly, based on the *resource-based view* of the firm and the *intellectual capital-based view*, this paper has a twofold purpose. First, it analyses the existing relationship between sustainable intangible capital and performance. Second, it analyses the role played by corporate social responsibility and strategic knowledge management as mediator capabilities in the relationship between sustainable intangible capital and performance. Three hypotheses are proposed and a quantitative methodology based on PLS on 120 Spanish hotels with three or more stars is used. The findings do not support the hypothesis that sustainable intangible capital directly influences hotel performance. However, the two mediating hypotheses are supported, showing that corporate social responsibility and strategic knowledge management act as mediators by creating the values, philosophy and necessary foundations for sustainable intangible capital to have a significant influence on hotel performance.

Introduction

The increasingly dynamic environment requires firms to respond to market changes quickly and flexibly to survive the competition and to maintain their long-term existence. "Amongst the forces that drive changes, requirements for corporate responsibility and sustainability are becoming more and more urgent" (Dao et al., 2011, p. 63). Evidence of this is the call made by various political, economic, social and academic institutions for companies to make a greater effort to develop three essential pillars: economic, social, and environmental (also known as Triple Bottom Line, TBL) (Govindan et al., 2013; Purvis et al., 2019).

The *resource-based view* provides opportunities to develop these three pillars: firstly, combining the identification and management of intangible assets (Reed et al., 2006; Subramaniam & Youndt, 2005); and secondly, considering the ideas put forward by Hart (1995), that the strategy and competitive advantage of a company should rely on resources and capabilities which facilitate environmentally sustainable economic activity. This can be observed in the works of Martínez-Martínez et al. (2019), Martínez-Martínez et al. (2015), Delgado-Verde et al. (2014),

Chang and Chen (2012), Huang and Kung (2011), López-Gamero et al. (2011), Cegarra-Navarro et al. (2010) or Cheng (2008), which focus on green intellectual capital or environmental knowledge. However, focusing exclusively on environmental aspects within the company's set of intangible assets is not enough to achieve the sustainability called for by the TBL approach; economic and social aspects should also be considered.

Seeking to fill this existing gap in the literature, this paper will propose a definition of Sustainable Intangible Capital (SIC) according to the TBL approach. To this end, we focus on the *resource-based view* of the firm (Barney, 1991; Grant, 1991) and the *intellectual capital-based view* (Reed et al., 2006; Subramaniam & Youndt, 2005). From the *resource-based view*, the endogenous factors of the company constitute a more solid basis for the maintenance of its competitive advantages (Barney, 1991; Grant, 1991). An extension of this theory is the *intellectual capital-based view*, which focuses exclusively on examining intangible resources and capabilities, paying special attention to the stocks and flows of knowledge incorporated into the company (Reed et al., 2006; Subramaniam & Youndt, 2005).

The literature contains more and more works that link the fields related to intangible assets, Corporate Social Responsibility (CSR) and Performance (PFM) (Chang & Chen, 2012; Chen, 2007; Huang & Kung, 2011; López-Gamero et al., 2011). However, our intention is to go a step further. Although intangible assets are currently seen as the basic production factor to improve competitiveness (Barney, 1991; Grant, 1991), it needs to be stressed that simply owning intangible assets will not guarantee better performance. As Grant (1991, p. 119) points out, "while resources are the source of a firm's capabilities, capabilities are the main source of its competitive advantage". Therefore, considering that the capabilities of a firm result from sets of resources working together (Grant, 1991), this paper highlights the role played by CSR and Strategic Knowledge Management (SKM) as mediator capabilities for SIC to ensure improved PFM. To our knowledge, no previous works have proposed these relationships in a holistic way.

Consequently, this paper has a twofold purpose. First, it analyses the existing relationship between SIC and PFM. Second, it analyses the role played by CSR and SKM as mediator variables in the relationship between SIC and PFM.

To achieve our aim, we analyse the tourism sector and, more specifically, the hotel sector. Although the literature on tourism and hospitality has grown significantly in the past five years (Font & Lynes, 2018) the sector needs to reinvent itself around a new model based on economic, social and environmental innovation, productivity and sustainability (Palacios-Florencio et al., 2018). To fill this gap, this work sheds light on the existing relationship between SIC, CSR, SKM and PFM within the hotel industry.

Several theoretical contributions are made with this paper. Firstly, it extends the understanding of intangible assets, proposing a definition of SIC from the TBL perspective, incorporating not only environmental, but also economic and social issues. Secondly, it delves deeper into the link between SIC and PFM in the hotel industry, offering a new model for the sector. Until now, the literature has not often dealt with these two topics by considering SIC in an integrative way as we have done in this paper. Thirdly, this study has made it clear that the simple possession of sustainable intangibles alone does not guarantee better PFM. Therefore, two capabilities —CSR and SKM— are introduced in the model and they have proved especially useful in setting the necessary values and creating the right climate for the company's sustainable intangibles to adequately capitalise on its PFM (Castelo Branco & Lima Rodrigues, 2006; Lee & Raschke, 2020; Surroca et al., 2010). From a managerial point of view, firstly, we consider that the definition of SIC is a starting point for managers to identify sustainable intangibles and how they could classify them. Secondly, it is necessary for managers to know not only the two dimensions of SIC but also the best way to exploit them, in order to translate this knowledge into the creation of competitive advantages. Thirdly, this study could help managers to become aware of the importance of CSR and SKM as drivers of the sustainable intangibles that hotels own.

The paper is structured as follows. After the introduction, a literature review forms the basis of the model design and the hypotheses proposals. An explanation of the methodology used and the description of findings follows. The paper concludes with a discussion of the results and the conclusions drawn from the study.

Literature review and proposed model

Sustainable intangible capital and performance

Intellectual capital can be defined as the sum of knowledge and knowledge capabilities that the company can use to obtain competitive advantages (Stewart, 1997). It is widely accepted that intellectual capital groups intangibles around three main blocks: human capital, structural capital and relational capital. The first refers to the (explicit or tacit) useful knowledge owned by the company's personnel, as well as to its ability to regenerate through learning. The second, "is made up of organizational culture, management philosophies, organisational processes, systems and informational resources" (Benevene & Cortini, 2010, p. 125). Finally, relational capital is the value provided to the firm by the set of relationships that it maintains with its external environment.

As discussed in the Introduction section, sustainability issues are increasingly featured in the specialised literature on intangible management and hospitality, mainly from an environmental perspective. This can be seen in the works of Martínez-Martínez et al. (2019, 2015) and Cegarra-Navarro et al. (2010) which focus on environmental knowledge in the hospitality sector. Nevertheless, considering only the environmental aspects takes us away from the sustainability approach proposed by the TBL.

Seeking to fill this existing gap in the literature, this paper attempts to define SIC under the TBL approach. To this end, we define SIC as the set of human, structural and relational intangibles that a company can exploit to carry out economic, social and environmental management, which allows it to achieve competitive advantages. Being coherent with the TBL philosophy, this definition enables us to break down SIC into two main dimensions: Green Intangible Capital (GIC) and Social and Economic Intangible Capital (SEIC).

(1) GIC: constituted by the human, structural and relational capital intangibles linked to the conservation and management of natural resources (minimising pollution, reducing water and energy consumption or conserving biodiversity). Martínez-Martínez et al. (2015) state that the "preservation of the environment becomes a crucial factor influencing hotel operations".

(2) SEIC: constituted by the human, structural and relational capital intangibles linked to the impact that the company has on the social system in which it operates and to the generation of prosperity at different social levels as well as to profitability through economic activity. It comprises employees (fair salaries, good working conditions), customers (safety and durability of finished products) and society as a whole (respect for heritage, culture and traditions, hiring of employees and suppliers from the local community, offering typical local products, etc.) (GRI, 2018).

Both dimensions, GIC and SEIC must be considered together and not independently of each other and it is expected that SIC can lead to a better hotel's PFM. On the one hand, environmental knowledge will lead to increased company benefits such as cost savings resulting from eco-efficiency, enhanced corporate image, improved relationships with local communities, access to new green markets and superior competitive advantage (Cegarra-Navarro et al., 2010). This is why the optimal use of environmental resources is key for hotel competitiveness, and this dimension plays a very important role through its close connection with tourism product quality (Benavides-Velasco et al., 2014; Quintana-García et al., 2018). On the other hand, SEIC is a must in the hotel industry due to the strong impact that this sector has on its social environment and because it positively influences both organisational confidence and consumer perception, which is critical to differentiate products and services from those of competitors (Benavides-Velasco et al., 2014).

According to the above, for the purpose of this paper, hotel's PFM could take the form of Environmental Performance (EP) or Hotel Performance (HP).The strategic nature of SIC, which stems from its heterogeneity, specificity and difficulty to be imitated and transferred, will provide companies owning it with higher PFM (Barney, 1991; Grant, 1991). Similarly, Bontis et al. (2015) and Kim et al. (2012), point out the degree to which intangible assets affect the financial results of hotels. NemecRudez and Mihalic (2007) highlight the new opportunities that knowledge assets bring to the hotel sector, while Engström et al. (2003) see intangible assets as the key resources and drivers of organisational performance and value creation in the hotel sector.

In the light of all the above, we formulate the first hypothesis.

H1: A hotel's sustainable intangible capital positively influences its performance.

The mediator role of CSR in the SIC-PFM link

CSR can be defined as "the voluntary integration by companies of social and environmental aspects into their business operations and interactions with their stakeholders" (Commission of the European Communities, 2001, p. 6). According to this definition, the implementation of CSR practices implicitly includes the need for companies to go beyond complying with the established legislation by investing in human capital, in environmental aspects and in relationships with their environment.

Waddock (2008) states that one reason for paying greater attention to CSR is that more than half of corporations' assets today are found not in tangible but rather in intangible assets, which in turn rely on the quality of stakeholder relationships that the company has developed.

According to the *resource-based view of the firm*, intangible assets are not productive on their own as they need to be integrated into capabilities to achieve competitive advantages. Parisi and Hockerts (2008) point out that treating intangible assets as stock offers the possibility of examining the way companies use them to create future wealth. The same authors consider that intellectual capital and CSR are the source of future prosperity. Therefore, not only the stock, but also the capability of managing intangible and CSR related activities are critical to companies.

In the context of our research, we consider that sustainable intangibles must be put to work and that CSR can be a good capability to leverage them. In this line, White (2006, p. 2) states, "the link between intangibles and CSR is intimate and multifaceted. Understanding how value is created through intangible assets is integral to understanding how long-term wealth is created through CSR".

CSR activities are considered to have a positive relationship with intellectual capital dimensions. Surroca et al. (2010) and Castelo Branco and Lima Rodrigues (2006) highlight the potential of the *resource-based view* as an analytical tool to study the relationship between CSR and financial results through their mutual connection with company resources. Amongst these resources, intangibles such as innovation capability, human capital, reputation and culture can greatly help to improve the results obtained with CSR actions through: (1) the incorporation of more responsible attributes within products and services (redesign, packaging, inputs, etc.); (2) the introduction of *commitment-based human resource practices* (advanced training, participation in teams and empowerment); (3) the development of a good reputation in terms of social responsibility; and (4) the rise of a *humanistic culture* (which encourages employees to seek solutions that can reduce the impact caused by the company on the natural environment).Based on Popoli (2015) and extending its brand image idea to the company's intangible assets, we can consider that CSR is an important driver for reinforcing sustainable intangibles. From this point of view, SIC must be considered as a vector that allows CSR strategy to translate into competitive advantages. Organizations that integrate CSR principles into their operations can yield both meaningful sustainability performance and long-term financial performance by leveraging its intangible qualities (Lee & Raschke, 2020).

Garay and Font (2012) point out that CSR actions will most probably have a positive correlation with a company's financial results, while simultaneously becoming a source of competitiveness in the sector. This is what PepsiCo calls *performance with purpose*, thus demonstrating its efforts to align competitiveness and sustainable growth (Busco et al., 2017). However, despite having been the study object in numerous empirical studies, no consensus seems to have been reached on the relationship between CSR and financial results (Saeidi et al., 2015). If firms that adopt socially responsible policies become more profitable, socially responsible investments will provide an incentive for businesses to increase investments in CSR programs (Lin et al., 2018). In fact, the study by Holcomb et al. (2007) showed that leading hotels such as Hilton, Accor or Marriott embrace the inclusion of social and environmental objectives in their operations and use them as a basis for the development of unique competitive advantages.

The arguments explained above lead us to pose the following hypothesis:

> H2: A hotel's corporate social responsibility acts as a mediating capability between its sustainable intangible capital and performance.

The mediator role of SKM in the SIC-PFM link

It is widely known that intangible assets underpin value creation in the hotel sector. However, on their own, these intangibles will not always create value. For the company to achieve competitive advantages, intangibles will have to be integrated so they can work together. To this end, knowledge management could be the organisational capability able to coordinate and integrate intangibles.

As Bolisani and Bratianu (2018) point out, knowledge management bridges the gap between operational management and strategic management since knowledge represents strategic resources playing a crucial role in a firm's competitive advantage. The same authors consider that the term *knowledge strategy* reflects the integration of knowledge management and strategic management (Bolisani & Bratianu, 2017; 2018; Bratianu & Bolisani, 2015).Taking these ideas as a reference, in this paper we use the term SKM to define a strategic process that includes a knowledge vision and diagnosis, the formulation of knowledge strategies and the existence of an infrastructure to support their implementation. Similarly to Bolisani and Bratianu (2017), we consider that SKM is associated with the necessity to include a company's knowledge as one of the objects of strategic planning, and it represents the formulation of long-term plans for knowledge management programs and activities. The three stages of a SKM process are explained below.

Vision and diagnosis

Intangibles must be prioritised by top management and included amongst the company's goals. Von Krogh et al. (2000) stress the need to instil a knowledge vision that requires emphasising knowledge creation as an essential activity for senior management. It is also essential to perform a diagnosis to reveal the strengths and weaknesses not only of the sustainable intangibles available in the hotel but also of those which still need to be built or promoted.

Formulation

Strategic diagnosis must be followed by the formulation of a knowledge strategy which, according to Zack (1999), will describe the global approach adopted by an organisation to align its intangible resources to the intellectual requirements associated with its strategy. From the SIC point of view in the hotel industry, the formulation of strategies should focus: (a) on the creation of sustainable intangibles; and (b) on making these intangibles visible to the hotel's internal and external stakeholders. In addition to allowing the hotel to improve its credibility in terms of sustainability, this will strengthen the relationship between SIC and PFM.

Implementation

Once the knowledge strategy has been formulated, it will be necessary to provide the company with mechanisms to ensure its efficient application, such as:

- A humanistic culture, which helps to promote a good working climate, trust and commitment between all organisation members, while enhancing stakeholders' satisfaction. Hotels need a corporate culture based on the principles of sustainability, continuous learning, fluid communications and the appreciation of errors as a means of improvement.

- Human resource practices, through employee empowerment, training, team collaboration and well-designed reward systems, with the purpose of giving workers the power, knowledge and motivation needed to understand problems, to identify solutions and to implement best practices associated with sustainability (Surroca et al., 2010).

- Organisational design and technological platform. How a firm is organised determines the extent to which knowledge flows internally and externally, it being advisable to adopt horizontal structures —as opposed to bureaucratic ones— so that maximum knowledge transfer and creation levels will be achieved. A technological platform which makes the flow of information and communication between the hotel and its stakeholders easier and faster is also needed. Disseminating social responsibility actions has important effects on the creation or reduction of fundamental intangible resources, such as those associated with employees or with corporate reputation (Castelo Branco & Lima Rodrigues, 2006).

Stakeholders' awareness of these social responsibility actions will allow sustainable intangibles, through the capability of SKM, to positively influence the PFM of the hotel. In this line of thinking, several authors point out a positive relationship between SKM processes and PFM (Andreeva & Kianto, 2012; Lee et al., 2012; Palacios & Garrigós, 2006; Zack et al., 2009).

All the considerations above lead us to formulate the third hypothesis:

H3: A hotel's strategic knowledge management acts as a mediating capability between its sustainable intangible capital and performance.

Figure 1 shows the developed model and the hypotheses proposed.

Methodology

Population

As pointed out in the Introduction section, for this research we focus on the hotel sector in Spain. Several reasons led us to focus on this sector. Firstly, according to the OMT-UNWTO. (2018), Spain has improved its position in the world ranking, its almost 82 million foreign tourists making it the second most visited country after France. The contribution made by tourism to the Spanish GDP is 12.3%, while its contribution to employment amounts to 12.7% (INE. , 2019). From the accommodation point of view, 16,967 establishments were located in Spain in 2018 —with a total of 876,147 rooms (Hosteltur, 2019). These figures justify the analysis of the proposed topics in a sector that is consolidating its weight in the national economy year after year. Secondly, we agree with Chung and Parker (2010) that the issues of sustainability and social responsibility deserve to be analysed due both to the way in which hotel establishments relate with the community and the environment, and to the strong impact that this causes not only on nature but also on society.

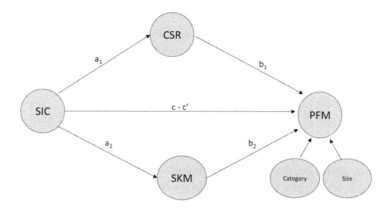

H1: SIC → PFM = c (total effect) or c' (mediated effect)
H2: SIC → CSR → PFM = a_1b_1
H3: SIC → SKM → PFM = a_2b_2

Figure 1. Proposed model.

It was considered advisable that the hotels to be analysed should belong to hotel chains and have a certain level of recognised quality. We restricted the study to hotels with three or more stars. This should guarantee a high level of top management qualification, continuous learning thanks to the social relations between the establishments and the implementation of actions related to the topics to be studied. We obtained our population from two databases (SABI-Iberian Balance Sheet Analysis System and Alimarket). After removing the hotels that did not meet the specified criteria as well as any which were inactive at the time of the research, our population finally consisted of 1,000 Spanish hotels belonging to hotel chains and with three or more stars. No procedure was applied to select a sample from this population and, therefore, the study adopted a census-format and had a cross-sectional nature.

Data collection

To collect the information a questionnaire was used and its preparation went through several stages: (1) The scientific literature focussed on the study's topics was thoroughly reviewed; (2) As the literature consulted was written in English, it was necessary to translate the potential questions for the questionnaire into Spanish. After this phase, a preliminary draft was discussed with academics and tourism experts; (3) A pilot test was carried out with the CEOs and Human Resources Managers (HRM) of five firms, in order to establish the questions to be incorporated in the questionnaire. After completing this stage, between October 2018 and May 2019, the final questionnaire (Annex I) was sent to both the CEO and the HRM of the hotels by postal and electronic mail. The questionnaire was designed to avoid revealing any sensitive information about the organisations involved and was preceded by a cover letter about the research study.

We received 168 questionnaires, although only 120 were considered valid (answered by both CEO and HRM). Therefore, 120 hotels finally participated in the study, which represents 12% of the population. The hotels participating in the study come from 14 different Spanish regions[1], have an average of 136 rooms and 53 employees; 28 are three-star hotels, 85 four-star hotels and 7 five-star hotels. As for the respondents, all of them have at least a higher university degree; 72% of CEOs are men, while 65% of Human Resources Managers are women; the average age is 43.

Apart from trying to control the common method variance by obtaining information from two different sources, considering the recommendations of Podsakoff et al. (2012), we have adopted a series of procedural and statistical remedies: (1) Interviewees remained anonymous and were told that they had to answer as sincerely and honestly as possible and that there were no 'good' or 'bad' answers. This approach is aimed at reducing their fear of being evaluated and at preventing them from giving socially desirable or appropriate answers; (2)Item construction was very careful, always trying to avoid any potential ambiguities. For this reason, the questionnaire included simple and concise questions in order to facilitate their understanding; (3)Interviewees were informed in detail about the object of the research and the importance of their participation in it. We also implemented Harman's one-factor test (Podsakoff et al., 2012). All variables were entered into an exploratory factor analysis. The results revealed that no single factor emerged; nor was there a general factor that could account for the largest proportion of variance in these variables. The above evidence suggests that common method bias did not represent a major problem in our study.

Possible non-response bias was also checked. The Student's t-test showed no significant differences for means comparison based on the control variables(category and size) between the hotels which did not answer the questionnaire and those which did.

Statistical technique

Structural Equation Modelling (SEM) is the statistical technique used in this research. "Its ability to model latent variables, to take various forms of measurement error into account, and to test entire theories make it useful for a plethora of research questions" (Henseler, 2017a, p. 361). More specifically, the relationships proposed in the model were tested using a variance-based SEM, which is the most appropriate method when using composites; that is, latent variables generated from artefacts or designs created by the researcher.

Of the variance-based SEM methods, Partial Least Squares (PLS) path modelling is one of the most developed (Henseler, 2017a), and one of its main features is the possibility of including both factors and composites in the same model(Dijkstra &Henseler, 2015a, 2015b; Henseler, 2017a, 2017b).This is one of the reasons for choosing this methodology. Other reasons can be found in the fact that PLS does not demand data normality and that it provides a flexible approach to sample size (Hair et al., 2011). According to Chin et al. (2003), this methodology is better suited to the causal analysis of highly complex phenomena whose theory has not been sufficiently developed. PLS can additionally operate with unobserved variables, and it helps to estimate values of latent variables when establishing predictions. Likewise, PLS works efficiently when used to predict the behaviour of path models which comprise many constructs, several structural path relationships and/or many indicators per construct. We deemed it appropriate to use this structural equation modelling because subjective assessments of the constructs constitute our starting point and the theoretical model considers many constructs and path relationships.

Measures

Sustainable intangible Capital

We defined SIC as the set of human, structural and relational intangibles that a company can exploit to carry out economic, social and environmental management to achieve competitive advantages. This variable was regarded as a second-order construct made up of two first-order formative constructs: Green Intangible Capital (GIC) and Social and Economic Intangible Capital (SEIC). GIC was measured by means of a seven-point Likert-type scale with seven items, taking as a reference —and adapting— the measures provided in the studies carried out by Chang and

Chen (2012), Huang and Kung (2011) and Chen (2007). A seven-point Likert-type scale with 14 items served to measure SEIC, taking as a reference —and adapting— the measures supplied by Subramaniam and Youndt (2005).

Corporate social responsibility
Based on a convention that we adopted in this paper, the implementation of CSR practices implicitly includes the need for hotels to go beyond complying with the established legislation, investing not only in human capital but also in environmental aspects and in their relationship with their environment. This variable was considered a second-order construct made up of two first-order reflective constructs: Employee and Customer Social Responsibility (ECSR) and Environment and Society Social Responsibility (ESSR). Both of them were measured through a seven-point Likert-type scale using the measures previously developed by Bai and Chang (2015), Chang and Chen (2012) and Turker (2009). Seven items served to measure ECSR, as opposed to four in the case of ESSR.

Strategic knowledge management
SKM is a process which should contain a set of major initiatives that must be undertaken to achieve certain economic, social and environmental goals. To perform this task, an SKM process should ideally include a knowledge vision and diagnosis, the formulation of knowledge strategies and the existence of an infrastructure to support their implementation. This variable was treated as a first-order construct which comprised seven formative indicators derived from the insights developed in a previously undertaken multiple-case study (Hill & Birkinshaw, 2014) and adapted from the paper authored by Claver-Cortés et al. (2018). All of them were measured by means of a seven-point Likert-type scale.

Performance
This variable was treated as a second-order construct shaped by two first-order reflective constructs: EP and HP. EP was measured by means of a seven-point Likert-type scale with five items, using the measures included in the studies performed by Paillé et al. (2014) and Chow and Chen (2012). EP shows the results derived from the implementation of environmental management measures, such as: reduction of waste, emissions, and direct or indirect energy consumption; increased recycled materials, the rate of renewable energy consumption and the number of ecological and services products developed. As for HP, perception measures based on Gibson and Birkinshaw (2004) were used. More precisely, we selected eight items to capture: (a) general performance criteria (market share growth, brand recognition, firm market image and sales growth); and (b) performance variables better suited to hotel sector firms (revenues per room, average occupancy, customer satisfaction level and employee satisfaction). All these items were measured through a seven-point Likert-type scale.

Control variables
In this research, we monitor potential explanations for the relationships proposed in the model through the inclusion of two control variables: hotel category and hotel size. The former is a little used variable in scientific papers focused on the hotel sector. However, authors such as Pine and Phillips (2005) have shown that the higher the category, the higher the hotel performance levels. Therefore, we decided to use hotel category (three-, four- or five-star) as a control variable. Hotel size, measured as the number of rooms in the hotel, was also introduced as a control variable in order to check if it is positively linked to PFM. Previous studies focused on the hotel

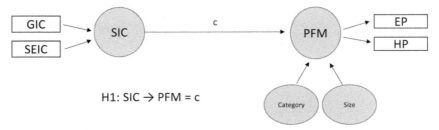

Figure 2. Model with total effect.

sector also included this control variable (Garay & Font, 2012; García & Armas, 2007; Pine & Phillips, 2005; Quintana-García et al., 2018).

Findings

The PLS methodology does not allow for calculations directly referred to second-order constructs. Hence our decision to use the *two-stage approach* —with *"latent variable scores"* or aggregated scores (Wright et al., 2012) — for the treatment of multidimensional constructs. After estimating the aggregate scores of first-order dimensions in the first stage, the scores were used to model the second-order construct in the second stage. Once the final model was designed (Figures 2 and 3), we proceeded to evaluate it following the three main model assessment stages in PLS, namely: global, measurement and structural. The Smart PLS3 software was used to obtain the results.

Global model assessment

Several measures can be used to evaluate the global fit of the model. The most commonly used is the SRMR (standardised root mean square residual) index. However, the most recent advances in PLS suggest the use of *Exact Model Fit*. This model tests the statistical inference (based on bootstrap) of the discrepancy between the empirical covariance matrix and the covariance matrix implied by the composite factor model. Dijkstra and Henseler (2015a) consider that d_ULS (unweighted least squares discrepancy) and d_G (geodesic discrepancy) are two different ways of calculating this discrepancy. For a good model fit, d_ULS and d_G discrepancies should be below the 95% (HI95) or 99% (HI99) percentiles of the bootstrap (Albort-Morant et al., 2018; Cepeda-Carrión et al., 2019; Henseler, 2017a; Henseler et al., 2014). Table 1 shows the values obtained for d_ULS and d_G. As can be seen, both values are below the values of HI95 and HI99.

Following Hu and Bentler (1998), the SRMR index should be less than 0.08 for a good model fit. In our model, the value for SRMR is 0.068. Therefore, both analyses indicate a good global adjustment of the proposed model.

Measurement model assessment

Our model includes both reflective (Mode A) and formative (Mode B) constructs, each group being evaluated differently in the context of PLS. More specifically, reflective constructs are evaluated according to the individual reliability of the item and the construct, as well as to convergent and discriminant validity; the evaluation of formative constructs takes as a reference the analysis of potential multicollinearity between the indicators, along with the value and significance of their weights.

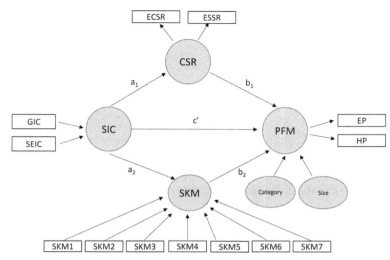

H1: SIC → PFM = c'
H2: SIC → CSR → PFM = a_1b_1
H3: SIC → SKM → PFM = a_2b_2

Figure 3. Model with a two-path mediated effect.

Table 1. Exact model fit.

	95% (HI95)	99% (HI99)
d_ULS = 0.480	0.575	0.882
d_G = 0.297	0.556	0.573

Table 2. Measurement model assessment (Mode A).

Loadings (λ)			
	PFM		CSR
ESSR			0.778
ECSR			0.887
HP	0.869		
EP	0.831		

Construct reliability and convergent validity coefficients			
	Cronbach α	Composite reliability	AVE
PFM	0.817	0.839	0.722
CSR	0.773	0.821	0.697

Discriminant validity (HTMT)	
	PFM
PFM	
CSR	0.737

Reflective constructs assessment (mode a): PFM and CSR

The individual reliability of indicators was evaluated through the value of their loadings (λ), which should exceed the value of 0.7 ($\lambda > 0.7$). As shown in Table 2, this requirement is fulfilled in our case: all loadings exceeded the value of 0.7.

Construct reliability is evaluated by means of Cronbach's α index and the composite reliability index. They both should exceed the critical value of 0.7 in every variable. The existence of convergent validity can be verified through the examination of extracted mean variance (AVE), which should lie above 0.5. As we can see in Table 2, all these values exceed the critical values of 0.7 and 0.5, respectively.

Finally, discriminant validity evaluation takes place through the Heterotrait-Monotrait Ratio (HTMT), which has a 0.85 threshold. It can be inferred from Table 2 that the data in our model confirm the existence of discriminant validity.

Table 3. Measurement model assessment (Mode B).

Multicollinearity analysis

	VIF
SEIC	1.110
GIC	1.110
SKM1	2.007
SKM2	1.848
SKM3	2.781
SKM5	2.666
SKM6	3.123
SKM7	3.057
Category	1.000
Size	1.000

Weight assessment and significance

	Weight	p-value	Confidence intervals 5.0%	95.0%	Significance
SEIC→SIC	0.763***	0.000	0.537	0.964	YES
GIC→SIC	0.449**	0.003	0.108	0.690	YES
SKM1→SKM	0.489***	0.000	0.201	0.731	YES
SKM2→SKM	−0.035	0.371	−0.210	0.138	NO
SKM3→SKM	0.180**	0.006	0.071	0.414	YES
SKM5→SKM	0.101**	0.009	0.134	0.304	YES
SKM6→SKM	0.434**	0.002	0.142	0.713	YES
SKM7→SKM	0.181**	0.006	0.105	0.455	YES
Category	1.000		1.000	1.000	
Size	1.000		1.000	1.000	

**p < 0.01, ***p < 0.001.

Formative constructs assessment (mode B): SIC and SKM

Firstly, potential multicollinearity between indicators needs to be analysed using the Variance Inflation Factor (VIF). In the case of formative indicators, we do not want multicollinearity to exist between them, because it would mean that they measure identical aspects of the construct. VIF values below 3.3 suggest that no multicollinearity exists between indicators. VIF calculation for SIC and SKM indicators revealed that one of them, more precisely SKM4, had a VIF value above 3.3; hence why this indicator was eliminated. The remaining indicators showed VIF values below 3.3, thus meeting the established requirement and confirming the absence of multicollinearity between them (see Table 3).

Secondly, weights and their significance are examined. The 5,000-sample non-parametric bootstrapping technique was used to obtain the *t* statistics and the confidence intervals which serve to assess coefficient significance. According to the theory, all weights should be positive and have a *p* value below 0.05 to be significant. Table 3 shows positive weights in every case and also that these weights are all significant, except for the one corresponding to the SKM2 indicator. Because formative indicators are viewed as causes of constructs, eliminating an indicator could decrease the information to explain it. Roberts and Thatcher (2009, p. 30) point out that "even if an item contributes little to the explained variance in a formative construct, it should be included in the measurement model". Hence our decision not to eliminate this indicator.

Structural model assessment

Structural model evaluation must go through five stages: (1) assessment of possible problems regarding collinearity between constructs (2) assessment of path coefficients and their significance (3) R^2 evaluation (4) assessment of f^2-effect size and (5) assessment of model predictive relevance based on the Stone-Geisser Q^2 test.

Table 4. VIF, f^2 and Q^2 values.

VIF values

	SKM	CSR	PFM
SIC	1.000	1.000	1.472
SKM			2.611
CSR			2.842
Category			1.104
Size			1.231

f^2 values

	SKM	CSR	PFM
SIC	0.246	0.386	0.029
SKM			0.153
CSR			0.133
Category			0.014
Size			0.023

Q^2 values

	Q^2
SKM	0.099
PFM	0.345
CSR	0.178

We firstly evaluated possible collinearity problems. Hair et al. (2014) argue that there will be signs of collinearity when the VIF value is above 5. As none of the values in our model exceed the value of 5, we can confirm the absence of collinearity problems. Table 4 shows the VIF values.

A second analysis focused on the algebraic sign, magnitude and significance of the path coefficients which show the estimates of structural model relationships, i.e. the hypothesised relationships between constructs. As explained above, the 5,000-sample bootstrapping technique was used to assess coefficient significance. Path coefficients and their significance appear in Table 5.

It can be observed in Table 5 that the direct effects corresponding to the relationships Category→ PFM, Size→ PFM and SIC→ PFM (c) are not significant in the model with total effect (Figure 2). These results show, on the one hand, that control variables (hotel category and size) do not significantly influence hotel PFM. On the other hand, H1 proposed a positive relationship between SIC and PFM and, although the path coefficient (c) is positive —thus showing a positive relationship between the two constructs— the relationship lacks significance. In other words, H1 cannot be confirmed.

It can also be inferred from Table 5 that four of the seven direct effects turned out to be significant in the model with two-path mediation effect (Figure 3). As with the model with total effect, the three non-significant direct effects appear in the relationships Category→ PFM, Size→ PFM and SIC→ PFM (c'). Control variables do not significantly influence hotel PFM in this case either. However, we found that when the mediating variables (CSR and SKM) were introduced, the path coefficient (c') which relates SIC and PFM was not only non-significant but also negative, which contradicts our H1. The mediation analysis carried out below will allow us to check whether the hypotheses corresponding to mediation, i.e. H2 and H3, are confirmed or not.

The third analysis involved the assessment of R^2 values. According to the theory, R^2 values should lie between 0 and 1. Falk and Miller (1992) consider that R^2 should be ≥ 0.10. In our work, the R^2 values for SKM, PFM and CSR were 0.197, 0.411 and 0.278, respectively, which suggests that almost 20% of SKM variance was explained by SIC, that 41% of PFM variance was accounted for by SIC, SKM and CSR, and that SIC explained 27.8% of CSR variance.

The fourth analysis consisted in assessing the sizes of f^2 effects. F^2 assesses the degree to which an exogenous construct contributes to explain a given endogenous construct in terms of R^2. Table 4 shows the f^2 values obtained for our study and, as can be seen, the exogenous variable which contributes most to explaining the endogenous variable PFM is SKM. The greatest f^2 effect appears in the relationship between SIC and CSR.

Table 5. Path coefficients and significance.

	Weight	p-value	Confidence intervals 5.0%	95.0%	Significance
Model with total effect					
SIC→ PFM (c)	0.196	0.059	−0.009	0.154	NO
Category→PFM	0.093	0.072	−0.012	0.217	NO
Size→PFM	0.106	0.051	−0.027	0.232	NO
Model with a two-path mediated effect					
SIC→ PFM (c)	−0.127	0.092	−0.296	0.029	NO
SIC→ CSR (a_1)	0.528***	0.000	0.422	0.633	YES
SIC→ SKM (a_2)	0.444***	0.000	0.291	0.608	YES
CSR→PFM (b_1)	0.231**	0.003	0.011	0.448	YES
SKM→PFM (b_2)	0.453***	0.000	0.216	0.652	YES
Category→PFM	0.093	0.072	−0.012	0.217	NO
Size→PFM	0.106	0.051	−0.027	0.232	NO

**p < 0.01, ***p < 0.001.

Finally, the structural model was also evaluated using the Stone-Geisser test Q^2 through a blindfolding procedure. A Q^2 greater than zero implies that the model has predictive relevance. The findings in Table 4 confirm the predictive relevance of the proposed model for every dependent variable.

Mediation analysis

According to the proposed model (Figure 3), H2 and H3 represent mediation hypotheses, which means that an independent variable (SIC) affects a dependent variable (PFM) through mediating variables or mediators (CSR and SKM). This study tests a two-path mediation model.

Figure 2 describes the total effect of SIC on PFM, (c) being the path coefficient. Figure 3 expresses the total effect of SIC on PFM as the sum of direct and indirect effects, the latter being estimated by the product of path coefficients for each path in the mediational chain. Thus, c = c′ + $a_1 b_1$ + $a_2 b_2$, with the last two terms being specific indirect effects and their sum representing the total indirect effect, while (c′) constitutes the direct effect of SIC on PFM (H1), controlling both mediators (CSR and SKM). The advantage of this approach is that it can isolate the indirect effect of both mediating variables, i.e. CSR (H2: $a_1 b_1$) and SKM (H3: $a_2 b_2$).

The bootstrapping method served to test the significance of indirect effects. We were able to verify the mediation hypotheses (i.e. H2 and H3) thanks to the analytical approach put forward by Hayes and Scharkow (2013). The indirect effects are specified and tested with the mediators (CSR and SKM) (Table 6).

Attention was also paid to the total effect (c) and the direct effect (c′) of the independent variable (SIC) on the dependent variable (PFM). Chin (2010) suggests a two-stage process to test mediation in PLS: 1) using the specific model —including both the direct and the indirect effects— and performing N bootstrap resampling, in addition to explicitly calculating the product of the direct paths that form the indirect path under assessment; and 2) estimating significance by means of percentile bootstrap. This generates a 95% confidence interval for the mediators: CSR (H2) and SKM (H3). If the interval for a mediation hypothesis does not contain the zero value, the indirect effect significantly differs from zero at a 95% confidence level.

Figure 2 and Table 6 reveal that SIC does not have a significant total effect on PFM (c). When the mediating variables are introduced (Figure 3), SIC has no significant effect on PFM (c′) either. The results also show that the indirect effects are highly significant. This means that CSR and SKM are mediating variables between SIC and PFM, thus confirming H2 (a1b1) and H3 (a2b2).

Variance Accounted For (VAF)[2] was calculated to ascertain whether partial or total mediation took place. VAF < 0.8 implies partial mediation, whereas VAF > 0.8 means that full mediation exists. Mediation can be described as being full in our study, since VAF reaches a value of 1.64.

Table 6. Mediating effect test.

Total effect of SIC on PFM (c)		Direct effect of SIC on PFM (c')		Indirect effect of SIC on PFM	Confidence intervals	
Path coefficient	p-value	Path coefficient	p-value		5%	95%
0.196 (ns)	0.059	−0.127 (ns)	0.092	H2= a_1b_1= 0.122***	0.004	0.250
				H3= a_2b_2 = 0.201***	0.080	0.339

***$p < 0.001$.

Discussion and conclusions

Based on the *resource-based view* of the firm (Barney, 1991; Grant, 1991) and the *intellectual capital-based view* of the firm (Reed et al., 2006; Subramaniam & Youndt, 2005), this work has analysed the relationship between SIC and PFM in 120 Spanish hotels with three or more stars. The need for hotels to behave as intelligent organisations so that they can cope with the continuous challenges imposed by their environment led us to test the extent to which CSR and SKM behave as mediating capabilities in the relationship between SIC and PFM.

Three hypotheses were posed in order to achieve our aim, using the PLS quantitative methodology to test them. After performing the corresponding evaluation and mediation analyses, the results shed light on the following aspects:

According to H1, a hotel's SIC (defined as the set of human, structural and relational intangibles that a company can exploit to carry out economic, social and environmental management) positively influences its PFM. However, H1 cannot be supported, because SIC has no significant direct effect on PFM (c). Our findings tell us that although hotels may own sustainable and strategic intangible capital -coming from the conservation and management of natural resources, the generation of prosperity at different social levels, the economic activity profitability, and the impact that the company has on the social system where it operates (employees, customers, society as a whole)- this will not always lead them to improve their results in terms of better business performance or greater competitive advantages.

This outcome matches those obtained by Bontis et al. (2015) and Kim et al. (2012).The former authors pointed out that, although the impact of intangible assets on PFM seems obvious and logical conceptually speaking, in practice this relationship cannot be fully confirmed for every sector. Their research shows that investment in intellectual capital is not always adequately capitalised. The latter authors stated that intellectual capital does not always have a direct influence on hotel PFM, as it is necessary for hotels to manage and improve their intellectual capital in an integrative manner. Under these premises, our findings reveal that we cannot expect the effects of SIC exploitation to be automatically visible in hotel PFM, showing the poor efficiency in SIC exploitation. Bontis et al. (2015, p. 1378) think that this result "opens up a new field of research regarding the relationship between the style of managing intellectual capital and corporate PFM".

In the light of this research, we can observe that the mere possession of sustainable intangibles is not enough to achieve a better PFM. Although intangibles are a reflection of the sustainable actions that hotels have implemented, the results indicate that they do not have a direct impact on PFM. We believe that such sustainable intangibles must be recognized by the top management of the hotel as highly strategic resources and, subsequently, a set of processes must be put in place that allow them to be exploited, capitalized and visualized both internally and externally to the hotel. Hence our conviction about the need to establish an infrastructure that is able to take full advantage of the sustainable intangibles that the hotels possess, and thus achieve a positive and significant relationship between SIC and PFM. This gave rise to the formulation of two mediating hypothesis.

H2 and H3 proposed that CSR and SKM act as mediating capabilities between hotel SIC and hotel PFM, leveraging the stock of sustainable intangibles. Our findings provide support for both hypotheses, showing full mediation and the existence of a multiple mediation effect. This means that, in terms of CSR, hotels with a good reputation for social responsibility can improve their relationships with external and internal stakeholders(Jamali et al., 2008). With regard to internal stakeholders, the result suggests that CSR not only attracts the best employees but also increases their motivation, loyalty and commitment to the company (Castelo Branco & Lima Rodrigues, 2006), which translates into better PFM. Regarding external stakeholders, the fact that hotels assume their duties as citizens and grant due diligence to their external stakeholders (economic and social) and the natural environment (Jamali et al., 2008), will also lead them to differentiate from their competitors, obtaining competitive advantages around corporate responsibility issues. In terms of SKM, considering the importance of sustainable intangibles within the vision of the hotel, together with the formulation of knowledge strategies to exploit them and cover existing needs, emerges as a fundamental capability that must be undertaken for hotels to reach certain economic, social and environmental objectives (Castelo Branco & Lima Rodrigues, 2006; Dayan et al., 2017; Lee & Raschke, 2020; Surroca et al., 2010).

Expressed differently, CSR and SKM capabilities create the values, the philosophy and the necessary foundations for SIC to significantly influence PFM.

The control variables did not show any evidence for their influence on hotel PFM.

Contributions

This paper contributes to the literature in the following aspects. Firstly, until now, sustainability issues have been considered in the specialised literature on intellectual capital mainly from an environmental point of view, focusing mainly on the study of green intellectual capital (Chang & Chen, 2012; Cheng, 2008; Delgado-Verde et al., 2014; Huang & Kung, 2011; López-Gamero et al., 2011). However, this paper extends the understanding of intangible assets, proposing a definition of SIC from the TBL perspective, incorporating not only environmental, but also economic and social issues. SIC is defined as the set of human, structural and relational intangibles that a company can exploit to carry out economic, social and environmental management, which allows it to achieve competitive advantages. This is a novel way of defining SIC in the strategic management literature. Moreover, to be coherent with the TBL philosophy, SIC has been divided into two dimensions: GIC and SEIC (Benavides-Velasco et al., 2014; GRI, 2018; Martínez-Martínez et al., 2015; Quintana-García et al., 2018). Secondly, our study delves deeper into the link between SIC and PFM in the hotel industry, offering a new model for the sector. Until now, the literature has not often dealt with these two topics by considering SIC in an integrative way as we have done in this paper. Thirdly, this study has made it clear that the simple possession of sustainable intangibles alone does not guarantee better PFM. As a consequence, two capabilities —CSR and SKM— are introduced in the model and they have proved especially useful in setting the necessary values and creating the right climate for the company's sustainable intangibles to adequately capitalise on its PFM (Lee & Raschke, 2020; Surroca et al., 2010; Castelo Branco & Lima Rodrigues, 2006).

From a practical point of view, authors such as Holcom et al. (2007) believe that the accommodation sector must be proactive and live up to the expectations that its establishments will be hospitable and take care of the world around them. Nonetheless, they also stress that the way to integrate these activities into the core business and to demonstrate the real impacts and positive changes still remains unclear. With this work we try to shed light on these aspects. First, we consider that the definition of SIC is a starting point for managers to identify sustainable intangibles and how they could classify them. This will allow them to make an inventory of them, know their strengths and weaknesses and adopt the appropriate strategies, covering the gaps that exist or exploiting the most strategic sustainable intangibles (Dayan et al., 2017).Second, it is necessary for managers to know not only the two dimensions of SIC but also the best way to exploit them. The SIC's exploitation will require establishing an action plan that pursues the conservation and management of natural resources, along with respect for customers, employees and society as a whole. The savings resulting from eco-efficiency and the optimal use of environmental resources, together with the care of culture and traditions, the establishment of a fair salary system and the safety of the service offered will finally translate into the creation of competitive advantages for hotels (Martínez-Martínez et al., 2015; Cegarra-Navarro et al., 2010).Third, this study could help managers to become aware of the importance of CSR and SKM as drivers of the sustainable intangibles that hotels own. They should especially focus on creating an SIC supported by a set of CSR and SKM values (aimed at satisfying internal and external stakeholders)which can provide these intangibles with the infrastructure required to enhance them and make them visible in order to positively influence PFM (Andreeva & Kianto, 2012; Lee et al., 2012; Palacios & Garrigós, 2006; Zack et al., 2009).

Limitations and further research

Despite the contributions mentioned above, this research has some limitations which have to be overcome with future research. First, SIC and CSR, both of them second-order constructs, have been analysed in an integrated way, without analysing each of the dimensions separately. We consider that, for future research, it would be interesting to extend the analysis to know how each of the dimensions behaves separately over the rest of the variables of the model. Second, the study has a cross-sectional nature, which means that the results can only be explained for the period of time in which the study was conducted. We consider that future longitudinal analysis may help to validate the results. Third, researchers often emphasize that predictive capabilities are a strength of the PLS method. The assessment of the predictive capabilities of PLS through the Stone-Geisser Q^2 criterion and the q^2 predictive effect size, both of them used in the present research, have been the only standard evaluation criteria thus far (Cepeda-Carrión et al., 2016). However, several researchers emphasize the importance of accounting for unobserved heterogeneity which has become a key concern to ensure the validity of results when applying PLS-SEM (Sarstedt et al., 2017). Considering these ideas, a future line of research would be to incorporate some recent advances in prediction-oriented results assessment of PLS-SEM, such as finite mixture-PLS (FIMIX-PLS) and PLS prediction-oriented segmentation (PLS-POS). Finally, this research has focused exclusively on Spanish hotels, so its extension to other geographical areas would be recommended in order to validate the results obtained.

Notes

1. Madrid (15), Andalusia (18), Catalonia (19), Valencian Community (18), Estremadura (2), Aragon (3), Canary Islands (10), Balearic Islands (12), Cantabria (2), Asturias (3), Navarra (1), Castilla la Mancha (6), Castilla Leon (8) and Galicia (3).
2. VAF=(Indirect effect)/(Total effect)

Disclosure statement

No potential conflict of interest was reported by the authors.

References

Albort-Morant, G., Henseler, J., Cepeda-Carrión, G., & Leal-Rodríguez, A. (2018). Potential and realized absorptive capacity as complementary drivers of green product and process innovation performance. Sustainability*Sustainability*, *10*(2), 381. https://doi.org/10.3390/su10020381

Andreeva, T., & Kianto, A. (2012). Does knowledge management really matter? Linking knowledge management practices, competitiveness and economic performance. *Journal of Knowledge ManagementManagement*, *16*(4), 617–636. https://doi.org/10.1108/13673271211246185

Bai, X., & Chang, J. (2015). Corporate social responsibility and firm performance: The mediating role of marketing competence and the moderating role of market environment. *Asia Pacific Journal of ManagementManagement*, *32*(2), 505–530. https://doi.org/10.1007/s10490-015-9409-0

Barney, J. (1991). Firm resources and sustained competitive advantage. *Journal of ManagementManagement*, *17*(1), 99–120. https://doi.org/10.1177/014920639101700108

Benavides-Velasco, C., Quintana-García, C., & Marchante-Lara, M. (2014). Total quality management, corporate social responsibility and performance in the hotel industry. *International Journal of Hospitality ManagementManagement*, *41*(August), 77–87. https://doi.org/10.1016/j.ijhm.2014.05.003

Benevene, P., & Cortini, M. (2010). Interaction between structural capital and human capital in Italian NPOs: Leadership, organizational culture and human resource management. *Journal of Intellectual CapitalCapital*, *11*(2), 123–139. https://doi.org/10.1108/14691931011039642

Bolisani, E., & Bratianu, C. (2017). Knowledge strategy planning: An integrated approach to manage uncertainty, turbulence, and dynamics. *Journal of Knowledge ManagementManagement*, *21*(2), 233–253. https://doi.org/10.1108/JKM-02-2016-0071

Bolisani, E., & Bratianu, C. (2018). *Emergent knowledge strategies. Strategic thinking in knowledge management*. Springer International Publishing AG.

Bontis, N., Janošević, S., & Dženopoljac, V. (2015). Intellectual capital in Serbia's hotel industry. *International Journal of Contemporary Hospitality ManagementManagement*, *27*(6), 1365–1384. https://doi.org/10.1108/IJCHM-12-2013-0541

Bratianu, C., & Bolisani, E. (2015, September). Knowledge strategy: An integrated approach for managing uncertainty. In *Proceedings of the 16th European cConference on Knowledge Management*, Italy, pp. 169–177.

Busco, C., Fiori, G., Frigo, M., & Riccaboni, A. (2017, September). Sustainable development goals: Integrating sustainability initiatives with long-term value creation. *Strategic Finance*, 28–37.

Castelo Branco, M., & Lima Rodrigues, L. (2006). Corporate social responsibility and resource-based perspectives. *Journal of Business EthicsEthics, 69*(2), 111–132. https://doi.org/10.1007/s10551-006-9071-z

Cegarra-Navarro, J. G., Eldridge, S., & Martinez-Martinez, A. (2010). Managing environmental knowledge through unlearning in Spanish hospitality companies. *Journal of Environmental PsychologyPsychology, 30*(2), 249–257. https://doi.org/10.1016/j.jenvp.2009.11.009

Cepeda-Carrión, G., Henseler, J., Ringle, C. M., & Roldán, J. L. (2016). Prediction-oriented modeling in business research by means of PLS path modeling: Introduction to a JBR special section. *Journal of bBusiness Researchresearch, 69*(10), 4545–4551. https://doi.org/10.1016/j.jbusres.2016.03.048

Cepeda-Carrion, G., Cegarra-Navarro, J. G., & Cillo, V. (2019). Tips to use partial least squares structural equation modelling (PLS-SEM) in knowledge management. *Journal of Knowledge ManagementManagement, 23*(1), 67–89. https://doi.org/10.1108/JKM-05-2018-0322

Chang, C. H., & Chen, Y. S. (2012). The determinants of green intellectual capital. *Management DecisionDecision, 50*(1), 74–94. https://doi.org/10.1108/00251741211194886

Chen, Y. S. (2007). The positive effect of green intellectual capital on competitive advantages of firms. *Journal of Business EthicsEthics, 77*(3), 271–286. https://doi.org/10.1007/s10551-006-9349-1

Chin, W. W. (2010). How to write up and report PLS analyses. In *Handbook of partial least squares* (pp. 655–690). Springer.

Chin, W. W., Marcolin, B. L., & Newsted, P. R. (2003). A partial least squares latent variable modeling approach for measuring interaction effects: Results from a Monte Carlo simulation study and an electronic-mail emotion/adoption study. *Information Systems ResearchResearch, 14*(2), 189–217. https://doi.org/10.1287/isre.14.2.189.16018

Chow, W., & Chen, Y. (2012). Corporate sustainable development: Testing a new scale based on mainland Chinese context. *Journal of Business EthicsEthics, 105*(4), 519–533. https://doi.org/10.1007/s10551-011-0983-x

Chung, L., & Parker, L. (2010, March). Managing social and environmental action and accountability in the hospitality industry: A Singapore perspective. *AccountingForum, 34*(1), 46–53.

Claver-Cortés, E., Zaragoza-Sáez, P., Úbeda-García, M., Marco-Lajara, B., & García-Lillo, F. (2018). Strategic knowledge management in subsidiaries and MNC performance. The role of the relational context. *Journal of Knowledge ManagementManagement, 22*(5), 1153–1175. https://doi.org/10.1108/JKM-07-2017-0305

Commission of the European Communities. (2001, July 18). Green paper-promoting a European framework for corporate social responsibility. DOC/01/9.

Dao, V., Langella, I., & Carbo, J. (2011). From green to sustainability: Information technology and an integrated sustainability framework. *The Journal of Strategic Information SystemsSystems, 20*(1), 63–79. https://doi.org/10.1016/j.jsis.2011.01.002

Dayan, R., Heisig, P., & Matos, F. (2017). Knowledge management as a factor for the formulation and implementation of organization strategy. *Journal of Knowledge ManagementManagement, 21*(2), 308–329. https://doi.org/10.1108/JKM-02-2016-0068

Delgado-Verde, M., Amores-Salvadó, J., Martín-de Castro, G., & Navas-López, J. E. (2014). Green intellectual capital and environmental product innovation: The mediating role of green social capital. *Knowledge Management Research & Practice, 12*(3), 261–275.

Dijkstra, T. K., & Henseler, J. (2015a). Consistent and asymptotically normal PLS estimators for linear structural equations. *Computational Statistics & Data AnalysisAnalysis, 81*, 10–23. https://doi.org/10.1016/j.csda.2014.07.008

Dijkstra, T. K., & Henseler, J. (2015b). Consistent partial least squares path modeling. *MIS QuarterlyQuarterly, 39*(2), 297–316. https://doi.org/10.25300/MISQ/2015/39.2.02

Engström, T., Westnes, P., & Westnes, F. (2003). Evaluating intellectual capital in the hotel industry. *Journal of Intellectual CapitalCapital, 4*(3), 287–303. https://doi.org/10.1108/14691930310487761

Falk, R. F., & Miller, N. B. (1992). *A primer for soft modelling*. University of Akron Press.

Font, X., & Lynes, J. (2018). Corporate social responsibility in tourism and hospitality. *Journal of Sustainable TourismTourism, 26*(7), 1027–1042. https://doi.org/10.1080/09669582.2018.1488856

Garay, L., & Font, X. (2012). Doing good to do well? Corporate social responsibility reasons, practices and impacts in small and medium accommodation enterprises. *International Journal of Hospitality ManagementManagement, 31*(2), 329–337. https://doi.org/10.1016/j.ijhm.2011.04.013

García, F., & Armas, Y. (2007). Relation between social-environmental responsibility and performance in hotel firms. *International Journal of Hospitality Management, 26*(4), 824–839.

Gibson, C. B., & Birkinshaw, J. (2004). The antecedents, consequences and mediating role of organizational ambidexterity. *Academy of Management JournalManagement Journal, 47*(2), 209–226. https://doi.org/10.2307/20159573

Govindan, K., Khodaverdi, R., & Jafarian, A. (2013). A fuzzy multi criteria approach for measuring sustainability performance of a supplier based on triple bottom line approach. *Journal of Cleaner Productionproduction, 47*, 345–354. https://doi.org/10.1016/j.jclepro.2012.04.014

Grant, R. (1991). The resource-based theory of competitive advantage: Implications for strategy formulation. *California Management ReviewReview, 33*(3), 114–135. https://doi.org/10.2307/41166664

GRI. (2018). *GRI 101: Foundation 2016*. Global Reporting Initiative.

Hair, F., Jr, Sarstedt, M., Hopkins, L., & Kuppelwieser, V. (2014). Partial least squares structural equation modeling (PLS-SEM). An emerging tool in business research. *European Business ReviewReview, 26*(2), 106–121. https://doi.org/10.1108/EBR-10-2013-0128

Hair, J. F., Ringle, C. M., & Sarstedt, M. (2011). PLS-SEM: Indeed a silver bullet. *Journal of Marketing Theory and PracticePractice, 19*(2), 139–152. https://doi.org/10.2753/MTP1069-6679190202

Hart, S. L. (1995). A natural-resource-based view of the firm. *Academy of Management ReviewReview, 20*(4), 986–1014. https://doi.org/10.5465/amr.1995.9512280033

Hayes, A. F., & Scharkow, M. (2013). The relative trustworthiness of inferential tests of the indirect effect in statistical mediation analysis: Does method really matter? *Psychological Sciencescience, 24*(10), 1918–1927. https://doi.org/10.1177/0956797613480187

Henseler, J. (2017a). Partial least squares path modeling. In P. Leeflang, P., J. Wieringa, J., T. Bijmolt, T. & K. Pauwels, K. (Eds.), *Advanced methods for modeling markets* (pp. 361–381). Springer.

Henseler, J. (2017b). Bridging design and behavioral research with variance-based structural equation modeling. *Journal of AdvertisingAdvertising, 46*(1), 178–192. https://doi.org/10.1080/00913367.2017.1281780

Henseler, J., Dijkstra, T. K., Sarstedt, M., Ringle, C. M., Diamantopoulos, A., Straub, D. W., Ketchen, D. J., Hair, J. F., Hult, G. T. M., & Calantone, R. J. (2014). Common beliefs and reality about PLS: Comments on Rönkkö and Evermann (2013). *Organizational rResearch Methodsmethods, 17*(2), 182–209. https://doi.org/10.1177/1094428114526928

Hill, S. A., & Birkinshaw, J. (2014). Ambidexterity and survival in corporate venture units. *Journal of ManagementManagement, 40*(7), 1899–1931. https://doi.org/10.1177/0149206312445925

Holcomb, J. L., Upchurch, R. S., & Okumus, F. (2007). Corporate social responsibility: What are top hotel companies reporting? *International Journal of Contemporary Hospitality ManagementManagement, 19*(6), 461–475. https://doi.org/10.1108/09596110710775129

Hosteltur. (2019). *Los hotelesfacturan 16.600 M. €en 2018, un 2,5% más, lejos de lo previsto*. https://www.hosteltur.com/128851_el-sector-hotelero-espanol-factura-16600-m-en-2018-un-25-mas.html

Hu, L. T., & Bentler, P. M. (1998). Fit indices in covariance structure modelling: Sensitivity to underparameterized model misspecification. *Psychological MethodsMethods, 3*(4), 424–453. https://doi.org/10.1037/1082-989X.3.4.424

Huang, C. L., & Kung, F. H. (2011). Environmental consciousness and intellectual capital management: Evidence from Taiwan's manufacturing industry. *Management DecisionDecision, 49*(9), 1405–1425. https://doi.org/10.1108/00251741111173916

INE. (2019). *Cuenta Satélite del Turismo en España*. https://www.ine.es/dyngs/INEbase/es/operacion.htm?c=Estadistica_C&cid=1254736169169&menu=ultiDatos&idp=1254735576863

Jamali, D., Safieddine, A. M., & Rabbath, M. (2008). Corporate governance and corporate social responsibility synergies and interrelationships. *Corporate Governance: An International ReviewReview, 16*(5), 443–459. https://doi.org/10.1111/j.1467-8683.2008.00702.x

Kim, T., Kim, W., Park, S., Lee, G., & Jee, B. (2012). Intellectual capital and business performance: What structural relationships do they have in upper-upscale hotels? *International Journal of Tourism ResearchResearch, 14*(4), 391–408. https://doi.org/10.1002/jtr.1868

Lee, M. T., & Raschke, R. L. (2020). Innovative sustainability and stakeholders' shared understanding: The secret sauce to "performance with a purpose. *Journal of Business ResearchResearch, 108*, 20–28. https://doi.org/10.1016/j.jbusres.2019.10.020

Lee, S., Gon, B., & Kim, H. (2012). An integrated view of knowledge management for performance. *Journal of Knowledge ManagementManagement, 16*(2), 183–203. https://doi.org/10.1108/13673271211218807

Lin, W., Ho, J., & Sambasivan, M. (2018). Impact of corporate political activity on the relationship between corporate social responsibility and financial performance: A dynamic panel data approach. *SustainabilitySustainability, 11*(1), 60. https://doi.org/10.3390/su11010060

López-Gamero, M. D., Zaragoza-Sáez, P., Claver-Cortés, E., & Molina-Azorín, J. F. (2011). Sustainable development and intangibles: Building sustainable intellectual capital. *Business Strategy and the EnvironmentEnvironment, 20*(1), 18–37. https://doi.org/10.1002/bse.666

Martínez-Martínez, A., Cegarra-Navarro, J. G., & García-Pérez, A. (2015). Environmental knowledge management: A long-term enabler of tourism development. *Tourism ManagementManagement, 50*, 281–291. https://doi.org/10.1016/j.tourman.2015.03.006

Martínez-Martínez, A., Cegarra-Navarro, J. G., García-Pérez, A., & Wensley, A. (2019). Knowledge agents as drivers of environmental sustainability and business performance in the hospitality sector. *Tourism Management, 70*, 381–389.

NemecRudez, H., & Mihalic, T. (2007). Intellectual capital in the hotel industry: A case study from Slovenia. *International Journal of Hospitality Management, 6*(1), 188–199.

OMT-UNWTO. (2018). *Panorama OMT dDel tTurismointernacional 2017*, .ISBN: 978-92-844-1988-3.

Paillé, P., Chen, Y., Boiral, O., & Jin, J. (2014). The impact of human resource management on environmental performance: An employee-level study. *Journal of Business EthicsEthics, 121*(3), 451–466. https://doi.org/10.1007/s10551-013-1732-0

Palacios, D., & Garrigós, F. J. (2006). The effect of knowledge management practices on firm performance. *Journal of KnowledgeManagement, 10*(3), 143–156.

Palacios-Florencio, B., García del Junco, J., Castellanos-Verdugo, M., & Rosa-Díaz, I. (2018). Trust as mediator of corporate social responsibility, image and loyalty in the hotel sector. *Journal of Sustainable TourismTourism, 26*(7), 1273–1289. https://doi.org/10.1080/09669582.2018.1447944

Parisi, C., & Hockerts, K. N. (2008). Managerial mind sets and performance measurement systems of CSR-related intangibles. *Measuring Business ExcellenceExcellence, 12*(2), 51–67. https://doi.org/10.1108/13683040810881199

Pine, R., & Phillips, P. (2005). Performance comparisons of hotels in China. *International Journal of Hospitality ManagementManagement, 24*(1), 57–73. https://doi.org/10.1016/j.ijhm.2004.04.004

Podsakoff, P. M., MacKenzie, S. B., & Podsakoff, N. P. (2012). Sources of method bias in social science research and recommendations on how to control it. *Annual rReview of Psychologypsychology, 63*, 539–569. https://doi.org/10.1146/annurev-psych-120710-100452

Popoli, P. (2015). Reinforcing intangible assets through CSR in a globalized world. *Journal of Management Policies and Practice, 3*(1), 23–30.

Purvis, B., Mao, Y., & Robinson, D. (2019). Three pillars of sustainability: In search of conceptual origins. *Sustainability ScienceScience, 14*(3), 681–695. https://doi.org/10.1007/s11625-018-0627-5

Quintana-García, C., Marchante-Lara, M., & Benavides-Chicón, C. (2018). Social responsibility and total quality in the hospitality industry: Does gender matter? *Journal of Sustainable TourismTourism, 26*(5), 722–739. https://doi.org/10.1080/09669582.2017.1401631

Reed, K. K., Lubatkin, M., & Srinivasan, N. (2006). Proposing and testing an intellectual capital-based view of the firm. *Journal of Management StudiesStudies, 43*(4), 867–893. https://doi.org/10.1111/j.1467-6486.2006.00614.x

Roberts, N., & Thatcher, J. (2009). Conceptualizing and testing formative constructs: Tutorial and annotated example. *ACM SIGMIS Database: The DATABASE ffor Advances in Information SystemsSystems, 40*(3), 9–39. https://doi.org/10.1145/1592401.1592405

Saeidi, S., Sofian, S., Saeidi, P., Saeidi, S., & Saaeidi, S. (2015). How does corporate social responsibility contribute to firm financial performance? The mediating role of competitive advantage, reputation, and customer satisfaction. *Journal of Business ResearchResearch, 68*(2), 341–350. https://doi.org/10.1016/j.jbusres.2014.06.024

Sarstedt, M., Ringle, C. M., & Hair, J. F. (2017). Treating unobserved heterogeneity in PLS-SEM: A multi-method approach. In *Partial least squares path modelling.*, (pp. 197–217). Springer.

Stewart, T. (1997). *Intellectual capital: The new wealth of organizations*. Doubleday Currency.

Subramaniam, M., & Youndt, M. A. (2005). The influence of intellectual capital on the nature of innovative capabilities. *Academy of Management JournalJournal, 48*(3), 450–464. https://doi.org/10.5465/amj.2005.17407911

Surroca, J., Tribó, J., & Waddock, S. (2010). Corporate responsibility and financial performance: The role of intangible resources. *Strategic Management JournalJournal, 31*(5), 463–490. https://doi.org/10.1002/smj.820

Turker, D. (2009). Measuring corporate social responsibility: A scale development study. *Journal of Business EthicsEthics, 85*(4), 411–427. https://doi.org/10.1007/s10551-008-9780-6

Von Krogh, G., Ichijo, K., & Nonaka, I. (2000). *Enabling knowledge creation: How to unlock the mystery of tacit knowledge and release the power of innovation*. Oxford University Press.

Waddock, S. (2008). Building a new institutional infrastructure for corporateresponsibility. *Academy of Management PerspectivesPerspectives, 22*(3), 87–108. https://doi.org/10.5465/amp.2008.34587997

White, A. L. (2006). Business brief: Intangibles and CSR. *Business for Social Responsibility, 6*, 1–10.

Wright, R. T., Campbell, D. E., Thatcher, J. B., & Roberts, N. H. (2012). Operationalizing multidimensional constructs in structural equation modelling: Recommendations for IS research. *Communications of the Association for Information SystemsSystems, 30*(23), 367–412. https://doi.org/10.17705/1CAIS.03023

Zack, M. (1999). Developing a knowledge strategy. *California Management ReviewReview, 41*(3), 125–145. https://doi.org/10.2307/41166000

Zack, M., McKeen, J., & Singh, S. (2009). Knowledge management and organizational performance: An exploratory analysis. *Journal of Knowledge ManagementManagement, 13*(6), 392–409. https://doi.org/10.1108/13673270910997088

ANNEX I: Questionnaire

To be answered by the Human Resources Manager
  Age _____
  Educational background_____
  Gender_____

Express your degree of agreement or disagreement for the following statements related to Sustainable Intangible Capital of your hotel (1 = strongly disagree; 7 = strongly agree):

GIC 1 Our employees care about environmental issues	1	2	3	4	5	6	7
GIC 2 Our employees have knowledge and skills to protect the environment							
GIC 3 Our employees cooperate in working groups to address environmental protection issues							
GIC 4 Our employees cooperate with our suppliers to protect the environment							
GIC 5 Our employees cooperate with our customers / distributors to protect the environment							
GIC 6 Our company carries out innovations to protect the environment (development of "green" products / services)							
GIC 7 Our company invests in facilities to protect the environment							
SEIC 1 Our employees are highly qualified							
SEIC 2 Our employees are considered the best in the sector							
SEIC 3 Our employees are creative and bright							
SEIC 4 Our employees are experts in their jobs and functions							
SEIC 5 Our employees develop new ideas and knowledge							
SEIC 6 Our employees are experts in collaborating with each other to diagnose and solve problems							
SEIC 7 Our employees share information and learn from each other							
SEIC 8 Our employees interact and exchange ideas with people from different areas of the company							
SEIC 9 Our employees partner with customers, suppliers, partners, etc., to develop solutions							
SEIC 10 Our employees apply knowledge of one area of the company to problems and opportunities that arise in another							
SEIC 11 Our organization uses patents and licenses as a way of storing knowledge							
SEIC 12 Much of our organization's knowledge is contained in manuals, databases, etc.							
SEIC 13 The culture of our organization (stories, rituals) contains valuable ideas, ways of doing business, etc.							
SEIC 14 Our organization incorporates much of its knowledge and information in structures, systems and processes.							

Express your degree of agreement or disagreement with the following statements related to Corporate Social Responsibility (1 = strongly disagree; 7 = strongly agree):

ESSR 1 Our company implements programs to minimize its negative impact on the environment	1	2	3	4	5	6	7
ESSR 2 Our company participates in activities that aim to protect and improve the quality of the natural environment							
ESSR 3 Our company aims for sustainable growth that considers future generations							
ESSR 4 Our company emphasizes the importance of its social responsibilities towards society							
ECSR 1 Our company provides complete and accurate information to our customers							
ECSR 2 Our company respects the rights of the consumer beyond the legal requirements							
ECSR 3 Customer satisfaction is very important for our company							
ECSR 4 Our company supports employees who wish to acquire additional training							
ECSR 5 Our company's policies encourage employees to develop their skills and careers							
ECSR 6 Our company implements flexible policies to provide a good work and personal balance to its employees							
ECSR 7 Management is involved with the needs and wishes of employees							

Express your degree of agreement or disagreement with the following statements related to the Strategic Knowledge Management (1 = strongly disagree; 7 = strongly agree):

	1	2	3	4	5	6	7
SKM 1 The company's vision recognizes the need and commitment to create and transfer knowledge							
SKM 2 The company has an inventory of the most critical and essential skills							
SKM 3 The processes to develop and distribute knowledge among the members of the organization allow the company to enjoy a superior position to its competitors							
SKM 4 The staff is characterized by being entrepreneurial, willing to innovate and committed to sharing their knowledge with the rest							
SKM 5 The organizational structure is increasingly horizontal, promoting multifunctional work teams							
SKM 6 The organizational culture tends to be more open to new initiatives, experimentation and oriented to continuous learning							
SKM 7 The company has information and communication technologies to store the most valuable knowledge and disseminate it among its members							

To be answered by the Chief Executive Officer
Age _____
Educational background_____
Gender_____

Rate the following performance indicators of your hotel in relation to its competitors (1 = very low; 7 = very high) during the last three years.

	1	2	3	4	5	6	7
HP 1 Market share growth							
HP 2 Average sales growth							
HP 3 Brand recognition							
HP 4 Firm market image							
HP 5 Average hotel occupancy							
HP 6 Customer satisfaction level							
HP 7 Employee satisfaction level							
HP 8 Revenue per available room (RevPAR)							

Assess the extent to which the actions developed by your hotel to protect the environment have had an impact on the following aspects (1 = strongly disagree; 7 = strongly agree):

	1	2	3	4	5	6	7
EP 1 Our hotel has reduced waste and emissions of toxic products							
EP 2 Our hotel has reduced total direct and indirect energy consumption							
EP 3 Our hotel has increased the volume of recycled materials							
EP 4 Our hotel has increased the rate of renewable energy consumption							
EP 5 Our hotel has increased the number of ecological products/services developed/offered to customers							

Developing sustainable business models: local knowledge acquisition and tourism lifestyle entrepreneurship

Álvaro Dias, Graça Miranda Silva, Mafalda Patuleia and Maria Rosario González-Rodríguez

ABSTRACT
Tourism lifestyle entrepreneurs' (TLEs) businesses are associated with sustainable business models (SBMs) due to a link to the place. This link is a source of essential local knowledge that provides differentiation, competitiveness, and sustainability. Given the importance of local knowledge to SBMs, this article explores knowledge management by examining how TLEs acquire and integrate knowledge as well as its effects on innovativeness and self-efficacy. We use a sequential mixed-methods approach in which we first conducted a qualitative study with four in-depth semi-structured interviews with TLEs, followed by a quantitative study through a survey of 115 TLEs, and third we conducted another qualitative study based on four semi-structured interviews. The results indicate that entrepreneurial communication has a significantly positive and direct effect on both the innovativeness and self-efficacy of TLEs. A community-centered strategy has a positive influence on innovativeness and self-efficacy but via the indirect effect of entrepreneurial communication. Local knowledge assimilation plays a mediating role between the acquisition of local knowledge and innovativeness and self-efficacy. These findings provide a general understanding and framework about how TLEs link the elements of an SBM to greater innovativeness and self-efficacy.

Introduction

A traditional business model outlines the architecture of a company's value creation, delivery, and capture mechanisms (Teece, 2010). In turn, sustainable business models (SBMs) "incorporate a triple bottom line approach and consider a wide range of stakeholder interests, including environment and society" (Bocken et al., 2014, p. 42). A SBM transcends the narrow perspective of for-profit models (Schaltegger et al., 2016a) by extending the focus on organizational value creation to incorporate social and ecological values (Schaltegger et al., 2016b). Boons and Lüdeke-Freund (2013) state that a SBM incorporates these values as generic elements: value proposition, organizational infrastructure, customer interface, and financial model.

Tourism lifestyle entrepreneurs (TLEs) constitute an important group within the tourism business (Thomas et al., 2011). The literature considers them different from entrepreneurs in other economic activities (Carlsen et al., 2008) because they are also governed by nonfinancial criteria (Ateljevic & Doorne, 2000; Wang et al., 2019), such as environmental and social goals, that are core features of a SBM (Stubbs, 2017). For them, business is a way of life in which the boundaries between personal life and work are blurred (Sun et al., 2020). TLEs also tend to differentiate themselves with an "ideological concept of sustainability, derived from their intrinsic lifestyle motivation" (Wang et al., 2019, p. 1156). In opposition to large firms, they are more likely to adopt a sustainable behavior (Bosworth & Farrell, 2011; Morrison, 2006) that contributes to sustaining "the natural environment or adding value to local communities" (Morrison, 2006, p. 200).

TLEs' place-based conception of sustainability (Shrivastava & Kennelly, 2013) reflects concerns with the preservation of the natural environment and the local culture and traditions (Sun et al., 2020) as well as purchasing from local suppliers, trading at the community level, and providing local employment (Jack & Anderson, 2002; Morrison, 2002). As argued in the SBM literature, "community spirit" is a distinctive characteristic in which social embeddedness plays a key role (Neumeyer & Santos, 2018; Schaltegger et al., 2016b) by providing access to valuable local knowledge and to a network of local stakeholders (Yachin, 2019), as compared to traditional business models (Stubbs & Cocklin, 2008).

In this study, we explore the link between the place as a source of local knowledge for TLEs and their SBMs to address three theoretical gaps. First, the research on SBMs has focused on their elements that misses a general understanding and a framework of the link between SBMs and how they contribute to innovation (Schaltegger et al., 2016b). Second, although there is a growing body of research on sustainable entrepreneurship, the role of the link to the place is still underexplored in the TLE context (Kibler et al., 2015). Third, although both gaps can be addressed independently, the link between the elements of the SBM and the connection to the place is not separable in the context of knowledge management. Knowledge management represents an essential issue in the relations between the elements of a business model (Teece, 2010). Although business theory recognizes the existence of studies related to knowledge acquisition and assimilation (c.f. Liao et al., 2007; Liao et al., 2010), the tourism research has made few contributions regarding the way TLEs manage knowledge (Hoarau, 2014). This is especially true for the specificities of this group of entrepreneurs that are not conducive to the existing traditional models in the business literature (Bosworth & Farrell, 2011). There are few studies that focus on the mechanisms that TLEs use to acquire and assimilate local knowledge that is in a state constant flux (García-Rosell et al., 2019). Specifically, as indicated by Hoarau (2014) and Yachin (2019), these entrepreneurs have reduced management and organizational capabilities; therefore, how they translate this knowledge into innovation is unclear (Marchant & Mottiar, 2011). Thus, considering the four elements of a SBM, the objectives of this study are (i) to understand the key role of the place as a source of local knowledge, (ii) to identify the link between the SBMs through which TLEs covert local knowledge into innovation and self-efficacy, and (iii) to propose a model to develop a SBM.

The contribution of this study is threefold. First, it addresses the local knowledge management of TLEs by providing a framework for how they link knowledge to the elements of a SBM. This is an underexplored topic despite the representativeness of TLEs in tourism and their importance to sustainability. Specifically, by addressing SBMs, we examine the processes by which TLEs acquire and assimilate local knowledge and the way local knowledge translates into innovation. Second, to the best of our knowledge, this is the first study to explore the relation between the assimilation and acquisition of local knowledge and a community-centered strategy and entrepreneurial communication as well as the mediating role of assimilation as an enabling factor in transforming knowledge into the innovativeness and self-efficacy of TLEs. Third, the sequential mixed-methods approach this study applies is a methodological contribution. We conduct a qualitative study that leads to a better understanding of the relevance of the variables and relations proposed in our conceptual model. After this study, we conduct a quantitative study through a survey to test the conceptual model. Finally, we conduct qualitative follow-up interviews with TLEs.

The study proceeds as follows: Section 2 presents the theoretical background and the conceptual model. In Section 3, we describe the research design and detail it in the next sections (4, 5 and 6). In Section 7, we discuss the empirical findings. Section 8 concludes by presenting theoretical, practical, and managerial implications; limitations: and future research.

Literature review

Local knowledge management and TLEs

Tles and sustainable business models

In the context of TLEs, the four elements of the SBM are associated with the place. The *value proposition* is the result of the TLEs' place embeddedness that allows tourists to participate in creative and genuine experiences that are associated with the place (Kibler et al., 2015). The quality of the local natural environment and social and cultural practices provide uniqueness (Shrivastava & Kennelly, 2013; Thompson et al., 2018) and a source of competitiveness (Stamboulis & Skayannis, 2003).

The *supply chain infrastructure* is related to the development of the value networks in which community spirit (Stubbs & Cocklin, 2008) and social embeddedness constitute distinctive features of the SBM (Neumeyer & Santos, 2018). By being embedded in local communities, TLEs benefit from the network effect with local stakeholders (Bredvold & Skålén, 2016; Yachin, 2019). Furthermore, the community, heritage, and environmental preservation represent a central concern of the TLE activities that contribute to a more sustainable tourism (de la Barre, 2013) in which environmental training contributes to the employee in-role green performance (Pham et al., 2020).

As a part of the local community, TLEs are able to co-create unique and authentic experiences (Schilar & Keskitalo, 2018) and to target specific market niches (Ateljevic & Doorne, 2000). The TLEs also integrate local stakeholders and communities in the SBM going beyond the classic customer concept as the primary beneficiary (Bocken et al., 2014). These *customer interfaces* represent an unrivaled path to transfer the value proposition. Further, by pursuing economic and non-economic goals (Sun et al., 2020), the *financial model* is strongly related to the TLEs' environmental and social performance (Stubbs, 2017). All the components of the TLEs' SBMs are linked to the place that represents a source of valuable knowledge (Yachin, 2019). Local knowledge gives meaning to the services and experiences they offer to tourists (Anderson, 2012) and simultaneously is unique and difficult to imitate (Shrivastava & Kennelly, 2013). Thus, knowledge plays an important role in the value proposition.

TLEs' knowledge management as a unique field of research

Knowledge management in tourism has particularities inherent to the sector. When compared to other sectors, the context of tourism is very complex, uncertain, and relational (Hall, 2019). The knowledge management models in tourism envisage structured approaches (Cooper, 2015). However, the characteristics of small-scale tourism firms do not facilitate knowledge management in these circumstances for several reasons: small businesses are predominant and often consist of just the founder who may have little training and management experience; lack of trust between partners; knowledge is instrumental and is only relevant if the results for the business are evident and immediate; the tourist product may be fragmented by various agents; the business and staff may be seasonal; and the entrepreneur may be risk averse (Cooper, 2015; Czernek, 2017).

The reality of TLEs is even more distinctive. Most of them are not exclusively governed by economic and financial criteria (Ateljevic & Doorne, 2000; Wang et al., 2019). Furthermore, the option to enter tourism is more related to the detection of opportunities than to thoughtful business decisions (Hjalager et al., 2018). Those opportunities can be low entry barriers like low investment or the inexistence of specific or formal training prerequisites (Ioannides & Petersen, 2003). As such, TLEs likely have little experience and few resources (Marchant & Mottiar, 2011).

TLEs' knowledge management

Knowledge can be divided into two groups: tacit and explicit. While tacit knowledge cannot be codified because it is associated with what people know, explicit knowledge is easily codified and transferable (Cooper, 2015). The superior strategic value of tacit knowledge is well recognized (Hoarau, 2014; Weidenfeld et al., 2010) because it is difficult to replicate (Stamboulis & Skayannis, 2003). As TLEs are highly associated with the place, the strategic value of tacit local knowledge is even higher for the following reasons: this knowledge can only be accessed through interpersonal interaction in that place (Yachin, 2019); local knowledge is difficult to access and imitate by competitors (Cooper, 2015); local knowledge increases the likelihood of sustainable value creation (Shrivastava & Kennelly, 2013); and it improves co-creation processes (García-Rosell et al., 2019).

Knowledge management can be divided into two phases: *potential* that integrates the steps of acquisition and assimilation of knowledge, and *realized* that consists of the transformation or exploitation of knowledge (Jansen et al., 2005; Zahra & George, 2002). The latter means that knowledge cannot be applied without first having acquired it (Hoarau, 2014). As such, the starting point in knowledge management is the way external knowledge (tacit and explicit) is acquired and assimilated in the tourism business processes (Hoarau, 2014). To exploit external knowledge, firms should translate it into useful forms that are market oriented in order to build competitive advantage through innovation and more responsive processes (Zahra & George, 2002). However, TLEs use their own mechanisms to manage local knowledge. Table 1 summarizes these mechanisms.

Table 1. TLE-specific mechanisms for knowledge management.

Acquisition	Assimilation	Outcomes
Informal and practical channels (Local embeddedness) • Living and spending time locally; sharing experiences, and stories • Participating in conversations • Observation and listening • Acting with other stakeholders • Being close to customers	Organizational dimension (processes and capabilities) • Routines to transform newly acquired knowledge • Incorporation in the organization knowledge stocks	Innovativeness • New experiences • Relevant interpretations of new local knowledge • Tailor-made innovations to niche markets • Resource exploitation
Community-centered strategy (active channels) • Partnership with stakeholders • Collaborative practices with the community to "attract" new knowledge • Cooperative strategies	Communication entrepreneurial orientation dimension (transformation in client-oriented narratives) • Knowledge diffusion within the organization • Free idea sharing • Transform new local knowledge into new stories and meaning-making experiences • "Selling the place" • Identity building	Entrepreneurial self-efficacy • Subjective measures of performance

Knowledge acquisition

Although the acquisition of tacit knowledge can be accomplished through socialization (Zhang et al., 2015), TLEs have unique mechanisms to acquire local knowledge (Bosworth & Farrell, 2011; Ioannides & Petersen, 2003; Kibler et al., 2015). Two complementary approaches for knowledge acquisition arise from the literature, namely, local embeddedness and a community-centered strategy. The acquisition of local knowledge stems from the fact that the TLEs are embedded locally (Bredvold & Skålén, 2016). This embeddedness provides access to local knowledge by merely living and spending time locally (Valtonen, 2009). Embeddedness is "the mechanism whereby an entrepreneur becomes part of the local structure" (Jack & Anderson, 2002, p. 467) that allows them to monitor the continuously evolving local knowledge through the sharing of experiences, stories, and tools (García-Rosell et al., 2019). Zhang et al. (2015) have found interactive relationships to be crucial to knowledge spillover. As such, place embeddedness allows the entrepreneur to align with the local cultural and social environment (Bredvold & Skålén, 2016).

Richards (2011) emphasizes the role of participating in conversations at cafes or in squares; and Valtonen (2009) also finds that observing, listening, and acting jointly with other stakeholders are mechanisms to acquire new knowledge. Furthermore, being close to customers is also a valuable source of tacit knowledge (Shaw & Williams, 2009). These mechanisms can be described as informal knowledge channels (Ioannides & Petersen, 2003; Marchant & Mottiar, 2011) with a distinctive practical nature (Valtonen, 2009). This approximation between learning and practice establishes a close relation between the processes of acquisition and the assimilation of knowledge (Cooper, 2015; Weidenfeld et al., 2010). As such, we hypothesize:

> H1. Local knowledge acquisition positively relates to local knowledge assimilation.

The second approach to acquiring knowledge is to more actively promote or participate in community-centered activities. The access to tacit local knowledge is mostly practice-based (Hoarau, 2014) and exists in a multiplicity of knowledge sources that require the ability to read symbolic and non-verbal evidence (Hall, 2019). In this context, knowledge acquisition benefits from the involvement of stakeholders through partnerships (Czernek, 2017) and the realization of collaborative practices (García-Rosell et al., 2019). The implementation of cooperative strategies also overcomes any barriers to knowledge sharing such as distrust and high competition (Czernek, 2017). As such, "forming and utilizing links to external actors is a practice which owner-managers of micro-tourism firms can develop and should apply. After all, such links embed entrepreneurial opportunities" (Yachin, 2019, p. 61-62). In this sense, TLEs benefit from acquiring local knowledge through actively cooperating with other local stakeholders, that is, community-centered strategies. These strategies transform new local knowledge into new stories and meaningful experiences and to "selling the place" that means TLEs not only acquire the knowledge but also share it with tourists (Schilar & Keskitalo, 2018). Formally, we propose the following hypothesis:

> H2. Pursuing a community-centered strategy positively relates to entrepreneurial communication.

Knowledge assimilation and TLEs' self-efficacy and innovativeness

The assimilation capacity refers to the firms' ability to integrate external knowledge into the organizational knowledge stock (Hoarau, 2014). The assimilation of knowledge also requires specific skills and experience from the entrepreneur (and his/her staff). The assimilation is the result of the existing routines, life and market experiences, and "certain person-specific competencies" (Ioannides & Petersen, 2003). More precisely, it combines the "knowledge corridor (ability to imagine resources as products), personal traits (creative thinking) and social network (access to information and inspiration)" (Yachin, 2019, p. 59). Thus, two dimensions exist. First, the organizational dimension represents the processes and capabilities to assimilate knowledge. It is related to the routines that transform newly acquired knowledge and incorporate it in the organization knowledge stock (Weidenfeld et al., 2010). This stock is destination-specific and user-oriented and thus provides an intangible and difficult to replicate source of competitive advantage (Stamboulis & Skayannis, 2003). Second, the communicational dimension comprises the entrepreneurs' user-oriented activities. Complementarily to the organizational capabilities, TLEs must be able to convert communication into client-oriented narratives (Yachin, 2019) by capitalizing on their connection with customers (Marchant & Mottiar, 2011) through a producer-oriented context (Richards, 2011). This connection demands that the TLE has important traits such as communication and interaction (Yachin, 2019). These abilities develop knowledge assimilation by stimulating its diffusion within the organization through the free sharing of ideas (Hoarau, 2014).

Knowledge management can provide TLEs with significant benefits in terms of innovation and competitiveness (Cooper, 2015; Weidenfeld et al., 2010). However, in the TLE context, performance should be contextualized. TLEs assess performance based on criteria that are not necessarily economic (Wang et al., 2019). In addition to the maintenance of the quality of life (Thomas et al., 2011), they also use social (Morrison, 2006), ideological, environmental (Ateljevic & Doorne, 2000), and cultural (Bredvold & Skålén, 2016) indicators. This myriad of options indicates that the most appropriate ways to assess TLEs' performance are subjective measures of performance (Wang et al., 2019), such as TLE's perceived self-efficacy that is defined as the TLEs' beliefs in their capabilities to achieve the business goals (Hallak et al., 2012) and their innovativeness (Hoarau, 2014).

Considering this definition of self-efficacy, the TLEs' performance is subjectively perceived through a combination of financial and nonfinancial indicators. The perceived self-efficacy depends on the ability to transform assimilated knowledge into enhanced performance (Marchant & Mottiar, 2011; Shaw & Williams, 2009). This transformation occurs through poorly structured activities (Cooper, 2015). Considering the contextual nature of local knowledge, the assimilation capacity depends on the interaction between the organization and the community and its stakeholders that is associated with life experience (Yachin, 2019). This valorization of knowledge as practice-based and context-specific contributes to overcoming TLEs' low qualification levels (Czernek, 2017; Hoarau, 2014). Additionally, these entrepreneurs usually follow an unstructured approach to knowledge management through a process of trial and error (Cooper, 2015). As such, previous experience plays an important role in the way knowledge is assimilated and transformed into increased performance (Martínez-Martínez et al., 2019). As such, assimilated knowledge generates growing returns in which the more it is used, the greater the benefits it delivers (Cooper, 2015) that then increases TLEs' perceived self-efficacy. As such, we hypothesize:

H3a. Local knowledge assimilation positively relates to TLEs' perceived self-efficacy.

In addition to self-efficacy, knowledge assimilation also supports innovation which is the basis of organizations' competitiveness (Shaw & Williams, 2009). Innovation is a recognized outcome of the TLE activities with important effects on both the organization and the destination (Sun et al., 2020). To do so, they should bridge the gap between their activity and the market (Eikhof & Haunschild, 2006). However, in tourism, converting knowledge into innovation requires certain abilities, especially when it concerns tacit knowledge (Hoarau, 2014). Weidenfeld et al. (2010) argue that exchange practices between organizations are essential for small-scale businesses to assimilate knowledge. Conducting collective learning practices, peer-to-peer relationships (Cooper, 2015), and active participation in networks (Weidenfeld et al., 2010) foster knowledge transfers and increase trust and shared values. As such, by influencing local knowledge assimilation, social participation plays a key role in the innovation success of small-scale businesses (Hoarau, 2014). The involvement of the local stakeholders facilitates knowledge assimilation (Czernek, 2017), stimulates innovation spillovers and collaborative efforts to generate local innovation (Zhang et al., 2015), and feeds TLEs with new local knowledge that is translated into innovative client-oriented narratives (Yachin, 2019). In this vein, knowledge assimilation supports

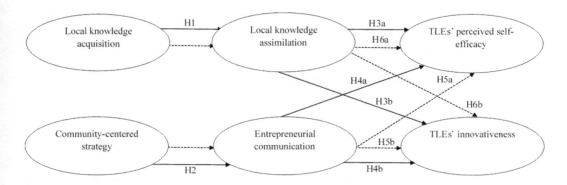

------→ Mediating hypotheses

Figure 1. Conceptual model.

innovation (Marchant & Mottiar, 2011; Shaw & Williams, 2009), even if it is the result of spontaneous and unstructured processes (Cooper, 2015). Thus:

> H3b. Local knowledge assimilation positively relates to TLEs' innovativeness.

Communication and interaction skills with stakeholders, clients, and the community also contribute to the innovation process (Yachin, 2019) by facilitating the translation of acquired knowledge and its application to new experiences (Hoarau, 2014). TLEs are generally effective communicators who exploit their "resources far more inclusively and thoroughly" than other workers (Eikhof & Haunschild, 2006: p. 240). They provide tourists with experiences associated with host and place values by offering a glimpse of local life (Sun et al., 2020), where new relevant interpretations of the place are implemented and validated through feedback from the tourists (Cooper, 2015). This process encourages innovation by adding value to the experiences delivered to the consumers (Eikhof & Haunschild, 2006). Community interaction also increases the sense of contribution and accomplishment of more sustainable practices (Morrison, 2006) that enables the TLEs to achieve their goals (Schilar & Keskitalo, 2018). By exchanging knowledge with other local stakeholders and customers, TLEs increase their ability to operate in highly segmented tourist markets with very demanding tourists that increases the likelihood of generating tailor-made innovations for niche markets (Ateljevic & Doorne, 2000). Thus, we formulated the following hypotheses:

> H4a. Entrepreneurial communication positively relates to TLEs' perceived self-efficacy.

> H4b. Entrepreneurial communication positively relates to TLEs' innovativeness.

Moreover, the business literature finds that the process of knowledge assimilation has a mediating role between its acquisition and performance (c.f. Zahra & George, 2002). Czernek (2017) argues that the conversion of acquired knowledge into better innovation requires its adequate assimilation. By being part of the community, TLEs interact face-to-face to leverage the acquired knowledge from innovation (Hoarau, 2014). It indicates that the transformation of the acquired knowledge into enhanced performance requires an adequate assimilation of this new knowledge (Czernek, 2017). Hoarau (2014) argues that this ability to assimilate knowledge enables TLEs to innovate and improve their performance. The ability to assimilate local tacit knowledge and use it to differentiate themselves from their competitors enables TLEs to achieve a competitive advantage (Cooper, 2015). Thus, we propose the following mediating hypotheses:

> H5a. Entrepreneurial communication mediates the relation between a community-centered strategy and TLEs' perceived self-efficacy.

H5b. Entrepreneurial communication mediates the relation between a community-centered strategy and TLEs' innovativeness.

H6a. Local knowledge assimilation mediates the relation between local knowledge acquisition and TLEs' perceived self-efficacy.

H6b. Local knowledge assimilation mediates the relation between local knowledge acquisition and TLEs' innovativeness.

Figure 1 shows the conceptual model and hypotheses.

Method

We use a sequential mixed-methods approach that combines two qualitative studies with a quantitative study.

The target population of this study is Portuguese and Spanish TLEs. We selected the TLEs based on the following inclusion criteria: (i) had a tourism related business; (ii) independently ran business (not part of larger chains or franchising networks); (iii) committed to expressing the local character of the destination; and (iv) sustained the local environment, heritage, and traditions. These criteria come from Bosworth and Farrell (2011) and Morrison (2006). The participants were from the center region of Portugal and the Andalucía autonomous community (Spain).

To increase the confidence of the participants, confidentiality and anonymity were assured in all studies.

Qualitative research I

Qualitative method

The first study is qualitative and seeks to gain insight into the variables and relations proposed in our conceptual model on TLEs and the SBM elements. The research team performed face-to-face in-depth interviews with four TLEs (1 hostel, 2 tour guides, and 1 cooking experience restaurant) that were selected using a purposive sampling technique. Although there was an interview script, a flexible approach was followed so that respondents could feel free to address the most important topics. Thus, in line with Bosworth and Farrell (2011) approach, the interviewer fulfilled the role of facilitator, although probing questions were used to explore some topics more deeply. Each interview took, on average, two hours and was held at the entrepreneurs' facilities. Two of the researchers conducted the interviews while taking notes and recording.

Qualitative results

From the interviews we learned about the various elements of SBM and how they facilitated knowledge management. Sustainability practices were integrated in the elements of the SBM, namely at the level of value proposal (tradition, nature preservation), infrastructure (community relationship), and customer relationships (narratives, products) which benefited from the inclusion of local knowledge in the SBM. Knowledge acquisition strategies such as the involvement of people from the community were also verified. Some of the respondents' comments were:

> "Twice a year we hold a local festival with tradition recreations [...] which allows us to publicize our activity".
>
> "Our hostel is decorated with themes alluding to the past of this place [...]. It allows us to have a storytelling with our guests".
>
> "Our customers value very much the traditional dishes made by old ladies of the neighborhood [...] and also our care with the recycling and reuse of materials".

The results of the interviews allowed us to verify the adequacy of the knowledge management variables used in the study. The acquisition of knowledge was essentially achieved informally through conversations with locals and customers. Community-centered strategies arose from cooperation with local stakeholders or from holding events and other festivities. The assimilation of knowledge was quite variable among respondents, but it was linked to transforming knowledge into new experiences and creating new stories and narratives (communication). Some examples taken from the interviews were as follows:

"We are constantly learning new things. We use several sources for that, but the conversations with people from the village are the most important."

"The old ladies who come to cook with us revealed to be a source of new knowledge and a way to improve our experiences, increasing authenticity at the same time."

"The festival we organize always brings new people, functioning as a magnet [...] in which we catch stories, photos, legends and other local traditions".

"As a result of talking with local people, we have a lot of new ideas, which allows us to quickly offer new tours".

"We feel that we are pioneers because we innovate within the tradition of this neighborhood."

These ideas show that a correspondence existed between what was observed in the field and the variables identified in the literature. They were: community-centered strategy (e.g., festivals, workshops, and cooking instruction), knowledge acquisition (talk with local people), communication (new stories and narratives, use of local people for marketing activities), and knowledge assimilation (offering new tours, pioneerism).

Quantitative research

Quantitative method

Data collection and sample

The target population for the quantitative study was Portuguese and Spanish TLEs who met the inclusion criteria previously presented. As obtaining a sampling frame in this case was difficult, we used a non-probability sampling, or more specifically a convenience sampling. One of the researchers recruited TLEs during three tourism entrepreneurship meetings (i.e., Tourism-Up, Taste-Up, and Green-Up) and invited them to participate in the quantitative study. An internet based-questionnaire was used for data collection. The questionnaire was initially developed through a review of the literature and revised following a two-step approach. First, we consulted three tourism academics to assess the content validity of the scales. After that, the questionnaire was pilot tested by using face-to-face semi-structured interviews with five TLEs (1 hostel, 1 tour guide, 1 cooking experiences restaurant, 2 nature tourism) to validate the wording and the survey design. The final internet-based questionnaire was sent by email to the 115 TLEs. A total of 115 complete questionnaires were received. Data collection occurred between February 2019 and October 2019.

Of the respondents, 66% were male, and 62% were born in the place where they currently had their tourism business. Most of the respondents were from the center region of Portugal (85), and the remaining were from the Andalucía autonomous community of Spain. In terms of age, 7.5% were less than 30 years old, 12.5% were between 30 and 40 years old, 25.6% were between 40 and 50 years old, 44.4% were between 50 and 60 years old, and the remaining were older than 60. Regarding firm size, 68% of the TLEs stated that their firms had 10 or less employees, 16.6% stated they had between 11 and 20 employees, and the remaining stated that their firms had more than 20 employees. The average years in operation of a business was 7.26 with a standard deviation of 5.47 years (minimum: 1 year; maximum: 43 years).

Variables

This study adopted existing scales to measure all variables. The acquisition and assimilation of local knowledge were measured using four and two items, respectively, that were adapted from Jansen et al. (2005). The entrepreneurial orientation to communication and the TLEs' innovativeness were measured using a five- and a four-item scale adapted from Kropp et al. (2006). The four items used to measure the TLEs' perceived self-efficacy were adapted from Zhao et al. (2005). Community-centered strategy was measured through a six-item scale adapted from Besser and Miller (2001) and Hallak et al. (2012). The acquisition and assimilation of local knowledge, the entrepreneurial orientation to communication, and the innovativeness of TLEs were measured using seven-point Likert-type scales anchored by one (strongly disagree) and seven (strongly agree). The perceived self-efficacy of TLEs was measured by asking respondents to indicate the degree of confidence with a specific statement (e.g., creating new products, commercializing an idea, or new development) on a five-point Likert-type scale (one equals no confidence disagree to five equals complete confidence). A community-centered strategy was assessed by asking TLEs to evaluate on a five-point Likert-type scale (one equals not important to five equals extremely important) the importance of specific strategies.

Statistical analysis

To test our conceptual model we used structural equation modelling (SEM). More specifically, we used partial least squares (PLS), which is a variance-based structural equation modelling technique, by means of SmartPLS 3 software (Ringle et al., 2015). The analyses and interpretation of the results followed a two-stage approach. We first evaluated the reliability and validity of the measurement model and then assessed the structural model.

To assess the quality of the measurement model, we examined the individual indicators of reliability, convergent validity, internal consistency reliability, and discriminant validity (Hair et al., 2017). The results showed that the standardized factor loadings of all items were above 0.6 (with a minimum value of 0.62) and were all significant at $p < 0.001$, which provided evidence for the individual indicator reliability (Hair et al., 2017). Internal consistency reliability was confirmed because all the constructs' Cronbach alphas and composite reliability (CR) values surpassed the cut-off of 0.7 (See Table 2) (Hair et al., 2017).

Convergent validity was also confirmed for three key reasons. First, as noted before all items loaded positively and significantly on their respective constructs. Second, all constructs had CR values higher than 0.70. Third, as Table 2 shows, the average variance extracted (AVE) for all constructs exceeded the threshold of 0.50 (Bagozzi & Yi, 1988). The discriminant validity was assessed using two approaches. First, we used the Fornell and Larcker criterion. This criterion requires that a construct's square root of AVE (shown on the diagonal with bold values in Table 2) is larger than its biggest correlation with any construct (Fornell & Larcker, 1981). Table 2 shows that this criterion is satisfied for all constructs. Second, we used the heterotrait-monotrait ratio (HTMT) criterion (Hair et al., 2017; Henseler et al., 2015). As Table 2 shows, all HTMT ratios

Table 2. Composite reliability, average variance extracted, correlations, and discriminant validity checks.

Latent Variables	α	CR	AVE	1	2	3	4	5	6
(1) Entrepreneurial communication	0.850	0.893	0.627	**0.792**	0.274	0.427	0.429	0.570	0.726
(2) Local knowledge aquisition	0.760	0.845	0.578	0.228	**0.760**	0.735	0.623	0.190	0.183
(3) Local knowledge assimilation	0.831	0.922	0.856	0.362	0.607	**0.925**	0.425	0.604	0.542
(4) Community-centered strategy	0.746	0.829	0.553	0.388	0.433	0.334	**0.744**	0.399	0.368
(5) TLEs' perceived self-efficacy	0.810	0.874	0.635	0.481	0.126	0.514	0.308	**0.797**	0.794
(6) TLEs' innovativeness	0.915	0.941	0.800	0.648	0.123	0.468	0.353	0.682	**0.895**

Note: α -Cronbach Alpha; CR -Composite reliability; AVE -Average variance extracted. Bolded numbers are the square roots of AVE. Below the diagonal elements are the correlations between the constructs. Above the diagonal elements are the HTMT ratios.

Table 3. Structural model assessment.

Path	Path coefficient	Standard errors	t statistics	p values
Local knowledge acquisition→ Local knowledge assimilation	0.607	0.067	9.071	0.000
Community-centered strategy→ Entrepreneurial communication	0.390	0.059	6.596	0.000
Local knowledge assimilation→ TLEs' perceived self-efficacy	0.391	0.097	4.043	0.000
Local knowledge assimilation→ TLEs' innovativeness	0.269	0.073	3.704	0.000
Entrepreneurial communication→ TLEs' perceived self-efficacy	0.340	0.090	3.765	0.000
Entrepreneurial communication→ TLEs' innovativeness	0.551	0.085	6.456	0.000

Table 4. Bootstrap results for indirect effects.

Indirect effect	Estimate	Standard errors	t statistics	p value
Community-centered strategy→ Entrepreneurial communication→ TLEs' perceived self-efficacy	0.133	0.043	3.064	0.002
Community-centered strategy→ Entrepreneurial communication→ TLE's innovativeness	0.215	0.050	4.334	0.000
Local knowledge acquisition→Local knowledge assimilation→ TLEs' perceived self-efficacy	0.237	0.059	4.020	0.000
Local knowledge acquisition→Local knowledge assimilation→ TLEs' innovativeness	0.164	0.046	3.544	0.000

are below the more conservative threshold value of 0.85 (Hair et al., 2017; Henseler et al., 2015). They provide additional evidence of discriminant validity.

The structural model was assessed using the sign, magnitude, and significance of the structural path coefficients; the magnitude of R^2 value for each endogenous variable as a measure of the model's predictive accuracy; and the Stone Stone-Geisser's Q^2 values as a measure of the model's predictive relevance (Hair et al., 2017). However, we checked for collinearity before evaluating the structural model (Hair et al., 2017). The VIF values ranged from 1.00 to 1.15, which was below the indicative critical value of 5 (Hair et al., 2017). These values indicated no collinearity. The coefficient of the determination R^2 for the four endogenous variables of entrepreneurial communication, local knowledge assimilation, and the TLEs' perceived self-efficacy and innovativeness were 15.2%, 36.9%, 36.4%, and 48.3%, respectively. These values surpassed the threshold value of 10% (Falk & Miller, 1992). The Q^2 values for all endogenous variables (0.08, 0.29, 0.20, and 0.35 respectively) were above zero that indicated the predictive relevance of the model. We used bootstrapping with 5,000 subsamples to evaluate the significance of the parameter estimates (Hair et al., 2017).

Quantitative results

The results in Table 3 show that acquiring local knowledge has a significantly positive effect on assimilating local knowledge ($\beta = 0.607$, $p < 0.001$) and that a community-centered strategy has a significant effect on entrepreneurial communication ($\beta = 0.390$, $p < 0.001$). These results provide support for H1 and H2, respectively. Local knowledge assimilation has a significantly positive relation with the perceived self-efficacy ($\beta = 0.391$, $p < 0.001$) and innovativeness of TLEs ($\beta = 0.269$, $p < 0.001$), which supports H3a and H3b, respectively.

Entrepreneurial communication has a significantly positive relation with the perceived self-efficacy ($\beta = 0.340$, $p < 0.001$) and innovativeness ($\beta = 0.551$, $p < 0.001$) of TLEs. These results provide support for H4a and H4b, respectively.

To test the mediation hypotheses (H5a-H6b), we followed the recommendations of Hair et al. (2017; p. 232). Thus, we used a bootstrapping procedure to test the significance of the indirect effects via the mediator (Preacher & Hayes, 2008). Table 4 presents the results of the mediation effects.

The indirect effects of a community-centered strategy on TLEs' perceived self-efficacy and innovativeness via the mediator of entrepreneurial communication are significant with ($\beta = 0.133$;

$p<0.01$) and ($\beta=0.215$; $p<0.001$), respectively. These results provide support for the mediation hypotheses H5a and H5b, respectively. In the same vein, the indirect effects of local knowledge acquisition on TLEs' perceived self-efficacy and innovativeness via the mediator of local knowledge assimilation are significant with ($\beta=0.237$; $p<0.001$) and ($\beta=0.164$; $p<0.001$), respectively. Thus, H6a and H6b have support.

Qualitative research II

Qualitative method

The second qualitative study was conducted to explore the results from the quantitative study in more detail. Thus, the researchers returned to the field to conduct additional face-to-face in-depth interviews. In order to not bias the interviews, four other TLEs (1 photographic tour guide, 1 hostel, and 2 handcraft workshop) were contacted who did not belong to the survey sample and did not participate in the first study. The aim of this study was to test whether the relationships found made sense. The same procedures for study 1 were used (open questions, anonymity, recording, note taking, transcript). Each interview took, on average, 1 hour and 13 minutes and was held at the entrepreneurs' facilities.

Qualitative results

The results of qualitative study II support the empirical results obtained in the quantitative study. Knowledge acquisition through informal means with locals and visitors was part of daily life, although it also turned out to be a deliberate approach to gather information and feedback on the activity. Cooperation with other local entrepreneurs represented a common practice with an emphasis on implementing community-centered strategies. The assimilation of local knowledge that results in learning was addressed in two ways: either it was quickly operationalized through the development of new experiences or narratives in which their communication abilities were essential, or it was accumulated in potential ideas for future innovation. Respondents acknowledged a strong competition between them. In this sense, the agility with which they made this conversion was essential for competitiveness and tourist satisfaction. Some of the answers were transcribed below.

"The experience and the narrative associated with it (newly acquired knowledge) are adapted throughout the realization and delivery of unique experiences with a high degree of creativity".

"... the knowledge obtained through local events does not always translate into innovation, but that they are 'stored' to be materialized in the future, when time is available".

"The municipality's is focused on promoting surf, contributing to disfigure the local commerce and traditions of the locality [...]. In response to this, I and other local entrepreneurs have held several events and a documentary with the aim of identifying and collecting ancestral practices and showing visitors the local way of life".

We also examine how a community-centered strategy relates to innovativeness and self-efficacy. The realization of events or other forms of collaboration within the community are important to acquire new knowledge and to increase the proximity to the potential market. However, the ability to capitalize on these opportunities is dependent on communication with the market. If TLEs do not approach customers with interesting proposals and new narratives, they cannot make a profit. This ability means that learning contributes only indirectly to innovation and self-efficacy but clearly benefits from the entrepreneur's communication skills.

One interviewee (photographic tour) stated:

"Our great difficulty is communication with the market. The tourists are dispersed, being very difficult to reach them so that we can fill the necessary vacancies to carry out the experiments".

Discussion

Entrepreneurial communication: creating new narratives and experiences

Our model considers TLEs' innovativeness and self-efficacy as outcomes. By considering the social goals for their businesses, TLEs incorporate a triple bottom line in their business model. The ability to communicate influences both outcomes and is an important TLE trait, as recognized by Yachin (2019). This ability is intrinsically linked to the producer-oriented form of experience (Richards, 2011). Indeed, these small-scale businesses provide close contact with tourists (Marchant & Mottiar, 2011), which is an important source of knowledge (Yachin, 2019). Furthermore, the indirect link between community-centered strategy and TLEs' innovativeness and self-efficacy reinforces the importance of the entrepreneurial communication. While there is a clear recognition that this area is essential, these businesses need to fill this gap at the same time.

The quantitative results show that there is a sequence in the SBM that goes from local knowledge acquisition to innovativeness and self-efficacy. The starting point is the local knowledge acquisition and the active participation in the community, that is, the community-centered strategy. However, the second qualitative study shows that it is not always easy to get community members involved. All those interviewed said that a lot of communication effort was necessary to generate trust in the local communities that traditionally were averse to change and the presence of strangers. This finding extends the knowledge on SBM by providing a better understanding of the knowledge links across it. Boons and Lüdeke-Freund (2013) and Porter et al. (2018) recognized the need to understand how these links were established and how they contributed to innovation.

Community-centered strategy: an active knowledge magnet

In line with the research (Binkhorst & Den Dekker, 2009), the results from the quantitative study show that knowledge acquisition and community-centered strategy are also typical mechanisms in the small-scale tourism business. This finding proves they are privileged channels for the TLEs to participate in the so-called "playgrounds of creativity" (Richards, 2011). The interviews conducted in the second qualitative study showed that organizing local events worked like a "magnet" to attract knowledge and visitors. In their words, the holding of events promoted the participation of members of the community to which they generally had no access to or contact with. They always brought new practices, theories, or traditions. Since TLEs are poorly structured and with few resources, these strategies for local knowledge acquisition represent the most common path (Cooper, 2015). Furthermore, the TLEs saw community-centered strategies as a way of preserving local traditions and identities, even when contradicting the official institutions that manage tourism locally. The studies from both the TLE and the SBM fields recommend more active strategies that involve stakeholders, communities, and visitors to promote trust and networking as ingredients for innovation in small-scale businesses (García-Rosell et al., 2019; Yachin, 2019). Furthermore, the community participation is a distinctive feature of SBM (Porter et al., 2018; Schaltegger et al., 2016). Our findings expand these relations by identifying a community-centered strategy as an important tool for knowledge acquisition that is appropriate for the limitations of these small-scale businesses.

Leveraging local knowledge outcomes

Our findings from the quantitative study show that local knowledge assimilation mediates the relation between local knowledge acquisition and TLEs' self-efficacy and innovativeness. As such, local knowledge needs to be integrated and applied in tourist experiences and narratives. As

Hjalager et al. (2018) point out, innovation depends on the ability of TLEs to capitalize on opportunities.

The learning that results from the community-centered strategy influences the ability of the TLEs to communicate new narratives to the market. Although the proximity of clients and the community allows them access to knowledge, the research has identified TLEs as having limited capabilities to use this knowledge (Yachin, 2019) that is evidence of an unstructured approach to innovation (Cooper, 2015). As such, they have difficulties in turning new knowledge into innovation (Hoarau, 2014; Morrison, 2006). Thus, the ability to acquire local knowledge is not all that matters, but also the ability to translate it into something meaningful for the business that is dependent on their ability to communicate with the market, as suggested by Yachin (2019). Thus, a community-centered strategy influences TLEs' innovativeness and self-efficacy indirectly through entrepreneurial communication. The interviews from the second qualitative study showed another possible complementary explanation. The accumulated knowledge not yet converted into innovation reflects the concept of "knowledge stock", as suggested by Weidenfeld et al. (2010).

This study contributes to the SBM literature by providing evidence of the importance of acquiring and assimilating local knowledge, community-centered strategy, and entrepreneurial communication for the innovativeness and self-efficacy of TLEs. Furthermore, by exploring the underlying relations between these elements, this study expands the knowledge on more competitive and integrative solutions for SBM development, as prompted in the recent research (c.f. Neumeyer & Santos, 2018; Schaltegger et al., 2016). Another important contribution for the TLE and SBM literature is the mediating roles of assimilating local knowledge and entrepreneurial communication. Although previous research has identified knowledge management as a mediator by creating the values, philosophy, and the necessary foundations for more sustainable businesses (Zaragoza-Sáez et al., 2020), this study expands existing knowledge by assessing the role of local knowledge assimilation and entrepreneurial communication in leveraging the effects of a community centered-strategy and local knowledge acquisition on TLEs' innovativeness and self-efficacy. Considering that local knowledge is the basis for the TLE's differentiation, mechanisms for knowledge assimilation in the SBM can benefit competitiveness.

Developing more sustainable business models

Based on our findings, the following links in the SBM can be considered. The TLEs acquire knowledge through formal mechanisms and a community-centered strategy. They transform this knowledge through very specific mechanisms: the capability to assimilate knowledge and the capability to communicate entrepreneurial activities. The innovativeness and self-efficacy are important outcomes of the TLEs' SBM. Furthermore, there are two streams for knowledge management in the SBM. One stream is related to organizational informal processes (knowledge acquisition and assimilation). A second stream is linked to the TLEs' ability to cooperate and communicate with local stakeholders, the community, and tourists.

Thus, the strategies for acquiring this knowledge (local and market) can result from being close to clients and to the community and other stakeholders. But it can also arise from active participation in the community that favors the involvement of stakeholders both in obtaining new knowledge and in participating in the experiences they offer to tourists. In this sense, Figure 2 displays four scenarios.

In a situation where the TLE poorly engages the community, the local knowledge acquisition requires greater local participation (*embed*). In this case, the development of charitable actions or the preservation of local traditions together with other stakeholders may be a route to explore. In this way, the access to the continuously evolving local knowledge and stakeholder participation increases because of sharing experiences and stories (García-Rosell et al., 2019). However,

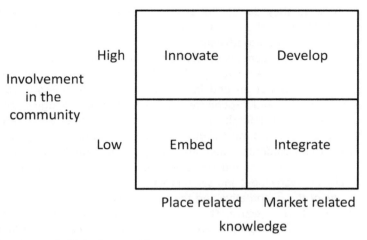

Figure 2. Actions for more sustainable business model.

collaboration is not an easy path, especially for those from abroad due to socio-cultural distance (Czernek, 2017).

When community involvement is low, TLEs need to seek market knowledge. In this situation, the TLE needs to *integrate* the business into the value chain, as suggested by Yachin (2019), or to maximize the power of networks with agents, companies, and organizations (Binkhorst & Den Dekker, 2009).

When a community-centered strategy already exists, the acquisition of knowledge is more assured. In this case, TLEs need to capitalize on it and *innovate*. The experiences offered can be leveraged with the existing link to the community and local stakeholders, which can be an integral part of the strategy. This strategy can be a playground for co-creation and creative experiences (Richards, 2011).

The last quadrant refers to the acquisition of market-related knowledge in situations where TLEs promote active strategies in the community. Here the important step is to *develop* the experiences in line with what the market seeks. Indeed, tourists that seek involvement in the experiences are fragmented into niches that demand tailor-made experiences (Ateljevic & Doorne, 2000). Thus, local experiences need to be adapted and developed in line with these specific expectations.

Conclusion

In this research, we used a mixed-methods approach to achieve our objectives. The first objective concerns the comprehension of the key role of the place as a source of local knowledge. Our results show that local knowledge is the source of the TLEs' competitiveness (innovativeness and self-efficacy) by providing a distinctive value proposition that materializes the specificities of the place and the network developed by the entrepreneur. Local knowledge is also a key factor in the business model. TLEs are particularly interested in the preservation of the environment and local social traditions and way of life. Those were the reasons they were attracted to the place. As stated by Stubbs (2017), TLEs integrate sustainability goals into their business because economic success is linked to their environmental and social performance. Furthermore, the networks of local stakeholders that add value to the experiences empower them. This valuable distinctiveness is operationalized through innovative narratives and new products and services that embody this new knowledge. This is the customer relation element of the SBM.

The question is how do they do it? The answer comes with the response to the second objective. This research identifies the links between the elements of the SBM that convert local knowledge into entrepreneurial innovativeness and self-efficacy. Specifically, the first element is local knowledge acquisition that consists of the collection of local knowledge through informal channels and a community-centered strategy. This element concerns the infrastructure of the SBM. Knowledge acquisition is not an end in of itself. It must be transformed both into the knowledge stocks of narratives and experiences. As such, local knowledge must be integrated into organizational routines and embedded in the tourist experiences and the communication strategies. Furthermore, these issues must align with the growing tourist exigencies, that is, market-focused experiences and communication. Knowledge acquisition is leveraged by knowledge assimilation, while a community-centered strategy is leveraged by entrepreneurial communication in relation to TLEs' innovativeness and self-efficacy.

Based on the results of the quantitative and the two qualitative studies, we proposed a model to develop an SBM, the third objective. The model proposes four situations according to the degree of the TLE's integration into the community and the source of local knowledge: place related or market related.

This study provides important practical and managerial implications. Local knowledge increases the probability of sustainable value creation from the destination (Shrivastava & Kennelly, 2013). Since TLEs are in the best position to promote sustainable practices (Bosworth & Farrell, 2011), destinations should create favorable conditions for the development of this type of business. By understanding the connections in the SBM managed by these entrepreneurs, some recommendations are possible. In order to improve the sustainability of small-scale businesses in the destination, it will be important to promote better knowledge management. First, TLEs must improve the acquisition of knowledge and the spillover effect. Based on the results, this research shows the importance of informal meetings with stakeholders that prevents maximum diversity and origins. Encouraging festivals and other events that involve the community is another important strategy. But improving knowledge assimilation skills is also important, which can be achieved through training (e.g., new product development, interpersonal communication, and marketing). Also, by stimulating the formation of clusters, destinations can not only boost this development of skills but can also act as a trigger for innovation in tourism in the destination (Czernek, 2017).

This study contains limitations that indicate different avenues for future research. First, the cross-sectional nature of this study limits our ability to fully establish causality. Thus, future research should follow a longitudinal data approach. Second, this study uses a non-probabilistic convenience sampling procedure for the survey which may create representativeness problems for the population under study. Third, it limited the sample to Portuguese and Spanish TLEs and hence may not be generalizable to the TLEs in other countries. Thus, some caution should be taken in the generalization of the results. Consequently, in order to achieve better generalization, future research should test our conceptual model by using data from TLEs from other countries and by using a probability sampling procedure.

An important topic is the knowledge stocks. TLEs learn from the local context, but they do not transform all of this knowledge into innovation. This topic was also identified by other studies (c.f. Weidenfeld et al., 2010). However, it was not sufficiently developed, and key questions emerged for both small-scale businesses and destination competitiveness; such as, which factors increase the conversion rate of new knowledge into innovation?

Considering the links between the elements of the SBM, another important issue is the exploration of other dimensions or variables. Human resources influence TLEs' ability to compete that poses a challenge due to seasonality and low qualifications, as pointed out by Czernek (2017). The implications for the SBM elements are an important avenue for researchers. This research also shows that the local knowledge flows along those elements until it is converted into TLEs' innovativeness and self-efficacy. However, other links need to be explored. Since TLEs follow a triple bottom line approach to their SBM, they seek to balance environmental and social goals with economic ones. However, as argued by Zhang et al. (2015) and Bredvold and Skålén (2016), these elements are not equally reflected in their ambitions. Is there a difference between a business orientation and a purely lifestyle orientation in relation to assimilation strategies and innovation? To answer this question researchers can explore the effectiveness of the Google keywords as suggested by Huynh (2019).

Disclosure statement

The authors report no potential conflict of interest.

ORCID

Álvaro Dias http://orcid.org/0000-0003-4074-1586
Graça Miranda Silva http://orcid.org/0000-0001-5396-395X
Mafalda Patuleia http://orcid.org/0000-0002-8401-1860
Maria Rosario González-Rodríguez http://orcid.org/0000-0002-6484-4128

References

Anderson, J. (2012). Relational places: The surfed wave as assemblage and convergence. *Environment and Planning D: Society and Space, 30*(4), 570–587. https://doi.org/10.1068/d17910

Ateljevic, I., & Doorne, S. (2000). Staying within the fence': Lifestyle entrepreneurship in tourism. *Journal of Sustainable Tourism, 8*(5), 378–392. https://doi.org/10.1080/09669580008667374

Bagozzi, R. P., & Yi, Y. (1988). On the evaluation of structural equation models. *Journal of the Academy of Marketing Science, 16*(1), 74–94. https://doi.org/10.1007/BF02723327

Besser, T. L., & Miller, N. (2001). Is the good corporation dead? The community social responsibility of small business operators. *The Journal of Socio-Economics, 30*(3), 221–241. https://doi.org/10.1016/S1053-5357(01)00094-4

Binkhorst, E., & Den Dekker, T. (2009). Agenda for co-creation tourism experience research. *Journal of Hospitality Marketing & Management, 18*(2-3), 311–327. https://doi.org/10.1080/19368620802594193

Bocken, N. M., Short, S. W., Rana, P., & Evans, S. (2014). A literature and practice review to develop sustainable business model archetypes. *Journal of Cleaner Production, 65*, 42–56. https://doi.org/10.1016/j.jclepro.2013.11.0

Boons, F., & Lüdeke-Freund, F. (2013). Business models for sustainable innovation: state-of-the-art and steps towards a research agenda. *Journal of Cleaner Production, 45*, 9–19. https://doi.org/10.1016/j.jclepro.2012.07.007

Bosworth, G., & Farrell, H. (2011). Tourism entrepreneurs in Northumberland. *Annals of Tourism Research, 38*(4), 1474–1494. https://doi.org/10.1016/j.annals.2011.03.015

Bredvold, R., & Skålén, P. (2016). Lifestyle entrepreneurs and their identity construction: A study of the tourism industry. *Tourism Management, 56*, 96–105. https://doi.org/10.1016/j.tourman.2016.03.023

Carlsen, J., Morrison, A., & Weber, P. (2008). Lifestyle oriented small tourism firms. *Tourism Recreation Research, 33*(3), 255–263. https://doi.org/10.1080/02508281.2008.11081549

Cooper, C. (2015). Managing tourism knowledge. *Tourism Recreation Research, 40*(1), 107–119. https://doi.org/10.1080/02508281.2015.1006418

Czernek, K. (2017). Tourism features as determinants of knowledge transfer in the process of tourist cooperation. *Current Issues in Tourism, 20*(2), 204–220. https://doi.org/10.1080/13683500.2014.944107

de la Barre, S. (2013). Wilderness and cultural tour guides, place identity and sustainable tourism in remote areas. *Journal of Sustainable Tourism, 21*(6), 825–844. https://doi.org/10.1080/09669582.2012.737798

Eikhof, D. R., & Haunschild, A. (2006). Lifestyle meets market: Bohemian entrepreneurs in creative industries. *Creativity and Innovation Management, 15*(3), 234–241. https://doi.org/10.1111/j.1467-8691.2006.00392.x

Falk, R. F., & Miller, N. B. (1992). *A primer for soft modelling*. University of Akron Press.

Fornell, C., & Larcker, D. F. (1981). Evaluating structural equation models with unobservable variables and measurement error. *Journal of Marketing Research, 18*(3), 382–350. https://doi.org/10.2307/3151312

García-Rosell, J. C., Haanpää, M., & Janhunen, J. (2019). Dig where you stand': values-based co-creation through improvisation. *Tourism Recreation Research, 44*(3), 348–358. https://doi.org/10.1080/02508281.2019.1591780

Hair, J. F., Hult, G. M., Ringle, C., & Sarstedt, M. (2017). *A primer on partial least squares structural equation modeling*. Sage Publications.

Hall, C. M. (2019). Constructing sustainable tourism development: The 2030 agenda and the managerial ecology of sustainable tourism. *Journal of Sustainable Tourism, 27*(7), 1044–1060. https://doi.org/10.1080/09669582.2018.1560456

Hallak, R., Brown, G., & Lindsay, N. J. (2012). The Place Identity–Performance relationship among tourism entrepreneurs: A structural equation modelling analysis. *Tourism Management, 33*(1), 143–154. https://doi.org/10.1016/j.tourman.2011.02.013

Henseler, J., Ringle, C. M., & Sarstedt, M. (2015). A new criterion for assessing discriminant validity in variance-based structural equation modeling. *Journal of the Academy of Marketing Science, 43*(1), 115–135. https://doi.org/10.1007/s11747-014-0403-8

Hjalager, A. M., Kwiatkowski, G., & Østervig Larsen, M. (2018). Innovation gaps in Scandinavian rural tourism. *Scandinavian Journal of Hospitality and Tourism, 18*(1), 1–17. https://doi.org/10.1080/15022250.2017.1287002

Hoarau, H. (2014). Knowledge acquisition and assimilation in tourism-innovation processes. *Scandinavian Journal of Hospitality and Tourism, 14*(2), 135–151. https://doi.org/10.1080/15022250.2014.887609

Huynh, T. L. D. (2019). Which Google keywords influence entrepreneurs? Empirical evidence from Vietnam. *Asia Pacific Journal of Innovation and Entrepreneurship, 13*(2), 214–230. https://doi.org/10.1108/APJIE-11-2018-0063

Ioannides, D., & Petersen, T. (2003). Tourism 'non-entrepreneurship'in peripheral destinations: a case study of small and medium tourism enterprises on Bornholm. *Tourism Geographies, 5*(4), 408–435. https://doi.org/10.1080/1461668032000129146

Jack, S. L., & Anderson, A. R. (2002). The effects of embeddedness on the entrepreneurial process. *Journal of Business Venturing, 17*(5), 467–487. https://doi.org/10.1016/S0883-9026(01)00076-3

Jansen, J. J., Van Den Bosch, F. A., & Volberda, H. W. (2005). Managing potential and realized absorptive capacity: how do organizational antecedents matter? *Academy of Management Journal, 48*(6), 999–1015. https://doi.org/10.5465/amj.2005.19573106

Kibler, E., Fink, M., Lang, R., & Muñoz, P. (2015). Place attachment and social legitimacy: Revisiting the sustainable entrepreneurship journey. *Journal of Business Venturing Insights, 3*, 24–29. https://doi.org/10.1016/j.jbvi.2015.04.001

Kropp, F., Lindsay, N. J., & Shoham, A. (2006). Entrepreneurial, market, and learning orientations and international entrepreneurial business venture performance in South African firms. *International Marketing Review, 23*(5), 504–523. https://doi.org/10.1108/02651330610703427

Liao, S. H., Fei, W. C., & Chen, C. C. (2007). Knowledge sharing, absorptive capacity, and innovation capability: an empirical study of Taiwan's knowledge-intensive industries. *Journal of Information Science, 33*(3), 340–359. https://doi.org/10.1177/0165551506070739

Liao, S. H., Wu, C. C., Hu, D. C., & Tsui, K. A. (2010). Relationships between knowledge acquisition, absorptive capacity and innovation capability:an empirical study on Taiwan's financial and manufacturing industries. *Journal of Information Science, 36*(1), 19–35. https://doi.org/10.1177/0165551509340362

Marchant, B., & Mottiar, Z. (2011). Understanding lifestyle entrepreneurs and digging beneath the issue of profits: Profiling surf tourism lifestyle entrepreneurs in Ireland. *Tourism Planning & Development, 8*(2), 171–183. https://doi.org/10.1080/21568316.2011.573917

Martínez-Martínez, A., Cegarra-Navarro, J. G., Garcia-Perez, A., & Wensley, A. (2019). Knowledge agents as drivers of environmental sustainability and business performance in the hospitality sector. *Tourism Management, 70*, 381–389. https://doi.org/10.1016/j.tourman.2018.08.030

Morrison, A. (2002). Small hospitality businesses: enduring or endangered? *Journal of Hospitality and Tourism Management, 9*(1), 1–12.

Morrison, A. (2006). A contextualisation of entrepreneurship. *International Journal of Entrepreneurial Behavior & Research, 12*(4), 192–209. https://doi.org/10.1108/13552550610679159

Neumeyer, X., & Santos, S. C. (2018). Sustainable business models, venture typologies, and entrepreneurial ecosystems: A social network perspective. *Journal of Cleaner Production, 172*, 4565–4579. https://doi.org/10.1016/j.jclepro.2017.08.216

Pham, N. T., Vo-Thanh, T., Shahbaz, M., Huynh, T. D., & Usman, M. (2020). Managing environmental challenges: Training as a solution to improve employee green performance. *Journal of Environmental Management, 269*, 110781 https://doi.org/10.1016/j.jenvman.2020.110781

Porter, B. A., Orams, M. B., & Lück, M. (2018). Sustainable entrepreneurship tourism:An alternative development approach for remote coastal communities where awareness of tourism is low. *Tourism Planning & Development, 15*(2), 149–165. https://doi.org/10.1080/21568316.2017.1312507

Preacher, K. J., & Hayes, A. F. (2008). Asymptotic and resampling strategies for assessing and comparing indirect effects in multiple mediator models. *Behavior Research Methods, 40*(3), 879–891. https://doi.org/10.3758/BRM.40.3.879

Richards, G. (2011). Creativity and tourism: The state of the art. *Annals of Tourism Research, 38*(4), 1225–1253. https://doi.org/10.1016/j.annals.2011.07.008

Ringle, C. M., Wende, S., Will, A. (2015). SmartPLS3.0. Hamburg: www.smartpls.de.

Schaltegger, S., Hansen, E. G., & Lüdeke-Freund, F. (2016a). Business Models for Sustainability: Origins, Present Research, and Future Avenues. *Organization & Environment, 29*(1), 3–10. https://doi.org/10.1177/1086026615599806

Schaltegger, S., Lüdeke-Freund, F., & Hansen, E. G. (2016b). Business models for sustainability: A co-evolutionary analysis of sustainable entrepreneurship, innovation, and transformation. *Organization & Environment, 29*(3), 264–289. https://doi.org/10.1177/1086026616633272

Schilar, H., & Keskitalo, E. H. (2018). Tourism activity as an expression of place attachment–place perceptions among tourism actors in the Jukkasjärvi area of northern Sweden. *Scandinavian Journal of Hospitality and Tourism, 18*(sup1), S42–S59. https://doi.org/10.1080/15022250.2017.1389123

Shaw, G., & Williams, A. (2009). Knowledge transfer and management in tourism organisations: An emerging research agenda. *Tourism Management, 30*(3), 325–335. https://doi.org/10.1016/j.tourman.2008.02.023

Shrivastava, P., & Kennelly, J. J. (2013). Sustainability and place-based enterprise. *Organization & Environment, 26*(1), 83–101. https://doi.org/10.1177/1086026612475068

Stamboulis, Y., & Skayannis, P. (2003). Innovation strategies and technology for experience-based tourism. *Tourism Management, 24*(1), 35–43. https://doi.org/10.1016/S0261-5177(02)00047-X

Stubbs, W. (2017). Sustainable entrepreneurship and B corps. *Business Strategy and the Environment, 26*(3), 331–344. https://doi.org/10.1002/bse.1920

Stubbs, W., & Cocklin, C. (2008). Conceptualizing a "sustainability business model. *Organization & Environment, 21*(2), 103–127. https://doi.org/10.1177/1086026608318042

Sun, X., Xu, H., Köseoglu, M. A., & Okumus, F. (2020). How do lifestyle hospitality and tourism entrepreneurs manage their work-life balance? *International Journal of Hospitality Management, 85*, 102359. https://doi.org/10.1016/j.ijhm.2019.102359

Teece, D. J. (2010). Business models, business strategy and innovation. *Long Range Planning, 43*(2-3), 172–194. https://doi.org/10.1016/j.lrp.2009.07.003

Thomas, R., Shaw, G., & Page, S. J. (2011). Understanding small firms in tourism: A perspective on research trends and challenges. *Tourism Management*, *32*(5), 963–976. https://doi.org/10.1016/j.tourman.2011.02.003

Thompson, B. S., Gillen, J., & Friess, D. A. (2018). Challenging the principles of ecotourism: insights from entrepreneurs on environmental and economic sustainability in Langkawi. *Journal of Sustainable Tourism*, *26*(2), 257–276. https://doi.org/10.1080/09669582.2017.1343338

Valtonen, A. (2009). Small tourism firms as agents of critical knowledge. *Tourist Studies*, *9*(2), 127–143. https://doi.org/10.1177/1468797609360600

Wang, C., Li, G., & Xu, H. (2019). Impact of lifestyle-oriented motivation on small tourism enterprises' social responsibility and performance. *Journal of Travel Research*, *58*(7), 1146–1160. https://doi.org/10.1177/0047287518800389

Weidenfeld, A., Williams, A. M., & Butler, R. W. (2010). Knowledge transfer and innovation among attractions. *Annals of Tourism Research*, *37*(3), 604–626. https://doi.org/10.1016/j.annals.2009.12.001

Yachin, J. M. (2019). The entrepreneur–opportunity nexus: Discovering the forces that promote product innovations in rural micro-tourism firms. *Scandinavian Journal of Hospitality and Tourism*, *19*(1), 47–65. https://doi.org/10.1080/15022250.2017.1383936

Zahra, S. A., & George, G. (2002). Absorptive capacity: A review, reconceptualization, and extension. *Academy of Management Review*, *27*(2), 185–203. https://doi.org/10.5465/amr.2002.6587995

Zaragoza-Sáez, P. C., Claver-Cortés, E., Marco-Lajara, B., & Úbeda-García, M. (2020). Corporate social responsibility and strategic knowledge management as mediators between sustainable intangible capital and hotel performance. *Journal of Sustainable Tourism*, (published ahead or print). https://doi.org/10.1080/09669582.2020.1811289

Zhang, C., Xiao, H., Gursoy, D., & Rao, Y. (2015). Tacit knowledge spillover and sustainability in destination development. *Journal of Sustainable Tourism*, *23*(7), 1029–1048. https://doi.org/10.1080/09669582.2015.1032299

Zhao, H., Seibert, S. E., & Hills, G. E. (2005). The mediating role of self-efficacy in the development of entrepreneurial intentions. *The Journal of Applied Psychology*, *90*(6), 1265–1272. https://doi.org/10.1037/0021-9010.90.6.1265

Greening hotels: does motivating hotel employees promote in-role green performance? The role of culture

Nhat Tan Pham, Charbel Jose Chiappetta Jabbour, Tan Vo-Thanh, Toan Luu Duc Huynh and Clarice Santos

ABSTRACT
In the new global economy, environmentally friendly policies have become a central issue for firms. The increasing attention given to the benefits of those policies has prompted research on the development of environmental management systems that encourage employees to engage in environmental activities. However, there is limited evidence concerning the relationship between employee motivation and employees' in-role green performance, in addition to the potential impact of culture and organizational citizenship behavior for the environment. Through a quantitative study of 301 managerial and non-managerial employees working in three- to five-star hotels, this study makes a major contribution by demonstrating that practices aimed at motivating hotel employees (e.g. green reward and performance management) are significantly linked with employees' in-role green performance and organizational citizenship behavior for the environment. The findings also indicate that the influence of green rewards on employees' in-role green performance and organizational citizenship behaviors for the environment is stronger when hotels are managed by Western corporations. Conversely, the study showed that the effect of green performance management on these two dependent variables is not moderated by culture. This article supports efforts to widen national cultural perspectives in the development and application of green human resource management.

Introduction

In recent years, companies have become more aware of the importance of environmental protection due to the enhanced environmental pressure from governments and consumers (Pham, Tučková, & Jabbour, 2019). In order to achieve a successful implementation of green strategy, the role of human resource management (HRM), including motivating employees' green behavior, is essential. The integration of environmental management and HRM, namely green human resource management (GHRM) (Renwick et al., 2013), has been embraced by a number of scholars, including those in the hospitality industry (e.g. Pham, Tučková, & Jabbour, 2019). In hospitality, environmental management practices have been increasingly adopted by hotels (Tritto, 2020), because these businesses are major actors in causing negative environmental impacts, due to their extensive use of natural resources (Chan & Hawkins, 2012; Molina-Azorín et al., 2009). In addition, along with the expected benefits associated with green behavior (e.g. cost, competitive advantage), external pressures (e.g. from customers) have encouraged hotels to consider green practices (Alonso-Almeida et al., 2017).

Researchers have focused on GHRM practices, especially motivating employees through green rewards (REW) and green performance management (PEM), to investigate the importance of these factors to the sustainable development of organizations (e.g. Saeed et al., 2019). Renwick et al. (2013) state that motivating employees involves both REW and PEM, and is one of three key components in developing GHRM strategies for organizations. Scholars have recognized such green practices as critical elements for building green strategy, since the successful implementation of policies aimed at motivating employees can stimulate individuals' environmental commitment and organizational citizenship behavior for the environment (OCBE) (Pinzone et al., 2016), as well as environmental knowledge, skills and awareness (Jabbour et al., 2010).

Despite the relevance of GHRM, three key emergent issues must be addressed. First, the existing research has concentrated on how REW and PEM influence extra-role green behavior, such as OCBE (e.g. Pinzone et al., 2016) and firm's environmental performance (e.g. Masri & Jaaron, 2017), rather than employee's environmental performance; for instance, employee in-role green performance (EIGP). Following Janssen and Yperen (2004), EIGP may be viewed as a set of environmental actions specified and required by the organization and outlined in the job description. For example, many companies ask their employees to behave "green", which may translate into jobs that prohibit employees to pour toxic waste into the water systems or where employees have to manage hazardous material in accordance with organizational policies as well as government regulations (Dumont et al., 2017). Similar to the hospitality sector, hotel employees are carefully monitored in a variety of activities aimed at cutting waste, reducing water usage, and saving energy as important tasks. In the literature, few scholars (e.g. Dumont et al., 2017) have empirically investigated EIGP and its antecedents, for example REW and PEM policies in management, and in particular, hospitality management. It can be argued that in addition to achieving person-organization fit (Hoffman & Woehr, 2006) and Ability-Motivation-Opportunity (AMO) (Appelbaum et al., 2000), HRM policies aimed at helping employees "fit" into the workplace also motivate their involvement in green activities. This process may in turn influence employees' green performance, through reward and performance management systems. GHRM practices, including REW and PEM, may boost employees' environmental knowledge, skills and awareness (Jabbour et al., 2010), green commitment and behavior in order to meaningfully stimulate environmental activities (Ren et al., 2018). Such practices help employees better understand their role and responsibility to be actively involved in green activities and to handle environmental problems effectively in the workplace, consequently promoting green performance. Furthermore, different GHRM practices may have various impacts on employee outcomes. For instance, Saeed et al.'s (2019) study indicates that green training has a stronger influence on pro-environmental behaviors than other practices (e.g. empowerment, reward). Thus, investigating the separate effects of each practice (REW and PEM) on EIGP is necessary to contribute to the literature, especially to the body of knowledge on hospitality. Although Dumont et al. (2017) and Zhang et al. (2019) explore the linkage between GHRM and employee in-role green behavior, their findings do not shed light on the separate effects of each individual GHRM practice.

Moreover, authors have called for papers to investigate the role of cultural perspectives (e.g. Western and local) in the application of GHRM (Ren et al., 2018), as organizations are likely to be impacted by the context in which they operate. Indeed, Hofstede (1983) emphasizes that national culture may constrain organizational culture. Therefore, even if a parent company's national culture is transferred to overseas subsidiaries through the firms' organizational culture (Lau & Ngo, 2001), the latter is likely to be impacted by the host country's national culture. Thus, one may find organizational culture differences between companies managed by international and domestic organizations, even in the same environment. Furthermore, institutional theory complements cultural approaches by suggesting that firms may be exposed to similar management practices when they are embedded in the same business system (DiMaggio & Powell, 1983). More specifically, Pham, Tučková, and Jabbour (2019) propose a study that explores potential differences in the GHRM system between hotels managed by Western and local companies in Vietnam. This approach aligns with Ryan's (2018) recommendation regarding the relevance of national culture differences for future investigations in the tourism sector. Despite this, the suggestion has not yet been addressed by the extant literature in hospitality management.

Finally, based on the AMO framework, HRM policies such as reward and performance management systems have the ability to boost employees' motivation and effort, which in turn influence employee performance (Jiang, Lepak, Han, et al., 2012). In the green context, authors have examined the connection between GHRM practices and OCBE (e.g. Luu, 2019; Pinzone et al., 2016). As previously mentioned, although Dumont et al. (2017) and Zhang et al. (2019) provide empirical evidence to support the direct effect of GHRM on employee in-role green behavior, evidence on the separate impacts of REW and PEM on EIGP is still lacking, especially in the hospitality sector. According to the AMO framework, an emerging research gap concerns the mediating effect of OCBE on the link between such green practices and EIGP, which remains largely neglected by the extant literature. Our study highlights this important gap because we argue that green policies aimed at motivating employees may boost their voluntary behavior in environmental activities, contributing to the individual achievement of environmental tasks.

In sum, the existing literature lacks studies which explore (1) the relationship between REW and PEM (separately) with EIGP; (2) the mediating role of OCBE in these relationships; and (3) the role of cultural perspectives (Western and local) in relationships between green practices (REW and PEM), EIGP and OCBE.

To address the uncertain status of the existing research on GHRM in the hospitality industry, our work aims to attain a better understanding of how green practices which motivate employees (e.g. REW and PEM) may enhance EIGP and OCBE. Additionally, this study provides an insight into the role of culture (Western and local) in the relationship between such green practices, EIGP and OCBE. The research questions include *RQ1: What is the influence of motivating employees on EIGP and OCBE?; RQ2: What is the mediating role of OCBE regarding the influence of motivating employees on EIGP?; and RQ3: What is the role of culture (Western and local) in influencing the motivation of employees for EIGP and OCBE?*

Theoretical framework and development of hypotheses

Motivating employees, OCBE, and EIGP

Motivating employees is seen as one of three core components of GHRM strategy and covers topics related to REW and PEM (Renwick et al., 2013). REW refers to a system of monetary and non-monetary workplace rewards for those who contribute to the firm's environmental management goals (Jabbour et al., 2010). PEM involves policies used by organizations which aim to monitor and evaluate employee performance and advancements made towards attaining environmental goals (Govindarajulu & Daily 2004).

OCBE is a component of organizational citizenship behavior (OCB) (Raineri & Paillé, 2016). It can be understood as *"individual and discretionary social behaviors not explicitly recognized by the formal reward system and contributing to improve the effectiveness of environmental management of organizations"* (Boiral, 2009, p. 223). Individuals' discretionary behaviors include green initiatives; for example, sharing knowledge to protect the environment and proposing suggestions to reduce pollution (Boiral, 2009).

Employee in-role performance can be understood as those activities specified and required by the job description and thus mandated, monitored and rewarded by the organization (Janssen & Yperen, 2004). In the green context, Paillé and Meija-Morelos (2019) define employee environmental performance via evaluations not only for preventing environmental crises and complying with environmental regulations, but also for educating others and the public about the environment. However, our study concerns EIGP, which focuses on the employees' green role, as specified in their job description. Following Janssen and Yperen (2004), this study extends employee in-role performance into the environmental perspective, meaning that EIGP can be considered to cover those environmental actions specified and required by the organization and outlined in the job description, and which are mandated, monitored and rewarded by the organization.

Links between motivating employees and EIGP

Following the AMO framework, HRM practices aim to enhance employees' motivation, thus affecting firms' organizational performance. To provide an insight into the HRM-performance relationship, it is necessary to explore the role of employees, since employee performance may be a key element in the link between HRM and organizational performance (Dyer & Reeves, 1995). Jiang, Lepak, Hu, and Baer (2012) point to employee performance as a reasonable outcome that is directly linked with HRM practices, including reward and performance management. Similarly, "person-organization fit" refers to the compatibility between an employee's attributes and their organization, which influences individual behavior (Hoffman & Woehr, 2006). Based on this theory, HRM policies aimed at helping employees to "fit" with the workplace, for example rewards and performance management, could affect employee outcomes (Lauver & Kristof-Brown, 2001). Therefore, two such practices may bring benefits to employees by improving employee performance; namely, encouraging employees to perform tasks actively and effectively and providing feedback to employees to minimize mistakes at work.

In the hospitality context, few studies have examined the separate impacts of GHRM practices on EIGP. Based on the AMO and person-organization fit frameworks, both REW and PEM policies may encourage employees to become more involved in environmental activities and help them understand the organizations' green goals, which play an essential role in directly predicting EIGP. Indeed, when hotels are focused on REW, and when monetary (e.g. bonuses, cash) and non-monetary rewards (e.g. recognition) are communicated clearly to employees, employees tend to better understand the tangible and intangible benefits embedded within environmental tasks in the workplace. This continuously motivates and stimulates environmental responsibilities based on employee commitment (Govindarajulu & Daily, 2004), which in turn enhances green performance.

Similarly, setting up a PEM system may boost employees' environmental understanding of, for example, the environmental targets and responsibilities of each employee. This helps to align individual behaviors with the hotel's environmental objectives (Guerci et al., 2016) and encourages employees to contribute to the hotel's green activities (Renwick et al., 2013). In turn, employees learn how to avoid environmental mistakes in order to meet environment-related requirements from their managers. For instance, hotel employees may enrich their environmental knowledge, skills and abilities when they regularly receive green feedback from managers (Pham, Tučková, & Jabbour, 2019). This is necessary to increase employees' green understanding, which helps them to actively address environmental problems, such as how to reduce and recycle waste, and to use water and electricity effectively. EIGP is, therefore, enhanced. Consequently, we expect such practices to emerge as important elements in predicting EIGP. We hypothesize that:

H1a: REW positively and significantly influences EIGP.

H1b: PEM positively and significantly influences EIGP.

The role of OCBE

Scholars have debated whether OCB should be a function of policies that aim to reward and monitor employees. Some argue that extra-role behaviors, for example OCB, are voluntary activities that are not a part of employees' tasks, and should be recognized by the reward system (Organ, 1988). The competing pressures of work may lead employees to feel overworked, resulting in difficulties with work-life balance; hence it can be challenging to improve employees' willingness to engage in OCB. Besides, organizations usually informally encourage their employees to participate in green behaviors, rather than setting up a system to appraise such behaviors. Consequently, even though organizations may invest significantly in reward and performance management systems, the question as to whether such systems boost discretionary behavior or not is still under debate. Therefore, from a traditional viewpoint, HRM policies such as those aimed at monitoring and rewarding employees may not be necessary to encourage employees' OCB.

However, this argument may be somewhat misleading. According to Jiang, Lepak, Hu, et al. (2012), social exchange theory suggests that if employees perceive benefits to their organization's actions, they may feel obligated to reciprocate and be inclined to exert more effort in the workplace. With HRM practices (e.g. reward and performance management), when employees have positive perceptions of organizational support for such practices, they are likely to express increased affective commitment based on the norm of reciprocity, which in turn influences employees' work behaviors (Kehoe & Wright, 2013). Additionally, person-organization fit may help explain direct connections between HRM practices and employees' voluntary behavior. These behaviors may be a function of the fit between employees and their work context, through the development of reward and performance management systems. Therefore, such systems could be used to encourage individuals to effectively perform both in-role and extra-role tasks. Schnake and Dumler (1997) also suggest that managers who hope to stimulate employees' OCB should reward their workers in order to involve them in these behaviors.

GHRM practices (e.g. REW and PEM) may be interpreted as aspects of environmental support from the organization, consequently these practices may be factors in predicting employees' green behavior (e.g. OCBE). For instance, Paillé et al. (2013) highlight the impact of environmental management practices on OCBE. We argue that employees may perceive such practices as benefits which help align their behaviors with the organization's green goals and motivate green commitment at work. As a consequence, individuals may wish to reciprocate by discretionarily changing their environmental behaviors with the aim of improving environmental effectiveness. For hotels, when they concentrate on developing REW systems (e.g. bonus, recognition), which are regarded as "goodwill" signals from the hotel, employees are likely to feel respected and recognized and understand the green goals of their organization. This may lead to a positive perception toward the hotel's policies, which may boost employees' environmental commitment at work (Pham, Tučková, & Phan, 2019) and encourage them to reciprocate. In turn, this motivates and stimulates employees to make more of an effort at work. In fact, Renwick et al. (2013) suggest that environmental rewards and recognition (e.g. daily praise) are important factors that can bring a number of benefits for companies, because this practice may encourage employees who are willing to generate eco-initiatives, an aspect of OCBE.

Similar with PEM, this practice helps guide hotel employees in aligning their behaviors with the hotel's green goals (Govindarajulu & Daily, 2004). Indeed, setting up such a system provides employees with clear information about their role in green activities and solidifies their environmental responsibilities, through receiving feedback and appraisals. Based on green feedback and information from managers and customers, hotel employees may learn the necessary green knowledge and skills to handle environmental issues themselves. Also, employees can recognize and react to what needs to change in order to avoid a negative impact on the environment. In terms of empirical evidence, Pham, Tučková, and Jabbour (2019) suggest that when hotels pay attention to developing PEM systems, employees are encouraged to become involved in OCBE. Saeed et al. (2019) also demonstrate that the effective implementation of both REW and PEM policies, as two of the most important GHRM practices, can enhance voluntary green behavior. Thus, our related hypotheses are that:

H1c: REW positively and significantly influences OCBE.

H1d: PEM positively and significantly influences OCBE.

Following AMO theory, Jiang, Lepak, Han, et al. (2012) argue that individual performance is a function of motivation and effort (e.g. OCB) and may be facilitated by HRM practices, including reward and performance management policies. According to the social exchange perspective, Ogbonnaya and Valizade (2018) state that HRM practices (e.g. reward and performance management) may provide signals about management's desire to motivate the workforce, and employees may perceive these signals as "goodwill" from an organization, thus contributing to improving performance. However, scholars argue that OCB represents an employee's voluntary commitment within the company and is not formally required by the organization (Organ, 1988), and thus that it is illogical to assume that employee in-role performance depends on their OCB. On the other hand, we argue that through voluntary behaviors in the workplace, employees may better understand the company's functioning because they gain more knowledge of the big picture and purpose of the organization, resulting in enhanced employee job performance. An empirical study by Bommer et al. (2007) indicates the importance of stimulating employees' OCB to enhance their in-role performance. Thus, employees' OCB can be boosted by HRM polices (e.g., reward and performance management), which may continuously affect employee in-role performance. Based on these arguments, in the green context, GHRM practices aimed at motivating employees may be expected to boost EIGP through employees' discretionary efforts, such as OCBE.

As discussed above, effective implementation of REW policy in hotels can help employees feel more environmental responsibility, which in turn stimulates them to consider potential ramifications of their actions which may affect the environment and to actively participate in green events at work. Consequently, employees may behave in ways that minimize the negative impact of their organization on the environment, as well as meet the green requirements of their job. Thus, OCBE becomes an important element in mediating the connection between REW and EIGP. In line with this reasoning, PEM is an important practice to align employees' behavior (e.g. OCBE) with the green goals of organizations (Guerci et al., 2016). Previous studies have demonstrated the importance of PEM policy in boosting OCBE in hotels (e.g. Pham, Tučková, & Jabbour, 2019). When hotel employees understand how to behave proactively to protect the environment, they voluntarily apply the green knowledge, skills and experience they have gained from the feedback of guests and managers to solve environmental issues. Consequently, these employees' discretionary green behaviors positively enhance their performance in implementing green tasks (Paillé & Meija-Morelos, 2019). EIGP is, therefore, increased. Thus, we expect that the connection between PEM and EIGP will be mediated by OCBE. We hypothesize that:

H1e: REW has an indirect effect on EIGP via OCBE.

H1f: PEM has an indirect effect on EIGP via OCBE.

The role of culture (Western and local)

The context in which an organization operates is instrumental in gaining a better understanding of organizational phenomena. The operational environment can differ between countries in various aspects, and institutional and cultural perspectives provide useful lens to examine organizations and individuals. Based on the institutional perspective (DiMaggio & Powell, 1983), firms operating in the same environment tend to behave similarly since they are exposed to the same institutional actors and have a need to gain legitimacy. This means that different companies are likely to adopt a similar set of business management practices if they are operating in the same country. From a cultural perspective, one expects national culture to underpin individuals' basic assumptions and shared meanings about the world around them. As such, national culture may be one of the main factors leading to variations in organizational culture (Johns, 2006). This is in line with Hofstede's (1983) argument, which states that organizational culture may be constrained by national culture. Consequently, multinational companies must consider the extent to which their organizational culture may be impacted by the host country's national culture and whether they should localize their business practices.

Researchers have supported the roles of institutional and cultural theories in examining multinationals' business practices. In this paper, we argue for a perspective that moves beyond the cultural perspective to emphasize the essential role of a unique organizational culture that is transferred from a firm's headquarters to overseas subsidiaries. Indeed, the cultural perspective has been applied in HRM research to study organizational operations in Western-owned or -managed subsidiaries of multinational companies (e.g. Hoang et al., 2018). According to Lau and Ngo (2001), the parent organizations' national culture has an influence on the operation and management decisions of subsidiaries in other countries. The beliefs and values of the parent organization are transferred to overseas subsidiaries and affect organizational systems and employees' values. Thus, the cultural values of both organizations and individuals within foreign companies operating in Vietnam – especially Western companies – may be affected by the culture of the organization's headquarters. For instance, Hoang et al. (2018) state that Vietnamese employees working in Western companies in Vietnam may learn and absorb the national culture and values of their parent company. They also suggest that ownership type (Western and local) is an important factor, which is expected to affect an organizations' HRM system and operation as well as employee behavior.

Our study focuses on the hospitality industry in Vietnam, where hotels have been managed either by local companies or by international hospitality corporations originating in Western countries (e.g. Marriott, Accor). Therefore, two distinct cultural influences – Western and local – dominate hotels in Vietnam. In this paper, we refer specifically to national culture and organizational culture in some instances as well as to a broader notion of cultural perspective associated with firm ownership or management as Western or local. Regarding the environmental aspect, we have found no published empirical studies focusing on the moderating effect of culture in the application of GHRM in either Western or local companies. However, Witt and Stahl (2016) have discussed the connections between manager-oriented corporate social responsibility and national cultural perspectives. They emphasize that business leaders from national cultures with strong power distance, for example, Vietnam, may be less likely to enact behaviors linked with responsible orientations (e.g. concern for environmental issues, community) than managers impacted by cultures with low power distance. In addition, Hoang et al. (2018) state that Western companies are more individualistic, and thus have a closer fit with interventions at the individual level (e.g. employee rewards and autonomy), whereas companies from emerging Asian markets, such as Vietnam, tend to be more collectivistic, group-oriented, and thus have a better fit with task/performance-oriented or group interventions (e.g. performance management and appraisals). This is consistent with Lau and Ngo's (2001) arguments about cultural perspective in HRM.

Consequently, this leads to different priorities for applying GHRM policies between hotels managed by Western and local companies, which in turn influence individuals' green output, including OCBE and EIGP. In terms of REW, at hotels managed by Western companies, employees may learn and adopt socially and environmentally responsible behaviors because of Western managers. Therefore, individual-oriented green policies (e.g. reward policy) are easily translated to all local employees. This is necessary to stimulate employees to concentrate on green

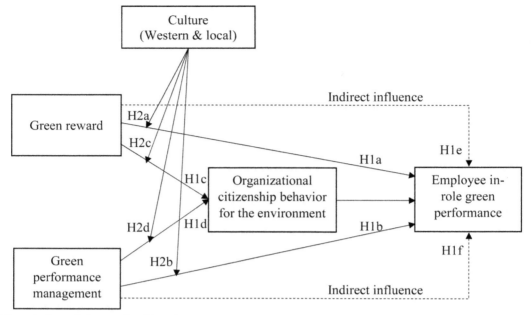

Figure 1. Research framework and hypotheses.

voluntary behavior at work, as well as to improve their performance in green tasks. In line with the above reasoning, a further step is to examine the role of culture in PEM's effect on EIGP and OCBE. Pham, Tučková, and Jabbour's (2019) study in Vietnam suggests that PEM has been implemented more often by local-run hotels than by Western-run hotels. As argued above, since employees working in hotels with local cultures are likely to be monitored by supervisors, managers or even customers, they might attempt to actively change their green behaviors (e.g. OCBE) to fit with the organization's green goals, and this may motivate them to meet green requirements (Figure 1). Thus, we hypothesize that:

> *H2a&c:* Culture (Western and local) moderates the effect of GHRM practices aimed at motivating employees on EIGP and OCBE, such that the effect of REW on EIGP (H2a) and OCBE (H2c) is higher in Western-managed hotels than local-managed hotels.

> *H2b&d:* Culture (Western and local) moderates the effect of GHRM practices aimed at motivating employees on EIGP and OCBE, such that the influence of PEM on EIGP (H2b) and OCBE (H2d) is greater in local-managed hotels than Western-managed hotels.

Methodology

Research design

Our research followed a deductive approach, which included a qualitative study to help develop and improve the quantitative questionnaire. The following step consisted of a quantitative study aimed at testing proposed hypotheses. With regard to our sample, respondents were both managerial and non-managerial employees working in three- to five-star hotels in Vietnam. Such hotels are more likely to be involved in environmental practices. This is consistent with Molina-Azorín et al. (2009), who state that environmental problems have been considered by many hotels, especially three- to five-star hotels, because of the industry's negative impact on nature and the environment. To ensure reliability, respondents were directly involved in environmental activities and had at least one year of work experience in such hotels, as they must be able to understand the hotel's environmental tasks and activities and provide reliable information for the study. Thus, we chose employees working in various departments, such as housekeeping, front office, food and beverages (F&B), administration (or HR) and maintenance for data collection.

The original questionnaire, written in English, was translated into Vietnamese by two native and bilingual researchers, and was then translated back into English. Due to the quantitative nature of the research, the questionnaire contained mainly closed questions, using a five-point Likert-type (Agree-Disagree) scale. Along with a covering letter, these questionnaires were provided to employees either by hard copy or e-mail. We contacted all three- to five-star hotels in Vietnam (880 hotels) in order to request their agreement to distribute these questionnaires to relevant employees, with 127 hotels allowing us to collect this data. For each hotel, we ensured that the questionnaires were answered separately by both managerial and non-managerial employees in order to reduce common method bias.

Among the constructs of the questionnaire, data on REW, PEM, OCBE and cultural perspectives were collected during the first round (Period 1), while EIGP was completed during the second round (Period 2). All responses collected in Period 1 were analyzed based on coding. In this stage, from 508 questionnaires sent to respondents (two for managerial employees and two for non-managerial employees within each hotel), we successfully received 375 completed responses. After carefully checking the returned questionnaires, we eliminated those which were invalid due to reasons such as missing data or major differences between managerial and non-managerial employees' evaluation of REW and PEM. A total of 355 individuals completed the survey to a usable level. At the end of the data collection process, we obtained their agreement to allow us to carefully store personal information (e.g., telephone number, e-mail), with the aim of contacting them again in the second round. In Period 2, these individuals were invited to respond to our questionnaire concerning EIGP, but only 301 respondents ultimately provided valid feedback at this stage. According to Hair et al.'s (2014) guidelines, the sample size of 301 is appropriate for this work. Specifically, 165 (54.8%) and 136 (45.2%) employees worked at hotels managed by local and Western companies, respectively.

In this study, the respondents consisted of 184 females (61.1%) and 117 males (38.9%). The participants came from a wide range of departments: the most prevalent were F&B and housekeeping, with 87 (28.9%) and 80 (26.6%) respondents respectively, followed by maintenance (51 employees [16.9%]), administration/HR (43 employees [14.3%]), and front office (40 employees [13.3%]). Of the sample, most respondents (255%–84.7%) had under ten years of work experience at their present hotel, with only 46 respondents (15.3%) having ten years or more. Regarding the hotels' length of operation, there were 157 (52.2%) and 111 (36.9%) respondents working at hotels which had been established for less than ten years and from 10 to 20 years, respectively, while 33 participants (10.9%) worked in hotels which had been in operation for over 20 years.

In the data analysis stage, we first applied the SMART-PLS software to assess the reliability and validity of the measurements. According to Hair et al. (2011), PLS-SEM may be a suitable method for researchers because it offers advantages such as fewer identification issues, data with much smaller as well as larger sample sizes, and compatibility with a complex structural model and many constructs and relationships. By doing a critical review of applying PLS-SEM in HRM papers published in leading journals, Ringle et al. (2020) revealed that PLS-SEM is an increasingly important method for empirical HRM studies. Next, the PROCESS package was used to test the direct and indirect effects of both REW and PEM practices on OCBE and EIGP and the moderating influence of cultural perspectives (Western and local) on these effects.

Assessment of common method variance

First, Harman's single factor analysis was applied in order to test common method variance. A significant level of common method variance is detected when the first factor's variance is

Table 1. Factor loadings and Descriptive statistics.

Constructs/items	Factor loading	Mean
Green performance management		
Employees know the specific environmental targets, goals and responsibilities	0.754	3.581
Employee's environmental behavior and contributions to hotels' environmental performance are assessed	0.767	3.615
Providing regular feedback to employees or teams to achieve environmental goals or improve hotel's environmental performance	0.765	3.711
Achievement of environmental goals is seen as one of the criteria in system of employee performance appraisal	0.825	3.787
Roles of managers in achieving environmental outcomes included in appraisals	0.803	3.728
Green reward		
Link suggestion schemes into reward system by introducing rewards for innovative environmental initiative/performance	0.847	3.575
Hotel has non-monetary rewards for environmental achievements	0.844	3.542
Hotel has monetary rewards based on environmental achievements	0.850	3.475
Environmental performance is recognized publicly	0.880	3.528
Organizational citizenship behavior for the environment		
I suggest new practices that could improve the hotel's environmental performance	0.760	3.605
I encourage my colleagues to adopt more environmentally conscious behaviors	0.717	3.684
I stay informed of the hotel's environmental efforts	0.772	3.648
I make suggestions about ways to protect the environment more effectively	0.761	3.678
I volunteer for projects or activities that address the hotel's environmental issues	0.718	3.608
I spontaneously give my time to help colleagues take the environment into account	0.726	3.605
I undertake environmental actions that contribute positively to the hotel's image	0.760	3.661
Employee in-role green performance		
I complete the environmental duties specified in the job	0.875	3.598
I fulfill all environmental responsibilities required by the job	0.911	3.635
I never neglect environmental aspects of the job which I am obligated to perform.	0.887	3.575

greater than 50% of the total variance (Podsakoff et al., 2003). Our results depicted four factors established at eigenvalues above 1.0, while the overall variance explained by the first factor was less than 50%. Second, based on Kock's (2015) suggestion, we tested for common method bias using the full collinearity assessment method. The results revealed that the values of all VIFs are less than 3.33, and thus common method bias was not present. Finally, in order to reduce data bias, the authors randomly arranged the order of the different question sections before the questionnaires were provided to respondents. We can therefore conclude that common method variance did not have serious implications for these findings.

Measurement

To measure EIGP, we developed three items based on the scale used by Janssen and Yperen (2004). This scale is widely used in the HRM literature to measure employee performance in general and may be extended into particular domains, for example extending it into the green context. We also employed seven items from Raineri and Paillé (2016) to evaluate OCBE. In fact, other publications in sustainable tourism management, such as Pham, Tučková, and Jabbour (2019) and Pham et al. (2020), have also applied these items to measure this factor. With respect to HRM practices aimed at motivating employees, on the basis of our case study findings and previous studies (Jabbour et al., 2010; Masri & Jaaron, 2017), items relating to both REW and PEM were adopted. Table 1 illustrates all items adopted in this study.

Tables 1 and 2 indicate acceptable reliability, as all values of Cronbach's alpha (CrA) and Composite reliability (CR) are better than the benchmark of 0.7 (Hair et al., 2014). The results also suggest reasonable convergent validity, since all Average Variance Extracted (AVE) values exceed 0.5 and all factor loading values are higher than the threshold level of 0.7 (Hair et al., 2014).

Table 2. Reliability and validity assessment.

				REW		PEM		OCBE		EIGP	
	CR	CrA	AVE	FLC	HTMT	FLC	HTMT	FLC	HTMT	FLC	HTMT
REW	0.916	0.878	0.732	**0.855**	—	—	—	—	—	—	—
PEM	0.888	0.843	0.614	0.507	0.591	**0.783**	—	—	—	—	—
OCBE	0.897	0.867	0.555	0.587	0.667	0.499	0.574	**0.745**	—	—	—
EIGP	0.921	0.870	0.794	0.594	0.678	0.556	0.647	0.669	0.766	**0.891**	—

Note: CR = composite reliability; CrA = Cronbach's alpha; FLC = Fornell-Larcker criterion; HTMT = Heterotrait-Monotrait ratio. Square roots of AVE in bold font are on the main diagonal.

Table 3. Path coefficients of direct effects.

Paths	Coefficient (b)	p-value
REW -> EIGP	0.420*	0.000
PEM -> EIGP	0.342*	0.001
REW -> OCBE	0.448*	0.000
PEM -> OCBE	0.274*	0.009

*Confidence interval at the 0.05 level.

Finally, to test discriminant validity, the study considered the Fornell-Larcker criterion and the Heterotrait-Monotrait ratio (HTMT). As shown in Table 2, the square root of the AVE of each construct, ranging from 0.745 to 0.891, must be greater than all correlation values with any other construct (Fornell & Larcker, 1981). In addition, Table 2 shows all HTMT ratios, between 0.574 and 0.766, are less than the threshold of 0.9 (Ringle et al., 2020). Thus, we can conclude that there was an adequate level of discriminant validity for this study.

Findings

Direct effects

As illustrated in Table 3, the results of bootstrap analysis (the 95% confidence intervals with bootstrapping 5000 samples) indicate that all path coefficients suggest significant effects of REW and PEM on EIGP and OCBE. Specifically, REW ($b = 0.420$, $p < 0.05$) and PEM ($b = 0.342$, $p < 0.05$) have positive and significant influences on EIGP, indicating that H1a and H1b are accepted. Similarly, there are positive and significant connections between REW and OCBE ($b = 0.448$, $p < 0.05$) and between PEM and OCBE ($b = 0.274$, $p < 0.05$), indicating that hypotheses H1c and H1d are supported.

Indirect effects

By analyzing bootstrap with 5000 samples and 95% conference intervals, Table 4 shows a significant and indirect effect of REW on EIGP via the mediating role of OCBE ($b = 0.183$, $p < 0.05$). Furthermore, the indirect effect of PEM on EIGP via OCBE is confirmed at a 95% confidence interval ($b = 0.300$, $p < 0.05$). Thus, hypotheses H1e and H1f are accepted.

Moderation analysis

In terms of the moderating effects, Table 5 shows the important role of the interaction between culture and REW in enhancing two dependent variables. Specifically, the interaction of both cultural perspectives and REW significantly impacts EIGP ($b = 0.551$, $p < 0.05$) and OCBE ($b = 0.397$, $p < 0.05$). By contrast, there are no significant influences arising from the interaction between culture and PEM on EIGP ($b = 0.022$, $p > 0.05$) and OCBE ($b = 0.038$, $p > 0.05$).

Table 4. Path coefficients of indirect effects.

Paths	Coefficient (b)	p-value
REW -> OCBE -> EIGP	0.183*	0.012
PEM -> OCBE -> EIGP	0.300*	0.000

*Confidence interval at the 0.05 level.

Table 5. Path coefficients of moderation analysis.

Paths	Coefficient (b)	p-value
Culture x REW -> EIGP	0.551*	0.000
Culture x PEM -> EIGP	0.022	0.859
Culture x REW -> OCBE	0.397*	0.000
Culture x PEM -> OCBE	0.038	0.678

*Confidence interval at the 0.05 level.

Table 6. Conditional effect at moderators.

Moderator	Coefficient (b)	p-value	LLCI–ULCI
Culture x REW -> EIGP			
Local	0.386*	0.000	0.253–0.518
Western	0.936*	0.000	0.797–1.076
Culture x REW -> OCBE			
Local	0.259*	0.000	0.166–0.352
Western	0.656*	0.000	0.558–0.754

*Confidence interval at the 0.05 level.

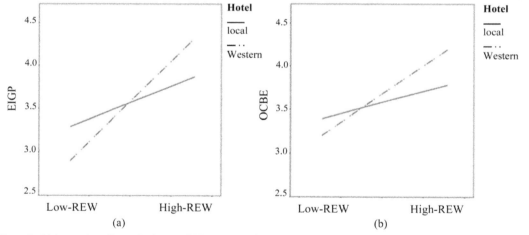

Figure 2. (a) Interactive effects of culture and REW on EIGP. (b) Interactive effects of culture and REW on OCBE.

Further analysis involved conditional effect assessment of the moderator factors, with the aim of deeply analyzing the interactive influences of culture and REW on the two dependent variables. Based on the data shown in Table 6, REW significantly influences EIGP and OCBE at both local- and Western-managed hotels. However, on the basis of coefficient values and the range of confidence intervals, it can be suggested that the size of REW's influence on EIGP at Western-managed hotels ($b = 0.936$, $p < 0.05$) is higher than at local hotels ($b = 0.386$, $p < 0.05$). Similarly, REW's influence on OCBE at Western hotels ($b = 0.656$, $p < 0.05$) is greater than at local hotels ($b = 0.259$, $p < 0.05$). This is visualized clearly in the positive slopes shown in Figure 2(a,b), where the slopes of the broken lines (Western hotels) are greater than the slopes of the solid lines (local hotels) in each figure. Thus, the results of this analysis suggest support for hypotheses H2a and H2c, whereas H2b and H2d are rejected.

Discussion

Theoretical implications

Embracing practices aimed at motivating employees to develop EIGP and OCBE

Underlining the theories of AMO and person-organization fit, we argue that GHRM practices, such as REW and PEM, may play a critical role in enhancing EIGP. EIGP can be given an important role in pursuing organizations' environmental sustainability strategies, but the absence of EIGP-related hospitality studies in the past represents a necessity for scholars. Therefore, our investigation of the connections between green practices and EIGP offers empirical evidence to contribute to the existing literature on GHRM and hospitality and tourism management. The findings of this work confirm the significant influence of REW and PEM on EIGP, in support of both AMO and person-organization fit theories. This is because, when hotels pay attention to green policies linked to both monetary and non-monetary rewards and communicate this to employees, employees are more likely to understand their hotel's green values and culture and actively participate in green activities. Thus, this policy can motivate employees' sense of responsibility to fulfill the environmental tasks included in their job description.

Similarly, developing a performance management system to monitor the green activities of hotel employees (e.g. employees receive environmental feedback from hotel managers or guests) helps employees understand how to avoid mistakes when performing green tasks at their hotel, consequently improving EIGP. These findings are important for the theoretical aspect of bridging this gap in the literature, because although the GHRM-EIGP connection has been suggested by Ren et al. (2018), published papers have not yet empirically demonstrated this relationship by extending these two theories in the green context, especially in the hospitality sector.

This work highlights the two perspectives of social exchange and person-organization fit as the ideal theoretical underpinnings to predict the effects of REW and PEM on OCBE. However, these relationships have been the subject of considerable scholarly debate. Some scholars argue that extra-role behaviors (e.g. OCBE) may not be recognized by the reward system and that real work-related pressures may not allow employees to engage in such behaviors voluntarily. Despite this argument, the results indicate the statistically significant effects of such practices on OCBE, in support of these two theories. This emphasizes the importance of applying green policies in hotels such as REW and PEM to motivate employees, encouraging employees to willingly involve themselves in environmental activities and events. Thus, if a hotel intends to implement reward policies for employees with high green performance along with a system for monitoring environmental tasks performed by employees, this encourages employees to reciprocally support their hotel through green behavior and attitude.

We argue that employees may perceive benefits from such policies implemented by the hotel, as these practices help to align their behavior with the hotel's green goals and stimulate commitment to the environment. Consequently, they may wish to reciprocate by voluntarily changing their environmental behaviors in the workplace; for example, they may be willing to provide green suggestions to protect the environment more effectively. This result is supported by previous studies, such as Saeed et al. (2019), who indicate that a strong green reward policy is critical to enhancing pro-environmental behavior among employees, and Pinzone et al. (2016), who suggest that PEM is a significant predictor to boost OCBE. Thus, these findings are in line with the existing literature, and demonstrate that these two theories can be extended to investigate these relationships in the hospitality context. Additionally, we contribute to the current literature on GHRM and hospitality and tourism management by providing empirical evidence that although OCBE is not rewarded and monitored by the organization, this behavior can be predicted by REW and PEM policies.

The mediating role of OCBE

One controversial topic in this area is whether employees' voluntary behavior (e.g. OCB) may boost in-role performance. Scholars have argued that such behavior is not rewarded and monitored by firms, and hence that it is irrational to assume that there is a relationship between these two variables. Based on AMO theory, however, individual performance can be considered as a function of motivation and effort (e.g. OCB), which may be advanced by HRM practices (Jiang, Lepak, Han, et al., 2012). This suggests that HRM practices such as REW and PEM may potentially enhance EIGP via the mediating role of OCBE. We argue that this expectation must be considered by hotels, as such practices may help employees to gain green knowledge, avoid unwanted environmental mistakes and boost their commitment to the environment (Pham, Tučková, & Phan, 2019). Consequently, this may stimulate employees' efforts and behaviors to willingly participate in green tasks and events at hotels. In turn, this can increase the responsibility they feel to fulfill environmental tasks required in their job description. From the results of our analysis, the findings support this argument and are in line with AMO theory. Thus, our study reveals the significant indirect effects of REW and PEM on EIGP through the mediation of OCBE, thus making an important contribution to the literature, and emphasizing this finding as a new perspective in investigating the role of GHRM application in hotels.

So far, this stream of research has generally been overlooked by scholars in GHRM as well as hospitality and tourism management. In fact, there are prior sudies which focus on the GHRM-OCBE relationship (Saeed et al., 2019) and the GHRM-EIGP relationship (Dumont et al., 2017). Nevertheless, the mediating role of OCBE in separate influences on GHRM practices and EIGP – especially REW and PEM – remains a gap in the literature, especially in the context of sustainable tourism. Accordingly, this paper offers an essential piece of evidence to fill this research gap and provides insight for scholars to reflect on the importance of OCBE in enhancing employees' green effectiveness in their roles. Also, these findings contribute to a clear understanding of the role of discretionary behavior in stimulating not just individuals' extra-role performance, but also in-role performance.

The role of cultural perspectives and unexpected findings

The country of origin and the national culture of a parent company (or headquarters) is likely to influence the operational and managerial processes and decisions of subsidiaries (Lau & Ngo, 2001). As a consequence, we would expect that in the hotel sector, not only green practices, but also green beliefs and values, would be transferred from headquarters to overseas subsidiaries, thus affecting hotel employees' green activities, behavior and performance. In this paper, we attempt to understand the moderating role of culture (operationalized as Western and local) in the connections between green practices aimed at motivating employees (REW and PEM), EIGP and OCBE. This is consistent with calls for papers to investigate the contribution of cultural influences to GHRM application (Pham, Tučková, & Jabbour, 2019; Ren et al., 2018). This stream of research has been under-researched in GHRM, and in particular, in the hospitality and tourism sectors. Thus, these findings make an essential contribution to the existing literature by bridging this research gap.

Our results indicate that culture significantly moderates the effect of REW on EIGP and OCBE at hotels. More specifically, these influences are found to be stronger at Western-managed hotels than at locally managed hotels. It is suggested that the hotels' development of green policies to reward employees (e.g. bonuses, cash, recognition from organizations) is important to motivate employees' OCBE and generate EIGP. Thus, it is clear that reward policies have a significant effect on EIGP and OCBE at both local and Western hotels. However, this effect seems to be stronger at hotels managed by Western companies.

A likely explanation for this effect may be that employees working at Western hotels are largely impacted by the green beliefs and values of top management and Western-based corporations. Furthermore, HRM practices that make interventions at the individual level (e.g. employee rewards) are considered more appropriate in Western enterprises as their culture tends to be more individualistic (Hoang et al., 2018). Consequently, at such hotels, policies aimed at rewarding employees who demonstrate effective green skills, strongly and positively boosts their pro-environmental behavior and green performance. Hotels managed by Western companies operating in Vietnam tend to be concerned with the role of employees in developing their professional green strategy. Environmental policies (e.g. rewards) aimed at boosting employees' green behaviors, especially voluntary green behavior, are valued by these hotels' top management (Pham, Tučková, & Jabbour, 2019); for example, non-monetary rewards (e.g. recognition from managers), which may stimulate employees' willingness to become involved in green activities. Additionally, these companies often exhibit top-down consistency in applying green policies to ensure that all employees understand and embrace the hotel's green values and culture. This is paramount for the effective implementation of green strategies. Locally-managed hotels that do not attempt to replicate Western hotels' professional green image seem to lack interest in this strategy often due to budgetary and people issues.

Contrary to expectations, the study found that culture does not moderate PEM's impact on EIGP and OCBE. We found no differences between the two types of hotel management in terms of the role of policies aimed at monitoring employees' green activities in boosting OCBE and EIGP. It is somewhat surprising that the effects of PEM on EIGP and OCBE in hotels managed by local companies are not higher than in those managed by Western companies. Employees working at local hotels are affected by local management, which tends to be more collectivistic than the management style at Western hotels, as a result, policies such as PEM are important in enhancing employees' voluntary green behavior and green effectiveness.

A possible explanation for such results might be that although employees work at Western hotels, they are Vietnamese and living in Vietnam, and hence are still largely affected by the local culture. Besides, after many years of operating in Vietnam, some of the Western hotels might have become more similar to local hotels due to influences from the environmental and institutional contexts. This argument is in line with the institutional perspective (DiMaggio & Powell, 1983), which suggests that organizations and individuals may be shaped by the social environment in which they exist. On the other hand, employees who work at hotels managed by local companies are likely located in major cities, such as Ho Chi Minh City/Hanoi, where the cultural exchange between Western and Vietnamese cultures is strong. Therefore, to a certain extent, Western culture will also have affected these employees. As a consequence, we may not see differences in the effects of PEM on EIGP and OCBE between these two types of hotels. Thus, by adopting the cultural lens, these findings provide an insight into Hofstede's (1983) argument, which emphasizes that organizational culture may be impacted or shaped by national culture.

Taken together, our findings shed light on the role of culture in explaining the importance of green practices in predicting employees' green behavior in the hospitality sector. Results indicate that culture moderates the effect of REW on EIGP and OCBE, but not the impact of PEM on EIGP and OCBE. We believe it is important to examine the intersection between green rewards, green performance management and culture as they shed light on the impact of the wider context on the GHRM system and its meaning to individuals (Ren et al., 2018). By and large, HRM practices are not all the same, and their degrees of transfer between headquarters and subsidiaries might differ (Björkman & Lervik, 2007; Myloni et al., 2004). Western-managed hotels are likely to be aligned with the cultural norms of their parent organizations which have already had to adjust to environmental-related norms for competition and survival (Martínez-Martínez, Cegarra-Navarro, García-Pérez, & Wensley, 2019). This impact was observed for green rewards but not for green performance management. A potential explanation for this difference may be that PEM is a construct that is much more affected by the role of local line management and the local culture – in the form of appraisals and feedback for example. Whilst the culture moderator addresses the potential influence of top management and headquarters on individuals (which is observed on compensation as rewards provided by the hotel), PEM is operationalized and conceptualized with a focus on the local context (which has similar dynamics for Western-managed and locally-managed hotels). This is in line with previous research in that MNC subsidiaries adapt to local conditions up to a certain extent, depending on the nature of the HRM policy or practice. While the transferability of compensation practices (green rewards) may be implemented when in alignment with government legislation, performance practices are highly dependent on (local) cultural norms and tend to be integrated as part of a wider HR system (Verburg et al., 1999).

Through these results, this paper supports efforts to widen national cultural perspectives in the GHRM field, which have previously been neglected. These findings offer the potential to inform future works on cultural perspective, especially in exploring their role in the application of GHRM, such as reward policies in organizations. Additionally, it may be argued that although culture does not moderate the connections of PEM with EIGP and OCBE, this result suggests that the cultural or institutional approaches may help explain such links in further studies.

Practical implications

From the results analyzed here, environmental action for sustainability may bring about positive green behavior, consequently enhancing EIGP. The first implication is the need to apply both REW and PEM policies in order to develop sustainability at hotels. Therefore, policies regarding both monetary (e.g. bonuses, cash) and non-monetary (e.g. gifts, promotion) rewards need to be considered by hotel management, especially for hotels managed by Western hospitality corporations. Rewards may be focused on encouraging employees to provide green suggestions for innovative green performance. Additionally, managers should concentrate on public recognition for employees with good environmental effectiveness. Similarly, PEM policy helps to boost employees' pro-environmental behavior, subsequently advancing their environmental effectiveness. Thus, setting up a green performance management system is important for hotels. For instance, hotels may carefully assess employees' environmental targets and results and set up a department for receiving feedback from guests or managers.

Second, the findings show that OCBE is an important mediating element in indirectly enhancing EIGP, suggesting that improving OCBE must be considered by hotels' top management. Thus, understanding how employees can actively involve themselves in green activities allows for a better result in enhancing employees' green performance. When employees have a tendency towards environmental protection at work, this helps them easily absorb their hotel's green values, mission and culture. Accordingly, green policies, such as REW and PEM, may strongly boost employees' positive behavior towards the environment, which in turn can help to achieve the required green targets and goals. With hotels, it is important to inspire employees to provide green suggestions for protecting the environment, to volunteer for environmental projects or activities, and to encourage their colleagues to adopt green behaviors in the workplace. These implications are necessary not only for achieving green performance for employees and hotels, but also for spreading green behavior and social values to communities where employees work and live.

Finally, one major suggestion for hotel managers is that a focus on cultural values could be an effective way of developing their hotel's green strategy. As mentioned in the findings section, although the reward policy in hotels managed by local companies can be an important component to predict employees' green behavior, such hotels need to place more emphasis on this policy. Thus, these hotels should guarantee top-down consistency in terms of using environmental resources and implementing environment-oriented policies, such as a reward system. Moreover, employees and managers should be encouraged to share their green experiences with others. This is essential to ensure that not only people working at present, but also employees recruited in the future, clearly understand the hotel's green values and culture.

Limitations and suggestions for further research

Although this work contributes significantly to the existing literature, it nevertheless contains several limitations that may suggest pathways for future investigations. First, while the authors expect that cultural perspectives can be applied to explain the moderating role of different cultures (Western and local) regarding the influence of REW and PEM on EIGP and OCBE, the results here indicate different outcomes between these two green practices. This may be an interesting area for further studies to examine; for example, a qualitative study, aimed at explaining why cultural differences do not moderate PEM's effects on EIGP and OCBE, leading to a result which was contradictory to our expectations. As mentioned above, the institutional perspective may be considered for exploring this area.

Second, following AMO theory, along with practices for motivating employees (e.g. REW and PEM), practices aimed at developing green ability (e.g. green training) and providing green opportunities (e.g. employee involvement) are two of the three core components of GHRM (Renwick et al., 2013), and have not been the focus of this paper. For instance, green training may develop employees' environmental knowledge (Jabbour et al., 2010), which can help them understand how to avoid behaviors and activities which negatively impact the environment as well as drive hotels' environmental sustainability and business performance (Martínez-Martínez et al., 2015; Martínez-Martínez, Cegarra-Navarro, García-Pérez, & Moreno-Ponce, 2019) Thus, a study to investigate the contributions of GHRM practices (e.g. green training, employee involvement) towards EIGP and hotel's success is suggested for further investigation.

Third, this paper tests these hypotheses via data collected within Vietnam. Employees working in organizations within different national cultures can differ in the ways they perceive emotions (Matsumoto, 1989), and thus an examination of these relationships and the moderating role of culture within different countries or between countries is likely to yield new insights. Fourth, all constructs in this study are based on self-assessment. One of the disadvantages of the self-assessment method is a low level of objectivity. Therefore, future studies may use more objective methods for data collection. For instance, EIGP can be evaluated by supervisors or department managers. Finally, it is important to recognize that any survey in sustainability-related topics can face the challenge of social desirability bias in data collection (Roxas & Lindsay, 2012).

Conclusion

By employing quantitative data, this paper theoretically argues and empirically tests the influences of REW and PEM on EIGP and OCBE, the mediating role of OCBE, and the role of cultural perspectives (Western and local) in these connections. The results show evidence which supports investing in hotels' green policies to advance EIGP and OCBE. OCBE also plays a mediating role in the effects of REW and PEM on EIGP. Importantly, we indicate that REW's effects on EIGP and OCBE at hotels managed by Western corporations are significantly stronger than in hotels managed by local companies. By contrast, connections between PEM, EIGP and OCBE do not depend on culture.

Acknowledgement

The authors gratefully acknowledge the great supports of hotels in Vietnam. We are also grateful for insightful comments from anonymous reviewers, Editor-in-Chief Prof Xavier Font, and Guest Editors Prof. Aurora Martínez-Martínez, Prof. Juan Gabriel Cegarra-Navarro, and Prof. Alexeis Garcia-Perez.

Disclosure statement

No potential conflict of interest was reported by the authors.

ORCID

Nhat Tan Pham http://orcid.org/0000-0001-9927-2257
Charbel Jose Chiappetta Jabbour http://orcid.org/0000-0002-6143-4924
Tan Vo-Thanh http://orcid.org/0000-0001-9964-3724
Toan Luu Duc Huynh http://orcid.org/0000-0002-1486-127X
Clarice Santos http://orcid.org/0000-0003-0326-8638

References

Alonso-Almeida, M. M., Robin, C. F., Pedroche, M. S. C., & Astorga, P. S. (2017). Revisiting green practices in the hotel industry: A comparison between mature and emerging destinations. *Journal of Cleaner Production*, *140*, 1415–1428. https://doi.org/10.1016/j.jclepro.2016.10.010

Appelbaum, E. R., Bailey, T., Berg, P., & Kalleberg, A. L. (2000). *Manufacturing advantage: Why high-performance work systems pay off*. Cornell University Press.

Björkman, I., & Lervik, J. E. (2007). Transferring HR practices within multinational corporations. *Human Resource Management Journal*, *17*(4), 320–335. https://doi.org/10.1111/j.1748-8583.2007.00048.x

Boiral, O. (2009). Greening the corporation through organizational citizenship behaviors. *Journal of Business Ethics*, *87*(2), 221–236. https://doi.org/10.1007/s10551-008-9881-2

Bommer, W. H., Dierdorff, E. C., & Rubin, R. S. (2007). Does prevalence mitigate relevance? The moderating effect of group-level OCB on employee performance. *Academy of Management Journal*, *50*(6), 1481–1494. https://doi.org/10.5465/amj.2007.28226149

Chan, E. S., & Hawkins, R. (2012). Application of EMSs in a hotel context: A case study. *International Journal of Hospitality Management*, *31*(2), 405–418. https://doi.org/10.1016/j.ijhm.2011.06.016

DiMaggio, P. J., & Powell, W. W. (1983). The iron cage revisited: Institutional isomorphism and collective rationality in organizational fields. *American Sociological Review*, *48*(2), 147–160. [Database] https://doi.org/10.2307/2095101

Dumont, J., Shen, J., & Deng, X. (2017). Effects of green HRM practices on employee workplace green behavior: The role of psychological green climate and employee green values. *Human Resource Management*, *56*(4), 613–627. https://doi.org/10.1002/hrm.21792

Dyer, L., & Reeves, T. (1995). Human resource strategies and firm performance: What do we know and where do we need to go? *International Journal of Human Resource Management*, *6*(3), 656–670. https://doi.org/10.1080/09585199500000041

Fornell, C., & Larcker, D. F. (1981). Evaluating structural equation models with unobservable variables and measurement error. *Journal of Marketing Research*, *18*(1), 39–50. https://doi.org/10.1177/002224378101800104

Govindarajulu, N., & Daily, B. F. (2004). Motivating employees for environmental improvement. *Industrial Management & Data Systems*, *104*(4), 364–372. https://doi.org/10.1108/02635570410530775

Guerci, M., Longoni, A., & Luzzini, D. (2016). Translating stakeholder pressures into environmental performance – The mediating role of green HRM practices. *International Journal of Human Resource Management*, *27*(2), 262–289. https://doi.org/10.1080/09585192.2015.1065431

Hair, J. F., Hult, G. T. M., Ringle, C., & Sarstedt, M. (2014). *A primer on partial least squares structural equation modeling (PLS-SEM)*. Sage Publications.

Hair, J. F., Ringle, C. M., & Sarstedt, M. (2011). PLS-SEM: Indeed a silver bullet. *Journal of Marketing Theory and Practice, 19*(2), 139–152. https://doi.org/10.2753/MTP1069-6679190202

Hoang, H. T., Rao Hill, S., Lu, V. N., & Freeman, S. (2018). Drivers of service climate: An emerging market perspective. *Journal of Services Marketing, 32*(4), 476–492. https://doi.org/10.1108/JSM-06-2017-0208

Hoffman, B. J., & Woehr, D. J. (2006). A quantitative review of the relationship between person–organization fit and behavioral outcomes. *Journal of Vocational Behavior, 68*(3), 389–399. https://doi.org/10.1016/j.jvb.2005.08.003

Hofstede, G. (1983). The cultural relativity of organizational practices and theories. *Journal of International Business Studies, 14*(2), 75–89. https://doi.org/10.1057/palgrave.jibs.8490867

Jabbour, C. J. C., Santos, F. C. A., & Nagano, M. S. (2010). Contributions of HRM throughout the stages of environmental management: Methodological triangulation applied to companies in Brazil. *International Journal of Human Resource Management, 21*(7), 1049–1089. https://doi.org/10.1080/09585191003783512

Janssen, O., & Yperen, N. W. (2004). Employees' Goal Orientations, the Quality of Leader-Member Exchange, and the Outcomes of Job Performance and Job Satisfaction. *Academy of Management Journal, 47*(3), 368–384.

Jiang, K., Lepak, D. P., Han, K., Hong, Y., Kim, A., & Winkler, A. L. (2012). Clarifying the construct of human resource systems: Relating human resource management to employee performance. *Human Resource Management Review, 22*(2), 73–85. https://doi.org/10.1016/j.hrmr.2011.11.005

Jiang, K., Lepak, D. P., Hu, J., & Baer, J. C. (2012). How does human resource management influence organizational outcomes? A meta-analytic investigation of mediating mechanisms. *Academy of Management Journal, 55*(6), 1264–1294. https://doi.org/10.5465/amj.2011.0088

Johns, G. (2006). The essential impact of context on organizational behavior. *Academy of Management Review, 31*(2), 386–408. https://doi.org/10.5465/amr.2006.20208687

Kehoe, R. R., & Wright, P. M. (2013). The impact of high-performance human resource practices on employees' attitudes and behaviors. *Journal of Management, 39*(2), 366–391. https://doi.org/10.1177/0149206310365901

Kock, N. (2015). Common method bias in PLS-SEM: A full collinearity assessment approach. *International Journal of e-Collaboration, 11*(4), 1–10. https://doi.org/10.4018/ijec.2015100101

Lau, C. M., & Ngo, H. Y. (2001). Organization development and firm performance: A comparison of multinational and local firms. *Journal of International Business Studies, 32*(1), 95–114. https://doi.org/10.1057/palgrave.jibs.8490940

Lauver, K. J., & Kristof-Brown, A. (2001). Distinguishing between employees' perceptions of person–job and person–organization fit. *Journal of Vocational Behavior, 59*(3), 454–470. https://doi.org/10.1006/jvbe.2001.1807

Luu, T. T. (2019). Green human resource practices and organizational citizenship behavior for the environment: The roles of collective green crafting and environmentally specific servant leadership. *Journal of Sustainable Tourism, 27*(8), 1167–1196. https://doi.org/10.1080/09669582.2019.1601731

Martínez-Martínez, A., Cegarra-Navarro, J. G., & García-Pérez, A. (2015). Environmental knowledge management: A long-term enabler of tourism development. *Tourism Management, 50*, 281–291. https://doi.org/10.1016/j.tourman.2015.03.006

Martínez-Martínez, A., Cegarra-Navarro, J. G., García-Pérez, A., & Moreno-Ponce, A. (2019). Environmental knowledge strategy: Driving success of the hospitality industry. *Management Research Review, 42*(6), 662–680. https://doi.org/10.1108/MRR-02-2018-009 https://doi.org/10.1108/MRR-02-2018-0091

Martínez-Martínez, A., Cegarra-Navarro, J. G., García-Pérez, A., & Wensley, A. (2019). Knowledge agents as drivers of environmental sustainability and business performance in the hospitality sector. *Tourism Management, 70*, 381–389. https://doi.org/10.1016/j.tourman.2018.08.030

Masri, H. A., & Jaaron, A. A. M. (2017). Assessing green human resources management practices in Palestinian manufacturing context: An empirical study. *Journal of Cleaner Production, 143*, 474–489. https://doi.org/10.1016/j.jclepro.2016.12.087

Matsumoto, D. (1989). Cultural influences on the perception of emotion. *Journal of Cross-Cultural Psychology, 20*(1), 92–105. https://doi.org/10.1177/0022022189201006

Molina-Azorín, J. F., Claver-Cortés, E., Pereira-Moliner, J., & Tarí, J. J. (2009). Environmental practices and firm performance: An empirical analysis in the Spanish hotel industry. *Journal of Cleaner Production, 17*(5), 516–524. https://doi.org/10.1016/j.jclepro.2008.09.001

Myloni, B., Harzing, A. W., & Mirza, H. (2004). Human resource management in Greece: Have the colours of culture faded away? *International Journal of Cross Cultural Management, 4*(1), 59–76. https://doi.org/10.1177/1470595804041527

Ogbonnaya, C., & Valizade, D. (2018). High performance work practices, employee outcomes and organizational performance: A 2-1-2 multilevel mediation analysis. *International Journal of Human Resource Management, 29*(2), 239–259. https://doi.org/10.1080/09585192.2016.1146320

Organ, D. W. (1988). *Organizational citizenship behavior: The good soldier syndrome.* Lexington Books.

Paillé, P., Boiral, O., & Chen, Y. (2013). Linking environmental management practices and organizational citizenship behaviour for the environment: A social exchange perspective. *International Journal of Human Resource Management, 24*(18), 3552–3575. https://doi.org/10.1080/09585192.2013.777934

Paillé, P., & Meija-Morelos, J. H. (2019). Organisational support is not always enough to encourage employee environmental performance. The moderating role of exchange ideology. *Journal of Cleaner Production, 220*, 1061–1070. https://doi.org/10.1016/j.jclepro.2019.02.192

Pham, N. T., Tučková, Z., & Jabbour, C. J. C. (2019). Greening the hospitality industry: How do green human resource management practices influence organizational citizenship behavior in hotels? A mixed-methods study. *Tourism Management, 72*, 386–399. https://doi.org/10.1016/j.tourman.2018.12.008

Pham, N. T., Tučková, Z., & Phan, Q. P. T. (2019). Greening human resource management and employee commitment toward the environment: An interaction model. *Journal of Business Economics and Management, 20*(3), 446–465. https://doi.org/10.3846/jbem.2019.9659

Pham, N. T., Vo-Thanh, T., Shahbaz, M., Huynh, T. L. D., & Usman, M. (2020). Managing environmental challenges: Training as a solution to improve employee green performance. *Journal of Environmental Management, 269*, 110781. https://doi.org/10.1016/j.jenvman.2020.110781

Pinzone, M., Guerci, M., Lettieri, E., & Redman, T. (2016). Progressing in the change journey towards sustainability in healthcare: The role of "green" HRM. *Journal of Cleaner Production, 122*, 201–211. https://doi.org/10.1016/j.jclepro.2016.02.031

Podsakoff, P. M., MacKenzie, S. B., Lee, J. Y., & Podsakoff, N. P. (2003). Common method biases in behavioral research: A critical review of the literature and recommended remedies. *The Journal of Applied Psychology, 88*(5), 879–903. https://doi.org/10.1037/0021-9010.88.5.879

Raineri, N., & Paillé, P. (2016). Linking corporate policy and supervisory support with environmental citizenship behaviors: The role of employee environmental beliefs and commitment. *Journal of Business Ethics, 137*(1), 129–148. https://doi.org/10.1007/s10551-015-2548-x

Ren, S., Tang, G., & Jackson, S. E. (2018). Green human resource management research in emergence: A review and future directions. *Asia Pacific Journal of Management, 35*(3), 769–803. https://doi.org/10.1007/s10490-017-9532-1

Renwick, D. W. S., Redman, T., & Maguire, S. (2013). Green human resource management: A review and research agenda. *International Journal of Management Reviews, 15*(1), 1–14. https://doi.org/10.1111/j.1468-2370.2011.00328.x

Ringle, C. M., Sarstedt, M., Mitchell, R., & Gudergan, S. P. (2020). Partial least squares structural equation modeling in HRM research. *The International Journal of Human Resource Management, 31*(12), 1617–1643. https://doi.org/10.1080/09585192.2017.1416655

Roxas, B., & Lindsay, V. (2012). Social desirability bias in survey research on sustainable development in small firms: An exploratory analysis of survey mode effect. *Business Strategy and the Environment, 21*(4), 223–235. https://doi.org/10.1002/bse.730

Ryan, C. (2018). Future trends in tourism research – Looking back to look forward: The future of 'Tourism Management Perspectives'. *Tourism Management Perspectives, 25*, 196–199. https://doi.org/10.1016/j.tmp.2017.12.005

Saeed, B. B., Afsar, B., Hafeez, S., Khan, I., Tahir, M., & Afridi, M. A. (2019). Promoting employee's proenvironmental behavior through green human resource management practices. *Corporate Social Responsibility and Environmental Management, 26*(2), 424–438. https://doi.org/10.1002/csr.1694

Schnake, M., & Dumler, M. P. (1997). Organizational citizenship behavior: The impact of rewards and reward practices. *Journal of Managerial Issues, 9*(2), 216–229.

Tritto, A. (2020). Environmental management practices in hotels at world heritage sites. *Journal of Sustainable Tourism, 28*(11), 1911–1931. https://doi.org/10.1080/09669582.2020.1771566

Verburg, R. M., Drenth, P. J., Koopman, P. L., Muijen, J. J. V., & Wang, Z. M. (1999). Managing human resources across cultures: A comparative analysis of practices in industrial enterprises in China and The Netherlands. *International Journal of Human Resource Management, 10*(3), 391–410. https://doi.org/10.1080/095851999340396

Witt, M. A., & Stahl, G. K. (2016). Foundations of responsible leadership: Asian versus western executive responsibility orientations toward key stakeholders. *Journal of Business Ethics, 136*(3), 623–638. https://doi.org/10.1007/s10551-014-2534-8

Zhang, Y., Luo, Y., Zhang, X., & Zhao, J. (2019). How green human resource management can promote green employee behavior in China: A technology acceptance model perspective. *Sustainability, 11*(19), 5408. https://doi.org/10.3390/su11195408

Building dynamic capabilities in tourism organisations for disaster management: enablers and barriers

Yawei Jiang, Brent W. Ritchie and Martie-Louise Verreynne

ABSTRACT
Dynamic capabilities enable tourism organisations to manage crises and disasters, yet many do not possess these competencies. This paper investigates the factors that enable or impede the development of dynamic capabilities in tourism organisations that help them to survive and thrive in crises or disaster environments. These enablers and barriers to build dynamic capabilities are compared across tourism organisations considering their age, size, and sector. Findings from 40 in-depth interviews with tourism business operators and other stakeholders in a disaster-prone region over two years show that knowledge-based, human-related, relational, and financial slack resources are important enablers of building dynamic capabilities in times of disasters. Internal process restrictions and external over-regulation act as major barriers to develop dynamic capabilities. The findings show that tourism organisations should consider reliance on the broader system in which multiple levels of actors are actively engaged in resource integration and develop shared values to enable adaptive capacity. Policymakers and tourism organisations can use this study to evaluate the appropriateness of their resources and processes in developing dynamic capabilities and thus achieve a more sustainable future in uncertain times.

Introduction

Tourism organisations are especially vulnerable to unexpected and unpredictable environments caused by natural, health and economic crises and disasters (Ritchie & Jiang, 2019). Their vulnerability is again highlighted by the impact of the COVID-19 pandemic with a loss of US$30 to $50 billion in international visitor expenditure (UNWTO., 2020). The need for tourism organisations to proactively respond to and recover from these crises and disasters is urgent (Paraskevas et al., 2013). However, tourism organisations often lack the resources and knowledge to prepare for and recover from unexpected disasters. This can incur significant economic losses as a result of a reduction in tourist demand (Boukas & Ziakas, 2013) or even be rendered unsustainable. One way to address these challenges is to develop dynamic capabilities (DCs), which are important organisational capabilities that provide mechanisms to strategically adapt, adjust, or reconfigure resources and routines (Teece et al., 1997).

While ordinary capabilities enable organisations to do things right, DCs help them do the right things and so address the unusual changes found in post-disaster environments (Mansour et al., 2019). Natural disasters affect tourism organisations' operating environment through damage to infrastructure, changes in the labour market and customer demand, and supply availability and costs (Battisti & Deakins, 2017). These changes create the kind of turbulence that necessitates "continuous adaptation" through organisational learning in the aftermath of disruptions. How tourism organisations respond to these changes and achieve transformation depends on their ability to adapt, modify, and reconfigure their resources and routines (Teece, 2017).

Although it is well recognised that organisations need to develop DCs to deal with crisis and disaster environments (Dixon et al., 2007), the factors that enable tourism organisations to develop DCs remain unclear. The broader strategy literature identifies a range of interrelated factors from inside and outside the organisation that enable or hinder the development from DCs, such as experience, culture, resources, leadership, and external uncertainty (Schilke, Hu, & Helfat, 2018). For example, the discussion of how tourism organisations leverage organic organisational structures over those that are more mechanistic (e.g., Sollund, 2006) can explain adaptability and flexibility in uncertain environments. Coping better with changes in dynamic environments is associated with greater staff participation in organically structured firms where organisational members know their decision-making roles, responsibilities, and authorities (Verreynne et al., 2016). Organic structures can thus improve organisational performance in uncertain environments, which is missing from the DC literature in tourism settings. First, it helps organisations develop knowledge to provide competitive advantage (Ramezan, 2011) by enforcing teamwork and employee's participation (Kraleva, 2011). Second, it enables more accurate information assembly and results in higher levels of strategic consensus, greater buy-in, improved implementation and subsequent performance (Verreynne et al., 2016). We build on these factors in this study, understanding that tourism organisations and the industry in which they operate are complex systems, with a range of factors working together to influence their survival and sustainable growth.

The overall aim of this study is to explore the key enablers and barriers for tourism organisations to develop DCs in times of disaster. It contributes to existing knowledge in two ways. First, the focus on tourism organisations facing extreme environmental uncertainty extends those studies that broadly investigate antecedents of DCs in a dynamic service/market environment (e.g., Lee et al., 2011). Different from dynamic market, political, or technology environments; crisis and disaster environments have higher levels of uncertainty and disruptive outcomes on organisations (Barreto, 2010). These disruptions can range from business suspensions due to damaged property caused by natural disasters, to complete shutdowns due to global travel restriction caused by pandemics such as COVID-19. Tourism organisations in crisis and disaster environments may find it difficult to access key resources (e.g., knowledge, money, labour) and may need to abandon old routines to continue business operations. Thus, investigating antecedents (enablers and barriers) of DCs development in crisis and disaster environments is important not just for their sustained growth when facing severe uncertainty, but also for their survival. Second, few studies focus on how different types of organisations use their resources to influence DC development. For example, do small and large organisations access resources differently, are young or old organisations more likely to build DCs, or do sectorial differences change how enablers or barriers affect building DCs (Barreto, 2010)? This comparison helps to evidence how a range of tourism organisations accesses different mechanisms in crisis and disaster environments as they build DCs.

This study was undertaken in the context of the 2017 Tropical Cyclone (TC) Debbie in the Whitsunday region of Australia. This cyclone provided a unique context to understand the factors that helped or hindered the development of DCs to deal with the extreme turbulence tourism organisations faced. Our study context is elaborated in the methods section to strengthen its usefulness and applicability of the research, as suggested by Ritchie and Jiang (2019). Findings of this study could improve our knowledge and identify appropriate ways for businesses to cope with other crises and disasters such as COVID-19.

Literature review

What are dynamic capabilities?

This paper focuses on those factors that proceed dynamic capabilities, rather than the nature thereof, yet it is important to provide a brief definition here. Dynamic capabilities, which are underpinned by organisational routines and managerial skills, are the firm's abilities to integrate, build, and reconfigure internal competencies to address or bring about changes in the business environment (Teece, 2007). Strong dynamic capabilities can enable the creation of effective business models (Teece, 2018), drive strategic renewal through, for example, collaborative approaches and culture change (Warner & Wäger, 2019) and open innovation (e.g., technology development) (Bogers et al., 2019), and shape markets and ecosystems (Schilke et al., 2018). Warner and Wäger (2019) use the example of digital transformation to illustrate how firms use dynamic capabilities to *sense* (scanning trends, screening competitors, enabling digital mindset), *seize* (scaling up business model, reallocating resources), and *transform* (joining a digital ecosystem, leveraging digital knowledge). To tourism organisations faced with severe uncertainty, dynamic capabilities can therefore shape strategic responses that ensure survival and future sustainability.

In disaster management, DCs provide mechanisms that enable tourism organisations to respond to disruptive environmental changes through a process of routine transformation, resource allocation and utilisation (Jiang et al., 2019). Within strategic management, two theoretical perspectives informed the development of DCs as a field of study. The first is the resource-based view of the firm (RBV), emanating from the work of Penrose (1959) who argued that an organisation's growth is due to resource deployment within organisations. Barney's Barney (1991) resource-based view notes that organisations' heterogeneous and immobilised resources can be used to generate sustained competitive advantage. Organisations that understand their available resources and how to effectively utilise them can implement more value-creating strategies. Human decision and capabilities are critical in making the best use of diversified and unique resources to cope with environmental changes (Teece et al., 1997). The second is the evolutionary theory of firms (ETF), which acknowledges that DCs are embedded in organisational processes and that the learning mechanisms of organisations guide the evolution of dynamic capabilities (Nelson & Winter, 1982). In unexpected and unpredictable environments, like those caused by a crisis or disaster, organisations' abilities to reconfigure resources is crucial for survival in the short-term, and to capitalise on opportunities in the long term. DCs enable organisations to purposefully create, extend, renew, and reconfigure its resources and routine base in response to rapid and unexpected changes (Teece, 2017).

Dynamic capabilities in tourism crisis and disaster environment

A DCs lens has been applied to study destination management (Denicolai et al., 2010), sustainable competitive advantage (Leonidou et al., 2015), and innovation (Thomas & Wood, 2014) in the tourism literature. However, the operating environment in these contexts is more suitable to be described as "competitive or dynamic" rather than "turbulent or chaotic" – where changes are unexpected and unpredictable. In dynamic environments, tourism organisations can take time to develop dynamic capabilities, while in crisis/disaster environments, processes are shortened or eliminated, as firms address immediate crises/disasters. Dynamic environments change rapidly and require organisations to respond quickly and flexibly (Hine et al., 2014), for example through continuous technological advancement, market variation, industry transformation, and policy/regulation innovation. However, unexpected and unpredictable environments are usually caused by crises and disasters, which have higher levels of uncertainty and disruptive outcomes on organisations (Barreto, 2010), such as the global border and travel restriction caused by health crisis COVID-19, which damaged the tourism industry heavily. Thus, this study aims to extend the understanding of DCs development in a crisis and disaster environment.

To date, the latter point is only illustrated in a few tourism studies that discuss DCs in crisis and disaster environments. For example, Alonso-Almeida et al. (2015) examined the development of DCs and their effects on restaurant performance in the global financial crisis. They found that organisations that proactively developed DCs were able to improve competitive advantage. However, their study focuses on how the crisis might improve or inhibit the development of DCs using proactive or reactive strategies, rather than how DCs can assist tourism organisations to respond to and recover from crisis and disaster environments quickly. Mansour et al. (2019) discussed two types of crisis management capabilities (crisis assessment and response) that enabled tourism organisations to survive the Libyan civil war. However, the authors did not discuss what triggered or impeded tourism organisations to build these capabilities. The next section draws from the strategic management literature to identify potential enablers and barriers to DCs development for tourism organisations.

Building dynamic capabilities in tourism organisations

DCs help organisations to increase their adaptive capacity and therefore their capacity to cope (Barreto, 2010) when resource adequacy and process efficiency are challenged. Adaptive capacity can reduce an organisation's vulnerability and help it to manage environmental uncertainty by reducing exposure and sensitivity to perturbation, which can eventually increase the resilience of organisations (Gallopín, 2006). External events often precipitate the development and use of DCs, but at a minimum, they are developed through the identification and utilisation of internal factors such as resources, managerial capabilities (Wang et al., 2015), and collaborative processes informed by learning (Zollo & Winter, 2002).

Antecedents refer to the factors or conditions that affect the emergence of DCs, which include both enablers and barriers (Ambrosini et al., 2009). The literature identifies a set of interrelated internal and external factors that enable or hinder the development of DCs. On the one hand, enablers are generated from organisational practices, such as business model changes and leadership styles (Paraskevas et al., 2013) and organisational resources, such as financial capital (Dixon et al., 2014). These factors relate to the resources of the organisation and the processes it uses. Burns and Stalker (1961) argue that organic structures – characterised by a contributive nature of special knowledge and experience to the common task of the concern, flexible task performance, a spread of commitment to the concern, a network structure of control, authority, and communication and a lateral rather than a vertical direction of communication – are more likely to maximise organisations' flexibility and orientation in uncertain environments. For example, it can enable employees' participation in the decision-making process (Verreynne et al., 2016) and improve double-loop learning in the organisation (Kraleva, 2011). Organic structures also improve leader's ability to flexibly cope with unexpected and unpredictable environments without defined tasks (Sollund, 2006).

In contrast, the development of DCs can also be constrained by organisations' administrative heritage or inertia, such as its existing organisational attributes, the configuration of assets/capabilities, distribution of managerial responsibilities, as well as previous and ongoing relationships with other organisations (Jiang & Ritchie, 2017). This is also termed a "success trap", which can cause the organisation to focus on existing capabilities based on past success, which prevents it from adapting to the changing environment (Junni et al., 2013). Wang et al. (2015) argue that success traps have a strong negative effect on the development of DCs and can hinder the process of strategic renewal and resource/capability creation. In other words, older and larger organisations with more static structures may have higher inertia, reducing their ability to adapt to environmental change quickly and flexibly.

Importantly, crises and disasters – by their nature – can exceed the capacity of tourism organisations to cope using only its resources and thus they look to wider external agencies to help provide resources. Similarly, the development of DCs should draw on both internal and external resources. This calls for empirical evidence to identify the factors that could enable or hinder the development of DCs in tourism organisations during times of disaster (Zahra et al., 2006).

Method

Tourism operating context in Australia

According to the latest World Bank (2020) annual rating, Australia is ranked 14th among 190 economies in terms of ease of doing business. Australia provides a safe, stable, and friendly business environment through effective governance and strong ties with other countries. It has well-developed business legislation (complexity of tariff, equal opportunity, and efficiency of clearance processes) and rule of law, which underpins its economic resilience (Tourism Australia, 2018). While Australia ranks well for investment, its rankings for government planning processes and assessment timeframes are less stellar, which reflects its high level of bureaucracy. It is also rated as one of the most expensive places in the world to do business due to high operating costs, such as occupancy/rent, energy and administration charges and labour costs (payroll tax), which reduce businesses' profit margins (Cummins, 2013). Under the Tourism 2020 strategy, all levels of government are pursuing regulatory reforms to limit tax, red tape, and other regulatory burdens for the industry.

Research site and context

This study examined the 2017 TC Debbie in the Whitsunday Region of Australia, which interrupted tourism operations with a 14-day loss of water and power and substantial damage to business properties and destination image (QFES, 2017). This region has experienced several natural disasters (e.g., cyclones, floods, bushfires) over the last 20 years (WRC, 2019). The most substantive and deadliest disaster in the past decade was the 2017 Cyclone Debbie – chosen for in-depth analysis in this study. It caused more than AUS$2.5 billion in economic damage to the local region agriculture, tourism, and mining industries (Queensland Government, 2019).

Tourism is the local region's second largest economic sector, which is renowned for its rich natural assets (beach, reef, national parks). It contributes around AUS$840.5 million and supports 20.9 per cent of the total employment in the Whitsunday Region (REMPLAN., 2020). There are many government regulations to protect the unique local environment, (e.g., responsible reef practices, zoning permits), which necessitate tourism businesses to plan their operations accordingly. The regional and local support for business response and recovery of disasters is well developed and supportive of small tourism businesses that are resource poor. The local council has a well-developed disaster management plan, evacuation measures (e.g., flood cameras, cyclone shelters), recovery plan, and an instant emergency information dashboard (WDCC, 2020). Many local tourism organisations are experienced in dealing with disasters, as witnessed by the involvement of tourism business owners in the Committee of Cyclone Recovery Group.

We therefore chose this research setting for four main reasons: (1) TC Debbie is the most severe cyclone that occurred in the past 20 years in the local region, with great negative impacts on tourism; (2) the tourism industry is the second largest industry in the Whitsunday region; (3) Whitsunday is located in a disaster-prone area due to its tropical wet season that occurs every year, with the cyclone season beginning in November and ending in April; and (4) the lead author is located nearby with access to the regional tourism organisation for further business contacts.

Sampling

We follow Lincoln and Guba (1985) guidelines for purposeful sampling. We initially chose respondents who would be most able to inform the research aim of how tourism organisations develop DCs in times of disaster. These were top managers and owners of tourism organisations as they have important insights into their organisations' identities, and unique access to knowledge of structures, strategies and actions concerning capability building in disaster time (Brockman et al., 2012). Then we used a snowball sampling technique, asking respondents for their recommendations as to who else could best explicate the process. The entire procedure was iterative. We simultaneously collected and analysed data, while seeking new respondents based on important information from prior respondents. This approach helped to ascertain the point at which theoretical data saturation was obtained (Corley & Gioia, 2004).

To study the region and tourism industry more deeply, we also involved external stakeholders in this research, such as government, industry association, insurance companies, and consultancy groups. These data provided supplementary information on the industrial and regional level and verified information obtained from businesses. Table 1 presents a summary of sampled tourism organisations considering their sector, size, and age, as well as external stakeholders from both government and industry agencies.

Data collection

This study used semi-structured interviews to collect data. To maintain consistency, the lead author conducted all interviews. Each interview took on average 58 minutes, varying between 28 and 100 minutes. Interviews followed a protocol that involved questions about (1) daily business operations, (2) impacts of TC Debbie, (3) new activities/routines used for TC Debbie management, and (4) factors that can facilitate and impede the development of new activities/routines. A summary of the respondents is provided in Table 2.

The first-round data were collected from October to November 2018. Face-to-face interviews were undertaken with 20 respondents from 14 tourism organisations (*6 tour operators, 7 accommodations, 1 food & beverage*) and four key government authorities and industry associations in Brisbane, Airlie Beach, and Cannonvale. Second-round data collection with a further 20 respondents took place from October to November 2019. Eleven of the respondents (*3 tour operators, 3 accommodations, 1 food & beverage, 4 external stakeholders*) were also included in the first-round database and nine (*1 accommodation, 8 external stakeholders*) were new respondents to the study. A total of 40 interviews were conducted with 25 organisations *(15 tourism organisations, 10 external stakeholders)* over a two-year time span.

Data analysis

Complete verbatim transcripts of interviews were organised using QSR NVivo, which enabled the researchers to index and coordinate the analysis of text and assisted in shaping and understanding data. Interview transcripts were analysed through the categorisation and analysis of emergent concepts and ideas and constant comparison of these concepts to identify common categories and themes. Following Shepherd and Williams (2014), we took three main steps to analyse the data to ensure robustness and trustworthiness. Data were first analysed into first-order codes, identifying initial categories using descriptive phrases. These codes were then organised into theoretical categories (themes), using axial coding to understand linkages among the initial categories and create higher-order categories. Last, themes were synthesised into aggregate theoretical dimensions, which formed the basis of the emergent theoretical framework.

Table 1. A combination of tourism organisations with specific characteristics.

Organisation types	Organisation size Micro size (<5 employees)	Small size (5-19 employees)	Medium size (20-199 employees)	Large size (>200 employees)	Organisation Age (years)
Accommodation (8)		1	2	1	<10 years
			3		10–20 years
					>20 years
Food and Beverage (1)		1			<10 years
			1		10–20 years
					>20 years
Tour Operator (6)	1		3		<10 years
		1	1		10–20 years
					>20 years
Non-business Organisations – External Stakeholders (10)	Government departments or agencies: *State Department of Transport Agency *Local City Council *Regional Tourism Organisation *Regional Transport Agency Industry associations or agencies: *Local Chamber of Commerce *Local Industry Association *Marine Safety Organisation *Small Business Consultancy *Insurance Company/Broker				

Source: ABS Defining small businesses. https://www.abs.gov.au/ausstats/abs@.nsf/mf/1321.0.

Table 2. Summary of respondents.[a]

Respondent	Respondent role	Sector	Age (until 2019)	Size (staff no.)[b]	No. of interview	Principal product and services
1	CEO	Accommodation	21	30	3	Low-budget accommodation, boat tours
2	Owner	Tour	31	8	2	Day and overnight sailing trip, island visit and snorkelling
3	GM, Sales Manager	Tour	15	190	2	Island transfer and day tours on boats to attractions
4	Owner	Accommodation	49	7–10	1	Accommodation and dinner
5	Owner	Tour	3	1–2	2	Personalised private charter, food, and snorkelling experience
6	Operations Manager	Accommodation	26	45	2	Caravan park resort, entertainment
7	GM	Accommodation	32	160	2	Accommodation, restaurant and bar, conference, and weddings
8	Owner	Tour	20	27	1	Day boat tour to islands and snorkelling
9	GM	Accommodation	20	25–45	1	High-end accommodation, restaurant and bar, conference, and weddings
10	Managing director	Food and Beverage	15	65	2	Restaurant and day boat catering
11	Sales and Marketing Manager	Tour	11	25	1	Day and overnight boat tours to island and attractions
12	GM	Accommodation	10	17	1	Resort and port, restaurant and bar, conference, and weddings
13	Business Development Manager	Tour	31	55–65	2	Marina, function venue for weddings and conference, restaurant
14	Sales Director	Accommodation	20	300	1	Holiday island resort, accommodation, F&B, tour activities
15	GM	Accommodation	10	80	1	Accommodation, restaurant, bars
External Stakeholders (government agencies and industry associations)						
16	State Department of Transport Agency (Maritime Safety QLD)				1	Responsible for the safety of all water vessels in Queensland waterways
17	Regional City Council (WRC)				3	Provide the Whitsunday region with strong and responsive local government
18	Regional Tourism Organisation (TW)				3	Conduct marketing campaign for the Whitsunday region
19	Regional Transport Agency (Whitsunday Coast Airport)				1	

(continued)

Table 2. Continued.

Respondent	Respondent role	Sector	Age (until 2019)	Size (staff no.)[b]	No. of interview	Principal product and services
20	Local Chamber of Commerce				1	Provide air transport services and serve the mainland and offshore islands
21	Local Industry Association (WCBIA)				2	Represent members to continually improve business conditions in the region
22	Marine Safety Organisation				1	Represents members operating charter boat tourism industry within Whitsunday region of the Great Barrier Reef Marine Park
23	Small Business Consultancy (business development)				2	Provide sustainable marine service solutions and making ports and terminals safer and more efficient
24	Small Business Consultancy (marine ecosystem)				1	Provide consultancy services for small tourism businesses
25	Insurance Company/Broker				1	Provide expert advice to design and implement innovative solutions to environmental challenges
Total					40	Specialist Marine Insurance Broker

[a]Size (staff no.) includes all full-time, part-time, and casual staff.
[b]Include all full-time, part-time, and casual staff.

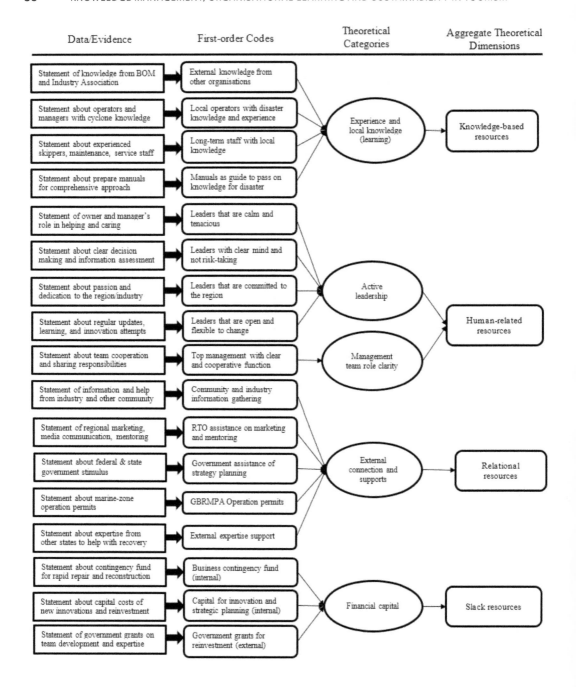

Figure 1. Data structure: enablers of DCs development.

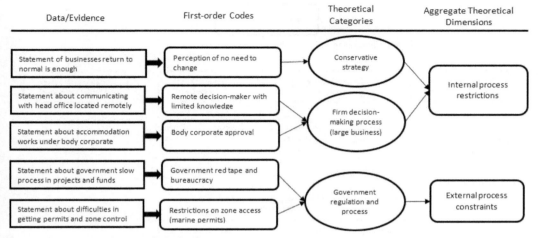

Figure 2. Data structure: barriers of DCs development.

In Figures 1 and 2 we show our data structure for DCs development analysis, comprised of the data/evidence, first-order codes, theoretical categories, and aggregate theoretical dimensions that emerged from the analysis. As illustrated in Figure 1, four main dimensions emerged from our data as the enablers of DCs development: (1) knowledge-based resources, (2) human-related resources, (3) relational resources, (4) financial slack resources. In Figure 2, two main dimensions emerged as the barriers to DCs development: (1) internal process restrictions and (2) external process constraints. Figure 1 and 2 are not causal or dynamic models, but rather a representation of the concepts and their relationships that emerged from the data.

Validity and trustworthiness

In this study, we adopted multiple strategies to improve validity and trustworthiness. The lead author spent a total of five weeks with participants in the field. This helped to build rapport and trust between the lead author and participants and ensure rich information for this study. By playing the role of an observer, the researcher was able to see the changes in the physical environment post-cyclone and note specific recovery works being progressed in the local region. This enabled more comprehensive conversations with participants and provided an improved context-based understanding for our data analysis. The long interview time (58 minutes on average) ensured rich information for this study. We also provide detailed contextual information and use direct quotes and thick description to convey our findings. Furthermore, semi-structured interview protocols were pre-designed and utilised throughout the data collection process to ensure consistency. We use NVivo, a well-established the qualitative software package, to manage the data and record the coding procedures to ensure data analysis consistency with clear steps and strategies.

Results

In the context of this paper, organisational changes are those processes and practices where organisations need to take proactive or reactive actions to prevent or manage negative impacts to maintain sustainability. DCs are actively used in these organisational change processes, including innovation (Lawson & Samson, 2001), strategic management (Ambrosini & Bowman, 2009), and branding (Brodie et al., 2017). The relationships between DCs and organisational resources are two-way and interactive. On the one hand, DCs can enable a more flexible use of resources

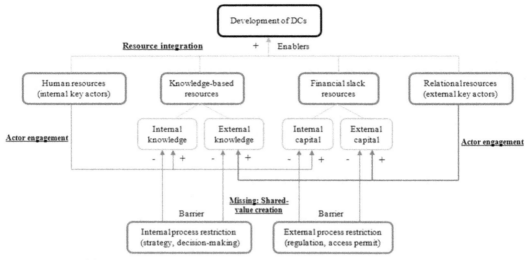

Figure 3. Framework for DCs development in tourism organisations (in times of disaster).

to enhance organisations' performance in a crisis and disaster environment (Makkonen et al., 2014). On the other hand, this paper also follows the resource-based view to argue that organisational resources can also influence the process of DC development. Organisations with more slack resources can pursue opportunities and can initiate or activate DCs to do so (Chen et al., 2013).

Key findings are summarised in Figure 3, which shows that tourism organisations should consider their reliance on the broader system in which multiple levels of actors are actively engaged in resource integration and develop shared values within the system to develop DCs. Three key components are discussed to interpret the development of DCs: resource integration, actor engagement, and shared value creation. First, four types of resources *(knowledge, financial, human-related, and relational)* are integrated within the tourism system to develop DCs. Second, both internal and external key actors (or stakeholders) play facilitating roles to create, modify and expand the knowledge-based and financial slack resources from within and outside tourism organisations. Third, key barriers to developing DCs exist in both internal and external processes. These are due to the absence of shared value creation, which hindered the development of DCs. For example, different values, norms, and governing principles can result in multi-layer leadership and government over-regulation that hinder the integration of resources to develop DCs.

Enablers in developing dynamic capabilities

Dimension 1: Knowledge-based resources

Experience and local knowledge (learning). Knowledge was one of the key elements contributing to DCs development. This study found four sources of knowledge that enable the development of DCs within tourism organisations. These were more relevant in the context of disaster management and gave weight to *staff-owned knowledge and experience*.

First, *long-term operators and managers with local disaster knowledge* were vital facilitators of DCs and helped to guide the process of disaster recovery. Managers' past experience dealing with natural disasters helped develop key capabilities to *read the situation through weather maps (R8) and draft safety management plans (R11, R13)* from past event learning: "… that is a pure consequence of my experience. It's my interpretation of what we should do in the event of a cyclone." (R13, Restaurant).

Managers' local knowledge of the community and strong networks was another key source of knowledge that drive organisations' capabilities to recover from disasters: "A couple of us who are just long-term operators in the region ... knowledge is what's going to win the day" (R1, Accommodation). This included an understanding of local circumstances, such as cyclone types, road condition and the knowledge of who in the community had certain ability or skills for repair work: " ... everything came down to keeping knowledge. The team's knowledge and my knowledge of the region are why we stayed ahead of the game of everyone else" (R16, Accommodation).

Second, **local knowledge embedded in long-term staff members** also accelerated organisations' ability to return to business as usual. For example, skippers with maritime experience who could observe weather changes, or maintenance team who understand the reef pontoon and vessels well knew how to prevent further damage in the storm or how to recover quickly after the storm. As respondents stated: "We're very fortunate in that we've collectively got 100 years of maritime experience in our skippers so we can send our skippers to anywhere in the Whitsundays and they've been there 100 times before and know what they're looking at" (R3&4, Tour Operator).

This knowledge embedded in staff members was passed on to other team members and thus became organisational knowledge through mutual learning and codification of tacit knowledge. The constant input to this set of information became powerful resources for organisations to cope with future disasters. As a respondent stated:

> Most of our staff are engaged in marine biology who take it on themselves to teach the other staff members ... there's a couple of outstanding staff members who are walking encyclopaedias about the coral. We video them, if those staff members then leave, we still continue to have that information and we're constantly adding to it (R15, Tour Operator).

Third, **knowledge input from external links** was vital for tourism organisations with limited resources. Examples of external sources of knowledge included: (1) government agency: "DITID handled the Cyclone Recovery Committee and the funding and so forth. They also have a great knowledge base that they brought into town for us" (R1, Accommodation); (2) industry associations: "We've got associations like ours and that Risk Management Group that we formed to make sure that the knowledge is available to all businesses" (R20, Industry Agency); and (3) other agencies: "you can provide better coverage by looking at the detail within the storm's information from the Bureau of Meteorology" (R8, Accommodation).

Fourth, **codification** of **manuals** was a common way to store knowledge from multiple sources and to guide organisational behaviours in times of disasters: "We don't just rely on the staff, but also the procedures and policies that the crew know about previously" (R15, Tour Operator). Regular updates of manuals were also necessary to keep organisations well-prepared as situations occurring in one cyclone may not necessarily happen in the next one, as one respondent stated: "we've just been updating it" (R9, Tour Operator). It is risky for organisations to rely on one standard manual and "one-size-fit-all" strategy: "Every storm is so different, but the manual tries to provide a comprehensive approach to covering all aspects" (R8, Accommodation).

Dimension 2: Slack resources (financial)
Financial capital. Cash flow was critical to enable organisations' ability to conduct product or service changes in times of disaster. Tourism organisations had to prepare and acquired three types of financial resources to enable their DCs development to rapidly adapt to the changing environment: *business contingency fund & insurance, business innovation fund, and government grants for disaster recovery*.

First, businesses that were *mindful of cash flows and insurance* were more prepared for unexpected crisis and events:

We are very mindful of cash flows on a daily and hourly basis in our companies ... our insurance is very extensive, and we certainly feel prepared and do not feel at risk going into another cyclone ... we always have contingency money for multiple types of events, not just cyclones (R1, Accommodation).

To achieve the goal of business recovery and back to normal, contingency funds were used to pay for emergency repair work and staff salaries, rather than waiting for the insurance money that took time to arrive *(R12, R16, Accommodation)*.

Second, **larger tourism organisations usually have more capital for regular renovation and development**, which was used as slack resources (e.g., contingency funds) for post-disaster recovery and redevelopment *(R1, Accommodation)*. Bigger businesses usually had financial backers (corporate group) able to provide investment funds to support renovations and extension programs, compared to other small or medium-sized organisations that rely solely on themselves *(R14, Government Agency)*.

In contrast, small businesses **lacked savings (slack resources) to be proactive** in the face of changing environment: "a lot of smaller businesses don't have that opportunity to be proactive because they don't have the [financial] resources to be, so they're very reactive" (R17, Tour Operator). Generators are critical for business operations after a cyclone – were not affordable to all small businesses and seen as a large investment. Businesses had to conduct a cost-benefit analysis and strike a balance between long-term capital outlay and short-term commercial return.

Third, apart from internal financial resources, governments also provided **financial assistance (grants and funding)** to support tourism recovery. Tourism organisations would benefit from external financial assistance (e.g., government funds) to enable their ability to recover from property losses and maintain their staff for operation: "if you take it to government injection of funds, straight away it starts to go up a level" (R10, Consultancy). This funding was required to rebuild and innovate, in areas such as digital marketing, staff retraining, and business reinvestment.

However, the complexity of government stimulus grants hindered the engagement of businesses and result in low uptake. Not all tourism organisations were eligible for grants or had time and resources to prepare application materials: "The priority is just running the business day to day ... " (R23, Marine Safety Agency). Also, some respondents argued that **external financial resources were lacking** for tourism organisations: " ... it's very challenging from a cashflow perspective, when you have no customers and got payroll. The government financial assistance needs to be looked at more thoroughly" (R32, Accommodation).

Furthermore, tourism organisations in Australia face **high operational costs** (Cummins, 2013), which also limited their ability to proactively change the changing environment. High staff cost was especially relevant: "staff is your most expensive commodity in Australia. I do most of the stuff myself these days because it's far too expensive and they're hard to get" (R5, Accommodation). Insurance cost was also an expensive fixed cost of doing business: "we're not a favourite for insurance companies definitely, our premiums are expensive" (R14, Government Agency). Other high operational costs were related to government taxes and compliance: "One of our issues is cost. People can travel overseas relatively inexpensively, our wages, our compliance, our levels of government, our GST, our taxation. Everything just adds so much cost, bureaucracy" (R28, COC).

Dimension 3: human-based resources (internal actors)
Active leadership. The engagement of leaders (usually operators and managers) was important in building organisations' DCs. This study found four leadership attributes that were critical in this regard: *calm and tenacity, clear-minded and coping, rather than taking risks, open and flexible to change, and with a commitment to the region.*

First, while leaders were stressed during the disaster, they had to outwardly display calm, drawing on leadership traits such as emotional stability (Huang et al., 2014) and conscientiousness (Christiansen & Tett, 2013). This is consistent with our study where respondents talked about their responsibility to keep calm: "The best quality you have is staying calm... They need to know you've got a plan and you instantly know you can get people organised" (R16, Accommodation). Leaders who could remain calm and tenacious in a crisis/disaster situation can better look after their team members and guided them through adversity. A high level of leaders' psychological capital (personality traits) increased their adaptive task performance as they managed adversity (Krauter, 2018), often by providing staff with a sense of security and keeping them engaged in the business. As one respondent stated: "There's a bit of a parent-child relationship that happens in natural disasters. People who are not used to experiencing natural disasters are looking for leadership to be in control and that have things organised" (R13, Restaurant).

Second, leaders who were able to **make clear decisions rather than take risks** were better at developing organisational DCs to get through the disasters. Emergency decision-making is important to improve the capability to respond to disasters. Normal decision-making involves selecting the optimal solution among alternatives. In contrast, emergency decision-making requires leaders to quickly collect relevant information, develop succinct emergency objectives and then design suitable programs for response and recovery (Zhou et al., 2018). For example, a careful risk assessment after the disaster helped some businesses to avoid an unnecessary secondary crisis *(R3, Tour Operator)*.

Third, leaders who were **open-minded and had the flexibility to make changes** after a disaster can develop DCs within the organisation. For example, a small ship operator could change their routes and customer experience quickly to adapt to the environment: "I guess the good thing is we are a vessel, we could look at doing longer trips and we could move locations" (R2, Tour Operator). Flexibility to change a plan was also required to build DCs, even for larger businesses who had comprehensive plans: "We had a plan in place, but you really have to depart from the plan because the plan wasn't big enough... so we started making decisions on the fly" (R3, Tour Operator).

Fourth, business owners and operators were **committed to the region,** which supported the tourism industry to recover faster. For example, some businesses helped the community to step up: "Opening up catering and feeding people just was a spur of the moment decision... we became this hub for assisting people" (R13, Restaurant). Passion and dedication were also important for community recovery: "It's really just the dedication or the passion to what you're doing that will give you that bump up" (R11, Accommodation).

Management team role clarity and collaboration. Disaster recovery and organisational adaptation were not the purview of one person but relied on broader cooperation within the organisation: "It's not always just a one-person job" (R15, Tour Operator). Apart from leadership, team role clarity and cooperation also contributed to the development of DCs since everyone knew what to do and how to do it, which led to effective operation during and after a disaster. As one respondent stated: "Each of us has different responsibilities in terms of their extract of the process, of the procedure... each of us renews that section that relates to their particular area" (R3, Tour Operator).

Dimension 4: Relational resources (external actors)

External connection and support. Natural disasters can exceed the capacity of organisations to cope with using their own resources and capabilities, thus looking to a wider range of external stakeholders to collaborate. The most mentioned external source of support was from the **wider community and industry practitioners**. For example, businesses who were members of the local Cyclone Recovery Committee or other industry associations had access to more information on regional recovery strategies and reconstruction plans. This helped to guide their business plans in the short-term after disasters: "The fact that I was on the Cyclone Recovery Committee gave me a very good insight into what was happening and the good messaging and what repairs were happening out to the national park tracks" (R1, Accommodation).

Furthermore, **community/industry-wide information sharing** was also key to enable a business to survive the disaster both mentally (showing caring) and physically and find contingency plans for business recovery. Businesses that were not members of any industry groups felt "isolated" in terms of information-sharing and people-connecting after a disaster: "we've got all these networks, when things happen, at least you can go and have meetings with other people and go how do we handle this as a group" (R9, Tour Operator). Government authorities were also looking for external resources to support local affected towns and businesses.

The regional tourism organisation (RTO) was an important source of information and assistance for local tourism organisations to develop their DCs, especially for conducting marketing campaigns and delivering positive messages to the outside world: "…having a strong RTO looking after your tourism interests is very important…we relied very heavily on them to be out there making sure that the messaging is right to government and marketing and those aspects" (R1, Accommodation). Furthermore, some businesses participated in mentoring sessions provided by RTO, which played a mentoring role: "I had some good mentoring sessions that were provided by the likes of Tourism Whitsundays. That was really good because I have a business coach…it's really turned my business forward" (R6, Tour Operator). A respondent from the RTO also justified these views and highlighted their role in crisis communication and training for businesses: "[we organised] forums for them to share and their processes and procedures and someone to review their processes and procedures for cyclones and making sure that they have solid things in place" (R19, RTO).

Barriers in developing dynamic capabilities

Dimension 1: Internal process restriction
Organisation decision-making process. For some medium and large-sized businesses with external management groups, the **decision-making hierarchy** from the headquarters limited their ability to rapidly adapt to circumstances: "we've been bought out by quite a large company. So, their bureaucracy slows us down sometimes" (R3, Tour Operator). Multiple stakeholder communications on new operations or new policies slowed the process. For example, the communication between harbour master – manager – head office to develop a refund strategy could be time-consuming. As the respondent stated:

> …as the warnings would come, we'd also communicate back to [the head office]. Once the harbour masters shut down the marina, the boats can't get from Hamilton to here… [the head office] send out a thing to all properties in this area saying your cancellation policy has now changed. You're allowed to refund people, or at this point, people can change their dates…then you set up a system to start doing that (R16, Accommodation).

Furthermore, often **remote leaders** were not involved in local operations and thus had a **lack of local knowledge** to make the right decisions: "…they don't have any expertise in this. They wouldn't know what a cyclone is…so I keep that in house and part of it is operational management" *(R3, Tour Operator)*. Some tourism organisations (mainly accommodation) used a body-corporate structure, which meant their decision-making processes were highly legislated and required committee approval for expenditure. This also resulted in slow decision-making in the post-disaster recovery stage: "…body corporate administrated the whole thing. It has to be works that are approved through the committee…to ensure that it is compliant with the Act" (R11, Accommodation).

Conservative strategy-making. Some confident senior managers had been through multiple disasters, especially those who operated in disaster-prone areas. A conservative mindset was embedded in their disaster management strategies. They held the view that they were well-prepared and there were not much they would change. This strategy-making mindset largely impeded an organisation's development of dynamic capabilities, regardless of their actual level of preparedness for then changing environment.

Dimension 2: External process constraints

Government regulation and process. Two major external constraints for DCs development in tourism organisations were government-related, especially regarding *red tape/bureaucracy and water zone access control*. First, respondents argued that government regulation led to a slow process due to **bureaucracy**, which impeded the development of new projects proposed by tourism organisations. For example, a feasibility study was only conducted nearly two years after the cyclone, with limited project design or construction going to happen. The same applied to local government projects. These varied from funding application from state and federal government, resilient structure design to insurance assessment, resulting in a very long process.

Second, local tour operators relied heavily on the Great Barrier Reef resources and **required a permit** to operate issued by the Great Barrier Reef Marine Park Authority (GBRMPA) and the Queensland Parks and Wildlife Service (QPWS) through a joint permission system. After the cyclone, tour operators needed to find new zones for snorkelling activities due to coral damage. Small businesses were limited by their permitted zones and cannot change their routes. As the respondent from a RTO stated: "The Great Barrier Reef Marine Park has different zonings for where people can go, so they're limited by the ones that they can go into and then they have to find good ones within that … The government doesn't open up any new zones [after cyclone]" (R19, RTO).

Cross-organisational comparison of enablers and barriers

Matrix-coding queries were used to compare how key enablers and barriers differ across tourism organisations from different sectors, ages and sizes. This comparison helps to understand the dimensions that are most valued by different tourism organisations in building DCs.

Table 3 compares key enablers among different types of tourism organisations. First, accommodation and restaurant sectors valued similar dimensions in building their DCs. Both tended to have prior cyclone knowledge and leadership with calm communication and limited risk-taking in a short-term post-disaster. Instead, tour operators relied more on long-term staff who had local knowledge and experience, and their leadership was open to other opinions and flexible to change. This could be because tour operators who run daily or overnight boat tours require experienced staff and their skills and knowledge of the marine industry, for example, to find new coral zones for snorkelling tours after cyclone damage *(R15, Tour Operator)*. Instead, accommodation and restaurants' operations were dependent on their top management teams' capabilities in decision-making and strategy-planning. Other industry and government stakeholders considered relational resources (e.g., RTO assistance) and government grants as the key factor to help tourism organisations build DCs.

Second, tourism organisations at all ages valued operators/managers' cyclone knowledge to build DCs, and organisations over 10 and 20 years also relied on manuals as guidebooks to articulate and transmit their knowledge. This is because older tourism organisations had more knowledge centred in their managers and staff, which could be easily lost due to regular turnover if not carefully articulated in manuals. Furthermore, older organisations had wider industry networks and appeared to obtain more innovative and strategic information to help develop their DCs. As one respondent said, more extensive knowledge was obtained by joining the Cyclone Recovery Committee and communicating with stakeholders from various sectors and agencies *(R1, Accommodation over 20 years)*. Also, older organisations were more likely to prepare business contingency funds (internal) and access to government grants (external) as their slack

Table 3. Top DC enablers cross-organisational comparison.

DC Enablers	Knowledge-based	Human-related	Relational	Slack
Sector				
Accommodation	• Long-term operators and managers with cyclone knowledge	• Leadership: clear mind and not risk-taking	• Community & Industry information	• Business contingency fund
Tour operator	• Long-term staff with local knowledge	• Leadership: open and flexible to change	• GBRMPA permits of boat operation	–
Restaurant	• Long-term operators and managers with cyclone knowledge	• Leadership: clear mind and not risk-taking	–	–
Other agencies	–	–	• RTO assist in marketing & mentoring	• Government grants for reinvestment and training
Age				
<10	• Long-term operators and managers with cyclone knowledge	• Leadership: open and flexible to change	–	–
10–20	• Long-term staff with local knowledge • Long-term operators and managers with cyclone knowledge • Manuals as guides to pass on knowledge	• Leadership: clear mind and not risk-taking	• GBRMPA permits of boat operation	–
>20	• Long-term operators and managers with cyclone knowledge • Manuals as guides to pass on knowledge	• Leadership: clear mind & not risk-taking	• Community & Industry information	• Business contingency fund • Government grants for reinvestment and training
Size				
Micro & small	–	• Leadership: open and flexible to change • Leadership: calm and tenacious	–	–
Medium	• Long-term staff with local knowledge • Long-term operators and managers with cyclone knowledge	• Leadership: clear mind and not risk-taking • Team: cooperative function	• GBRMPA permits of boat operation	• Business contingency fund
Large	• Long-term operators and managers with cyclone knowledge	• Leadership: open and flexible to change	–	• Capital for innovation and strategic planning

Table 4. Top DC barriers cross-organisational comparison.

DC Barriers	Internal resources	Internal process	External process
Sector			
Accommodation	• High operational costs • Lack of external assistance • No proper insurance	• Perception of no need to change • Body corporate approval • Remote decision-maker with limited knowledge	• Government red tape and bureaucracy
Tour operator	• Lack of spare money to be proactive	• Remote decision-maker with limited knowledge	–
Restaurant	• Lack of spare money to be proactive • High operational costs	–	–
Other agencies	• High operational costs • Lack of time • Lack of spare money to be proactive	–	• Government red tape and bureaucracy • Restrictions on zone access
Age			
<10	• Lack of time	–	• Restrictions on zone access
10-20	• Lack of spare money to be proactive • High operational costs	–	–
>20	• High operational costs • No proper insurance	• Perception of no need to change	• Government red tape and bureaucracy
Size			
Micro and Small	• High operational costs • No proper insurance • Lack of time	–	• Restrictions on zone access
Medium	• Lack of spare money to be proactive • High operational costs • No proper insurance	• Perception of no need to change • Remote decision-maker with limited knowledge	• Government red tape and bureaucracy
Large	–	–	–

financial resources in coping with disasters. In contrast, younger organisations were often restricted by their cashflow and networks.

Third, micro and small tourism organisations (fewer than 20 staff) relied on leaders' ability to stay calm and be flexible to change in coping with a disruptive environment. They had limited knowledge, relational and slack resources to build DCs quickly. Small or young businesses that had not developed their networks had limited access to external information. Apart from core leadership and staff with experience, medium tourism organisations (between 20 and 200 staff) also highlighted the team cooperative functions in developing their DCs. A management team with around five to six managers had to be clear with their respective responsibilities and can collaborate effectively with each other. Unlike small and medium-sized organisations, some large tourism organisations (over 200 staff) had slack capital for innovation and strategic planning, which built their DCs in disaster times.

Table 4 shows the key barriers compared across tourism organisations. First, high operational costs were the most common barrier for all types of tourism organisations to build DCs. However, different from other sectors, accommodation had internal process restrictions in building DCs (especially older ones). For example, administrative inertia was visible in the perception that there was no need to change, as respondents viewed their organisations as "ready enough" based on experience. This could be a "success trap" and can prevent organisations from adapting further to the changing environment (Junni et al., 2013; Wang et al., 2015). Furthermore, some tour operators and accommodations had head offices in other states and suffered from communication delays in making changes to cope with disasters *(R3&4, R16)*. Other industry and government agencies considered limited internal resources (e.g., high costs, lack of time and money) and government regulations as major barriers for tourism organisations to build DCs.

Second, younger tourism organisations lacked the time and/or money to adapt to the environment, while older organisations suffered more from high operational costs and insurance issues (too expensive to cover the whole property). Younger organisations (especially tour operators) were restricted by Great Barrier Reef zone access rules (*R6, Tour Operator less than 2 years*), while older organisations found government bureaucracy to be their main barrier to developing new projects or products (*R1, Accommodation over 20 years*).

Third, few differences related to barriers were found between small and medium-sized tourism organisations. They usually lacked time and money to cope with changing environments, while some medium-sized organisations also suffered from administrative inertia and remote leadership with little cyclone management knowledge. Large organisations seldom mentioned barriers in developing DCs, although it could be due to the small number of large organisations involved in this study due to the dominance of small and medium-sized organisations in the local tourism industry.

Discussion and conclusion

This study aims to investigate key enablers and barriers for tourism organisations to develop DCs in crisis and disaster environments, and to identify how these factors differ across tourism organisations considering their age, size, and sector. The DCs development framework (Figure 3) summarises these findings and identifies four resources-based enablers and two processes-based barriers.

Theoretical contribution

This study makes two important contributions to knowledge.

First, it highlights the development of DCs as an important aspect of disaster response and recovery. Studies on DCs tend to focus on dynamic environments, such as technology advancement and market variation, whereas crisis and disaster environments usually have higher levels of uncertainty and disruptive outcomes on organisations (Barreto, 2010). Access to adequate resources and process efficiency can be severely challenged in disaster contexts, thus it is important to examine DCs beyond just dynamic environments and extend it to unexpected and unpredictable environments such as crises and disasters. Three important themes were evident in this study in this regard.

Reliance on external resources: This study identifies the exposure to and reliance of tourism organisations on external processes and restrictions from industry and government agencies. Although tourism organisations are operating independently in a large service system, they are also emerged in broader networks based on interactions of resources and collaborative decision-making that leads to function stability and system resilience (Frow et al., 2019). For example, knowledge and financial input from external sources through information-sharing and government funding projects are indispensable for tourism organisations when internal resources are damaged and inaccessible in the short-term. This is consistent with discussions on "external links" as a core driver for dynamic knowledge articulation through rapid flow and acquisition of information (Lee et al., 2011). Examples of this could be industry-wide capability-training and government financial schemes (e.g., loans, payments, tax relief) to support business continuity. Paradoxically, these agencies can create over-regulation and bureaucracy that act as barriers to post-disaster transformation, such as new project proposition (land use in national parks, water area accessibility rules) and funding acquisition. Government bureaucracy has frequently been discussed as an obstacle for organisations to adopt better and faster innovation. In managing emergency situations, a decentralised bureaucracy structure that involves a diversity of organisations allows the local industry to adapt rapidly to changing environments (Kusumasari et al.,

2010). This is also in line with the enablers of DCs where personnel or organisations with more local knowledge and a better understanding of local needs can make rapid and optimal decisions.

Actor-embedded knowledge and attributes: The findings demonstrate that the possession of knowledge resources can facilitate and support the ongoing renewal of resources within organisations to adapt to these fast-changing environments (Penrose, 1959). Prior knowledge and skills embedded at an individual (managers and staff members) and organisational level (business-owned manuals or plans) can facilitate the development of DCs (Nieves & Haller, 2014). Local knowledge embedded in managers and staff is critical to facilitate new activities within organisations and adapt existing plans for future events. This reflects the requirement of an organic structure that allows employees to initiate changes and adapt quickly to changing environments, which in turn increase knowledge sharing across members within the organisation (Ramezan, 2011). Regular codification and dissemination of knowledge via artefacts such as manuals can help make tacit knowledge explicit for future crises/disasters (Blackman & Ritchie, 2008). Furthermore, organisational leadership that is open-minded and flexible to change can encourage the flow of knowledge among organisational members and foster exploratory learning for DCs development (Ambrosini et al., 2009). A tenacious, decisive, and authoritarian leadership style may be more efficient in the face of crises and disasters, where more emergent and fast responses are needed immediately after the event. Leaders' abilities to allocate or relocate employees to work within teams to ensure everyone knows what to do and how to do can result in more effective operation during and after a disaster (Ramezan, 2011). At the same time, external networking and information-sharing can produce new knowledge within tourism organisations through active learning, which in return contribute to DCs development.

Missing shared value within the system: Shared institutional arrangements and mutual value creation provide foundations for multiple actors to actively engage with each other guided by values and norms for effective interactions and collaborations (Jiang & Ritchie, 2017). In this study, while resources were integrated through active actor engagement, it was hampered by the absence of shared values in the tourism disaster management system leading the recovery practices, which constrained adaptation. Value creation occurs due to a process that provides more novel and appropriate benefits (economic profitability, societal and environmental value) for stakeholders (Lepak et al., 2007). Mutual value creation is critical for effective decision-making and the development of strategies for rapid response and recovery from disasters. Furthermore, an organic structure requires organisations to share common goals that guide actions in unstable environments (Ramezan, 2011). This would require an improved understanding of differences in how stakeholders create value during disaster impact mitigation and recovery (Räikkönen et al., 2017). In this study, we identified that missing shared value not only exists within tourism organisations where leaders and stakeholders can have different opinions and goals; but also outside tourism organisations where government regulations and red-tape can slow down the progress of new projects. For example, tourism organisations' uptake of government grants or other forms of support can be low due to the complexity of eligibility rules and bureaucracy. Therefore, mutual value creation that links government rules and tourism organisations' needs is needed in disaster management, where the common value should be assuring prompt and accurate assistance, achieving rapid recovery, business continuity, and sustainable tourism development in the fast-changing environment (Räikkönen et al., 2017).

Second, this study contributes to the literature by comparing differences and similarities of these dimensions across tourism organisations considering their age, size, and sector. Past studies on DCs often view organisations as homogeneous (Mansour et al., 2019), while its heterogeneity characterises the tourism industry. Overall, the findings suggest that accommodation and restaurants rely more on operators and leaderships' capabilities and knowledge to develop DCs, while tour operators rely more on long-term staff members with local knowledge. Older and larger tourism organisations have more established structures to sustain their knowledge and can absorb new information from wider networks to develop their DCs. They often have business contingency funds, such as financial slack resources to deal with unexpected changes, while younger and smaller tourism organisations often lack time and money to prepare for future crises/disasters and rely mainly on their leaderships' ability to stay calm and be flexible to change. Smaller organisations have also been found to focus on the operational and internal aspects of change in the short-term but are also more flexible to adapt to changes (Verreynne et al., 2016) as information flows more freely across the organisation (Burnard & Bhamra, 2011). Yet, they also need to improve their ability to use resources more strategically to achieve resilience, improve planning capabilities and learn to drive change proactively (Bhamra et al., 2011).

Practical implications

For small and medium-sized tourism organisations, this study demonstrates that focussing only on daily operations and cash flow does not lead to sustained recovery. Businesses need to consider their role in a broader ecosystem in which multiple levels of actors are actively engaged in resource integration, such as governments, suppliers and collaborators. Active networks and new technologies should be established and adopted with industry and government agencies to access necessary knowledge and financial-related resources in a crisis and disaster environment.

Three implications are evident from our study to assist tourism operators and managers in developing dynamic capabilities. First, tourism organisations located in disaster-prone areas need to develop a more flexible and open-to-change business culture. They need to be well-equipped with four types of resources to enable rapid and adaptive practices: (1) experienced labour with local knowledge (through local hiring or training), (2) active leadership that is open to new information and flexible to change, (3) sustained and cooperative relationships with industry associations and government agencies (through membership, volunteering service roles or other networking events), and (4) ongoing contingency funds for business reconstruction and reinvestment. Second, organisations with a hierarchical structure need to temporally compress their structure to empower front-line managers with instant decision-making power. This can improve communication across hierarchies and ensure the accuracy and comprehensiveness of information and thus increase optimal and timely decisions. Third, in a highly regulated operating environment, tourism operators and managers need to advocate for the creation of mutual value within the industry to pursue the best interest of community/industry recovery in times of crises/disasters. Collaboration to achieve common goals, rather than competition was found to be essential.

Although this study focussed on a cyclone (natural disaster) there are some implications that are useful to consider in the face of other disruptions (such as the COVID-19 pandemic). First, the tourism industry in the Whitsunday region is relatively mature in coping with unexpected crises/disasters and can guide the tourism businesses to available external resources to recover. In responding to other disruptive events, this study suggests that governments should improve and shorten the process for business reopening by simplifying the application process for support (e.g., JobKeeper payment and other stimulus schemes). Governments should conduct consistent information-sharing to the public and produce simple procedures to avoid confusion and low uptake of policies and programs (Ritchie et al., 2004). Second, although multiple resources were found to support the development of dynamic capabilities in coping with disasters, few tourism operators and managers can estimate their resource shortages and where/how to access these resources in times of emergency. This study suggests developing a simple "risk-assessment tool" for organisations to review and self-assess their resources and capabilities to prepare for unexpected crisis/disaster events (Group of Eight, 2020). Governments should also develop a consolidated information-sharing platform to increase transparency and accessibility of information and resources to support tourism recovery.

Limitations and future research

This study has several limitations that should be addressed in future research. First, this study only discussed key enablers and barriers in the tourism system that contribute to the development of DCs within tourism organisations. Future research should investigate how the new dynamic capabilities required in a crisis/disaster context are institutionalised in a tourism organisation. This could be progressed by discussing the development process of various dynamic capabilities in different environments (e.g., Hine et al., 2014) and its embedment in organisational processes/routines. In addition, future research needs to explore and investigate the process of how DCs can be developed to achieve tourism organisational resilience. For instance, what processes of existing resources integration (e.g., knowledge sharing) within the system can maximise disaster recovery outcomes; what learning mechanisms can be adopted by tourism organisations to acquire new resources outside the system to facilitate DCs (Penrose, 1959).

Second, this study focussed on post-disaster practices that may only reflect reactive behaviours in developing DCs. Future research could examine organisations' proactive behaviours in developing DCs to identify different challenges. For instance, pre-disaster scenarios should be tested to consider organisation's managerial perception of possible environmental changes, which acknowledged operators/managers' bounded rationality, imperfect understanding of the environment, and inability to accurately predict the outcomes (Smircich & Stubbart, 1985). Third, a broader system understanding of how tourism organisations can adapt to crisis and disaster environments is needed. The service ecosystem lens (Frow et al., 2019) could be used in future studies to understand resource-actor interactions under a shared worldview that facilitates adaptation to changes.

Disclosure statement

No potential conflict of interest was reported by the authors.

ORCID

Yawei Jiang http://orcid.org/0000-0003-3125-3732
Brent W. Ritchie http://orcid.org/0000-0003-1540-9389

References

Alonso-Almeida, M. D. M., Bremser, K., & Llach, J. (2015). Proactive and reactive strategies deployed by restaurants in times of crisis: Effects on capabilities, organisation and competitive advantage. *International Journal of Contemporary Hospitality Management, 27*(7), 1641–1661. https://doi.org/10.1108/IJCHM-03-2014-0117

Ambrosini, V., & Bowman, C. (2009). What are dynamic capabilities and are they a useful construct in strategic management? *International Journal of Management Reviews, 11*(1), 29–49. https://doi.org/10.1111/j.1468-2370.2008.00251.x

Ambrosini, V., Bowman, C., & Collier, N. (2009). Dynamic capabilities: An exploration of how firms renew their resource base. *British Journal of Management, 20*(s1), S9–S24. https://doi.org/10.1111/j.1467-8551.2008.00610.x

Barney, J. (1991). Firm resources and sustained competitive advantage. *Journal of Management, 17*(1), 99–120. https://doi.org/10.1177/014920639101700108

Barreto, I. (2010). Dynamic capabilities: A review of past research and an agenda for the future. *Journal of Management, 36*(1), 256–280. https://doi.org/10.1177/0149206309350776

Battisti, M., & Deakins, D. (2017). The relationship between dynamic capabilities, the firm's resource base and performance in a post-disaster environment. *International Small Business Journal: Researching Entrepreneurship, 35*(1), 78–98. https://doi.org/10.1177/0266242615611471

Bhamra, R., Dani, S., & Burnard, K. (2011). Resilience: The concept, a literature review and future directions. *International Journal of Production Research, 49*(18), 5375–5393. https://doi.org/10.1080/00207543.2011.563826

Blackman, D., & Ritchie, B. W. (2008). Tourism crisis management and organisational learning: The role of reflection in developing effective DMO crisis strategies. *Journal of Travel & Tourism Marketing, 23*(2-4), 45–57. https://doi.org/10.1300/J073v23n02_04

Bogers, M., Chesbrough, H., Heaton, S., & Teece, D. J. (2019). Strategic management of open innovation: A dynamic capabilities perspective. *California Management Review, 62*(1), 77–94. https://doi.org/10.1177/0008125619885150

Boukas, N., & Ziakas, V. (2013). Impacts of the global economic crisis on Cyprus tourism and policy responses. *International Journal of Tourism Research, 15*(4), 329–345. https://doi.org/10.1002/jtr.1878

Brockman, B. K., Jones, M. A., & Becherer, R. C. (2012). Customer orientation and performance in small firms: Examining the moderating influence of risk-taking, innovativeness, and opportunity focus. *Journal of Small Business Management, 50*(3), 429–446. https://doi.org/10.1111/j.1540-627X.2012.00361.x

Brodie, R. J., Benson-Rea, M., & Medlin, C. J. (2017). Branding as a dynamic capability: Strategic advantage from integrating meanings with identification. *Marketing Theory, 17*(2), 183–199. https://doi.org/10.1177/1470593116679871

Burnard, K., & Bhamra, R. (2011). Organisational resilience: Development of a conceptual framework for organisational responses. *International Journal of Production Research, 49*(18), 5581–5599. https://doi.org/10.1080/00207543.2011.563827

Burns, T., & Stalker, G. M. (1961). *The management of innovation*. London, England: Tavistock.

Chen, Y. C., Li, P. C., & Lin, Y. H. (2013). How inter- and intra-organisational coordination affect product development performance: the role of slack resources. *Journal of Business & Industrial Marketing, 28*(2), 125–136. https://doi.org/10.1108/08858621311295263

Christiansen, N., & Tett, R. (2013). *Handbook of personality at work*. Brunner-Routledge.

Corley, K. G., & Gioia, D. A. (2004). Identity ambiguity and change in the wake of a corporate spin-off. *Administrative Science Quarterly, 49*(2), 173–208.

Cummins, C. (2013). *High costs eat into profit margins of local hoteliers*. https://www.smh.com.au/business/high-costs-eat-into-profit-margins-of-local-hoteliers-20131105-2wzsh.html

Denicolai, S., Cioccarelli, G., & Zucchella, A. (2010). Resource-based local development and networked core-competencies for tourism excellence. *Tourism Management, 31*(2), 260–266. https://doi.org/10.1016/j.tourman.2009.03.002

Dixon, S. E., Meyer, K. E., & Day, M. (2007). Exploitation and exploration learning and the development of organisational capabilities: A cross-case analysis of the Russian oil industry. *Human Relations, 60*(10), 1493–1523. https://doi.org/10.1177/0018726707083475

Dixon, S., Meyer, K., & Day, M. (2014). Building dynamic capabilities of adaptation and innovation: A study of micro-foundations in a transition economy. *Long Range Planning, 47*(4), 186–205. https://doi.org/10.1016/j.lrp.2013.08.011

Frow, P., Mccoll-Kennedy, J. R., Payne, A., & Govind, R. (2019). Service ecosystem well-being: conceptualisation and implications for theory and practice. *European Journal of Marketing, 53*(12), 2657–2691. https://doi.org/10.1108/EJM-07-2018-0465

Gallopín, G. C. (2006). Linkages between vulnerability, resilience, and adaptive capacity. *Global Environmental Change, 16*(3), 293–303. https://doi.org/10.1016/j.gloenvcha.2006.02.004

Group of Eight. (2020). *COVID-19 Roadmap to recovery: A report for the nation*. https://cpb-ap-se2.wpmucdn.com/blogs.unimelb.edu.au/dist/8/401/files/2020/05/Go8-Roadmap-to-Recovery-A-Report-for-the-Nation-Full.pdf

Hine, D., Parker, R., Pregelj, L., & Verreynne, M. (2014). Deconstructing and reconstructing the capability hierarchy. *Industrial and Corporate Change, 23*(5), 1299–1325. https://doi.org/10.1093/icc/dtt046

Huang, J., Ryan, A., Zabel, K., & Palmer, A. (2014). Personality and adaptive performance at work: A meta-analytic investigation. *The Journal of Applied Psychology, 99*(1), 162–179. https://doi.org/10.1037/a0034285

Jiang, Y., & Ritchie, B. W. (2017). Disaster collaboration in tourism: Motives, impediments and success factors. *Journal of Hospitality and Tourism Management, 31*, 70–82. https://doi.org/10.1016/j.jhtm.2016.09.004

Jiang, Y., Ritchie, B. W., & Verreynne, M. L. (2019). Building tourism organisational resilience to crises and disasters: A dynamic capabilities view. *International Journal of Tourism Research, 21*(6), 882–900. https://doi.org/10.1002/jtr.2312

Junni, P., Sarala, R. M., Taras, V., & Tarba, S. Y. (2013). Organisational ambidexterity and performance: A meta-analysis. *Academy of Management Perspectives, 27*(4), 299–312. https://doi.org/10.5465/amp.2012.0015

Kraleva, N. (2011). Learning organisations: Prerequisite for successful tourism organisations. *UTMS Journal of Economics, 2*(1), 77–82.

Krauter, J. (2018). The adaptive leader: The influence of leaders' psychological capital on their task adaptive performance managing adversity. *International Journal of Knowledge. Culture & Change in Organisations: Annual Review, 18*(1), 19–45.

Kusumasari, B., Alam, Q., & Siddiqui, K. (2010). Resource capability for local government in managing disaster. *Disaster Prevention and Management. An International Journal, 19*(4), 438–451.

Lawson, B., & Samson, D. (2001). Developing innovation capability in organisations: a dynamic capabilities approach. *International Journal of Innovation Management, 5*(3), 377–400. https://doi.org/10.1142/S1363919601000427

Lee, P. Y., Chen, H. H., & Shyr, Y. H. (2011). Driving dynamic knowledge articulation and dynamic capabilities development of service alliance firms. *The Service Industries Journal, 31*(13), 2223–2242. https://doi.org/10.1080/02642069.2010.504820

Leonidou, L. C., Leonidou, C. N., Fotiadis, T. A., & Aykol, B. (2015). Dynamic capabilities driving an eco-based advantage and performance in global hotel chains: The moderating effect of international strategy. *Tourism Management, 50*, 268–280. https://doi.org/10.1016/j.tourman.2015.03.005

Lepak, D., Smith, K., & Taylor, M. (2007). Value creation and value capture: a multilevel perspective. *Academy of Management Review, 32*(1), 180–194. https://doi.org/10.5465/amr.2007.23464011

Lincoln, Y. S., & Guba, E. G. (1985). *Naturalistic inquiry*. Sage.

Makkonen, H., Pohjola, M., Olkkonen, R., & Koponen, A. (2014). Dynamic capabilities and firm performance in a financial crisis. *Journal of Business Research, 67*(1), 2707–2719. https://doi.org/10.1016/j.jbusres.2013.03.020

Mansour, H. E., Holmes, K., Butler, B., & Ananthram, S. (2019). Developing dynamic capabilities to survive a crisis: Tourism organisations' responses to continued turbulence in Libya. *International Journal of Tourism Research, 21*(4), 493–503. https://doi.org/10.1002/jtr.2277

Nelson, R., & Winter, S. (1982). *An evolutionary theory of technical change*. Belknap Press of Harvard University Press.

Nieves, J., & Haller, S. (2014). Building dynamic capabilities through knowledge resources. *Tourism Management, 40*, 224–232. https://doi.org/10.1016/j.tourman.2013.06.010

Paraskevas, A., Altinay, L., McLean, J., & Cooper, C. (2013). Crisis knowledge in tourism: Types, flows and governance. *Annals of Tourism Research, 41*, 130–152. https://doi.org/10.1016/j.annals.2012.12.005

Penrose, E. (1959). *The theory of the growth of the firm*. Oxford University Press.

Queensland Fire and Emergency Services (QFES). (2017). *Queensland State natural hazard risk assessment*. Retrieved October 12, 2020, from https://www.disaster.qld.gov.au/cdmp/Documents/Emergency-Risk-Mgmt/QLD-State-Natural-Risk-Assessment-2017.pdf.

Queensland Government (2019). *STATE RECOVERY PLAN 2017-2019: Operation Queensland Recovery*. Retrieved October 12, 2020, from https://www.qra.qld.gov.au/sites/default/files/2019-05/0415%20Op%20QLD%20Rec%20Plan%202017-19%20Update.pdf

Räikkönen, M., Molarius, R., Mäki, K., Forssén, K., Petiet, P., & Nieuwenhuijs, A. (2017). Creating stakeholder value through risk mitigation measures in the context of disaster management. *Infrastructures, 2*(4), 14. https://doi.org/10.3390/infrastructures2040014

Ramezan, M. (2011). Intellectual capital and organisational organic structure in knowledge society: How are these concepts related? *International Journal of Information Management, 31*(1), 88–95. https://doi.org/10.1016/j.ijinfomgt.2010.10.004

REMPLAN. (2020). *Economy, Jobs and Business Insights: Whitsunday Tourism*. Retrieved October 12, 2020, from https://app.remplan.com.au/whitsunday/economy/tourism/output?state=1AEYiQ!LWPYFbnjvFdWj2DHqNJ4euvidSZrjHAvDgdSGSG4uASghZh32E

Ritchie, B. W., Dorrell, H., Miller, D., & Miller, G. A. (2004). Crisis communication and recovery for the tourism industry: Lessons from the 2001 foot and mouth disease outbreak in the United Kingdom. *Journal of Travel & Tourism Marketing, 15*(2-3), 199–216. https://doi.org/10.1300/J073v15n02_11

Ritchie, B. W., & Jiang, Y. (2019). A review of research on tourism risk, crisis and disaster management: Launching the annals of tourism research curated collection on tourism risk, crisis and disaster management. *Annals of Tourism Research, 79*, 102812. https://doi.org/10.1016/j.annals.2019.102812

Schilke, O., Hu, S., & Helfat, C. E. (2018). Quo vadis, dynamic capabilities? A content-analytic review of the current state of knowledge and recommendations for future research. *Academy of Management Annals, 12*(1), 390–439. https://doi.org/10.5465/annals.2016.0014

Shepherd, D. A., & Williams, T. A. (2014). Local venturing as compassion organizing in the aftermath of a natural disaster: The role of localness and community in reducing suffering. *Journal of Management Studies, 51*(6), 952–994. https://doi.org/10.1111/joms.12084

Smircich, L., & Stubbart, C. (1985). Strategic management in an enacted world. *Academy of Management Review, 10*(4), 724–736. https://doi.org/10.5465/amr.1985.4279096

Sollund, R. (2006). Mechanistic versus organic organizations' impact on immigrant women's work satisfaction and occupational mobility. *Scandinavian Journal of Hospitality and Tourism, 6*(4), 287–307. https://doi.org/10.1080/15022250601003240

Teece, D. (2017). Towards a capability theory of (innovating) firms: implications for management and policy. *Cambridge Journal of Economics, 41*(3), 693–720. https://doi.org/10.1093/cje/bew063

Teece, D. J. (2007). Explicating dynamic capabilities: the nature and microfoundations of (sustainable) enterprise performance. *Strategic Management Journal, 28*(13), 1319–1350. https://doi.org/10.1002/smj.640

Teece, D. J. (2018). Business models and dynamic capabilities. *Long Range Planning, 51*(1), 40–49. https://doi.org/10.1016/j.lrp.2017.06.007

Teece, D. J., Pisano, G., & Shuen, A. (1997). Dynamic capabilities and strategic management. *Strategic Management Journal, 18*(7), 509–533. https://doi.org/10.1002/(SICI)1097-0266(199708)18:7<509::AID-SMJ882>3.0.CO;2-Z

Thomas, R., & Wood, E. (2014). Innovation in tourism: Re-conceptualising and measuring the absorptive capacity of the hotel sector. *Tourism Management, 45*, 39–48. https://doi.org/10.1016/j.tourman.2014.03.012

Tourism Australia. (2018). *Australia's business environment*. https://www.tourisminvestment.com.au/en/why-australia/easy-place-to-do-business.html

UNWTO. (2020). Tourism and COVID-19: Impact on tourism. https://www.unwto.org/tourism-covid-19

Verreynne, M., Meyer, D., & Liesch, P. (2016). Beyond the formal-informal dichotomy of small firm strategy-making in stable and dynamic environments. *Journal of Small Business Management, 54*(2), 420–444. https://doi.org/10.1111/jsbm.12143

Wang, C. L., Senaratne, C., & Rafiq, M. (2015). Success traps, dynamic capabilities and firm performance. *British Journal of Management, 26*(1), 26–44. https://doi.org/10.1111/1467-8551.12066

Warner, K. S., & Wäger, M. (2019). Building dynamic capabilities for digital transformation: An ongoing process of strategic renewal. *Long Range Planning, 52*(3), 326–349. https://doi.org/10.1016/j.lrp.2018.12.001

Whitsunday Disaster Coordination Centre. (WDCC) (2020). *Disaster Management*. Retrieved from https://www.whitsunday.qld.gov.au/140/Disaster-Management (accessed 12 Oct 2020).

Whitsunday Regional Council. (WRC) (2019). *Whitsunday Region Local Disaster Management Plan 2019-2020*. Retrieved October 12, 2020, from https://www.whitsunday.qld.gov.au/DocumentCenter/View/5436.

World Bank. (2020). *Doing Business 2020*. https://www.doingbusiness.org/

Zahra, S. A., Sapienza, H. J., & Davidsson, P. (2006). Entrepreneurship and dynamic capabilities: A review, model and research agenda. *Journal of Management Studies, 43*(4), 917–955. https://doi.org/10.1111/j.1467-6486.2006.00616.x

Zhou, L., Wu, X., Xu, Z., & Fujita, H. (2018). Emergency decision making for natural disasters: An overview. *International Journal of Disaster Risk Reduction, 27*, 567–576. https://doi.org/10.1016/j.ijdrr.2017.09.037

Zollo, M., & Winter, S. G. (2002). Deliberate learning and the evolution of dynamic capabilities. *Organisation Science, 13*(3), 339–351. https://doi.org/10.1287/orsc.13.3.339.2780

A safe space for local knowledge sharing in sustainable tourism: an organisational justice perspective

Raymond Rastegar and Lisa Ruhanen

ABSTRACT
Knowledge is recognised as having more value when it is created and shared amongst stakeholders. Applying knowledge management principles can assist tourism organisations in achieving a competitive advantage. Importantly though, one-way, top-down transfer of knowledge, particularly in developing countries, can result in ignoring valuable local knowledge and compromise sustainable development objectives. Certainly, when considering the context of sustainable tourism, relying solely on more powerful stakeholders' knowledge inputs to make decisions can result in injustice and undermine sustainability values. Given the importance of justice principles to sustainable tourism, this study applies the concept of organisational justice with a focus on the three dimensions of distributive, procedural and interactional justice to examine local knowledge sharing in tourism development. To address issues of justice and fairness in the context of sustainable tourism development, this study proposes a safe space framework to facilitate knowledge sharing in a local context that is based on recognition of diversity in social patterns and embedding multiple forms and sources of knowledge. This conceptual paper contributes to the framing of justice principles with regards to local knowledge sharing and discusses practical implications for how different claims of justice by local actors can be addressed in sustainable tourism development.

Introduction

Knowledge management (KM), a concept that arose in the 1980s, is recognised as a key factor in destination competitiveness (Cooper, 2018; Ruhanen & Cooper, 2004). In addition to gaining a sustainable competitive advantage (Awad & Ghaziri, 2004; Raisi et al., 2020), adopting a KM approach can assist tourism organisations with addressing environmental change (Dutta & Madalli Devika, 2015; Martinez-Martinez et al., 2019), becoming more efficient and profitable (Ruhanen & Cooper, 2004), reducing costs (Li et al., 2017), manage different types of knowledge (Yang & Wan, 2004), and facilitate innovation and organisational learning (Cooper, 2018). Certainly, the application of KM principles is particularly relevant to tourism given its susceptibility to continuous and unprecedented events (Nordin & Svensson, 2005; Su et al., 2019) such as the COVID-19 pandemic (Gössling et al., 2021) or political crises (Li et al., 2018). Further, it is argued that the application of KM can enable organisations to not only innovate, but also to support their sustainability objectives (Breznik, 2018; López-Torres et al., 2019), particularly when combining KM with an organisations' broader strategies (Davenport et al., 2019).

For KM to be effective, the development of a knowledge sharing (KS) culture between knowledge users and those generating knowledge to deliver knowledge-based innovation is required. Issues of injustice can arise when some forms of knowledge, usually that of more powerful stakeholders, is given priority over the knowledge of marginalised groups such as local communities and residents (Baker & Constant, 2020; Rastegar, 2020a, 2020b; Shrestha et al., 2019). Indeed, it has been widely recognised that top-down decision-making approaches often exclude local knowledge, with preference given to more powerful stakeholder voices or those seen as more legitimate such as experts with particular scientific knowledge (Kruger et al., 2015; Lecuyer et al., 2018; Shaw et al., 2008). Local knowledge can be defined as a body of knowledge and practices that evolve over time originating from a specific geographical location culture or tradition which can be transferred from one generation to another (Baker & Constant, 2020; Cuaton & Su, 2020; Thomas et al., 2020). Similarly, in tourism, ignoring such knowledge by policymakers is identified as a missed opportunity to "uncover new insights, needs, and perceptions" (De Lucia et al., 2020, p. 82). Ignoring the inputs of local communities can lead to 'monopolies of power' or 'monoculture' where some groups decide what is right and what is wrong for all (Schlosberg, 2004; Velicu, 2019; Wang et al., 2019).

Asymmetry in power is identified as a key challenge in developing countries where more powerful stakeholders such as government organisations usually lead the process of tourism decision-making (Rastegar, 2020b). In such situations, the lack of a safe space makes this difficult, if not impossible, for local people to share their knowledge with other stakeholders (Rastegar et al., 2021; Shrestha et al., 2019). A safe space in this context can include an environment that is free of discrimination or criticism, where local knowledge and values are recognised, and where justice prevails. Similarly, Rastegar et al. (2021 p. 2) call for a justice turn in tourism by "recognising local rights, needs and social spaces." This is particularly important as divergence of power has been found to undermine sustainability values (Allen, 2007; Hill et al., 2020), negatively affect local livelihoods and businesses (Kahmann et al., 2015), and result in an increase in injustice issues (Rastegar, 2020b; Shrestha et al., 2019).

Local stakeholders' willingness to contribute their knowledge will similarly be affected by their perception of justice. A willingness to share knowledge amongst individuals directly relates to the organisational environment or destination context (Raisi et al., 2020; Saulais & Ermine, 2020; Zhang et al., 2020), and has been found to play a key role in encouraging KS (Aguiar-Quintana et al., 2020; Akram et al., 2020; Bouazzaoui et al., 2020; Imamoglu et al., 2019; Li et al., 2017; Yeşil & Dereli, 2013). Despite the wide presence of such injustice issues in tourism contexts, "they often remain implicit or poorly theorised" in the literature (Jamal & Higham, 2021, p. 145).

Organisational justice has been identified as a useful tool in examining individuals' KS behaviour (Akram et al., 2020; Li et al., 2017). Given the important interrelationships between knowledge and justice, and these gaps in the literature, this paper uses an organisational justice perspective to conceptually explore KS in the context of sustainable tourism development. To achieve this aim, this study adopts a broad sectorial approach, drawing from various disciplines and perspectives to inform our understanding of these issues in a tourism context. Drawing on KS, local knowledge, and organisational justice principles, this paper proposes a safe space framework to support tourism sustainability outcomes in the context of local communities, particularly in developing countries where justice issues are more prevalent. The proposed framework helps initiating a conversation on the issues of justice and sustainability in local knowledge and opens new opportunities for future research. The framework provides a conceptual basis for recognising diverse values and worldviews to encourage local knowledge recognition and integration in just and sustainable tourism.

Knowledge and knowledge sharing

The concept of knowledge can be considered free from the tangible world and is divided into forms of tacit knowledge and explicit knowledge (Bétrisey et al., 2018). Explicit knowledge is easy to transfer and communicate (Cooper, 2018), can be codified (Abbas & Sağsan, 2019), and is usually available in written forms (Ooi, 2014). Scientific knowledge generated by experts is an example of such knowledge. Tacit knowledge however, is usually in unwritten form, resides within individuals' minds (Maravilhas & Martins, 2019), and is difficult to codify and communicate (Abbas & Sağsan, 2019; Cooper, 2018). Local knowledge such as that held by residents and local communities can be considered as 'on-the-ground' or tacit knowledge (Allen, 2007). KM process can be utilised to convert tacit to explicit knowledge with the aim of making it available and easy to share (Yang, 2008).

Knowledge is recognised as having more value when it is shared between stakeholders (Takeuchi, 2001). Indeed, some consider KS as the core element of KM (Park et al., 2009), particularly in terms of achieving sustainable development (López-Torres et al., 2019). KS can enable and facilitate organisations to develop new approaches to achieve sustainability (Abbas & Sağsan, 2019; Habib et al., 2019) and innovation (Bereznoy et al., 2021). For instance, by collaborating and sharing know-how to help others, solve problems, develop new ideas and/or implement policies or procedures (Wang & Noe, 2010). The link between KM, KS and sustainable development objectives can be seen through individuals' commitments to acquire, share and create knowledge. For instance, the findings of a study examining the role of KM in green innovation and corporate sustainable development indicated that there were significant positive impacts of KS on all sustainable development practices (Abbas & Sağsan, 2019). The positive impacts of KS have also been found to improve employee's innovation and organisation financial performance (Habib et al., 2019) and the creation of new ideas (Alhady et al., 2011) which in turn results in increased customer satisfaction (Abbas & Sağsan, 2019).

KS is an integral part of KM but does not come naturally. For instance, knowledge can be considered as personal intellectual property and a private asset (Zhang et al., 2020), so individuals are more likely to hoard knowledge rather than sharing it with others as they fear that by sharing their knowledge, they will lose their power and be less competitive (Yang & Wu, 2008; Zhang et al., 2020). However, in organisations where individuals feel respected and perceive their treatment to be fair, they are more committed to the organisation and feel more willing, or even obligated, to share their knowledge (Li et al., 2017). Therefore, in an effective KM system, KS behaviour cannot be forced but can instead be understood and facilitated (Gibbert & Krause, 2002).

Using and managing knowledge in a KM process requires understanding the flow of knowledge between different stakeholders (Ferreira et al., 2018; Styhre, 2004). For an effective knowledge transfer process from creator to user, learning and absorption are the key factors (Cooper, 2018). For example, in analysing characteristics of sharing knowledge between tourism organisations, Raisi et al. (2020) identified the importance of increasing collaboration and KS between tourism destinations. The findings show that one-way flows of limited knowledge from hubs such as public bodies to small and medium-sized enterprises does not fulfil the criteria of KS. Similarly, the presence of a top-down approach has been found to result in neglecting less powerful stakeholders' knowledge such as local people in decision-making (Kahmann et al., 2015; Shrestha et al., 2019). Therefore, in the process of generating and using knowledge, decisions have to be based on credibility, the legitimacy of knowledge and also whose knowledge counts (Vogel et al., 2007). Given the significance of multi-stakeholder participation to facilitate KM in tourism contexts, issues of diversity and inequality in KS are relatively under-examined in the literature. This is particularly important as locally tailored practices based on local rights, values and knowledge have been found to contribute not only to sustainable, but just tourism futures also (Higgins-Desbiolles, 2020; Rastegar et al., 2021).

Local knowledge: a sustainability issue

In tourism contexts, local knowledge provides insights and understanding of tourism from local perspectives (De Lucia et al., 2020; Dias et al., 2020; Tribe & Liburd, 2016). It is also recognised that local communities and organisations have different knowledge systems (Allen, 2007; Lecuyer et al., 2018). Local knowledge reflects beliefs, values, lived experiences and everyday observations that have been shaped over the long-term and "transmitted through myriad forms including song, dance, paintings and rituals" (Hill et al., 2020, p. 10). The key concepts of local knowledge have been identified as a) being dynamic in encompassing values and worldviews that is transmitted across generations b) highly diverse between ecosystems and cultural systems, and c) managed by cultural institutions rules about who holds what knowledge and how it can be shared (Hill et al., 2020). Recognition of such diversity in social patterns and the inherent multiple forms of knowledge is considered critical to addressing sustainability objectives and justice (Holifield, 2012; Ramos, 2015).

Issues of injustice arise when limited or no opportunity is given to local communities to effectively contribute their knowledge (Kruger et al., 2015; Rastegar, 2019), or participate in decision-making (Kahmann et al., 2015; Rastegar et al., 2021). Ignoring such local knowledge in decision-making processes has been found to result in a lack of KS among individuals and groups and ineffective knowledge exchange (Shrestha et al., 2019). Even when the opportunity is given to only a few members of the community, this is not sufficient to ensure the effective participation of the community to share and contribute their knowledge (Shrestha et al., 2019). In such situations, more powerful stakeholders such as government organisations will lead the process of decision-making (Rastegar, 2020b; Rastegar et al., 2021). Formation of "monopolies of thought" (Illich, 1972) or 'monopolies of power' (Velicu, 2019) in decision-making results in the loss of valuable local knowledge. For instance, a study examining perspectives of justice found that ignoring local ecological knowledge and relying on scientific data to make decisions resulted in the collapse of the fishery sector in Newfoundland, Canada (Kahmann et al., 2015). Another study exploring the relevance of Indigenous culture to natural resources management in Zimbabwe, found that practices based on local knowledge resulted in sustaining local livelihoods without significant adverse impacts on the natural environment (Reniko et al., 2018). Similar findings have emerged in studies of post disaster recovery in Nepal (Shrestha et al., 2019) and New Orleans, USA (Allen, 2007) where limited opportunities were given to local communities to participate and share their knowledge and local expertise to the detriment of the recovery effort.

Ignoring local knowledge has been suggested as a reason for injustice and in turn, undermining sustainability values (Allen, 2007; Baker & Constant, 2020; Hill et al., 2020; Kahmann et al., 2015; Mabudafhasi, 2002; Rastegar et al., 2021). As noted, the existence of such a relationship indicates that individuals' willingness to share knowledge is directly affected by the organisational environment or destination context (Raisi et al., 2020; Saulais & Ermine, 2020; Zhang et al., 2020). ; This is despite the fact that local KS has been documented to be effective in building community resilience to natural disasters (Cuaton & Su, 2020), play a key role in biodiversity conservation and sustainable harvesting (Baker & Constant, 2020), sustainable agriculture (Thomas et al., 2020), and capacity building for sustainable tourism (Buzinde et al., 2020; Mabudafhasi, 2002). The argument above indicates that exploring local KS requires an approach to provide a comprehensive understanding of the phenomenon in different bodies of knowledge.

Conceptual framework analysis

This paper aims to theorize the interdisciplinary term of local KS in the context of sustainable tourism development. To achieve this aim, we employed the qualitative method proposed by

Jabareen (2008, 2009) for building conceptual frameworks for phenomena that are linked to multidisciplinary bodies of knowledge. Jabareen suggests that conceptual analysis techniques are based on the grounded theory method and focus on providing a comprehensive understanding of the phenomenon, rather than description of the data or prediction. In step one, we embarked on a multidisciplinary approach regarding the phenomenon in question. In this step, we conducted an extensive review of texts on local KS in different disciplines. This process resulted in adopting a broad sectorial approach, drawing from various disciplines and perspectives including KM, KS and organisational justice to inform our understanding of the phenomenon. Such an approach of mapping the selected data sources ensured the validity of data collection (Jabareen, 2008; Morse & Mitcham, 2002).

In the next step, our aim was to recognise patterns in competing and contradictory themes and meanings that were identified in the previous phase. We conducted this step carefully as local KS is a complex phenomenon that links to different body of knowledge from multiple disciplines. Step three consisted of synthesising and categorising themes with similar meanings. The iterative process helped to deconstruct and categorise the concepts into smaller groups with distinctive meanings. In the final step, discussion and describing of the relationships amongst the derived concepts was undertaken to synthetise the concepts into a conceptual framework. Maxwell (2013) suggested that this step be repeated by reworking the concept map many times until it best communicates the ideas to provide an understanding of the phenomenon. The process led to proposing a safe space conceptual framework to support tourism sustainability based on the concepts of KM, KS, organisational justice, and local knowledge system.

Findings and discussion

Towards a sustainable framework: the application of organisational justice principles

The fair and just treatment of individuals is fundamental to encouraging KS (Akram et al., 2020; Li et al., 2017). The relationship can be explained through the direct effect of individuals perceptions of justice and fairness on KS behaviour (Aguiar-Quintana et al., 2020; Bouazzaoui et al., 2020; Imamoglu et al., 2019; Yeşil & Dereli, 2013). For instance, Zhou et al. (2020, p. 5) argue that "knowledge sharing can be integrated via an intangible exchange through a series of justice perception principles among members in collaboration."

In examining KS behaviour, it is suggested that organisational justice can be a useful tool in studying individuals' KS behaviour (Akram et al., 2020; Li et al., 2017). Organisational justice is developed based on the Equity Theory proposed by Adams (1965) and has been found to have a significant role in shaping the behaviours of organisational members (Chen et al., 2015). Organisational justice focuses on the concept of justice and fairness and can be used to examine individuals' perceptions about the degree of fairness. In this context, tourism destinations can be considered as complex organisations and their residents as employees (Buhalis, 2003; Su et al., 2019) that interact with other stakeholders in providing services to tourists and visitors (Su et al., 2018).

Organisational justice is generally studied through the three dimensions of *distributive, procedural* and *interactional* justice (Karkoulian et al., 2016). Distributive justice is concerned with fairness in allocating resources (Colquitt, 2001). Recognising the rights of the individuals to have their say, procedural justice suggests that individuals must have "equal participation in decision-making process" (Venn, 2019, p. 716). Interactional justice refers to individuals' perception of how they are treated (Su et al., 2019) and the level of perceived fairness in the communication process (Colquitt, 2001). Some have widened the debate to consider the interactional dimension as "justice-as-recognition" to cover the importance of cultural diversity, local values and knowledge systems (Lecuyer et al., 2018; Martin et al., 2016; Schlosberg, 2007).

Justice-as-recognition can therefore exist beyond the rights of individuals and address recognition of knowledge and KS among stakeholders. For instance, Lecuyer et al. (2018) categorise justice-as-recognition as 'conditional justice' and distributive and procedural justice as 'practical justice'. They argue that recognition-as justice underpins other dimensions by asking whose perception of costs and benefits matters (distributive) and whose knowledge counts (procedural).

The positive impacts of the dimensions of organisational justice on KS can be explained by Social Exchange Theory (Akram et al., 2020). It is suggested that individuals who perceive the treatment as fair are more likely to contribute their knowledge to achieve organisational goals (Pignata et al., 2016). Similarly, in tourism, Organisational Support Theory can be used to explain how residents personify with the organisation when they feel their contributions are valued and that destination managers care for their well-being and participation in tourism (Su et al., 2019). The study further suggests that to address sustainable tourism development, destinations managers must treat residents with respect by ensuring fairness in distribution, sharing of information and also provide the opportunity for residents to contribute. Another study on the relationship between organisational justice dimensions and job insecurity in hospitality industry identified the need to expand justice perspective to enhance business performance (Ruiz-Palomino et al., 2020). The application of organisational justice to investigate KS behaviour is therefore relevant as it is increasingly recognised that individuals are more likely to share their knowledge when they feel they receive fair treatment in their environment (Akram et al., 2020; Li et al., 2017).

From a just process to fair outcomes

KS has been found to play a vital role in local capacity building in sustainable tourism development process (Buzinde et al., 2020; Mabudafhasi, 2002). Indeed, the principles of sustainable development acknowledge the importance of creating a safe space that regulates KS via local people and their inclusion in the dialogue regarding tourism development (Ainsworth et al., 2020; Allen, 2007; Shrestha et al., 2019). This point is particularly relevant to the practical aspect of justice (procedural and distributive) as it works to define a 'just process' with 'fair outcomes' (Lecuyer et al., 2018). Similarly, in tourism, procedural justice is considered as an antecedent of distributive justice because individuals perceive the outcome as fair when the have control over the process (Aguiar-Quintana et al., 2020).

The practical aspect of justice is now becoming increasingly accepted as part of the development process by international, national and local governments, and tourism organisations (Aguiar-Quintana et al., 2020; Dirth et al., 2020; Le et al., 2016; Rastegar et al., 2021). However, issues of injustice arise with the failure to understand what justice means to local communities outside academia, legal frameworks and government agencies. To this end and with regards to local knowledge and KS behaviour, the pursuit of sustainable tourism will then be about exploring the dimensions of justice in creating a more democratic process of decision making that recognises different knowledge system and worldviews. Hence, understanding individuals' perceptions of justice will have a greater impact on tourism sustainability (Le et al., 2016).

Tourism policies and local inclusion

Both procedural and distribution equity has clearly been an important aspect of tourism development policies in many countries. Such tourism policies have claimed to improve local livelihoods (Rastegar, 2020a; Wang et al., 2019). However, knowledge production without the inclusion of all stakeholders has been identified as an unfair process (Baker & Constant, 2020) that can negatively affect KS (Yeşil & Dereli, 2013). In more traditional, top-down approaches, local development without meaningful local participation cannot be considered fair or sustainable. For example, while the establishment of protected areas are claimed to benefit local communities and the environment (Snyman & Bricker, 2019), there is a growing concern that in some cases they are established with the objective of increasing tourism (GEF, 2018). In such cases, local communities are often informed about the decisions that are made based on the knowledge produced by others (Baker & Constant, 2020; Rastegar, 2020b; Rastegar et al., 2021).

Tourism policies can be created around justice principles at the national level but when implemented at the local level, community interests are ignored (Wang et al., 2019). This is largely due to these programs focusing on outcomes rather than the process of engagement and collaboration. For example, the findings of a study investigating the case of tourism development in a World Heritage Site (WHS) that was established under the guise of benefitting local people, revealed that the local community were ignored in the decision-making process (Rastegar et al., 2021). The findings showed that tourism policies left local people "powerless to act upon concerns about tourism and cultural change" (Rastegar et al., 2021, p. 520). This case reinforces that top-down approaches minimise the meaningful involvement of local people in the decision-making process and prevent local knowledge recognition and sharing.

Discrimination of local knowledge

Prejudice and the lack of fair procedure can also negatively affect KS behaviour. For example, local people might be reluctant to share their knowledge because of negative previous experiences, fear of discrimination and being laughed at by others (Cuaton & Su, 2020). Similarly, cultural insensitivity can reduce the chance of local people willing to share their knowledge with outsiders (Peterson et al., 2010). Lack of local participation and KS will then be a missed opportunity (Baker & Constant, 2020). However, local people can express their willingness to share their knowledge when they realise how the process will ensure fairness in local KS and preservation. For example, investigating the contribution of local knowledge to disaster risk reduction in the Philippines, revealed that efforts in nurturing genuine local participation encouraged local leader cooperation in sharing their knowledge (Cuaton & Su, 2020). As procedural problems in tourism largely stem from an under appreciation and lack of attention to local people, their values and knowledge system (Muntifering et al., 2020), creating a fair social process (procedural justice) that leads to fair outcomes for local people (distributive justice), will therefore require recognition of diverse worldviews. To this end, tourism organisations should be required to embrace inclusion and diversity in their policies and practices (Le et al., 2016; Rastegar, 2020b; Rastegar et al., 2021).

Justice-as-recognition of local knowledge

Recognition injustice refers to a lack of respect for local culture, value and knowledge (Jamal, 2019). In the broader literature, recognition justice is usually linked to claims of self-determination (Martin et al., 2014; Rastegar, 2020a; Schlosberg, 2004). Here, when the discursive power suppresses the rights of local people and alternative ways of thinking, more powerful stakeholders will be the "legitimate source of justice norm" (Martin et al., 2014, p. 169). The exercise of such discursive power and imbalance in power relationships determines whose idea and knowledge is given priority over others. In such situations, conflicts usually stem from feelings of injustice by marginalised groups (Clayton et al., 2016; Lecuyer et al., 2018) as they are often the main victims of injustice (Camargo & Vázquez-Maguirre, 2021; Dirth et al., 2020). In this vein, the recognition of diversity in social patterns and multiple forms of knowledge is required to ensure sustainability and justice can occur (Holifield, 2012; Ramos, 2015).

Local worldviews and knowledge system

Local peoples' concept of justice and their perceptions of fairness is usually based on their values and knowledge system. Such diversity in perceived fairness may not necessarily be aligned with globally referenced justice principles defined in many development programs (Jamal, 2019; Martin et al., 2014). Some have even used the term "spatial justice" when referring to local areas to acknowledge that what is considered as fair and just may differ from place to place (Nordberg, 2020). For instance, Lecuyer et al. (2018, p. 364) proposed that "local actors would have diverse ways of seeing 'justice', and that justice appraisals would be tentative and likely to vary across communities, issues and contexts." Rastegar et al. (2021) also identified the importance of recognising and embracing diverse values as important factors in understanding local peoples' perceptions of justice in tourism development. To understand local perceptions of justice, we then need to learn how these perceptions are shaped based on their contextual knowledge and experiences (Dirth et al., 2020; Graness, 2015).

Justice-as-recognition, rather than focusing on what is fair and unfair, acknowledges different perceptions of justice and worldviews among individuals (Martin et al., 2013). This point can be supported by the findings of studies that have highlighted the impacts of wider social injustice issues such as socio-economic class, gender, caste, and ethnicity in each community on the perception of justice and how individuals are treated (Cuaton & Su, 2020; Dirth et al., 2020; Satyal et al., 2020; Shepherd & Gill, 1999). Therefore, what is considered as 'fair' by one may be seen as 'unfair' by another individual (Gross, 2011). Similar thinking can be seen in the environmental literature when acknowledging that local knowledge is key to sustainability at the local level (Hill et al., 2020). Indeed, attempts to understand local knowledge systems and their relationship with the environment provide a pathway to give space to different worldviews in managing natural resources (Hill et al., 2020; Rastegar, 2017, 2020b). Such approaches help to ensure the integrity of local knowledge systems to enable inclusion of different thinking on sustainability practices.

In response to justice concerns and with the growing and wide-spread recognition of the need to consider local knowledge, frameworks such as the Intergovernmental Platform on Biodiversity and Ecosystem Services (IPBES) were established to recognise social, cultural and environmental local knowledge and to ensure sustainability across large parts of the globe (Hill et al., 2020; Mistry & Berardi, 2016). Such approaches identify the synergies between local and scientific knowledge and recognise these as key in moving towards sustainability (Tengö et al., 2017; Ulicsni et al., 2019). Nevertheless, some have claimed that even such frameworks struggle to address the uneven power relations between stakeholders as they may not retain local knowledge authenticity when integrated with scientific knowledge (Ainsworth et al., 2020).

Power asymmetry and local knowledge

Power asymmetry is a key challenge in working with local and more powerful stakeholders' knowledge systems (Hill et al., 2020; Rastegar, 2020b). The literature exploring the relationships between knowledge and power has confirmed the presence of a discriminatory attitude towards non-western knowledge systems (Baker & Constant, 2020; Briggs & Sharp, 2004; Dotson, 2014). It has also been found that local communities are often subordinated to more powerful stakeholders such as government organisations, experts and the media (Rastegar, 2020b; Velicu, 2019). In places where professional and scientific knowledge "act as default," local communities struggle to find a safe space to share their knowledge with other stakeholders (Shrestha et al., 2019, p. 213). It might be the reason why activists call for policies to ensure the recognition of local knowledge and opportunities to enable a diverse group of residents and locals to participate in decision-making processes (Ainsworth et al., 2020; Allen, 2007; Schlosberg, 2007). For example, locals' traditional worldviews can be dominated by profit-focused worldviews of more dominant stakeholders (Persson et al., 2017). Similarly, expert views or scientific initiatives have resulted in mistrust, power inequality, and loss of original meanings and values of local knowledge (Agrawal, 2002; Hill et al., 2020; Reid et al., 2006). A feeling of mistrust can then emerge when local communities see that their knowledge and experiences are overlooked by experts and scientists (Baker & Constant, 2020). To overcome such an issue, the integration of local and scientific knowledges has been advocated, as opposed to knowledge extraction, where local people are involved in the process from the beginning to implementation based on equal power distribution (Buzinde et al., 2020).

The integration of local and scientific knowledge is not without its challenges. Local knowledge can be considered a part of cultural heritage that is shared by the members of a community (tacit knowledge), while scientific knowledge is based on continuous testing and conformation that is reported by experts (explicit knowledge) (Cuaton & Su, 2020). "Tacit knowledge is the property of those who possess it; it can be easily expressed by one person, but another may find it very difficult to explain" (Saulais & Ermine, 2020, p. 4). Therefore, when working with local people, access to and assessing local knowledge are two key challenges (Ainsworth et al., 2020).

Mistrust can also occur between parties when they are not able to assess the validity of different knowledge systems or have opposing worldviews (Ainsworth et al., 2020; Young et al., 2016). Some have cautioned the "romanticisation" of local knowledge as it may not "always geared towards the promotion of sustainable practices" (Baker & Constant, 2020, p. 2). On the other hand, a lack of local knowledge recognition can also limit the progress of scientific knowledge in addressing sustainability issues (Buzinde et al., 2020; Manuel-Navarrete & Pelling, 2015). Local and scientific knowledges can therefore be seen valid and effective when they are complementary and not mutually exclusive (Ainsworth et al., 2020; Cuaton & Su, 2020; Lejano et al., 2013). In such a way, integrating local knowledge with scientific knowledge can be an effective tool for decision-making and sustainable policies (Allen, 2007; Shaw et al., 2008).

A safe space framework to regulate local knowledge sharing

Based on the preceding discussion, arguably a *safe space framework* can contribute to regulating and facilitating KS in local contexts. Drawing on KM, KS, local knowledge, and organisational justice principles, a conceptual framework is proposed to support tourism sustainability outcomes in the context of local communities (Figure 1). The proposed framework attempts to reflect the importance of closing the gap between local knowledge recognition and KS in the complex context of tourism that involves more powerful stakeholder groups such as government bodies, experts, businesses and NGOs. The application of this framework to local level tourism development provides a conceptual basis for recognising diverse values and worldviews with the aim of encouraging local knowledge recognition and integration in just and sustainable tourism.

Exploring local knowledge systems through an organisational justice lens provides a number of valuable insights. As shown in the framework, the first step in facilitating KS behaviour among local actors is to understand local knowledge systems and the three key concepts of local knowledge. These are identified by Hill et al. (2020) as: dynamic, diversity and being managed by cultural institution rules. Local knowledge reflects the beliefs, values, lived experiences and everyday observations that have been shaped over time. In this regard, understanding local knowledge in its local context will facilitate the identification of how local people shape their worldview and build their perception of justice regarding tourism. Such perceptions of justice have been proven to affect individuals KS behaviour (Bouazzaoui et al., 2020; Imamoglu et al., 2019; Yeşil & Dereli, 2013). As such, a KM system based on the principles of justice and sustainability respects local values and worldviews and can facilitate the creation of a safe space to encourage KS behaviour among local stakeholders.

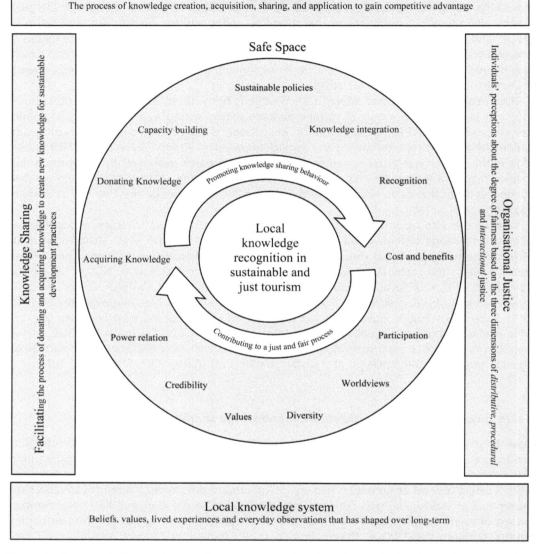

Figure 1. Framework for creating a safe space to regulate knowledge sharing in local context when mapping sustainable tourism development.

Issues of injustice in tourism however may not just be about acknowledging the principles of justice. There is now an increasing appreciation of justice and equity both in UN Sustainable Development Goals (SDGs) and legal frameworks (Dirth et al., 2020; UN, 2020). Nevertheless, policymakers in many cases and particularly in developing countries still fail to understand different perceptions of justice at the local level (Kahmann et al., 2015; Rastegar, 2020a, 2020b; Rastegar et al., 2021). Such negligence can threaten the sustainable future of the industry as in tourism, KS and knowledge generation are enhanced when stakeholders with different agendas work together (Dimmock et al., 2014).

Given this, we also recognise that the power relationships between stakeholders is complex and does not happen in a vacuum. Therefore, ensuring the sustainable future of any institution requires addressing the interests of different stakeholders (Plummer & Fennell, 2009). We have also now established that the romanticisation of local knowledge can undermine the credibility of knowledge as it may not always be geared towards the promotion of sustainable tourism practices. Therefore, recognition of local knowledge and worldviews where integrated with another stakeholders' knowledge, can contribute to the successful implementation of a program within real world constraints. Local people have context specific skills and knowledge that have been developed over centuries and when connected with scientific knowledge, have been proven to be credible and sustainable (Cuaton & Su, 2020; Gaillard & Mercer, 2013). Therefore, acknowledging the complexity of power relations between different tourism stakeholders, the proposed safe space facilitates knowledge integration via acquiring and donating knowledge based on equal recognition and participation of all.

Lastly, the framework proposes a two-way relationship between justice and KS behaviour. Local knowledge recognition in sustainable and just tourism requires a fair and just process to ensure KS behaviour. Demand for local inclusion and participation can be interpreted as an approach for bottom-up development in tourism destinations. Similarly, KS mechanisms can also promote local recognition and meaningful participation in the decision-making process (Mabudafhasi, 2002). Linking this back to the framework, information sharing between stakeholders based on mutual respect and recognition can contribute to sustainable tourism development. It is therefore proposed that the inclusion of different perspectives should inform tourism decision-making based on the principles of justice and fairness.

Conclusion

This paper has provided the first synthesis of the KM, KS and organisational justice theoretical approaches; particularly focused on local knowledge recognition in the contexts of justice and sustainability in tourism. Despite increasing attention to justice in the tourism literature, much more work is required to "clearly conceptualise and identify key principles and approaches to justice" (Jamal & Higham, 2021, p. 147). Similarly, limited research on the dimension of KS in the broader KM system has failed to address the important issue of justice and fairness in KS and decision-making in tourism contexts. Certainly, KS between tourism academics and the tourism industry has been identified as a missed opportunity (Hardy et al., 2018). The conceptual framework can therefore guide knowledge holders, policymakers and researchers to develop a just and ethical knowledge integration approach based on the recognition of different knowledge systems, values and worldviews.

In cases where marginalised groups' knowledge is ignored, often rights "are defined by an underlaying value structure" which "tend to mirror the interests of the powerful groups" (Shrestha et al., 2019, p. 207). However, this study proposes that KS in a just and sustainable approach is about the recognition of diverse values and worldviews to encourage local knowledge recognition and integration in achieving sustainable development objectives. Following the just process of recognition and participation for all in KS requires acceptance of the fact that stakeholders will have different views. Particularly, experts and scientists need to recognise that local knowledge can include practices that support sustainability. In this vein, integrating local knowledge with scientific knowledge can be an effective tool for decision-making and sustainable policies.

Increasing the awareness of justice amongst destination managers and practitioners is an important step in this process; particularly understanding and accommodating the crucial role perceptions of justice by local people play in achieving sustainable development objectives in tourism destinations. However, it is not just understanding that such feelings and perceptions about fairness and justice, but to provide platforms or a safe space in which local people can share their views. Similarly, providing the opportunities for stakeholders to collaborate via sharing their knowledge can promote KS behaviour as a social responsibility. Based on the safe space framework proposed in this study, facilitating the process in which stakeholders with different agendas work together can support the process of developing mutual understanding in tourism contexts.

Limitations and future directions

Despite a number of contributions made by this study, limitations remain. This paper presents a conceptual synthesis, discussion and framework. This paper has initiated a conversation on the issues of justice and sustainability in local knowledge recognition and KS in the complex context of tourism that offers some interesting insights and venues for new debates to open new opportunities for future research. Empirical research must engage more closely with notion of justice in sustainable tourism development particularly in the developing world. This article is only the first step in that direction, but future research avenues would be required to focus on operationalising the safe space framework proposed in this study to explore the relationship between the justice dimensions and KS behaviour across different contexts. Following this path, the research area can be deepened and expanded by examining how the application of justice principles can reconcile conflicting perspectives and promote KS behaviour among stakeholders. This study offers a conceptual framework and encourages qualitative and quantitative research to deeply investigate local knowledge recognition and KS in the complex context of tourism. In particular, scholars can examine how providing a safe space by ensuring a fair and just process and recognition of diverse values and worldviews can encourage KS behaviour. The findings of such empirical studies can propose approaches to decision-making that can assist in creating the just and sustainable development that the tourism sector requires to face the future.

Disclosure statement

No potential conflict of interest was reported by the authors.

ORCID

Lisa Ruhanen http://orcid.org/0000-0002-8495-8843

Raymond Rastegar http://orcid.org/0000-0002-5794-2096

References

Abbas, J., & Sağsan, M. (2019). Impact of knowledge management practices on green innovation and corporate sustainable development: A structural analysis. *Journal of Cleaner Production*, *229*, 611–620. https://doi.org/10.1016/j.jclepro.2019.05.024

Adams, J. S. (1965). Inequity in social exchange. In L. Berkowitz (Ed.), *Advances in experimental social psychology* (Vol. 2, pp. 267–299). Academic Press.

Agrawal, A. (2002). Indigenous knowledge and the politics of classification. *International Social Science Journal, 54*(173), 287–297. https://doi.org/10.1111/1468-2451.00382

Aguiar-Quintana, T., Araujo-Cabrera, Y., & Park, S. (2020). The sequential relationships of hotel employees' perceived justice, commitment, and organizational citizenship behaviour in a high unemployment context. *Tourism Management Perspectives, 35*, 100676. https://doi.org/10.1016/j.tmp.2020.100676

Ainsworth, G. B., Redpath, S. M., Wilson, M., Wernham, C., & Young, J. C. (2020). Integrating scientific and local knowledge to address conservation conflicts: Towards a practical framework based on lessons learned from a Scottish case study. *Environmental Science & Policy, 107*, 46–55. https://doi.org/10.1016/j.envsci.2020.02.017

Akram, T., Lei, S., Haider, M. J., & Hussain, S. T. (2020). The impact of organizational justice on employee innovative work behavior: Mediating role of knowledge sharing. *Journal of Innovation & Knowledge, 5*(2), 117–129. https://doi.org/10.1016/j.jik.2019.10.001

Alhady, M., Idris, A., Sawal, M., Azmi, N., & Zakaria, Z. (2011). *Knowledge sharing behavior and individual factors: A relationship study in the i-Class environment* [Paper presentation]. Paper presented at the International Conference on Management and Artificial Intelligence, Bali, Indonesia.

Allen, B. L. (2007). Environmental justice, local knowledge, and after-disaster planning in New Orleans. *Technology in Society, 29*(2), 153–159. https://doi.org/10.1016/j.techsoc.2007.01.003

Awad, E. M., & Ghaziri, H. M. (2004). *Knowledge management*. Pearson/Prentice Hall.

Baker, S., & Constant, N. L. (2020). Epistemic justice and the integration of local ecological knowledge for marine conservation: Lessons from the Seychelles. *Marine Policy, 117*, 103921. https://doi.org/10.1016/j.marpol.2020.103921

Bereznoy, A., Meissner, D., & Scuotto, V. (2021). The intertwining of knowledge sharing and creation in the digital platform based ecosystem. A conceptual study on the lens of the open innovation approach. *Journal of Knowledge Management*. https://doi.org/10.1108/JKM-10-2020-0769

Bétrisey, F., Bastiaensen, J., & Mager, C. (2018). Payments for ecosystem services and social justice: Using recognition theories to assess the Bolivian Acuerdos Recíprocos por el Agua. *Geoforum, 92*, 134–143. https://doi.org/10.1016/j.geoforum.2018.04.001

Bouazzaoui, M., Wu, H.-J., Roehrich, J. K., Squire, B., & Roath, A. S. (2020). Justice in inter-organizational relationships: A literature review and future research agenda. *Industrial Marketing Management, 87*, 128–137. https://doi.org/10.1016/j.indmarman.2020.02.003

Breznik, K. (2018). Knowledge management efrom its inception to the Innova tionLinkage. *Paper Presented at the SIM 2017/14 the International Symposium in Management*.

Briggs, J., & Sharp, J. (2004). Indigenous knowledges and development: A postcolonial caution. *Third World Quarterly, 25*(4), 661–676. https://doi.org/10.1080/01436590410001678915

Buhalis, D. (2003). *eTourism: Information technology for strategic tourism management*. Prentice Hall.

Buzinde, C. N., Manuel-Navarrete, D., & Swanson, T. (2020). Co-producing sustainable solutions in indigenous communities through scientific tourism. *Journal of Sustainable Tourism, 28*(9), 1255–1271. https://doi.org/10.1080/09669582.2020.1732993

Camargo, B. A., & Vázquez-Maguirre, M. (2021). Humanism, dignity and indigenous justice: The Mayan Train megaproject, Mexico. *Journal of Sustainable Tourism, 29*(2-3), 372–391. https://doi.org/10.1080/09669582.2020.1758707

Chen, S.-Y., Chang, Y.-C., Chang, C.-S., Lin, C.-T., Kung, J.-Y., Lin, Y.-T., & Lee, S.-I. (2015). Organizational justice, trust, and identification and their effects on organizational commitment in hospital nursing staff. *BMC Health Services Research, 15*, 363. https://doi.org/10.1186/s12913-015-1016-8

Clayton, S., Kals, E., & Feygina, I. (2016). Justice and environmental sustainability. In C. Sabbagh & M. Schmitt (Eds.), *Handbook of social justice theory and research* (pp. 369–386). Springer.

Colquitt, J. A. (2001). On the dimensionality of organizational justice: A construct validation of a measure. *Journal of Applied Psychology, 86*(3), 386–400. https://doi.org/10.1037/0021-9010.86.3.386

Cooper, C. (2018). Managing tourism knowledge: A review. *Tourism Review, 73*(4), 507–520. https://doi.org/10.1108/TR-06-2017-0104

Cuaton, G. P., & Su, Y. (2020). Local-indigenous knowledge on disaster risk reduction: Insights from the Mamanwa indigenous peoples in Basey, Samar after Typhoon Haiyan in the Philippines. *International Journal of Disaster Risk Reduction, 48*, 101596. https://doi.org/10.1016/j.ijdrr.2020.101596

Davenport, M., Delport, M., Blignaut, J. N., Hichert, T., & van der Burgh, G. (2019). Combining theory and wisdom in pragmatic, scenario-based decision support for sustainable development. *Journal of Environmental Planning and Management, 62*(4), 692–716. https://doi.org/10.1080/09640568.2018.1428185

De Lucia, C., Pazienza, P., Balena, P., & Caporale, D. (2020). Exploring local knowledge and socio-economic factors for touristic attractiveness and sustainability. *International Journal of Tourism Research, 22*(1), 81–99. https://doi.org/10.1002/jtr.2320

Dias, Á., Silva, G. M., Patuleia, M., & González-Rodríguez, M. R. (2020). Developing sustainable business models: local knowledge acquisition and tourism lifestyle entrepreneurship. *Journal of Sustainable Tourism*, 1–20. https://doi.org/10.1080/09669582.2020.1835931

Dimmock, K., Hawkins, E. R., & Tiyce, M. (2014). Stakeholders, industry knowledge and adaptive management in the Australian whale-watching industry. *Journal of Sustainable Tourism, 22*(7), 1108–1121. https://doi.org/10.1080/09669582.2013.879311

Dirth, E., Biermann, F., & Kalfagianni, A. (2020). What do researchers mean when talking about justice? An empirical review of justice narratives in global change research. *Earth System Governance, 6*, 100042. https://doi.org/10.1016/j.esg.2020.100042

Dotson, K. (2014). Conceptualizing epistemic oppression. *Social Epistemology, 28*(2), 115–138. https://doi.org/10.1080/02691728.2013.782585

Dutta, B., & Madalli Devika, P. (2015). Trends in knowledge modelling and knowledge management: An editorial. *Journal of Knowledge Management, 19*(1). https://doi.org/10.1108/JKM-10-2014-0442

Ferreira, J., Mueller, J., & Papa, A. (2018). Strategic knowledge management: Theory, practice and future challenges. *Journal of Knowledge Management, 24*(2), 121–126. https://doi.org/10.1108/JKM-07-2018-0461

Gaillard, J. C., & Mercer, J. (2013). From knowledge to action: Bridging gaps in disaster risk reduction. *Progress in Human Geography, 37*(1), 93–114. https://doi.org/10.1177/0309132512446717

GEF. (2018). *Mainstreaming biodiversity management into production sector activities*. https://www.thegef.org/project/mainstreaming-biodiversity-management-production-sector-activities

Gibbert, M., & Krause, H. (2002). *Practice exchange in a best practice marketplace in knowledge management case book: Siemens best practices*. Publics Corporate Publishing.

Gössling, S., Scott, D., & Hall, C. M. (2021). Pandemics, tourism and global change: A rapid assessment of COVID-19. *Journal of Sustainable Tourism, 29* (1), 1–20. https://doi.org/10.1080/09669582.2020.1758708

Graness, A. (2015). Is the debate on 'global justice' a global one? Some considerations in view of modern philosophy in Africa. *Journal of Global Ethics, 11*(1), 126–140. https://doi.org/10.1080/17449626.2015.1010014

Gross, C. (2011). Why justice is important. In Connell, D., & Quentin Grafton (Ed.), R. *Basin future. Water reform Murray-Darling basin* (pp. 149–162). ANU Press

Habib, M., Abbas, J., & Noman, R. (2019). Are human capital, intellectual property rights, and research and development expenditures really important for total factor productivity? An empirical analysis. *International Journal of Social Economics, 46*(6), 756–774. https://doi.org/10.1108/IJSE-09-2018-0472

Hardy, A., Vorobjovas-Pinta, O., & Eccleston, R. (2018). Enhancing knowledge transfer in tourism: An elaboration likelihood model approach. *Journal of Hospitality and Tourism Management, 37*, 33–41. https://doi.org/10.1016/j.jhtm.2018.09.002

Higgins-Desbiolles, F. (2020). Socialising tourism for social and ecological justice after COVID-19. *Tourism Geographies, 22*(3), 610–623. https://doi.org/10.1080/14616688.2020.1757748

Hill, R., Adem, Ç., Alangui, W. V., Molnár, Z., Aumeeruddy-Thomas, Y., Bridgewater, P., Tengö, M., Thaman, R., Adou Yao, C. Y., Berkes, F., Carino, J., Carneiro da Cunha, M., Diaw, M. C., Díaz, S., Figueroa, V. E., Fisher, J., Hardison, P., Ichikawa, K., Kariuki, P., ... Xue, D. (2020). Working with Indigenous, local and scientific knowledge in assessments of nature and nature's linkages with people. *Current Opinion in Environmental Sustainability, 43*, 8–20. https://doi.org/10.1016/j.cosust.2019.12.006

Holifield, R. (2012). Environmental justice as recognition and participation in risk assessment: Negotiating and translating health risk at a superfund site in Indian country. *Annals of the Association of American Geographers, 102*(3), 591–613. https://doi.org/10.1080/00045608.2011.641892

Illich, I. (1972). *Deschooling society*. Harper Row.

Imamoglu, S. Z., Ince, H., Turkcan, H., & Atakay, B. (2019). The effect of organizational justice and organizational commitment on knowledge sharing and firm performance. *Procedia Computer Science, 158*, 899–906. https://doi.org/10.1016/j.procs.2019.09.129

Jabareen, Y. (2008). A new conceptual framework for sustainable development. *Environment, Development and Sustainability, 10*(2), 179–192. https://doi.org/10.1007/s10668-006-9058-z

Jabareen, Y. (2009). Building a conceptual framework: Philosophy, definitions, and procedure. *International Journal of Qualitative Methods, 8*(4), 49–62. https://doi.org/10.1177/160940690900800406

Jamal, T. (2019). *Justice and ethics in tourism*. Routledge.

Jamal, T., & Higham, J. (2021). Justice and ethics: Towards a new platform for tourism and sustainability. *Journal of Sustainable Tourism, 29*(2-3), 143–157. https://doi.org/10.1080/09669582.2020.1835933

Kahmann, B., Stumpf, K. H., & Baumgärtner, S. (2015). Notions of justice held by stakeholders of the Newfoundland fishery. *Marine Policy, 62*, 37–50. https://doi.org/10.1016/j.marpol.2015.08.012

Karkoulian, S., Assaker, G., & Hallak, R. (2016). An empirical study of 360-degree feedback, organizational justice, and firm sustainability. *Journal of Business Research, 69*(5), 1862–1867. https://doi.org/10.1016/j.jbusres.2015.10.070

Kruger, F., Bankoff, G., Cannon, T., Orlowski, B., & Schipper, L. (2015). *Cultures and disasters: Understanding cultural framings in disaster risk reduction*. Routledge.

Le, H., Zheng, C., & Fujimoto, Y. (2016). Inclusion, organisational justice and employee well-being. *International Journal of Manpower, 37*(6), 945–964.

Lecuyer, L., White, R. M., Schmook, B., Lemay, V., & Calmé, S. (2018). The construction of feelings of justice in environmental management: An empirical study of multiple biodiversity conflicts in Calakmul, Mexico. *Journal of Environmental Management*, 213, 363–373.

Lejano, R. P., Tavares-Reager, J., & Berkes, F. (2013). Climate and narrative: Environmental knowledge in everyday life. *Environmental Science & Policy*, 31, 61–70. https://doi.org/10.1016/j.envsci.2013.02.009

Li, F., Wen, J., & Ying, T. (2018). The influence of crisis on tourists' perceived destination image and revisit intention: An exploratory study of Chinese tourists to North Korea. *Journal of Destination Marketing & Management*, 9, 104–111. https://doi.org/10.1016/j.jdmm.2017.11.006

Li, X., Zhang, J., Zhang, S., & Zhou, M. (2017). A multilevel analysis of the role of interactional justice in promoting knowledge-sharing behavior: The mediated role of organizational commitment. *Industrial Marketing Management*, 62, 226–233. https://doi.org/10.1016/j.indmarman.2016.09.006

López-Torres, G. C., Garza-Reyes, J. A., Maldonado-Guzmán, G., Kumar, V., Rocha-Lona, L., & Cherrafi, A. (2019). Knowledge management for sustainability in operations. *Production Planning & Control*, 30(10-12), 813–826. https://doi.org/10.1080/09537287.2019.1582091

Mabudafhasi, R. (2002). The role of knowledge management and information sharing in capacity building for sustainable development – An example from South Africa. *Ocean & Coastal Management*, 45(9-10), 695–707. https://doi.org/10.1016/S0964-5691(02)00094-7

Manuel-Navarrete, D., & Pelling, M. (2015). Subjectivity and the politics of transformation in response to development and environmental change. *Global Environmental Change*, 35, 558–569. https://doi.org/10.1016/j.gloenvcha.2015.08.012

Maravilhas, S., & Martins, J. (2019). Strategic knowledge management in a digital environment: Tacit and explicit knowledge in Fab Labs. *Journal of Business Research*, 94, 353–359. https://doi.org/10.1016/j.jbusres.2018.01.061

Martin, A., Coolsaet, B., Corbera, E., Dawson, N. M., Fraser, J. A., Lehmann, I., & Rodriguez, I. (2016). Justice and conservation: The need to incorporate recognition. *Biological Conservation*, 197, 254–261. https://doi.org/10.1016/j.biocon.2016.03.021

Martin, A., Gross-Camp, N., Kebede, B., McGuire, S., & Munyarukaza, J. (2014). Whose environmental justice? Exploring local and global perspectives in a payments for ecosystem services scheme in Rwanda. *Geoforum*, 54, 167–177. https://doi.org/10.1016/j.geoforum.2013.02.006

Martin, A., McGuire, S., & Sullivan, S. (2013). Global environmental justice and biodiversity conservation. *The Geographical Journal*, 179(2), 122–131. https://doi.org/10.1111/geoj.12018

Martinez-Martinez, A., Cegarra-Navarro, J.-G., Garcia-Perez, A., & Wensley, A. (2019). Knowledge agents as drivers of environmental sustainability and business performance in the hospitality sector. *Tourism Management*, 70, 381–389. https://doi.org/10.1016/j.tourman.2018.08.030

Maxwell, J. A. (2013). *Qualitative research design: An interactive approach* (3rd ed.). Sage.

Mistry, J., & Berardi, A. (2016). Bridging indigenous and scientific knowledge. *Science*, 352(6291), 1274–1275. https://doi.org/10.1126/science.aaf1160

Morse, J. M., & Mitcham, C. (2002). Exploring qualitatively derived concepts: Inductive-deductive pitfalls. *International Journal of Qualitative Methods*, 1(4), 28–35. https://doi.org/10.1177/160940690200100404

Muntifering, J. R., Clark, S., Linklater, W. L., Uri-Khob, S., Hebach, E., Cloete, J., Jacobs, S., & Knight, A. T. (2020). Lessons from a conservation and tourism cooperative: The Namibian black rhinoceros case. *Annals of Tourism Research*, 82, 102918. https://doi.org/10.1016/j.annals.2020.102918

Nordberg, K. (2020). Spatial Justice and local capability in rural areas. *Journal of Rural Studies*, 78, 47–58. https://doi.org/10.1016/j.jrurstud.2020.06.008

Nordin, S., & Svensson, B. (2005). *The significance of governance in innovative tourism destinations*. Mid-Sweden University Oestersund.

Ooi, K.-B. (2014). TQM: A facilitator to enhance knowledge management? A structural analysis. *Expert Systems with Applications*, 41(11), 5167–5179. https://doi.org/10.1016/j.eswa.2014.03.013

Park, H., Son, S. Y., Lee, S., & Yun, S. (2009). Organizational justice and knowledge sharing. *International Journal of Business Research*, 9(4), 180–185.

Persson, S., Harnesk, D., & Islar, M. (2017). What local people? Examining the Gállok mining conflict and the rights of the Sámi population in terms of justice and power. *Geoforum*, 86, 20–29. https://doi.org/10.1016/j.geoforum.2017.08.009

Peterson, R. B., Russell, D., West, P., & Brosius, J. P. (2010). Seeing (and doing) conservation through cultural lenses. *Environmental Management*, 45(1), 5–18. https://doi.org/10.1007/s00267-008-9135-1

Pignata, S., Winefield, A. H., Provis, C., & Boyd, C. M. (2016). A longitudinal study of the predictors of perceived procedural justice in Australian University Staff. *Frontiers in Psychology*, 7, 1271. https://doi.org/10.3389/fpsyg.2016.01271

Plummer, R., & Fennell, D. A. (2009). Managing protected areas for sustainable tourism: Prospects for adaptive co-management. *Journal of Sustainable Tourism*, 17(2), 149–168. https://doi.org/10.1080/09669580802359301

Raisi, H., Baggio, R., Barratt-Pugh, L., & Willson, G. (2020). A network perspective of knowledge transfer in tourism. *Annals of Tourism Research*, 80, 102817. https://doi.org/10.1016/j.annals.2019.102817

Ramos, H. (2015). Mapping the field of environmental justice: Redistribution, recognition and representation in ENGO press advocacy. *Canadian Journal of Sociology*, 40(3), 355–376. https://doi.org/10.29173/cjs25640

Rastegar, R. (2017). *Environmental protection and local resident attitudes at early stages of tourism development* [Doctoral dissertation]. The University of Queensland.

Rastegar, R. (2019). Tourism development and conservation, do local resident attitudes matter?*International Journal of Tourism Sciences*, 19(3), 181–191. https://doi.org/10.1080/15980634.2019.1663998

Rastegar, R. (2020a). *Exploring the dimensions of social justice in sustainable tourism development* [Paper presentation]. Paper presented at the CAUTHE2020, Auckland, New Zealand.

Rastegar, R. (2020b). Tourism and justice: Rethinking the role of governments. *Annals of Tourism Research*, 85, 102884. https://doi.org/10.1016/j.annals.2020.102884

Rastegar, R., Higgins-Desbiolles, F., & Ruhanen, L. (2021). COVID-19 and a justice framework to guide tourism recovery. *Annals of Tourism Research*, 103161. https://doi.org/10.1016/j.annals.2021.103161

Rastegar, R., Zarezadeh, Z., & Gretzel, U. (2021). World heritage and social justice: Insights from the inscription of Yazd, Iran. *Journal of Sustainable Tourism*, 29(2-3), 520–539.

Reid, W. V., Berkes, F., Wilbanks, T. J., & Capistrano, D. (2006). *Bridging scales and knowledge systems*. Island Press.

Reniko, G., Mogomotsi, P. K., & Mogomotsi, G. E. J. (2018). Integration of Indigenous knowledge systems in natural resources management in Hurungwe district, Zimbabwe. *International Journal of African Renaissance Studies - Multi-, Inter- and Transdisciplinarity*, 13(1), 96–112. https://doi.org/10.1080/18186874.2018.1475869

Ruhanen, L., & Cooper, C. (2004). Applying a knowledge management framework to tourism research. *Tourism Recreation Research*, 29(1), 83–87. https://doi.org/10.1080/02508281.2004.11081434

Ruiz-Palomino, P., Zoghbi-Manrique-de-Lara, P., & Ting-Ding, J. M. (2020). Gender differences in the relationship between justice perceptions and job insecurity in hotel outsourcing. *International Journal of Hospitality Management*, 91, 102412. https://doi.org/10.1016/j.ijhm.2019.102412

Satyal, P., Corbera, E., Dawson, N., Dhungana, H., & Maskey, G. (2020). Justice-related impacts and social differentiation dynamics in Nepal's REDD+ projects. *Forest Policy and Economics*, 117, 102203. https://doi.org/10.1016/j.forpol.2020.102203

Saulais, P., & Ermine, J. L. (2020). Knowledge transfer and knowledge sharing. In P. Saulais & J. L. Ermine (Eds.), *Knowledge management in innovative companies* (Vol. 2, pp. 1–77). Wiley

Schlosberg, D. (2004). Reconceiving environmental justice: global movements and political theories. *Environmental Politics*, 13(3), 517–540. https://doi.org/10.1080/0964401042000229025

Schlosberg, D. (2007). *Defining environmental justice: Theories, movements, and nature*. : Oxford University Press.

Shaw, R., Uy, N., & Baumwoll, J. (2008). *Indigenous knowledge for disaster risk reduction: Good practices and lessons learned from experiences in the Asia-Pacific Region*. United Nation International Strategy for Disaster Reduction.

Shepherd, G., & Gill, G. (1999). *Community forestry and rural livelihood in Nepal: Issues and options for the future of the Nepal UK Community Forestry Project*. Overseas Development Institute.

Shrestha, K. K., Bhattarai, B., Ojha, H. R., & Bajracharya, A. (2019). Disaster justice in Nepal's earthquake recovery. *International Journal of Disaster Risk Reduction*, 33, 207–216. https://doi.org/10.1016/j.ijdrr.2018.10.006

Snyman, S., & Bricker, K. S. (2019). Living on the edge: Benefit-sharing from protected area tourism. *Journal of Sustainable Tourism*, 27(6), 705–719. https://doi.org/10.1080/09669582.2019.1615496

Styhre, A. (2004). Rethinking knowledge: A Bergsonian critique of the notion of tacit knowledge*. *British Journal of Management*, 15(2), 177–188. https://doi.org/10.1111/j.1467-8551.2004.00413.x

Su, L., Huang, S., & Huang, J. (2018). Effects of destination social responsibility and tourism impacts on residents' support for tourism and perceived quality of life. *Journal of Hospitality & Tourism Research*, 42(7), 1039–1057. https://doi.org/10.1177/1096348016671395

Su, L., Huang, S., & Nejati, M. (2019). Perceived justice, community support, community identity and residents' quality of life: Testing an integrative model. *Journal of Hospitality and Tourism Management*, 41, 1–11. https://doi.org/10.1016/j.jhtm.2019.08.004

Takeuchi, H. (2001). Towards a universal management concept of knowledge. In I. Nonaka & D. J. Teece (Eds.), *Managing industrial knowledge: Creation, transfer and utilization* (pp. 315–329). SAGE Publications.

Tengö, M., Hill, R., Malmer, P., Raymond, C. M., Spierenburg, M., Danielsen, F., Elmqvist, T., & Folke, C. (2017). Weaving knowledge systems in IPBES, CBD and beyond – Lessons learned for sustainability. *Current Opinion in Environmental Sustainability*, 26-27, 17–25. https://doi.org/10.1016/j.cosust.2016.12.005

Thomas, E., Riley, M., & Spees, J. (2020). Knowledge flows: Farmers' social relations and knowledge sharing practices in 'Catchment Sensitive Farming. *Land Use Policy*, 90, 104254. https://doi.org/10.1016/j.landusepol.2019.104254

Tribe, J., & Liburd, J. J. (2016). The tourism knowledge system. *Annals of Tourism Research*, 57, 44–61. https://doi.org/10.1016/j.annals.2015.11.011

Ulicsni, V., Babai, D., Vadász, C., Vadász-Besnyői, V., Báldi, A., & Molnár, Z. (2019). Bridging conservation science and traditional knowledge of wild animals: The need for expert guidance and inclusion of local knowledge holders. *Ambio*, 48(7), 769–778. https://doi.org/10.1007/s13280-018-1106-z

UN. (2020). *About the sustainable development goals*.https://www.un.org/sustainabledevelopment/sustainable-development-goals/

Velicu, I. (2019). De-growing environmental justice: Reflections from anti-mining movements in Eastern Europe. *Ecological Economics, 159*, 271–278. https://doi.org/10.1016/j.ecolecon.2019.01.021

Venn, A. (2019). 24-Social justice and climate change. In T. M. Letcher (Ed.), *Managing global warming* (pp. 711–728). Academic Press.

Vogel, C., Moser, S. C., Kasperson, R. E., & Dabelko, G. D. (2007). Linking vulnerability, adaptation, and resilience science to practice: Pathways, players, and partnerships. *Global Environmental Change, 17*(3-4), 349–364. https://doi.org/10.1016/j.gloenvcha.2007.05.002

Wang, S., & Noe, R. A. (2010). Knowledge sharing: A review and directions for future research. *Journal of Human Resource Review, 20*, 115–131.

Wang, W., Liu, J., & Innes, J. L. (2019). Conservation equity for local communities in the process of tourism development in protected areas: A study of Jiuzhaigou Biosphere Reserve, China. *World Development, 124*, 104637. https://doi.org/10.1016/j.worlddev.2019.104637

Yang, H.-L., & Wu, T. C. T. (2008). Knowledge sharing in an organization. *Technological Forecasting and Social Change, 75*(8), 1128–1156. https://doi.org/10.1016/j.techfore.2007.11.008

Yang, J. (2008). Managing knowledge for quality assurance: An empirical study. *International Journal of Quality & Reliability Management, 25*(2), 109–124. https://doi.org/10.1108/02656710810846907

Yang, J.-T., & Wan, C.-S. (2004). Advancing organizational effectiveness and knowledge management implementation. *Tourism Management, 25*(5), 593–601. https://doi.org/10.1016/j.tourman.2003.08.002

Yeşil, S., & Dereli, S. F. (2013). An empirical investigation of the organisational justice, knowledge sharing and innovation capability. *Procedia - Social and Behavioral Sciences, 75*, 199–208. https://doi.org/10.1016/j.sbspro.2013.04.023

Young, J. C., Searle, K., Butler, A., Simmons, P., Watt, A. D., & Jordan, A. (2016). The role of trust in the resolution of conservation conflicts. *Biological Conservation, 195*, 196–202. https://doi.org/10.1016/j.biocon.2015.12.030

Zhang, Z., Song, F., & Song, Z. (2020). Promoting knowledge sharing in the workplace: Punishment v. reward. *Chaos, Solitons & Fractals, 131*, 109518. https://doi.org/10.1016/j.chaos.2019.109518

Zhou, M., Govindan, K., & Xie, X. (2020). How fairness perceptions, embeddedness, and knowledge sharing drive green innovation in sustainable supply chains: An equity theory and network perspective to achieve sustainable development goals. *Journal of Cleaner Production, 260*, 120950. https://doi.org/10.1016/j.jclepro.2020.120950

Conceptualising trust as a mediator of pro-environmental tacit knowledge transfer in small and medium sized tourism enterprises

Conor McTiernan, James Musgrave and Chris Cooper

ABSTRACT
This conceptual paper adds to the theoretical exploration of inter-organisational pro-environmental knowledge transfer in small and medium sized tourism enterprises (SMTEs). It does so by focusing on the role of trust, a concept which has received only scant attention in this context. Drawing on theoretical and empirical research, we argue that the willingness of SMTE managers to engage in the transference of pro-environmental tacit knowledge is based on their intrinsic and extrinsic motivations, coupled with the perceived trustworthiness of both the message and social actors involved. It remains a challenge for SMTE managers to receive, absorb and respond to appropriate pro-environmental knowledge, based on organisational needs. The paper makes an important contribution to the work on pro-environmental knowledge transfer in tourism by proposing a model of four key antecedents of trust in the knowledge transfer process – self- efficacy, social norms, credibility of knowledge source and social capital between actors. We identify a future research agenda including the need to assess the weighted impact of each antecedent of trust; establish the influence of tourism networks on trust formation and development; and explore if peer perception intervenes in tacit knowledge transfer between pro-active and reactive SMTE managers.

Introduction

This conceptual paper considers the under-researched, focal theme of trust as a mediator of pro-environmental tacit knowledge transfer in small and medium sized tourism enterprises (SMTEs) (Jaakkola, 2020). While trust is an emerging feature of debate in sustainable tourism, it has rarely been the subject of systematic research and it remains a diluted concept in studies on the importance of social capital in tourism development (Nunkoo, 2017). Equally, while it is encouraging to note the increasing research attention to trust in tourism, there are few attempts to link it explicitly to knowledge transfer, good governance of networks, and business relationships (Czernek & Czakon, 2016). Indeed, trust in these contexts seems to have been taken for granted by tourism researchers compared to other fields such as sociology and political science (Nunkoo, 2017).

This paper provides a theoretical contribution by conceptualising how trust informs SMTE managers' decisions to engage in the transfer of pro-environmental tacit knowledge. Drawing on Mayer et al.'s (1995) definition of trust, specifically the willingness to be vulnerable, this research presents a conceptual model of four key antecedents of trust-based decisions set within tourism networks (Cooper, 2015). We underline the crucial role that trust plays within these groupings, the importance of personal relationships and the social embedding of SMTEs within them to facilitate pro-environmental knowledge transfer partnerships. Researchers concur that while difficult, the effective transfer of pro-environmental tacit knowledge among individuals and organisations is crucial for competitiveness (Del Chiappa & Baggio, 2015), enhancing stakeholders' perceptions of the organisation (Teng et al., 2018), and satisfying the personal goals of pro-environmental orientated SMTE managers (Kornilaki et al., 2019).

We build on relevant research in tourism-specific contexts such as trust in sustainable tourism practice, implementation, policy formation and governance (Nunkoo & Gursoy, 2017), which influences SMTE managers' perceptions of, and behaviours toward, pro-environmental knowledge. The research also contributes to further understanding the process of trust development between tourism collaborators (Sun et al., 2020) and acknowledges the corresponding impact of uncertainty and vulnerability in such trust formation (Williams & Baláž, 2020). These insights highlight contextual challenges to the acceptance and adoption of pro-environmental knowledge at the SMTE level. Specifically, there remains concern that while sustainable development ideals are espoused by SMTE managers (Garay et al., 2019), there is a need to be *willing* to trust and accept new knowledge (Van der Werff et al., 2019) to implement pro-environmental knowledge and practices to achieve sustainability within the tourism sector.

We postulate that trust of both the knowledge and the knowledge source are key mediators in knowledge transfer in tourism (Higuchi & Yamanaka, 2017) and cumulatively these inform a manager's pro-environmental intentions and behaviours. This requires SMTE managers to discriminate not only between sustainable knowledge sources, they must also assess and trust the credibility of these sources (Buys et al., 2014). This research also considers the mediating influence of inter-personal and inter-organisational social capital on the knowledge transfer process (Liu, 2018). Specifically, the model contends that successful knowledge transfer in tourism necessitates both rational and relational trust of the knowledge source (Zach & Hill, 2017). Within SMTEs however, limited expertise and resources place stress on the success of knowledge transfer. Moreover, actors may lack prior experience and absorptive capacity in knowledge transfer and use (Cohen & Levinthal, 1990; Thomas & Wood, 2014). Equally, smaller organisational scale may enhance SMTE practitioners' willingness to trust, based on the degree of social capital a collaborating partner can exercise (Nahapiet & Ghoshal, 1998).

This paper begins by analysing challenges to knowledge management in tourism. It continues by exploring SMTE managers' willingness to trust pro-environmental knowledge before proposing a model which identifies four key antecedent conditions of said trust. We acknowledge different perspectives on this decision-making process and the challenge of uncertainty when embracing and integrating pro-environmental knowledge in SMTEs. The paper concludes by introducing potential themes for further research.

Challenges to the transfer of pro-environmental tacit knowledge in tourism

The efficacy of knowledge management (KM) is predicated upon an organisation's capability to create, curate, transfer and leverage information assets. This equates to the absorptive capacity of organisations to process and action new knowledge (Cohen & Levinthal, 1990). In tourism, this process often occurs in networks of organisations which can be based either on destinations or functions (such as value chains). Such networks support inbound open innovation where SMTEs build upon existing internal knowledge stocks through exploration and adoption of pro-environmental tacit knowledge residing in external yet knowledgeable peers (Singh et al., 2021). Here, the effectiveness and strength of a network is determined by social cohesion and the extent to which organisations are embedded within the network (Reagans & McEvily, 2003). In turn, the successful transfer of knowledge both within and between networks requires antecedents of trust and cooperation amongst network members (Czakon & Czernek, 2016; Williams & Baláž, 2020).

Within these networks, the transfer of pro-environmental knowledge in SMTEs faces two key sets of barriers. The first relates to the nature of the tourism sector itself, whilst the second relates to the nature of knowledge transfer within and between SMTEs. Taking the tourism sector first, it can be argued that the characteristics of the sector militate against the successful application of KM, and in particular knowledge transfer (Cooper, 2018; Czernek, 2017). For example, a transient and seasonal workforce limits organisational learning whilst the de-skilling of the workforce diminishes the aspiration to be innovative. In addition, not only is the tourism product fragmented across myriad providers, but also its varied contextualisation reduces the ability to transfer knowledge between contexts. The literature also suggests a widening gap between knowledge assets and the tourism sector's ability to use knowledge innovatively (Garay et al., 2017). For instance, in the private sector, de-centralised ownership structures reduce the sense of shared commitment across the sector, whilst for government, fragmented tourism policies limit transfer of information between destinations.

Tacit knowledge is often more common in SMTEs than explicit knowledge, and this creates the second barrier to the transfer of pro-environmental knowledge in tourism. There is evidence to suggest that tourism organisations, particularly SMTEs, leverage collective knowledge through their tacit knowledge stocks with limited use of explicit knowledge sources (Hjalager, 2010; Nonaka & Takeuchi, 1995). Yet, explicit knowledge transfer between known collaborators is easier than tacit knowledge transfer, as explicit knowledge is codified and made relevant to the recipient (Becerra et al., 2008; Cavusgil et al., 2003). In contrast, tacit knowledge transfer is more complex and can be likened to the transfer of knowledge between master and apprentice - the knowledge is not codified; rather it is highly personal. Identifying and transferring appropriate tacit knowledge is therefore increasingly recognised as an essential part of the successful management of sustainable practices in SMTEs for two reasons (Font et al., 2016; Garay et al., 2017). Firstly, the technical narrative in explicit pro-environmental knowledge limits the reach, acceptance and impact for SMTEs and secondly, SMTEs have limited resources and capabilities to create and codify new pro-environmental knowledge.

Pro-environmental knowledge constitutes two inter-linking elements: knowledge about environmental impacts and their causes and secondly knowledge pertaining to actions that minimise negative environmental impacts (Juvan & Dolnicar, 2017). A key consideration for SMTE managers when absorbing pro-environmental knowledge is the nature and credibility of the knowledge source (Kim & Stepchenkova, 2020). This is exacerbated by the technical complexity of the environmental issues themselves (Cainelli et al., 2015; Czernek, 2017) – take for example the complex science of climate change. The lack of immediacy and indirect experiences of these issues lead many SMTE owners to dismiss global environmental disputes as narrow scientific concerns (Buys et al., 2014). The authors also suggest an over-reliance on scientific models and expert judgment to explain particular phenomena. Buys et al. (2014) further suggest the use of experts engenders a deficit of understanding, proliferated by a misplaced assumption of knowledge in the audience. This chasm of knowledge between experts and intended audience evolves into antagonism, whereby lay knowledge sources are considered inferior. Thus, inertia follows and the management of sustainability in SMTEs stays bounded to the familiar rather than the unfamiliar (Sampaio et al., 2012).

The deteriorating transfer of knowledge between scientific institutions and the tourism sector also limits sustainable action in SMTEs (Campbell, 2011) and is compounded by SMTEs' limited resources and ability to create new sustainable knowledge, absorb and apply it (Garay et al., 2019; Russo & Perrini, 2010). Here, triadic constraints of time, finance and understanding are cited as barriers; indeed, Roux et al. (2006) emphasise this as *the* challenge of sustainable knowledge management.

Attempts have been made to explore these issues in SMTEs. For example, Garay et al. (2017) examined how SMTEs acquire sustainability information. Whilst the findings indicate a process, they fail to explore the mediating nature of tacit knowledge in absorptive capacity and environmental action. Building on Garay et al. (2017), Martínez-Martínez et al. (2018) asseverate knowledge agents as the conduit to updated environmental knowledge for competitive gain. Yet their study limits investigation into the level of sustainable understanding, acceptance and dissemination of environmental knowledge within other agents (employees). Theoretical insights to the barriers to pro-environmental knowledge transfer have also been explored by, for example Kornilaki et al. (2019), who applied aspects of Social Identity Theory to explain environmental behaviours in SMTEs. They found that environmental behaviours of SMTE owners are mediated by perceptions of efficacy and social acceptance. These findings confirm that effective tacit knowledge transfer is highly personal and takes place within social contexts (Boiral, 2002) such as "green committees" (Roux et al., 2006). Russo and Perrini (2010) refer to these committees as inter-stakeholder relationships; working across and between hierarchies, exploring environmental strategies and evaluating practices where knowledge transfer is less about process and more about social relationships.

Clearly then, the nexus between sustainability and knowledge is deeply rooted in personal experience, ideals, values and beliefs (Russo & Perrini, 2010). Arguably, levels of acceptance and understanding of pro-environmental knowledge are also mediated by these characteristics. In support, Holste and Fields (2010) argue that any future use of tacit knowledge depends upon the individual's affiliation and extent of positive relations with the organisation and its members.

Methodological approach

To ensure this conceptual paper adheres to academic rigour, we used Jaakkola's (2020) model-based research framework. First, this analytical approach required inspection of the contributory associations and mechanisms at play (Delbridge & Fiss, 2013). Secondly, we explored the literature to identify the novel connections between existing constructs (Brentani & Reid, 2012; Fiss, 2011), in this case trust-based knowledge transfer. Thirdly, we developed a conceptual model based on theoretical propositions to explain the relationships between constructs (MacInnis, 2011). Finally we debated the model to further understand the sequence of events that lead to an outcome (Jaakkola, 2020). Our position is derived from an examination and exploration of the relationship between pro-environmental knowledge, trust and tacit knowledge transfer set within the tourism context (Garay et al., 2019; Higuchi & Yamanaka, 2017; Yamagishi, 1986). However, we strongly support the contention that the advancement of further research in trust within the tourism sector necessitates firstly, returning to the theoretical conceptualisations of trust before situating them within a tourism specific context (Saunders et al., 2015). Secondly, we acknowledge cross-disciplinary insights are required to facilitate deductive reasoning (MacInnis, 2011).

To explicate the relationships between these existing constructs our conceptual model (Figure 1) offers a new theoretical lens based upon the fundamental position that tacit knowledge transfer in tourism networks necessitates interaction between two or more actors and that the outcome of such interaction is informed by the strength of relations between parties (Cooper, 2018;

Shaw, 2015). This focus complements the shift in scholarly research in the role of trust in tourism from a transactional to a relational perspective (Isaeva et al., 2020).

Fundamentally, trust is a psychological perception (Nunkoo & Gursoy, 2016) and the absence or presence of trust between SMTE actors has a direct influence on knowledge transfer behaviours (McTiernan et al., 2019). By emphasising the importance of the willingness to trust, our theoretical adaption builds on Van der Werff et al. (2019) position that trust is a self-regulatory process requiring active participation in pro-environmental behaviours. We also draw upon the psychological uncertainty of engaging in pro-environmental decision making (Roux et al., 2006; Russo & Perrini, 2010). In particular we consider Williams and Baláž's (2020) assertion that both cognitive and affective trust informs the behaviours of SMTE managers. Finally, we consider the socio-cognitive processes and social norms that lead SMTE managers to seek out, absorb and transform an organisation's pro-environmental tacit knowledge (Garay et al., 2017).

In summary, our model delineates the relationships, causal linkages and moderating conditions that impact the decision-making process and proposes an explanatory roadmap (Figure 1). The next section presents the context and integrates the aforementioned calls for further research.

Theoretical perspectives

Trust based decisions – exploring the knowledge transfer gap

As this paper focuses on the willingness of SMTE managers to make a trust-based decision, psychological and behavioural perspectives are considered. Specifically, we propose that the motivations and actions of individuals and organisations are based on their own beliefs, social norms, trust of knowledge sources and the strength of existing relationships impact the willingness to collaborate in pro-environmental knowledge transfer (Kornilaki et al., 2019; Nunkoo, 2017; Rousseau et al., 1998). Drawing on recommendations of Maak (2007), we place SMTE managers central to the advancement of a tacit knowledge transfer as studies note that SMTE managers' pro-environmental values have a direct influence on environmental sustainability in the sector (El Dief & Font, 2010; Han, 2015; Kornilaki & Font, 2019). Such trust facilitates the engagement with both internal and external stakeholders (Jang et al., 2017). Trusting relationships with external stakeholders allow responsible SMTE managers to consider the impact of their environmental actions on the broader community and consider these needs when formulating pro-environmental strategies (Epstein & Buhovac, 2014). Such relationships can be strengthened between partners who share integrity-based social norms promoting adherence to pro-environmental behaviours (Miller et al., 2010).

We prescribe that SMTE managers follow trust-based decisions that are conscious of external perceptions of their business's ethical values, and by extension, their trust in the organisation. These psychosocial conditions can directly influence external stakeholder's opinions of business behaviours and attitudes (Carroll & Buchholtz, 2008). Additionally, trust between responsible SMTE managers and internal stakeholders strengthens SMTE managers' ability to convince and motivate employees to recognise the importance of pro-environmental behaviours and adopt daily practices to achieve social and environmental goals (Alonso & Ogle, 2010). Cumulatively, these trust-based actions with internal and external stakeholders demonstrate altruistic, pro-environmental values which are pivotal to the perceptions of trustworthiness of the SMTE manager. Therefore, we suggest that the presence of such trusting relationships increases the willingness of SMTE managers to engage in pro-environmental knowledge transfer.

The nature of trust is contested by a variety of disciplines (Kelliher et al., 2018) and though many have attempted to develop a universal definition, no consensus is agreed (Molina-Morales et al., 2011; Nunkoo, 2017; Rousseau et al., 1998). Nevertheless, common phrases such as "willingness to be vulnerable" (Mayer et al., 1995) and "willingness to rely on another" (Doney et al., 1998) are often cited. At its core, trust is an expectation concerning the intentions and behaviours of others (Becerra et al., 2008). We purport that SMTE managers' willingness to trust others must be considered a lubricant to co-operation for mutual exchange. This resonates with the contention of Mayer et al. (1995) that trust is the willingness to be vulnerable to the behaviours and decisions of others. This willingness is a volitional act requiring the parties to be motivated, based on their cognitive processes, to risk exposing their vulnerabilities (Van der Werff et al., 2019). Importantly, this does not suggest that trust is a risk-taking behaviour, rather trust is the willingness to take a risk and such willingness to risk informs a SMTE manager's motivation to trust others in pro-environmental tacit knowledge transfer (McTiernan et al., 2019). Supporting this, Holste and Fields (2010) submit that a willingness to trust should be interpreted as a continuum; reflecting nuances naturally found in inter- and intra-personal relations. With this in mind, Van der Werff et al. (2019) study is noteworthy as it asserts that both the willingness and motivation to trust is a function of two variables of propensity to trust; 'trust goal setting' and 'trust regulation'. Based on intrinsic and extrinsic needs, the contextual decision to trust an actor is influenced by the motivations to expose vulnerabilities to the actor and their perceptions and experiences of the relationship in question: 'trust goal setting'. Once an actor achieves such trust motivation, the relationship will evolve based on 'trust regulation', the motivation and effort required to build and maintain such trust (Van der Werff et al., 2019). This suggests that the willingness and decision of SMTE managers to trust an actor in pro-environmental tacit knowledge transfer is both complicated and contextual as motivations are influenced by their personal values.

Notwithstanding, Gifford (2011) argues that trust is fragile and pro-environmental tacit knowledge transfer can be easily damaged if, for example, scientists exaggerate, or underestimate say, the impact of climate change. Supporting this perspective, Williams and Baláž (2020) contend that trust can act as a remedy to risk and uncertainty. Building on McKnight and Chervany's (2001) model of trust development in tourism, Williams and Baláž (2020) suggest that uncertainty directly informs SMTE managers' trust in institutions and indirectly counsels their beliefs and attitudes which cumulatively impact intentions and behaviours. The purpose of presenting these alternative perspectives is not to favour one over another. Rather, by doing so we consider the willingness of SMTE managers to make trust-based decisions from several outlooks. Collectively, the above perspectives emphasise the importance of personal values, motivations, attitudes and behaviours to pro-environmental measures and these, based on intrinsic and extrinsic motivations, are key influences in the decision to engage in pro-environmental knowledge transfer.

Thus, we return to positioning trust as both a psychological and behavioural phenomenon. This results in a two-fold challenge for SMTE managers engaging in pro-environmental tacit knowledge transfer. First, maintaining an equilibrium between these constructs, and second, applying this equilibrium to the complexities of sustainability knowledge and trust-based decisions. It is our proposition that trust intervenes in the decision to engage in pro-environmental tacit knowledge transfer in SMTEs. These decisions are made in conjunction with antecedents of trust – self-efficacy; social norms; credibility of knowledge source and social capital (see Figure 1). We see these as a combination of psycho-social elements, that is both context dependent and asynchronous. Arguably, maintaining and fostering these antecedents will minimise resistance to the transfer of pro-environmental knowledge. In extending the determinants of inter-organisational knowledge transfer to the management of psycho-social conditions of trust-based decisions, we argue that it is possible to better understand how SMTE managers receive, absorb and apply pro-environmental tacit knowledge. In the following section, each antecedent is examined and applied to the specific tourism context where nuanced barriers and enablers to tacit knowledge transfer in tourism are evident.

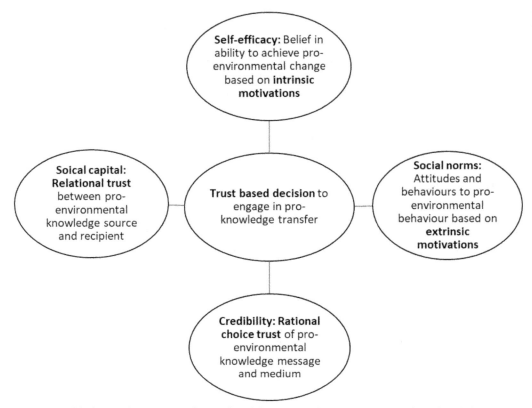

Figure 1. A model of antecedent conditions for trust-based decisions to adopt pro-environmental tacit knowledge.

Antecedents of trust

Self-efficacy: Belief in ability to achieve pro-environmental change based on intrinsic motivations

The model (Figure 1) highlights the blurring of personal and work values where SMTE managers not only desire to engage in pro-environmental behaviours but actively seek opportunities to access knowledge (Kim, 2020). To this end, self-efficacy is an important determinant in the adoption of pro-environmental behaviours (Kornilaki et al., 2019; Teng et al., 2018). In their study of pro-environmental behaviours in museums, Han (2015) suggests that self-efficacy is one of four cognitive factors that inform pro-environmental intentions, the other factors being environmental concern, environmental awareness and, importantly, pro-environmental knowledge. The literature also contends that self-efficacy, or the individual's belief that they can produce specific achievements (Chan et al., 2007) such as tacit knowledge transfer, acts as an enabler of a pro-environmental agenda (De Groot & Steg, 2009). Self-efficacy as a cognitive variable, coupled with a positive anticipated effect as an affective factor, not only increases the willingness of the SMTE manager to embrace pro-environmental knowledge, but we argue such an intrinsic motivation stimulates affect-based trust between potential knowledge transfer actors. Furthermore, as an antecedent of trust, we suggest self-efficacy inadvertently invokes genuine care and concern between partners and a belief in the intrinsic value of the relationship, reducing issues of trust in a transient workforce (Kelliher et al., 2018).

Bringing this back to pro-environmental policies, Steg et al. (2005) and Steg and Vlek (2009) suggest that actors' attitudes toward sustainable knowledge are determined by three factors. First, they must perceive the knowledge as acceptable to the group, reflecting conformity with personal norms. Second, sustainable knowledge must be deemed effective in achieving their remit (Eriksson et al., 2008), thus reinforcing collective efficacy in the network. Third, the individual's desire to reflect an environmental or sustainable social norm must be present (De Groot & Schuitema, 2012).

Building on these points, tourism research suggests that an individual's normative beliefs, motivations and attitudes toward pro-environmental behaviours can be deemed the decisive influence on their environmental behaviours, intentions and actions (Han, 2015). Jang et al. (2017) posit that SMTE managers with robust pro-environmental values are most likely to address internal environmental concerns, consider stakeholders' environmental interests and form ethically based relationships with similarly minded pro-environmental SMTE managers. Such desires and relationships can achieve the formulation of pro-environmental strategies (Black & Hartel, 2004). Though the creation of such strategies may seem aspirational for critics, researchers suggest that the sector is increasingly embracing the New Environmental Paradigm (NEP) (Dunlap et al., 2000). For example, Jang et al. (2017) suggest an emergence of SMTE managers committed to ensuring the sector engages in responsible environmental leadership practices. Studies also suggest that the adoption of such practices are based on two key antecedents: Firstly, the manager's personal, altruistic and eco-centric values (El Dief & Font, 2010); and secondly, the Value-Belief-Norm (VBN) theory of environmentalism. Here, Stern et al. (1999) contend that SMTE managers are increasingly developing their own pro-environmental values, often based on public opinions and social movements, which culminate in the development of a moral obligation to engage in pro-environmental actions.

Our view is that this sense of moral obligation develops and maintains attitudes and values that allow for the selective filtering of pro-environmental information and assists motivated, yet resource constrained, SMTE managers to select knowledge that appears consistent with their values. In doing so, we bring together findings from Kim (2020) whereby personal value constructs of SMTE managers inform the decision-making processes and that of Stern and Dietz (1994) whereby three value bases influence environmental based decisions: (i) Egoistic values predispose SMTE managers to protect those elements of the environment that positively affect them; (ii) Altruistic values suggest SMTE managers will engage with pro-environmental knowledge on the basis that they are both aware of the consequences of not acting and that they perceive a responsibility to act; and (iii) SMTE managers may make decisions based on biospheric values, often based on the NEP (Stern & Dietz, 1994). Cumulatively, such personal values are not only desirable to make SMTE managers pre-disposed to pro-environmental behaviours and knowledge, they can cognitively create abstract goals within the individual which ultimately can impact SMTE managers' actions (Roccas et al., 2002). We suggest engaging in pro-environmental knowledge transfer is one such action.

Empirical evidence to support this position includes the study by Upchurch and Ruhland (1996) which found that hotel managers who work, and are personally motivated to work, in ethical environments are inclined to seek appropriate knowledge to make pro-environmental decisions. This is furthered by Wenger et al. (2002) and Roux et al. (2006) who propose that the formation of independent groups founded on mutual self-interest facilitates tacit knowledge transfer via face-to-face interaction (socialisation). In support, self-categorisation theorists such as Brewer (1979) and Turner et al. (1987) argue social similarity, objectified by group conformity, can help institute personal norms. In turn, personal norms develop 'self-identification' and 'description of self by others' within a shared network. The reinforcing fashion of one's self, cultivates self-efficacy, and can strengthen a sense of trust towards the group. This utility can diminish the prevailing challenges associated with trust in the transient tourism workforce and enable such groups to quickly adapt to pro-environmental knowledge.

Based on the above we suggest that those SMTE managers who hold pro-social values and attitudes and who are infused by a moral obligation to pro-actively mitigate against the negative impacts of the sector, are intrinsically motivated to adopt pro-environmental knowledge.

Therefore, we build on Van der Werff et al. (2013) who highlight that intrinsic motivations to adopt pro-environmental behaviours are based not on external incentives but on the individual's environmental self-identity. This environmental self-identity, typically influenced by an internal desire to engage in environmentally friendly behaviours, creates an obligation-based intrinsic motivation.

Social norms: Attitudes and behaviour to environmental behaviour based on extrinsic motivations

While intrinsic motivations may enhance SMTE managers' willingness to engage in pro-environmental knowledge transfer, the model contends that extrinsic motivations are also influential. Extrinsic motivations differ from intrinsic motivations in that they refer to behaviours driven by external rewards.

We have applied Iorio et al.'s (2017) work to exemplify how extrinsic motivators promote a willingness to engage in pro-environmental tacit knowledge transfer. Based on their suggestion that extrinsic motivations to engage in pro-social behaviours can be monetary, learning and reputational (Iorio et al., 2017), it could be argued that SMTE managers with a desire to learn and develop a positive reputation within their professional network are motivated to engage in pro-environmental tacit knowledge transfer. Equally, we acknowledge that the model fails to ascertain if these are the only extrinsic motivations nor does it speculate on the weighted influence they exert on an SMTE's manager's motivations which can be predicated by pro-environmental social norms.

In this context, social norms create a social pressure to comply with pro-environmental policies (Cialdini et al., 2006) and this, in turn, increases the acceptability of the environmental policies (De Groot & Schuitema, 2012). We posit that conditions of social norms are determined by (i) mutual interest in and action to support sustainability (McAllister, 1995), and (ii) evidence of altruistic behaviour and good organisational citizenship as a prerequisite to engage in sustainable knowledge transfer (Zaheer et al., 1998). This proposition underlines the suggestion that relationships formed by individuals who are free to act independently are more likely to be deeper and more satisfying than those forced to partake in relationships by persons of authority, such as scientific experts or government agencies (Patrick et al., 2007). Equally relational-based affective trust and a freedom and willingness to act can only assist pro-environmental tacit knowledge transfer when the individual actors are intrinsically motivated and perceive social pressure to engage with SMTE network peers.

The potency of this social pressure is further influenced by people's expectations and perceptions of the effectiveness of the pro-environmental policies and ultimately these inform their acceptability (Eriksson et al., 2008). This is reinforced by Kornilaki and Font (2019) who maintain that sustainable (in)action is regulated by both a behavioural and moral framework that is determined by either social or industry comparisons. Equally, we acknowledge that pro-environmental social norms in tourism are difficult to determine as the sector is comprised of a wide population with multiple, often conflicting values. Noting this, Gifford (2011) reminds us that the challenge in achieving a trust-based pro-environmental collective remit within a self-interest group, occurs when one looks to adopt behaviours cognisant of the individual's needs, and sustainability values. This link between extrinsic motivations, social norms and the decision to engage in trust-based knowledge transfer was highlighted by Yamagishi (1986).

Yamagishi's (1986) research on goal acceptance suggests that strong pro-social norms can increase the likelihood that others will trust the pro-environmental policies and enhance the willingness of SMTE managers to participate in pro-environmental tacit knowledge transfer collaborations. Though extrinsic motivations can encourage adoption of acceptable pro-environmental behaviours, De Groot and Schuitema (2012) remind us that the 'pull' of intrinsic motivations to achieve environmental benefits is more coercive than the social 'push' to accept them. This suggests that where affect-based trust strengthens knowledge transfer collaborations between actors with similar intrinsic motivations (McAllister, 1995), extrinsic motivations trigger different indicators of inter-personal trust. In terms of the reputational benefits of engaging in pro-environmental tacit knowledge transfer, inter-personal trust can develop between parties when the trustor, or knowledge recipient, feels their work identity and reputation is somewhat defined by their ability to collaborate with peers (Weber et al., 2004). Yet to develop strong trust-based collaborative relationships with peers, SMTE managers must deem them to be credible sources of tacit knowledge.

Credibility: Rational choice trust of pro-environmental knowledge, message and medium
We contend that SMTE managers are best served by trusting knowledge sources based on rational choice. From their study of trust building in tourism networks, Kelliher et al. (2018) and Czernek and Czakon (2016) show that such a propensity to trust creates emotional bonds between individuals both at a cognitive and affective level. Cognitive trust is rooted in reasoning and logic (Heidari et al., 2014). Therefore SMTE managers should firstly choose credible sources of pro-environmental knowledge, and secondly, based on affective trust, the knowledge transfer partners develop a belief that emotional bonds between the parties will be enhanced through collaboration (McAllister, 1995). Such unity of practice is supported by Sharratt and Usoro (2003) and Bakker et al. (2006) who view trust as moderating the motivation to participate in knowledge transfer between trusted members of a network. Indeed, Du Plessis (2008) argues integrity-based trust formed through a network over time can fortify relational trust in social capital. We purport that credibility-based trust can be used in the absence of certainty (in this case pro-environmental knowledge) and where individuals need to make a 'leap of faith' (Nikolova et al., 2015) to engage in tacit pro-environmental knowledge transfer. As with all our antecedents, credibility behaves differently within different contexts. Importantly, we recognise that tacit knowledge transfer in tourism is further complicated by the fact that it constitutes the vast majority of desirable general knowledge resources (Scott et al., 2008), often induced by a transient and de-skilled workforce.

Drawing from notions of credibility, SMTE managers face two distinct barriers to pro-environmental tacit knowledge transfer. Firstly, environmental knowledge can often represent a technical narrative (Cainelli et al., 2015). For instance, sustainable and pro-environmental knowledge generally require organisations to master new knowledge, often linked to alternative production processes and systems which can require different inputs and technological solutions (Horbach et al., 2013). Acquiring such knowledge may emphasise technical ambiguity within SMTEs (De Marchi, 2012) and reinforce a lack of affective trust in such knowledge acquisition. Roux et al. (2006) suggests the credibility of scientists in the transfer of sustainable knowledge is dependent on the integrity of their message and the actor. Campbell (2011) found high trust of scientists in the transfer of sustainable messages was associated with perceptions of their competence, their reliability, their openness and perceptions that they cared. Conversely Buys et al. (2014) reports the perceived lack of integrity in government bodies is a key driver in responding to issues of climate change.

Returning to professional networks, (Hansen et al., 2011) conclude that any negative perceptions of sustainable sources can dilute trust in organisational networks and elucidate negative attitudes towards the organisation at large. Conversely, transparent and consistent social responsibility reinforces trust in all stakeholders. Given such change, SMTE managers may be required to firstly embrace new, and reconfigure existing, tacit knowledge stocks, and secondly introduce new, non-routine skills within their workforce (Barbieri et al., 2020).

The second contextual barrier, based on Czernek's (2017) study of collaborative knowledge transfer in the Polish tourism sector, is that SMTE managers can perceive such scientific knowledge as unnecessarily complicated and excessively sophisticated. This can result in managers choosing easily adopted solutions to pro-environmental challenges, yet such swift solutions may not address the core dilemma (Stamboulis & Skayannis, 2003). Given these contextual issues, SMTE managers are often required to engage in difficult knowledge sourcing efforts which may require new external knowledge providers (Ghisetti et al., 2015). Faced with such challenges, tourism practitioners could be advised to limit cooperation to credible knowledge sources only and Xiao and Smith (2007) suggest that credibility relates both to the quality of the knowledge available and the credibility of the knowledge source.

Social capital: Relational trust between pro-environmental knowledge source and recipient
The model considers SMTE managers' willingness to engage in pro-environmental tacit knowledge transfer based on levels of relational trust, which is directly influenced by the strength of social capital between potential partners. As pro-environmental tacit knowledge transfer requires two or more actors there is, naturally, a degree of social relationship in play.

There has been a marked increase in studies exploring the role of social capital and trust in knowledge transfer in the tourism literature (Liu, 2018). Tourism research suggests that trust is a facilitator of social capital development and acts as both an antecedent to, and outcome of, fruitful collaborations (Czernek & Czakon, 2016). Relational trust applies to specific partners where, within the dyad, trust follows a Bayesian-like process (Zaheer et al., 1998). Nunkoo (2017) affirms this, suggesting relational perspectives in SMTEs stimulate 'knowledge-based trust' over time. For example, through regular network interactions, tourism knowledge transfer partners' inter-personal and inter-organisational trust develops (Shaw, 2015). The resulting social capital facilitates the development of relational trust, a stronger bond between collaborators than calculus-based trust (Rousseau et al., 1998). Tourism researchers equally note that inter-organisational trust does not necessarily eliminate conflict, rather it facilitates the negotiation of conflict between partners and facilitates the return to conducive collaboration based on social capital between parties (Heidari et al., 2014; Williams & Baláž, 2020).

Applying the work of Rousseau et al. (1998) and Kramer (2009) we suggest these personal interactions utilise a range of psychological states, namely expectations and belief. These trust-based relations are assumed to be the magnet that attracts and binds networks together but equally, can be the repellent force. For Campbell (2011) and Supanti et al. (2014), misplaced trust can proliferate acceptance of (mis)information on issues of sustainability. The likelihood of misinformation in SMTEs is also highlighted by Russo and Perrini (2010), arguing that sustainable practices in SMTEs do not follow a typical Bayesian-like process, preferring personalised and localised perspectives.

Yet Kelliher et al.'s (2018) study of trust development in rural tourism networks notes that it is naïve to think that positive interactions alone build trust between individuals and organisations. Specifically, and of significance to our model, social capital based on relational trust is not as influential on a partner's willingness to trust as their prior experiences of collaboration, emotional standing and cognitive processes (Kelliher et al., 2018). Therefore, we acknowledge that while relational trust based on social capital can enhance pro-environmental tacit knowledge transfer partnership over time, SMTE managers' willingness to trust is based both on their expectations and their inherent propensity to trust. Equally, the model is conscious that SMTE managers' expectations and propensity to trust are not static. Social capital development between tourism partners can, again over time, alter expectations and such changes are typically based on developments in both emotional and cognitive experience (Heidari et al., 2014). Finally, SMTE managers' propensity to trust pro-environmental social partners can be positively and negatively impacted by the fact that trust is an evolving asset. Liu (2018) notes that, over time, trust-based social capital can encourage the creation, development and maturation of a relationship and generate mutually beneficial outcomes for partners based on shared understandings and learned practices. Equally, trust is a fragile resource in that when trust between parties is destroyed, it may never be repaired (Dovey, 2009). This implies that even the longest lasting, positive and mutually beneficial of pro-environmental knowledge exchange partnerships could cease based on a myriad of causes of relationship breakdowns.

Given such opposing perspectives, we suggest that pro-environmental tacit knowledge transfer based on relational trust may necessitate placing trust in specific partners without certainty of reciprocity. This underlines the importance of transparent governance of networks so all parties not only think that trust exists, but feel it too (Beesley, 2005). This underscores the findings of Russo and Perrini (2010), Cole (2015) and Font et al. (2016) in that any adoption of future sustainability-led interventions requires a reinforcement of relations to develop high levels of trust. In turn, this trust can exert influence on sustainable knowledge; determine application, evaluation and reporting of sustainable practices and enable pro-environmental behaviour change.

Conclusions and further research

This paper explores the sequence of SMTE managers' decision-making process to engage in pro-environmental tacit knowledge transfer (Delbridge & Fiss, 2013). It achieves this by drawing on literature from such diverse fields as tourism, sustainability, knowledge management, psychology and organisational behaviour to examine how the role of trust intervenes in the transfer of pro-environmental knowledge experienced by SMTE managers. We have drawn on this wide literature because the advancement of further research in trust within the tourism sector necessitates returning to theoretical conceptualisations of trust before situating them within a tourism specific context (Saunders et al., 2015). The paper argues that it is important to consider not only the trust of knowledge sources and the nature of the knowledge itself, but also the degree of trust that exists within SMTE networks and the personal and social relationships involved as they are important in fostering transfer. Of course, there has to be a willingness for SMTE managers to engage in the pro-environmental knowledge transfer process and the model presented considers the degree of risk-taking behaviour involved as this will either limit or foster adoption of pro-environmental behaviours based upon new knowledge received. Here, the analogy with networks is important as they represent purposeful and active groupings of organisations and individuals. Building on the tourism insights into trust-based co-operation in the sector (Czernek & Czakon, 2016; Kelliher et al., 2018), the conceptual model attempts to unpack SMTE managers' decision-making processes to engage in pro-environmental tacit knowledge transfer by collapsing the theoretical discussion into four sets of antecedents. Although based on a tourism perspective, we speculate that the model could be applicable in other fields.

We acknowledge this contribution to an emerging research agenda also presents avenues for future research. First, we have proposed that each antecedent be placed on a continuum, arguing each has a fluctuating asynchronous effect. In terms of this, there are gaps in our understanding on the extent of influence these antecedents have on trust-based decisions, and indeed, whether all four antecedents are required to enable such decisions. Ascertaining influence will confirm if such relationships exist between these antecedents and tacit knowledge transfer and help determine the underlying construct of the model; thus, supporting the call for theoretical constructs and scales drawn from tourism perspectives rather than allied to tourism setting (Han, 2015; Williams & Baláž, 2020).

Second, we have positioned these antecedents in a social context, reflecting the conditions of the operating constraints of the SMTEs and the nature of networks. Whilst the model takes account of these idiosyncrasies, it does not establish the level of impact these conditions have on the defining constructs of the model; or indeed, whether these antecedents can operate in isolation of such conditions. As such, determining the relationship between the social/industry conditions and antecedents of trust in SMTE's pro-environmental knowledge transfer will add to existing calls into situational normality (Williams & Baláž, 2020). Such studies would expand our understanding of how internal and external factors affect SMTE managers' willingness to trust at a local and broader social level (Kelliher et al., 2018).

Cumulatively there is considerable scope for evolving the model towards an ecological systems perspective; appreciating interdependent elements that form a holistic perspective (Musgrave & Woodward, 2016). In this sense we return to tacit knowledge transfer taking place within social contexts, reflecting inter-stakeholder relationships (Boiral, 2002; Roux et al., 2006; Russo & Perrini, 2010) and how internal/external factors effect methods of practice in SMTEs.

At numerous times this paper has alluded to a 'willingness to trust' and social capital evolving over time, implying a longitudinal approach. Whilst there are numerous research agenda that fit into such an approach (Nunkoo, 2017), we propose two: peer perception between tacit knowledge transfer partners and differences in pro-active and reactive SMTE managers. The first theme for future research focuses on the importance of peer perception between tacit knowledge transfer partners and how these evolve over time. Tourism studies have alluded to the importance of a perceived equality between trusted knowledge transfer partners, yet there is a dearth of empirical data to support this position (Hjalager, 2010; McTiernan et al., 2019). The second study could explore if the antecedent factors differ between pro-active and reactive SMTE managers over an extended period of study. Such research could determine if intrinsic motivations to seek opportunities to engage in pro-environmental behaviours differ from managers reacting to external changes such as modifications in customers' expectations of corporate social responsibility and developments in environmental legislation.

Disclosure statement

No potential conflict of interest was reported by the authors.

The authors declare that they have no relevant or material financial interests that relate to the research described in this paper.

References

Alonso, A. D., & Ogle, A. (2010). Tourism and hospitality small and medium enterprises and environmental sustainability. *Management Research Review*, 33(8), 818–826. https://doi.org/10.1108/01409171011065626

Bakker, M., Leenders, R., Gabbay, S., Kratzer, J., & Van Engelen, J. (2006). Is trust really social capital? Knowledge sharing in product development projects. *The Learning Organization*, 13(6), 594–605. https://doi.org/10.1108/09696470610705479

Barbieri, N., Marzucchi, A., & Rizzo, U. (2020). Knowledge sources and impacts on subsequent inventions: Do green technologies differ from non-green ones? *Research Policy*, 49(2), 103901. https://doi.org/10.1016/j.respol.2019.103901

Becerra, M., Lunnan, R., & Huemer, L. (2008). Trustworthiness, risk, and the transfer of tacit and explicit knowledge between alliance partners. *Journal of Management Studies*, 45(4), 691–713. https://doi.org/10.1111/j.1467-6486.2008.00766.x

Beesley, L. (2005). The management of emotion in collaborative tourism research settings. *Tourism Management*, 26(2), 261–275. https://doi.org/10.1016/j.tourman.2003.11.019

Black, L. D., & Hartel, C. E. J. (2004). The five capabilities of socially responsible companies. *Journal of Public Affairs*, 4(2), 125–144. https://doi.org/10.1002/pa.176

Boiral, O. (2002). Tacit knowledge and environmental management. *Long Range Planning*, 35(3), 291–317. https://doi.org/10.1016/S0024-6301(02)00047-X

Brentani, U., & Reid, S. E. (2012). The fuzzy front-end of discontinuous innovation: Insights for research and management. *Journal of Product Innovation Management*, 29(1), 70–87. https://doi.org/10.1111/j.1540-5885.2011.00879.x

Brewer, M. B. (1979). In-group bias in the minimal intergroup situation: A cognitive-motivational analysis. *Psychological Bulletin*, 86(2), 307–324. https://doi.org/10.1037/0033-2909.86.2.307

Buys, L., Mengersen, K., Johnson, S., van Buuren, N., & Chauvin, A. (2014). Creating a Sustainability Scorecard as a predictive tool for measuring the complex social, economic and environmental impacts of industries, a case study: Assessing the viability and sustainability of the dairy industry. *Journal of Environmental Management*, 133, 184–192. https://doi.org/10.1016/j.jenvman.2013.12.013

Cainelli, G., De Marchi, V., & Grandinetti, R. (2015). Does the development of environmental innovation require different resources? Evidence from Spanish manufacturing firms. *Journal of Cleaner Production*, 94, 211–220. https://doi.org/10.1016/j.jclepro.2015.02.008

Campbell, P. (2011). Understanding the receivers and the reception of science's uncertain messages. *Philosophical Transactions. Series A, Mathematical, Physical, and Engineering Sciences*, 369(1956), 4891–4912. https://doi.org/10.1098/rsta.2011.0068

Carroll, A., & Buchholtz, A. (2008). *Business & society: Ethics and stakeholder management* (7th ed.). South Western Educational Publishing.

Cavusgil, S. T., Calantone, R. J., & Zhao, Y. (2003). Tacit knowledge transfer and firm innovation capability. *Journal of Business & Industrial Marketing*, 18(1), 6–21. https://doi.org/10.1108/08858620310458615

Chan, H., Wan, L. C., & Sin, L. Y. M. (2007). Hospitality service failures: Who will be more dissatisfied? *International Journal of Hospitality Management*, 26(3), 531–545. https://doi.org/10.1016/j.ijhm.2006.02.004

Cialdini, R. B., Demaine, L. J., Sagarin, B. J., Barrett, D. W., Rhoads, K., & Winter, P. L. (2006). Managing social norms for persuasive impact. *Social Influence*, 1(1), 3–15. https://doi.org/10.1080/15534510500181459

Cohen, W. M., & Levinthal, D. A. (1990). Absorptive capacity: A new perspective on learning and innovation. *Administrative Science Quarterly*, 35(1), 128–152. https://doi.org/10.2307/2393553

Cole, D. H. (2015). Advantages of a polycentric approach to climate change policy. *Nature Climate Change*, 5(2), 114–118. https://doi.org/10.1038/nclimate2490

Cooper, C. (2015). Managing tourism knowledge. *Tourism Recreation Research*, 40(1), 107–119. https://doi.org/10.1080/02508281.2015.1006418

Cooper, C. (2018). Managing tourism knowledge: A review. *Tourism Review*, 73(4), 507–520. https://doi.org/10.1108/TR-06-2017-0104

Czakon, W., & Czernek, K. (2016). The role of trust-building mechanisms in entering into network coopetition: The case of tourism networks in Poland. *Industrial Marketing Management*, 57, 64–74. https://doi.org/10.1016/j.indmarman.2016.05.010

Czernek, K. (2017). Tourism features as determinants of knowledge transfer in the process of tourist cooperation. *Current Issues in Tourism*, 20(2), 204–220. https://doi.org/10.1080/13683500.2014.944107

Czernek, K., & Czakon, W. (2016). Trust-building processes in tourist coopetition: The case of a Polish region. *Tourism Management*, 52, 380–394. https://doi.org/10.1016/j.tourman.2015.07.009

De Groot, J. I. M., & Schuitema, G. (2012). How to make the unpopular popular? Policy characteristics, social norms and the acceptability of environmental policies. *Environmental Science & Policy*, 19–20, 100–107. https://doi.org/10.1016/j.envsci.2012.03.004

De Groot, J. I. M., & Steg, L. (2009). Morality and prosocial behavior: The role of awareness, responsibility, and norms in the norm activation model. *The Journal of Social Psychology, 149*(4), 425–449. https://doi.org/10.3200/SOCP.149.4.425-449

De Marchi, V. (2012). Environmental innovation and R&D cooperation: Empirical evidence from Spanish manufacturing firms. *Research Policy, 41*(3), 614–623. https://doi.org/10.1016/j.respol.2011.10.002

Del Chiappa, G., & Baggio, R. (2015). Knowledge transfer in smart tourism destinations: Analyzing the effects of a network structure. *Journal of Destination Marketing & Management, 4*(3), 145–150. https://doi.org/10.1016/j.jdmm.2015.02.001

Delbridge, R., & Fiss, P. C. (2013). Editors' comments: Styles of theorizing and the social organization of knowledge. *AMR, 38*, 325–331. https://doi.org/10.5465/amr.2013.0085

Doney, P., Cannon, J., & Mullen, M. (1998). Understanding the influence of national culture on the development of trust. *The Academy of Management Review, 23*(3), 601–620. https://doi.org/10.2307/259297

Dovey, K. (2009). The role of trust in innovation. *The Learning Organization, 16*(4), 311–325. https://doi.org/10.1108/09696470910960400

Du Plessis, M. (2008). The strategic drivers and objectives of communities of practice as vehicles for knowledge management in small and medium enterprises. *International Journal of Information Management, 28*(1), 61–67. https://doi.org/10.1016/j.ijinfomgt.2007.05.002

Dunlap, R. E., Liere, K. D. V., Mertig, A. G., & Jones, R. E. (2000). New trends in measuring environmental attitudes: Measuring endorsement of the new ecological paradigm: A revised NEP scale. *Journal of Social Issues, 56*(3), 425–442. https://doi.org/10.1111/0022-4537.00176

El Dief, M., & Font, X. (2010). The determinants of hotels' marketing managers' green marketing behaviour. *Journal of Sustainable Tourism, 18*(2), 157–174. https://doi.org/10.1080/09669580903464232

Epstein, M. J., & Buhovac, A. R. (2014). *Making sustainability work: Best practices in managing and measuring corporate social, environmental, and economic impacts.* Berrett-Koehler Publishers.

Eriksson, L., Garvill, J., & Nordlund, A. M. (2008). Acceptability of single and combined transport policy measures: The importance of environmental and policy specific beliefs. *Transportation Research Part A: Policy and Practice, 42*(8), 1117–1128. https://doi.org/10.1016/j.tra.2008.03.006

Fiss, P. C. (2011). Building better causal theories: A fuzzy set approach to typologies in organization research. *Academy of Management Journal, 54*(2), 393–420. https://doi.org/10.5465/amj.2011.60263120

Font, X., Garay, L., & Jones, S. (2016). Sustainability motivations and practices in small tourism enterprises in European protected areas. *Journal of Cleaner Production, 137*, 1439–1448. https://doi.org/10.1016/j.jclepro.2014.01.071

Garay, L., Font, X., & Corrons, A. (2019). Sustainability-oriented innovation in tourism: An analysis based on the decomposed theory of planned behavior. *Journal of Travel Research, 58*(4), 622–636. https://doi.org/10.1177/0047287518771215

Garay, L., Font, X., & Pereira-Moliner, J. (2017). Understanding sustainability behaviour: The relationship between information acquisition, proactivity and performance. *Tourism Management, 60*, 418–429. https://doi.org/10.1016/j.tourman.2016.12.017

Ghisetti, C., Marzucchi, A., & Montresor, S. (2015). The open eco-innovation mode. An empirical investigation of eleven European countries. *Research Policy, 44*(5), 1080–1093. https://doi.org/10.1016/j.respol.2014.12.001

Gifford, R. (2011). The dragons of inaction: Psychological barriers that limit climate change mitigation and adaptation. *The American Psychologist, 66*(4), 290–302. https://doi.org/10.1037/a0023566

Han, H. (2015). Travelers' pro-environmental behavior in a green lodging context: Converging value-belief-norm theory and the theory of planned behavior. *Tourism Management, 47*, 164–177. https://doi.org/10.1016/j.tourman.2014.09.014

Hansen, S. D., Dunford, B. B., Boss, A. D., Boss, R. W., & Angermeier, I. (2011). Corporate social responsibility and the benefits of employee trust: A cross-disciplinary perspective. *Journal of Business Ethics, 102*(1), 29–45. https://doi.org/10.1007/s10551-011-0903-0

Heidari, M., Najafipour, A., Farzan, S., & Pavaresh, S. (2014). The fundamental distinctive applications of networks in the tourism industry: A useful mechanism for trust. *Academic Research in Economics and Management Services, 3*, 263–285.

Higuchi, Y., & Yamanaka, Y. (2017). Knowledge sharing between academic researchers and tourism practitioners: A Japanese study of the practical value of embeddedness, trust and co-creation. *Journal of Sustainable Tourism, 25*(10), 1456–1473. https://doi.org/10.1080/09669582.2017.1288733

Hjalager, A.-M. (2010). A review of innovation research in tourism. *Tourism Management, 31*(1), 1–12. https://doi.org/10.1016/j.tourman.2009.08.012

Holste, J. S., & Fields, D. (2010). Trust and tacit knowledge sharing and use. *Journal of Knowledge Management, 14*(1), 128–140. https://doi.org/10.1108/13673271011015615

Horbach, J., Oltra, V., & Belin, J. (2013). Determinants and specificities of eco-innovations compared to other innovations—An econometric analysis for the French and German industry based on the community innovation survey. *Industry & Innovation, 20*(6), 523–543. https://doi.org/10.1080/13662716.2013.833375

Iorio, R., Labory, S., & Rentocchini, F. (2017). The importance of pro-social behaviour for the breadth and depth of knowledge transfer activities: An analysis of Italian academic scientists. *Research Policy, 46*(2), 497–509. https://doi.org/10.1016/j.respol.2016.12.003

Isaeva, N., Gruenewald, K., & Saunders, M. N. K. (2020). Trust theory and customer services research: Theoretical review and synthesis. *The Service Industries Journal, 40*(15–16), 1031–1063. https://doi.org/10.1080/02642069.2020.1779225

Jaakkola, E. (2020). Designing conceptual articles: Four approaches. *AMS Review, 10*(1–2), 18–26. https://doi.org/10.1007/s13162-020-00161-0

Jang, Y. J., Zheng, T., & Bosselman, R. (2017). Top managers' environmental values, leadership, and stakeholder engagement in promoting environmental sustainability in the restaurant industry. *International Journal of Hospitality Management, 63*, 101–111. https://doi.org/10.1016/j.ijhm.2017.03.005

Juvan, E., & Dolnicar, S. (2017). Drivers of pro-environmental tourist behaviours are not universal. *Journal of Cleaner Production, 166*, 879–890. https://doi.org/10.1016/j.jclepro.2017.08.087

Kelliher, F., Reinl, L., Johnson, T. G., & Joppe, M. (2018). The role of trust in building rural tourism micro firm network engagement: A multi-case study. *Tourism Management, 68*, 1–12. https://doi.org/10.1016/j.tourman.2018.02.014

Kim, M. (2020). A systematic literature review of the personal value orientation construct in hospitality and tourism literature. *International Journal of Hospitality Management, 89*, 102572. https://doi.org/10.1016/j.ijhm.2020.102572

Kim, M.-S., & Stepchenkova, S. (2020). Altruistic values and environmental knowledge as triggers of pro-environmental behavior among tourists. *Current Issues in Tourism, 23*(13), 1575–1580. https://doi.org/10.1080/13683500.2019.1628188

Kornilaki, M., & Font, X. (2019). Normative influences: How socio-cultural and industrial norms influence the adoption of sustainability practices. A grounded theory of Cretan, small tourism firms. *Journal of Environmental Management, 230*, 183–189. https://doi.org/10.1016/j.jenvman.2018.09.064

Kornilaki, M., Thomas, R., & Font, X. (2019). The sustainability behaviour of small firms in tourism: The role of self-efficacy and contextual constraints. *Journal of Sustainable Tourism, 27*(1), 97–117. https://doi.org/10.1080/09669582.2018.1561706

Kramer, R. (2009). Rethinking trust. *Harvard Business Review, 87*(6), 68–77.

Liu, C.-H. S. (2018). Examining social capital, organizational learning and knowledge transfer in cultural and creative industries of practice. *Tourism Management, 64*, 258–270. https://doi.org/10.1016/j.tourman.2017.09.001

Maak, T. (2007). Responsible leadership, stakeholder engagement, and the emergence of social capital. *Journal of Business Ethics, 74*(4), 329–343. https://doi.org/10.1007/s10551-007-9510-5

MacInnis, D. J. (2011). A framework for conceptual contributions in marketing. *Journal of Marketing, 75*(4), 136–154. https://doi.org/10.1509/jmkg.75.4.136

Martínez-Martínez, A., Zumel-Jiménez, C., & Cegarra-Navarro, J.-G. (2018). A theoretical framework for key processes on environmental knowledge management. *Anatolia, 29*(4), 605–613. https://doi.org/10.1080/13032917.2018.1519180

Mayer, R. C., Davis, J. H., & Schoorman, F. D. (1995). An integrative model of organizational trust. *Academy of Management Review, 20*(3), 709–734. https://doi.org/10.5465/amr.1995.9508080335

McAllister, D. (1995). Affect and cognition trust as foundations for interpersonal cooperation in organisations. *Academy of Management Journal, 38*(1), 24–59. https://doi.org/10.2307/256727

McKnight, H.D., Chervany, N.L., Trust and Distrust Definitions: One Bite at a Time , Trust in Cyber-Societies, Lecture Notes in Computer Science, Falcone, R., Singh, M., Tan, Y.H., Springer, Berlin, 2001, 27, 54,

McTiernan, C., Thomas, R., & Jameson, S. (2019). Focusing on knowledge exchange: The role of trust in tourism networks. In E. Fayos-Solà & C. Cooper (Eds.), *The future of tourism: Innovation and sustainability* (pp. 301–314). Springer International Publishing. https://doi.org/10.1007/978-3-319-89941-1_16

Miller, G., Rathouse, K., Scarles, C., Holmes, K., & Tribe, J. (2010). Public understanding of sustainable tourism. *Annals of Tourism Research, 37*(3), 627–645. https://doi.org/10.1016/j.annals.2009.12.002

Molina-Morales, F., Martinez-Fernandez, M., & Torlo, V. (2011). The dark side of Trust: The benefits, costs and optimal levels of trust for innovation performance. *Long Range Planning, 44*, 118–133.

Musgrave, J., & Woodward, S. (2016). Ecological systems theory approach to corporate social responsibility: Contextual perspectives from meeting planners. *Event Management, 20*(3), 365–381. https://doi.org/10.3727/152599516X14682560744712

Nahapiet, J., & Ghoshal, S. (1998). Social capital, intellectual capital and organisational advantage. *The Academy of Management Review, 23*(2), 242–266. https://doi.org/10.2307/259373

Nikolova, N., Möllering, G., & Reihlen, M. (2015). Trusting as a 'leap of faith': Trust-building practices in client–consultant relationships. *Scandinavian Journal of Management, 31*(2), 232–245. https://doi.org/10.1016/j.scaman.2014.09.007

Nonaka, I., & Takeuchi, H. (1995). *The knowledge creating company* (1st ed.). Oxford University Press.

Nunkoo, R. (2017). Governance and sustainable tourism: What is the role of trust, power and social capital? *Journal of Destination Marketing & Management, 6*(4), 277–285. https://doi.org/10.1016/j.jdmm.2017.10.003

Nunkoo, R., & Gursoy, D. (2016). Rethinking the role of power and trust in tourism planning. *Journal of Hospitality Marketing & Management, 25*(4), 512–522. https://doi.org/10.1080/19368623.2015.1019170

Nunkoo, R., & Gursoy, D. (2017). Political trust and residents' support for alternative and mass tourism: An improved structural model. *Tourism Geographies, 19*(3), 318–339. https://doi.org/10.1080/14616688.2016.1196239

Patrick, H., Knee, C., Canevello, A., & Lonsbary, C. (2007). The role of need fulfillment in relationship functioning and well-being: A self-determination theory perspective. *Journal of Personality and Social Psychology, 92*(3), 434–457. https://doi.org/10.1037/0022-3514.92.3.434

Reagans, R., & McEvily, B. (2003). Network structure and knowledge transfer: The effects of cohesion and range. *Administrative Science Quarterly, 48*(2), 240–267. https://doi.org/10.2307/3556658

Roccas, S., Sagiv, L., Schwartz, S. H., & Knafo, A. (2002). The Big Five personality factors and personal values. *Personality and Social Psychology Bulletin, 28*(6), 789–801. https://doi.org/10.1177/0146167202289008

Rousseau, D., Sitkin, S., Burt, R., & Camerer, C. (1998). Not so different after all: A cross discipline view of trust. *Academy of Management Review, 23*(3), 393–404. https://doi.org/10.5465/amr.1998.926617

Roux, D. J., Rogers, K. H., Biggs, H. C., Ashton, P. J., & Sergeant, A. (2006). Bridging the science–management divide: Moving from unidirectional knowledge transfer to knowledge interfacing and sharing. *Ecology and Society, 11*(1), 20. https://doi.org/10.5751/ES-01643-110104

Russo, A., & Perrini, F. (2010). Investigating stakeholder Theory and social capital: CSR in large firms and SMEs. *Journal of Business Ethics, 91*(2), 207–221. https://doi.org/10.1007/s10551-009-0079-z

Sampaio, A. R., Thomas, R., & Font, X. (2012). Small business management and environmental engagement. *Journal of Sustainable Tourism, 20*(2), 179–193. https://doi.org/10.1080/09669582.2011.602193

Saunders, M., Lyon, F., & Mollering, G. (2015). Researching trust in. tourism: Methodological issues and associated concerns. In R. Nunkoo & L. Smith (Eds.), *Trust, development and planning* (pp. 168–179). Routledge.

Scott, N., Baggio, R., & Cooper, P. C. (2008). *Network analysis and tourism: From theory to practice*. Channel View Publications.

Sharratt, M., & Usoro, A. (2003). Understanding knowledge-sharing in online communities of practice. *Electronic Journal of Knowledge Management, 1*, 18–27.

Shaw, G. (2015). Tourism networks, knowledge dynamics and co-creation. In M. McLeod & R. Vaughan (Eds.), *Knowledge networks and tourism* (pp. 45–61). London.

Singh, S. K., Gupta, S., Busso, D., & Kamboj, S. (2021). Top management knowledge value, knowledge sharing practices, open innovation and organizational performance. *Journal of Business Research, 128*, 788–798. https://doi.org/10.1016/j.jbusres.2019.04.040

Stamboulis, Y., & Skayannis, P. (2003). Innovation strategies and technology for experience-based tourism. *Tourism Management, 24*(1), 35–43. https://doi.org/10.1016/S0261-5177(02)00047-X

Steg, L., Dreijerink, L., & Abrahamse, W. (2005). Factors influencing the acceptability of energy policies: A test of VBN theory. *Journal of Environmental Psychology, 25*(4), 415–425. https://doi.org/10.1016/j.jenvp.2005.08.003

Steg, L., & Vlek, C. (2009). Encouraging pro-environmental behaviour: An integrative review and research agenda. *Journal of Environmental Psychology, 29*(3), 309–317. https://doi.org/10.1016/j.jenvp.2008.10.004

Stern, P. C., Dietz, T., Abel, T., Guagnano, G. A., & Kalof, L. (1999). A Value-Belief-Norm Theory of Support for Social Movements: The Case of Environmentalism. *Human Ecology Review, 6*, 81–97.

Stern, P. C., & Dietz, T. (1994). The value basis of environmental concern. *Journal of Social Issues, 50*(3), 65–84. https://doi.org/10.1111/j.1540-4560.1994.tb02420.x

Sun, J., Yang, Y., & de Jong, A. (2020). A geographical approach to trust in tourism. *Tourism Geographies, 22*(4–5), 768–786. https://doi.org/10.1080/14616688.2019.1652337

Supanti, D., Butcher, K., & Fredline, L. (2014). Understanding managers' engagement with corporate social responsibility (CSR) in the Thai hotel sector. [WWW Document]. *Proceedings of the International Association for Business and Society*. https://doi.org/10.5840/iabsproc20142512

Teng, C.-C., Lu, A. C. C., & Huang, T.-T. (2018). Drivers of consumers' behavioral intention toward green hotels. *International Journal of Contemporary Hospitality Management, 30*(2), 1134–1151. https://doi.org/10.1108/IJCHM-04-2017-0203

Thomas, R., & Wood, E. (2014). Innovation in tourism: Reconceptualising and measuring the absorptive capacity of the hotel sector. *Tourism Management, 45*, 39–48. https://doi.org/10.1016/j.tourman.2014.03.012

Turner, J. C., Hogg, M. A., Oakes, P. J., Reicher, S. D., & Wetherell, M. S. (1987). *Rediscovering the social group: A self-categorization theory, Rediscovering the social group: A self-categorization theory*. Basil Blackwell.

Upchurch, R. S., & Ruhland, S. K. (1996). The organizational bases of ethical work climates in lodging operations as perceived by general managers. *Journal of Business Ethics, 15*(10), 1083–1093. https://doi.org/10.1007/BF00412049

Van der Werff, L., Legood, A., Buckley, F., Weibel, A., & de Cremer, D. (2019). Trust motivation: The self-regulatory processes underlying trust decisions. *Organizational Psychology Review, 9*(2–3), 99–123. https://doi.org/10.1177/2041386619873616

Van der Werff, E., Steg, L., & Keizer, K. (2013). The value of environmental self-identity: The relationship between biospheric values, environmental self-identity and environmental preferences, intentions and behaviour. *Journal of Environmental Psychology, 34*, 55–63. https://doi.org/10.1016/j.jenvp.2012.12.006

Weber, J. M., Malhotra, D., & Murnighan, J. K. (2004). Normal acts of irrational trust: Motivated attributions and the trust development process. *Research in Organizational Behavior, 26*, 75–101. https://doi.org/10.1016/S0191-3085(04)26003-8

Wenger, E., McDermott, R. A., & Snyder, W. (2002). *Cultivating Communities of Practice: A Guide to Managing Knowledge*. Harvard Business Press.

Williams, A. M., & Baláž, V. (2020). Tourism and trust: Theoretical reflections. *Journal of Travel Research*, 1–16. https://doi.org/10.1177/0047287520961177

Xiao, H., & Smith, S. L. J. (2007). The use of tourism knowledge: Research propositions. *Annals of Tourism Research, 34*(2), 310–331. https://doi.org/10.1016/j.annals.2006.09.001

Yamagishi, T. (1986). The provision of a sanctioning system as a public good. *Journal of Personality and Social Psychology, 51*(1), 110–116. https://doi.org/10.1037//0022-3514.51.1.110

Zach, F. J., & Hill, T. L. (2017). Network, knowledge and relationship impacts on innovation in tourism destinations. *Tourism Management, 62*, 196–207. https://doi.org/10.1016/j.tourman.2017.04.001

Zaheer, A., McEvily, B., & Perrone, V. (1998). Does trust matter? Exploring the effects of interorganizational and interpersonal trust on performance. *Organization Science, 9*(2), 141–159. https://doi.org/10.1287/orsc.9.2.141

Systems thinking to facilitate "double loop" learning in tourism industry: a COVID-19 response strategy

Ayham A. M. Jaaron, Duong Thuy Pham and Marielyn Espiridion Cogonon

ABSTRACT
It is evident there is an urgent need for tourism companies to build highly responsive learning systems to adapt to COVID-19 threats and beyond. As such, only learning tourism companies that promote inquiry, challenging current actions, and departing away from adopted assumptions will be able to survive. However, there is paucity of studies exploring effective learning methods in tourism companies to adapt to unpredictable crisis consequences. This study argues that systems thinking approach for service delivery design can operationalize double loop learning in tourism companies of finding alternative service offerings. An exploratory case study was conducted in a leading cruise group company in Vietnam. Results show that systems thinking activated double-loop learning by promoting three different drivers: systematic judges and acts, problem-based task force teams, and service innovation. This paper theorizes systems thinking with double-loop learning as an organizational means to help tourism companies survive during COVID-19 global tragedy, and to transform their service offerings. It also extends current understanding of tourism companies' organisational learning by incorporating double loop learning with structural design issues based on the lens of organic structures and introduces managers of tourism companies to the significance of organic structures for competitive advantage creation during crisis.

Introduction

The outbreak of COVID-19 pandemic in early 2020 has had a catastrophic impact on the tourism industry worldwide (Conde Nast Traveller, 2020; Gössling et al., 2021). The pandemic scale and its projected impact on global economy also means that it poses major threats towards attaining the UN's 17 Sustainable Development Goals (SDGs) (Filho et al., 2020; Nhamo et al., 2020). According to G20 (Group of Twenty Countries) (2019), tourism sector plays a major role in the attainment of four SDGs, namely, decent work and economic growth (SDG8), responsible consumption and production (SDG12), life below water-blue/ocean economy (SDG14), and partnerships (SDG17). As it remains fundamentally unclear when things will go back to normal, tourism companies will not survive an extended period of lack of liquidity (Hoque et al., 2020;

Ranasinghe et al., 2020). Thus, aims towards those four SDGs face considerable setbacks due to COVID-19. It is, then, evident that COVID-19 will be transformative for the tourism industry if these SDGs are to be achieved (Nhamo et al., 2020). According to Quang et al. (2020), the COVID-19 crisis should be a catalyst for restructuring the tourism industry markets and offerings through continuous learning processes. Therefore, there is an urgent need for tourism companies to build highly responsive learning systems to fundamentally change their existing operations to adapt to threats and stressors of COVID-19 and beyond. Blackman and Ritchie (2008) explained that tourism companies faced with external crises, such as COVID-19, should adopt a learning method that allows for promoting inquiry, challenging current actions, and departing away from adopted assumptions. According to the authors, this type of learning, also known as double loop learning, is pivotal to achieving new insights that can stimulate innovative adaptation to crisis demands. Argyris and Schön (1996) defined "double loop" learning as that type of inquiry where existing business processes and operations are changed based on realities and identifying opportunities. Therefore, building double loop learning requires system-wide thinking to facilitate profound shifts in business offerings (Jaaron & Backhouse, 2017; Kraleva, 2011). However, if tourism companies are to successfully adopt double loop learning as their strategy to survive during COVID-19 and beyond, they need to create new operational models that will operationalize adaptation of their current offerings.

Although various earlier work discussed the adoption of learning approaches in tourism management literature (e.g., Ali et al., 2020; Bayraktaroglu & Kutanis, 2003; Bernsen et al., 2009; Božič & Cvelbar, 2016; Liu, 2018), there is a paucity of studies that have linked double loop learning with tourism industry performance and evolution capabilities. According to Ghaderi et al. (2014), the lack of empirical studies investigating double loop learning at different stages of tourism crisis management is due to the absence of integrative models of learning that can encourage system-wide knowledge creation. Much of the reasoning for the need for double loop learning during COVID-19 crisis and beyond emanates from the fact that current tourism management systems do not have effective tools to adapt to unpredictable crisis consequences (Khoshkhoo & Nadalipour, 2016). Second, responding to the vulnerability of the tourism industry (Kwok & Koh, 2020), double loop learning through a system approach provides tourism companies with opportunities to unfold new business opportunities (Jaaron & Backhouse, 2017). This was discerned by Stone and Nyaupane (2018) who found that systems thinking activates adaptive learning mechanisms in tourism businesses that can deliver more long-term sustainable solutions than the traditional "cause and effects" initiatives. A central tenet in systems thinking approach is its ability to provide an organizational structure that views the organization as a whole (Jaaron & Backhouse, 2014; Jackson et al., 2008). This guarantees interconnectedness of employees through open channels of interactions and social exchange, both within their teams and with other teams in other organizational parts (Seddon, 2008). Moreover, systems thinking approach is centered on the core element of dynamics of the organization that requires a great deal of coordination and power delegation to employees at all levels. According to Heslinga et al. (2017), it is systems thinking application in tourism companies that facilitates inter-functional coordination, decentralizes decision making, and, in turn, fuels operational adaptations necessary for quick response to environment volatility. Such realization warrants the need for this study.

Given the dearth of research on double loop learning and its connection with systems thinking application in tourism literature, this study aims to examine the impact of applying systems thinking approach for service operations design on operationalizing double loop learning in tourism companies amidst the COVID-19 crisis. This research inquiry uses a qualitative case study approach. The case study was conducted in a leading cruise group company in Vietnam. The company organizes private tours throughout the UNESCO's recognized World Heritage Ha Long Bay – Lan Ha Bay in Quang Ninh Province of Vietnam. The Vietnamese case was selected as the economic impact of the pandemic has been tremendous for tourism companies. In fact, Vietnamese tourism industry was the most affected industry in the country after the collapse of international travellers (Quang et al., 2020; Vietnam Tourism, 2020). The study contributes by theorizing systems thinking application with double loop learning in tourism management literature for the first time, thus, offering new insights on how transformation of tourism companies can be achieved for their survival and better sustainable performance. Therefore, this study provides a new dimension on how tourism companies should address shortfalls in their contribution to sustainable economic growth within the COVID-19 pandemic (i.e., the scope of SDG8). Also, the study provides a critical view on operational and employee's behavioural changes associated with double loop learning realization. In addition, this research explores the offerings of Seddon's (2003, 2008) systems thinking approach for operations design in the tourism industry context for the first time. Furthermore, the paper highlights the characteristics of an organic structure brought about by the systems thinking approach necessary for learning acquisition and sharing in tourism companies. The paper begins by providing the theoretical background, outlining the concepts of systems thinking including its associated organic structure, and the concept of "double loop" learning. Next, the case study methodology followed is explained with details about the case study company. Results are then reported based on data analysis from in-depth interviews and internal business documents. The paper is concluded by presenting a discussion of results and implications for theory and practice along with research limitations and suggestions for future research.

The systems thinking and tourism companies

Tourism companies are widely described as open, complex, and dynamic systems that are composed of interconnected parts dependent on each other to execute tourism operations (Rodriguez-Giron & Vanneste, 2019; Van Mai & Bosch, 2010). This would imply that tourism companies should be managed as a holistic entity to allow the necessary interaction between parts (Roxas et al., 2020). As posited by Gregory (2007), reductionist approach of separately managed standalone parts can inhibit dynamic ability of the organization and can harm organizational responsiveness to environment demands. Within this view, Comfort et al. (2001) asserted that interconnectedness of organizational parts activates team members' interactions and social exchange. This was supported by the work of Sollund (2006) who suggested that equipping workplace with cross-department coordination, power delegation, and free channel of communication provides tourism and hospitality companies with recovery ability during challenging events. This conceptualization gave rise to the concept of systems thinking in tourism literature (Ropret et al., 2014; Roxas et al., 2020).

Systems thinking is defined as a holistic approach to evaluate and analyze the interrelation of a system's integral parts. It allows an organization to connect its components and improve the service it delivers to clients (Jackson et al., 2008). Pham and Jaaron (2018) asserted that it is of importance to the leader of the organization to comprehend his or her organization as a system. However, since the term was coined, a reasonable number of researchers have attested its authentic elucidation in the tourism industry at a macro-level. For example, Mai and Smith (2015) investigated the links between systems thinking approach and tourism development in Vietnam to identify underlying system structures that can influence sustainability. Similarly, Stone and Nyaupane (2018), through a systems-thinking lens, studied whether wildlife tourism introduction in Botswana can lead to local community development outcomes. Peric and Djurkin (2014) developed an innovative community-based tourism business-model using systems thinking principles that aimed at serving local community needs. However, there is paucity of previous research in tourism literature that investigates the offerings of systems thinking at the organisational level.

Seddon's (2003, 2008) interpretation of systems thinking and its focus on the world of service industry generates an initiative and definition that is the most suitable view and approach for

Table 1. Principles of systems-thinking.

Comparative dimension	Command and control thinking (mechanistic)	Systems-thinking (organic)
Perspective	Top-down, hierarchy	Outside-in, system
Design of work	Functional specialization	Demand, value and flow
Decision making	Separated from work	Integrated with work
Measurement	Output, targets, standards: related to budget	Capability, variation: related to purpose
Attitude to customers	Contractual	What matters?
Attitude to suppliers	Contractual	Co-operative
Role of management	Manage people and budgets	Act on the system
Ethos	Control	learning
Change	Reactive, projects	Adaptive, integral
Motivation	Extrinsic	Intrinsic

Source: Seddon (2003).

the execution of this research paper. Jaaron and Backhouse (2017) asserted that Seddon's (2003, 2008) systems thinking approach has the best potential of ameliorating an organization through hard times. This approach offers the service industry the liberty to transfer from "command and control" design to "systems" design (Jackson et al., 2008; Seddon, 2008) as it gives better structure of analysis essential for an in-depth understanding of the organization. Table 1 conveys an intrinsic break-down of organic and mechanistic structures for a point of comparison analysis.

A service-delivery system grounded from the principles of systems-thinking is expressed into actions through the application of Seddon's (2003) three stages: check – plan – do. The stage "Check" provides an understanding of the system as it is and identifies what the purpose of the system is from the customers' point of view. This is usually done through a process of customers demand analysis. A flow chart is then prepared for each service operation to identify sources of waste that potentially blocking delivery of what the customers want. This stage usually shows managers and staff the failings of their system and provides an evidence for the need to alter their current operations. However, the stage "Plan" explores possible solutions to mitigate waste production to scout a better flow design of operation against customer demand. From "Check" stage, an improvement of the flow of work through service operation to mitigate wasteful activities from the customer's perspective is gained. Correspondingly, measures of performance for the newly designed operations to calculate the improvement once administered will occur; this process can commence value demands and reduce or prevent failure demand. The stage "Do" calls for the execution of the solutions provided by the experimentation done in the "Plan" stage, whereby the assessment of the newly designed service operations and improvements is monitored. A cautious observation of both employees' reaction and customer feedback to the implementation are reviewed continuously. The repetition of the process of redesigning and retesting the new service operation to ensure the maximum value from the expected service might be administered, as necessary.

Finally, after the "systems picture" and "logic picture" of the service organization is established in the "Check" step, the amelioration points of "Plan" and "Do" steps are initiated. Under the supervision of organizational sponsors and consultants, a reevaluation of the systems' purpose, and the principles of the reconstruction with the aim of achieving its new purpose, from customer's perspective, occur in "Plan" stage. "Do" stage is a straightforward action on the system, releases capacity, integrates and engrains new processes. The notion that "Check – Plan – Do" is a never-ending cycle to foster sustainable improvement must be considered.

Systems thinking and organic structure

Jackson et al. (2008) and Jaaron and Backhouse (2014) asserted that systems thinking has the propensity of providing an organizational structure that views and analyzes the organization as a whole. The provision of this viewpoint generates a free flow of interactions and social exchange of employees as it caters an open channel of interconnection from within their teams and with other teams that comprises the organization (Seddon, 2008). This underlying idea of systems thinking was confirmed to spawn a development of an organically structured tourism company (Kraleva, 2011). Defined as a non-custom sort of working pattern, organic structure initiates a high degree of individual authority, as well as power, at the lower levels of the tourism company (Ramezan, 2011). Therefore, organic structure insinuates a great deal of employee decision making authority, fundamentally practiced in systems thinking organizations, to allow flexibility and initiate quick response to unpredictable external environment circumstances (Pham & Jaaron, 2018). This implies that team members can practice informality in approaching a colleague as personal relationships spawn a vital aspect for the learning organization life (Bhat et al., 2012). In fact, the presence of non-barrier working environment results in an easier communication between departments. This entails the smooth flow of information needed to solve a problem.

These virtues of the organic structures were found quite useful for enhancing intellectual capital of organizations, which is defined as knowledge capabilities that can be used by organizations to create competitive advantages (Ramezan, 2011). Zaragoza-Sáez et al. (2020), in their study of strategic management impact on hotel performance, reported that intellectual capital has three main components. First, human capital which reflects the ability of employees to generate tacit and/or explicit knowledge through earning. Second, structural capital which contains organisational elements that fuel coordination and integration culture within employees, teams, and organisational units. Third, relational capital which reflects the values of maintaining open relationships with the external environment. While tacit is the knowledge used to increase expertise and experience of employees which is harder to codify, explicit is the knowledge that can be codified and transferred between employees and teams (Nonaka & Takeuchi, 1995). However, Dias et al. (2020) emphasized that interpersonal interactions between tourism employees and external stakeholders provide a superior mechanism for achieving both tacit and explicit knowledge. Consequently, this confirms that such interactions enabled by organic structure is cornerstone for enabling a knowledge culture within an organisation (Ramezan, 2011),

Systems thinking: the advent of double loop learning

An escalating economic crisis, disruption, and severe international travel reductions because of the COVID-19 pandemic generates the prevalence of the idea of learning organization in tourism companies (Kaushal & Srivastava, 2021; Su et al., 2021). Shipton et al. (2013) asserted that chaotic stressors and uncertain environments are inevitable: natural disasters, customer demand randomness, financial crisis, volatile customer tastes, and other unanticipated factors. Thus, to nourish viability and growth, tourism companies must develop a tremendously efficacious learning system to assimilate from stressors and uncertainty they encounter (Kaushal & Srivastava, 2021). This concept is relevant to Argyris (1977) idea of the learning organization. He viewed this belief to be the "process of detecting and correcting error." It was later flourished by the work of Senge (1990) as he asserted learning organizations are "organizations where people continually expand their capacity to create the results they truly desire, where new and expansive patterns of thinking are nurtured, where collective aspiration is set free, and where people are continually learning how to learn together." Senge (1990) contended that an essential component for building a learning organization is systems thinking of viewing the organization as a whole. In addition, the customers demand importance, which is a central tent in systems thinking, was present in Senge's (1990) definition. As such, customer demand aspect plays a major role in understanding external world events and found to be a significant element for aiming to be a learning organization.

Khoshkhoo and Nadalipour (2016) confirmed that customer needs and wants-orientation in tourism and travel companies provides an emphasis on customers' problems in the organization, which makes learning indispensable for worthwhile development. Consequently, further researchers examined Senge's (1990) conceptualization of learning organization in tourism context. For instance, Rao et al. (2018) emphasised that knowledge sharing between employees and customers in tourism companies can build organisational learning capabilities and service innovation. Similarly, Kraleva (2011) found that at times of uncertainty and constant change, tourism companies can only compete and survive if learning organisation concepts can be activated through changes to organisational design, culture, and leadership. Liu (2018), through his study of learning mechanisms in Taiwanese tourism companies, suggested that the creation of social capital where employees enjoy strong ties with each other and with the external business environment is a critical mechanism for enhancing absorptive capability and of turning new information into new opportunities. It can, thus, be discerned that some form of organic structure is needed for tourism organisations to learn and grow amidst instability and uncertainty (Sollund, 2006).

In unpredictable business environments, success comes to those who understand the realities quickly (Bagodi & Mahanty, 2013). Argyris and Schön (1996) generated the theory of double loop learning as a course of action to develop stronger knowledge. They addressed that single-loop learning encompasses the identification and rectification of an existing error. According to them, single-loop learning offers a straightforward problem analysis where the existing policies of decision-makers are not questioned. In contrast, double loop learning offers problem analysis and rectification of errors that are associated with a change in the rudimentary beliefs, boundaries, time horizon, goals, and values (Sterman, 1994). Argyris and Schön (1996) asserted that efficient decision-makers must analyse and question the pre-existing variables and be primed for inquiry in a double loop learning environment. They advocate the usage of double loop learning to promote inquiry, to challenge current assumptions and actions, and to lead to the implementation of new theories. For this reason, this higher-level learning offers an opportunity for organizations to go beyond mere transactional problems to dramatic changes that can develop new ways of working (Jaaron & Backhouse, 2017).

In tourism context, Blackman and Ritchie (2008) also explained that double loop learning, through reflection and dialogue with stakeholders and information analysis, challenge existing mental models in tourism companies and develop better crisis management capabilities. Therefore, active involvement of employees in tourism companies is required to apply generated knowledge that can shape the new working systems during and after a crisis, such as COVID-19 (Kaushal & Srivastava, 2021). It is as posited by Pham et al. (2020), such practices of using adaptive behavior and feedback exchange may help hotel employees fit with their workplace and minimize mistakes at work. This will inevitably encourage tourism employees to adopt a holistic view of the company as they evaluate the new working systems and effects on various parts of the business and external environment (Mustelier-Puig et al., 2018; Roxas et al., 2020). According to Rodriguez-Giron and Vanneste (2019), this evaluation of the new working systems is only possible when channels of communication within tourism companies and with external environment allow involved people to act together on the systems. Thus, adoption of systems thinking principle in such environments becomes a necessity (Mai & Smith, 2015; Van Mai & Bosch, 2010). Furthermore, double loop learning provides tourism companies with a way to be more flexible to change using innovations that involve the modification of standard operating procedures based on new knowledge (Ghaderi et al., 2014). The result is the creation of an innovative working place that views stressors as opportunities to further improve (Jaaron & Backhouse, 2017).

The process of adapting double loop learning exhibits a relationship with the norms of a learning organization. This promotes a culture where the organization members are motivated to actively use adaptive behavior and operational processes to improve the system based on continuous interaction, feedback, and knowledge-sharing between employees (Ghaderi et al., 2014), thus, representing the features of organic structures and systems thinking. Organic structures, enabled through applying systems thinking principles, stimulate dragging various resources and expertise from all parts of an organization to deal with unpredictable scenarios (Jaaron

& Backhouse, 2017). The value of systems thinking is in the process of organizations' growth, as seen through the practice of viewing the importance of linking organizational departments to nurture adaptability (Seddon, 2008). The connection of parts of a whole is seen as an integral portion of the success of an organization that leads to innovation (Ali et al., 2020). Therefore, systems thinking approach strategically strengthens the foundation of organizational adaptability that is necessary for creating learning opportunities leading to innovation (Jaaron & Backhouse, 2017).

Research methodology

To explore the impact of applying systems thinking approach to service operations design to combat the devastating impact of the COVID-19 pandemic on tourism industry in Vietnam, a case study methodology was conducted to collect data via interviews, reports, and archival documents from a leading Vietnamese cruise group company. The reason for the choice of the case study methodology is based on the premise that qualitative research methods are more appropriate than quantitative ones in exploring tourism phenomenon intricacies (Banki et al., 2016; Jennings, 2010). A case study is particularly suitable for dealing with "what," "how" and "why" questions that are focused on contemporary events in a natural sitting (Kyburz-Graber, 2004). Moreover, an exploratory case study is useful for studying a distinct phenomenon in real-life context using multiple sources of evidence (Yin, 2009). It is regarded by Benbasat et al. (1987) as an adequate research method for exploring a topic or an area where no previous research has been conducted, or where no previous theoretical propositions have been detected. Given the dearth of research on double loop learning and its connection with systems thinking application in tourism literature poses the case study methodology in this research as a novel method. Furthermore, case studies can help explain a complex issue in detail which quantitative data cannot do (Yin, 2009). In this study, the complex phenomenon is the application of systems thinking to tourism operations design and its impact on double loop learning capabilities. Also, case study research recognizes the inseparable nature between boundaries of phenomena and the context within which it occurs (Yin, 2009). Therefore, the intention of this research was to provide a preliminary attempt to explore the relationships between the implementation of the principles of systems thinking in a tourism service organization, and the building of its organic structure that can learn from shocks and disruptions, which further facilitates the operationalization of double loop learning capability in a tourism company.

Case study selection and characterization

This research inquiry took place from March to October 2020, when the COVID-19 pandemic had negatively and seriously affected every aspect of the tourism industries, globally and in Vietnam. The most severe effect has been on luxury cruise business, which serves 90 per cent of its customers from Europe and America, where the world's biggest and most complicated COVID-19 outbreak have occurred (Gössling et al., 2021). The chosen case study company was a leading cruise group organizing private tours throughout the UNESCO's recognized World Heritage Ha Long Bay – Lan Ha Bay. Its selection was in line with the work of Yin (2009), who suggested that when selecting a case, it is more appropriate to be of the extreme situation where the phenomenon of interest is "transparently observable." In this research, the case was selected since it adopted the principles of systems thinking as their strategy to quickly respond to the stressors of Covid-19 pandemic crisis. The company details, as well as those of the participants, are kept anonymous throughout this paper.

The Group has become one of the largest yacht groups in Ha Long - Cat Ba with 8 yachts offering 129 guest rooms. Every year, the number of tourists using the group's services reaches over 100,000 visitors. Having 6 brands in total, ranging from 3 to 5 star- luxury cruises, the company's business areas include ship construction, luxury cruise services, and tailor-made cruise services in Ha Long Bay and Lan Ha Bay in Vietnam. This 9-year-old private company, with 497 service employees, had no way but to quickly respond to the stressors of the COVID-19 pandemic to maintain its survival.

Data collection and analysis

In this qualitative exploratory study, the main sources of data were in-depth interviews with key informants and internal business documents. A total of 27 interviews were conducted which were all recorded and transcribed using Zoom meeting application. Interviewees were a mixture of eight front-line staff, five back-office staff, five team leaders, four middle managers, and five senior managers. The number of interviews was deemed appropriate as no significantly new information was achievable from extra interviews. This was in line with McCracken (1988), who found that in order to produce perceptive themes from in-depth interviews, eight interviewees are needed but subsequent to that number the returns become minimal for the effort required. The in-depth interviews were of the "one-to-one" type in which only one participant was interviewed at a time. Each interview lasted for 40 minutes on average. Interviewees were asked questions such as: How was your organization able to survive during this crisis? Can you describe the changes made to the way you operate during the period of closure, quarantine, separation and social distances? How were you able to change your service offerings? Do you use the lessons learned from the COVID-19 pandemic to create totally new services? How? and Do you think your organization is an adaptive organization to stressors/shocks? Why?

In addition to interviews, theoretical triangulation (Yin, 2009) was achieved through collecting other supplementary data such as organizational transformation project reports, service performance reports, brochures, and employee handbooks, itinerary sheet, menu, pricing information, promotion policies, travel agency policies, and special rates after COVID-19 period that provided a useful source of information.

The data analysis process from in-depth interviews was guided by the steps of Bryman and Bell (2007) for conducting thematic analysis of interviews data. This inductive analysis strategy is based on notion of finding patterns in the data through a process of segmenting and categorizing qualitative data before final interpretation (Patton, 2002). It was chosen in this research as it offers a highly flexible approach through which detailed, yet rich account of data can be achieved (Braun & Clarke, 2006). Furthermore, it allows examining the perspectives of different interviewees in a study, highlighting similarities and differences, and generating novel insights (Nowell et al., 2017). However, one of the distinctive characters of thematic analysis process is providing a well-structured approach to handling large data that can contribute to producing clear and well-organized findings (Braun & Clarke, 2006). Bryman and Bell (2007) steps followed in this study are illustrated below:

- Step 1: To sharpen understanding of the collected data, research questions and interviewees' transcripts were studied to shed light on general leading theoretical topics; also called coding schemes (Minichiello et al., 2008). A set of words or topics were then listed to represent a general meaning of what was recorded in the interviews, which was known as the coding framework of interviews' analysis (Attride-Stirling, 2001). The benefit of creating such a coding framework was the generation of a list of words which could be linked into common categories during analysis (Minichiello et al., 2008).
- Step 2: This step involved reading through the transcripts of interviews again and coding the content. The interviews transcripts were divided into meaningful fragments to facilitate dealing with data. Every text segment was then given a code from the developed coding framework that represented the meaning perceived (Attride-Stirling, 2001).

- Step 3: This step aimed to revise the divided transcripts to find codes with common basic themes. This was done by careful reading of the coded segments, thus enabling the identification of underlying structures and connections (Attride-Stirling, 2001).
- Step 4: The final step allowed authors to cluster basic themes around more central themes that were used later for interpretations.

Table 2 illustrates the coding framework and three central themes found. These emerging themes are further explained in the next section.

Research results

Systematic judges and acts

This theme refers to judges and acts on the system to produce an in-time response strategy for the company to survive amidst COVID-19 and beyond. As confirmed by a senior manager, "We are proud of being survived in such turbulent crisis as Covid −19… I think systems thinking principles works well here in our cruise group. Our organization is viewed as a whole structurally. We always act on systems whenever a change occurs." A front-line staff reconfirmed, "We have found new markets to fill vacant cabins on boat. I think that is the most fruitful achievements of acting on systems." A back-office interviewee explained, "When we face shocks like closure requests, we all think about how to make our company survival. We volunteered to have a work leave alternatively to help reduce operational cost for the company." Also, a senior manager interviewee stated, "We can only have enough readiness and adaptiveness to respond to shocks when we keep learning and absorbing the shocks and turning them into opportunities to learn new things, fix the problems, improve the situation, and learn at a higher level." Additionally, a number of measures were taken adaptively, such as minimizing the number of crews on cruise in Bays, encouraging staff to work from home, saving energy consumption on yachts as well as cutting off all the costs related to advertising or ineffective promotions. Interviewees believed that such actions on the systems helped the company reduce operational costs during this crisis.

Interviewees also learned collectively because of the problems that the whole company were faced with. Several multifunctional tasks were given to the employees on boat during the time of the pandemic. A front-line staff working on one of the boats explained, "We are only two people who helped each other become quickly familiar with covering all maintenance jobs that previously were made by 20 people… like cleaning, self-cooking, checking the engine operations, cabin clearing, pier management etc." This act on the whole system could contribute to saving costs and creating opportunities for self-cross-training for personnel.

A middle manager also explained, "… In a very short time we have experienced the two big shocks: the nearly two-month closure and the sudden reoperation in two days, thus it was compulsory for our organizational system to judge and act quickly and exactly to grasp the opportunities from the threats." Another middle manager stated, "The strict barriers between different departments have been replaced now by the soft ones of open communications, discussions and cooperation to quickly learn from each other and accomplish the tasks. Interviewees revealed that capturing these learning opportunities with its flexibility in an organically structured organization, the cruise company have judged the situation and acted in an appropriate way to unfold new business opportunities to survive.

Problem-based task force teams

This theme refers to the engagement and readiness to learn of problem-based Task Force Teams (TFTs) in the cruise firm and using systems-thinking principles to save the life of the company amid COVID-19. The interviewees shared that since the first day of closure, TFTs have been set

Table 2. In-depth interview analysis: from codes to central themes.

Variables	Codes	Issued discussed	Common basic themes	Central themes
Organic systems-thinking characteristics	• Interrelationships • Dynamics • Wholeness	• Interconnectedness of employees: open channels of interactions, social exchange within and across the teams • Readiness/ adaptiveness to respond to stressors/ shocks • An organizational structure views the organization as a whole	• Knowledge sharing • Team-based • Case analysis • Organic structure • Act on systems whenever changes occur.	• Systematic Judges and Acts
Learning organization	• organizational learning • learning at work • learning climate • learning structure	• power delegation to employees at all levels coordination • quick response to environment volatility • Inter-functional coordination, • Decentralized decision making by employees	• capturing learning opportunities from shocks and disruptions • problems based learning • expanding employees capacity	• Problem-based Task Force Teams
Double loop learning organization	• New ways of working (Jaaron & Backhouse, 2017) • Mental models (Bagodi & Mahanty, 2013) • Systems, operational, and behavioral changes	• ability to find new customers • customer need analysis • management role is different • Employee empowerment • Correction of detected errors • Change procedures and policies if possible	• new customers, new demand, new problems, new strategy • leadership support • learning behavior	• Innovative Changes

up in the cruise case. A team leader explained further: "At first there is only one Task Force Team with the participants of four sales staffs, two financial officers, two crews, two other logistics employees, one middle manager, and a top manager. We all worked together without any hierarchies in the reduction stage for searching for survival solutions while actively interacting with our existing loyal customers. Team members had chance to share their knowledge about customer change in demands during the pandemic as well as to learn from each other ideas.... Since then whenever we have specific problems to solve, TFTs have immediately been established with job-related participants from relevant departments." As quoted from one interviewed sales and marketing staff: "... My proposal of new service offerings was the result of firstly, the open discussions among members of the TFT and with loyal customers we have, secondly the shortening hierarchical distance among levels of management and operations, thirdly the ability to continuously learning from team members, customers new demands, from the problem, from the system, and from stressors." This was further asserted by a front-line staff, "We have been empowered to make decision for the specific tasks and have sufficient support from leader if needed."

As soon as the re-operation of cruise services was allowed, dozens of problem-based TFTs in both tangible and intangible forms were established and operated both online and offline smoothly to deal with specific tasks. A branch manager shared: "The problem-based TFTs have helped to develop and expand the employees' capacity via each time of problem solving... whenever the organization is exposed to a problem, a danger, or customer safety demands, employees from different departments and sections, from different levels of management could cooperate to give the best solution at the lowest cost." As exemplified by a front-line interviewee: "When we received an order from 22 Vietnamese visitors with various requests about discounts, safety measures, and tailored- make demands, we actively worked with a newly born TFT to identify the breakeven point for that cruise trip, then the TFT generated a plan that was shared with the customers for reflections and feedback. This provided opportunities to learn from case analysis and customer's requests for a matched negotiations and offerings." The problem-based learning project was successful with high levels of customer satisfaction and an acceptable profit for the company in the context of Covid-19 crisis.

Innovative changes

The theme of innovative changes refers to service innovations that the cruise group company created from building an organic structure in operations and a double loop learning ability from the turbulent shocks. Problem-based TFTs indicated, "Inbound vouchers and domestic visitors are the two major sources of innovative income which can save the company life at the moment." Accordingly, a great deal of new promotional policies and activities were simultaneously taken to stimulate domestic demand. During this period, the company gradually reached the breakeven point and then obtained an amount of profit. Added by a team leader interviewee: "Our current customers now are Vietnamese, who are totally new to us and to our luxury services. It urgently requests our company group to completely change our services as quickly as possible to satisfy the new demands received from local customers. For example, the menu, the decoration styles, entertaining activities on deck, prices, other services, etc... should be changed due to absolutely new customer's demands. To be survived, the organization structure was changed to be as organic and flexible as possible to set up new working structure."

Employees within their TFTs could test new ways of offering services. According to interviewees, this was the moment that their organization embraced the application of systems thinking approach for its service delivery design based on new customer demands. Interviewees explained that every TFT in the organization was encouraged to identify value demand, analyze failure demand, learn from errors, fix defects, seek new information, modify process and procedures, learn from knowledge sharing across TFTs, and eventually offer the exact services at the exact time the customers want.

The second significant service innovation was the creation of several brand new services by the cruise firm with the help of its TFTs. One of the best-selling services now is 3-year inbound vouchers. This kind of voucher offers international customers incentives, an expiry date of 3 years, and a variety of other beneficial customized-choices for customers when they use the vouchers after the pandemic. As revealed by an accountant interviewer, "We could collect immediately an amount of cash in advance for survival and even increase our revenue." Interviewees discussed that more innovative act in selling this creative type of vouchers was targeting local travel agents, who were willing to buy large numbers of these vouchers and transfer a lot of money into the cruise company's accounts at once. As it was reported, retail and wholesale vouchers have contributed roughly 40 percent to monthly revenues in May- September 2020. A senior manager highlighted, "From no customers during the period of March 5 – April 28, 2020; it took only few days for us to install the whole system to serve the totally new customers on May 1, 2020 with 80 percent of occupancy rate." This spectacular result was explained by a middle manager, "Only three things rescued us from the crisis are: in-time response, fostering the strength of the company as a whole, and learning from each other, travel agents, and also from our customers." Other interviewees explained further that an organization can only give a quick response to the shocks when it is really a dynamic one, otherwise, it will take time and opportunities fly away. Interviewees also suggested if the company followed the traditional management with hierarchical or separated structures, it could not have achieved such innovations. Concluded by a top leader interviewee: "We capture any learning opportunities both internally and externally; from inter-functional coordination of TFTs, from customer need analysis and even from shocks and disruptions .... we not only view stressors as problems to tackle but also view them as opportunities to improve continuously."

In addition, interviewees showed that the relationships with reserved customers were nurtured via phone, email, and social networks and the deposits from the booked orders persuaded to be kept until the pandemic crisis is over. This action not only improved customer relationships for future business but also kept the paid deposit for current operations. Finally, interviewees noted that to avoid dependence on such markets as the USA and Europe, the cruises have expanded cabin sales across multiple online travel agents' channels, attracting customers in many other regions of the world, for instance China and Asia. This renovation could help the cruise company extend its market in the future, which was considered as a lesson of back-up or contingency plans gained from the COVID-19 crisis.

Discussion

The data analysis process showed that the systems thinking approach enabled structuring the organization organically and that in return operationalized double loop learning by promoting three different drivers. These drivers are presented in a conceptual framework as shown in Figure 1, and further explained through discussion of results.

The results suggest that the theme of systemic judges and acts has clarified the impact of systems thinking approach on the working structure of the firm in the struggle for existence during this crisis. It is elicited here that continuous capturing and analysis of external stressors brough about by COVID-19 and performed by the company employees added to the competencies of the individuals and better prepared the knowledge-base of the organisation (Shipton et al., 2013). As a result, employees were able to question current methods of doing the work, and to propose alternative methods for reducing operational costs necessary for business survival during crisis. Furthermore, it was evident in the results that the mechanistic top-down structure, which emphasise standardisation, the elimination of variation and managers' monitoring

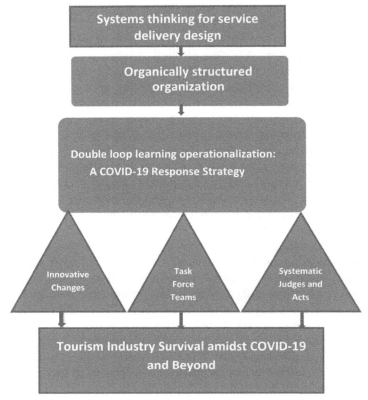

Figure 1. Three drivers for double loop learning: a COVID-19 response strategy.

(Seddon, 2008), was not found at the case company. On the contrary, managers had an active role in supporting employees to give solutions to the newly emerging problems. This outcome from results acted as a catalyst for translating employees' learning into organisational learning and allowed employees to adapt to the stressors of random and unfamiliar situations through calling on their managers support and experience. According to Hannah and Lester (2009), changing the role of leaders from monitors to supporters enhance double loop learning; by maintaining a tendency of employees to critically criticise current business methods and share their findings with leaders. This was also in line with Jaaron and Backhouse (2017) who explained that supportive role of leaders within systems thinking workplace would be essential to activate latent learning capabilities of employees. Therefore, employees in the cruise company recognised that systems thinking taught them to learn about their system through shifting the decision making from a top-down approach to horizontal collaboration approach between employees. This theme, thus, suggests that systems thinking enabled employees to practice double loop learning through questioning and modifying existing methods of doing the work in their search for survival opportunities.

The results also asserted that the second theme of problem-based TFTs has led to knowledge sharing and learning emergence from stressors and disruptions. This was shared by Shipton et al. (2013), who linked learning-oriented behaviour of organisations during chaotic situations with information sharing across team members. The cruise company had to become an adaptive service organisation, also referred to as "organic structures" (Burns & Stalker, 1961). It was recognised in this theme that when employees were relocated to work on emerging disruptions within problem-based TFTs, it was possible to make organizational changes systematically with a continuous learning ability. Thus, results propose that members of TFTs were equally levelled, trusted, and enjoyed informal open communication channels when working on emerging disruptions. Consequently, employees naturally developed a sense of freedom and responsibility as they were encouraged to share and try new methods as they collectively learn. In fact, this virtue of TFTs supported by organic structure facilitated the development of knowledge culture at the cruise company. This was evident through facilitating transfer of tacit knowledge through interaction between members of various TFTs. According to Dias et al. (2020), continuous interaction of employees during execution of organisational improvement projects has the potential to improve intellectual capital necessary for learning in the organisation. These results are also in line with the findings of Ghaderi et al. (2014), who stated that social relationship at the workplace is an integral part for knowledge creation- a cornerstone for organisational learning. It was also consistent with the views of Ramezan (2011) who showed that high levels of employee interactions are essential for creating strength and powerfulness that could bring a great deal of innovative learning opportunities to the system. Another interesting outcome reported in the second theme is the focus on external environment in the learning process. Taking customer demands and environment changes into account ensured that problem-based TFTs would be able to expand their knowledge on what the cruise company still needs to learn about its stressors. This has also ensured that learning is directed to continuously adapting service offerings to match external safety requirements during the COVID-19 crisis. This was similar to what Liu (2018) advocated learning tourism companies to do; effectively including external factors while simultaneously improving internal systems.

Perhaps the theme of innovative changes is the strongest theme identified through data analysis. It showed that the most significant change for the company's survival was to divert attention towards domestic customers in the recovery process. The results suggest that having a free conversation with domestic customers allowed for the exploration of "what matters" to these customers during COVID-19 pandemic if they to use the tourism service. Understanding what customers want were seen by the cruise company as source of new creative ideas. Subsequently, it was then possible to translate these creative ideas into new service offerings. It is as Jaaron and Backhouse (2017) have explained, taking into consideration customer demands and wants is vital for creating a learning organisation that aspire to create innovative updates to its service systems. This is the context of double loop learning as descried by Argyris and Schön (1996). The results also depict a culture where employees are expected by their managers to continuously monitor varying demand coming into the cruise company and collectively question current systems if a demand cannot be met with current arrangements. Arguably, this gave rise to a new mode of working where every unmet customer demand is treated as a unique opportunity that could potentially lead to a new innovative solution. This was congruent to the work of Rao et al. (2018) who explained that interaction between tourism customers and employees can fuel knowledge exchange necessary for enabling service innovation capabilities. At a more subtle level, the results also reflected a working environment resembled by a non-routine type of work that required high degree of individual authority and power. This further confirmed achieving organic structure at the cruise company. However, this fundamental process of encouraging interaction with customers and the associated inter-employees sharing of knowledge ensured operationalising double loop learning and system adaptability during uncertain times (Khoshkhoo and Nadalipour (2016). As it was asserted through results, double loop learning enabled the cruise company to identify the targeted domestic customers and allowed demand-stimulating policies to work effectively. This was evident through monthly financial reports of the cruise company which showed that revenue has increased from the first date of receiving the domestic visitors, leading to a surprising five per cent monthly profit during the four successive months. Therefore, it can be discerned that the new working system was able to contribute to sustainable economic growth of the company within the COVID-19 pandemic.

Theoretical and managerial implications

The findings of this research have some significant contributions for practitioners and researchers. First, while most of the literature has focused on the adoption of learning approaches in tourism and hospitality management literature (e.g., Ali et al., 2020; Bernsen et al., 2009; Božič & Cvelbar, 2016; Kaushal & Srivastava, 2021; Liu, 2018), this work has extended current understanding of organisational learning in tourism companies by incorporating double loop learning with structural design issues based on the lens of organic structures. This is a novel conceptualisation of organisational learning in tourism literature that was not dealt with before. The study delves deeper into the relationship between double loop learning and tourism companies' evolution capabilities amidst COVID-19 crisis, offering new insights for the type of knowledge-based structure needed for the new generation of tourism industry. The results have made it clear that relocating employees to work within teams in organically structured environment facilitates the creation of "knowledge culture" (Ramezan, 2011) through effectively involving external stakeholders (i.e., customers), while concurrently redesigning internal tourism operations. As a consequence, our investigation in this study adds new evidence to tourism literature on the ability to increase tacit and explicit knowledge creation through structuring self-improving tourism operations. More specifically, this research has theorized systems thinking with double loop learning as an organizational means for tourism companies to survive during COVID-19 global tragedy that can accelerate the transformation of tourism companies. Thus, this work provides empirical evidence of the possibility of using the systems thinking approach to build highly responsive learning systems to fundamentally change tourism organizations' existing operations and offerings to adapt to threats and stressors such as the recent COVID-19 crisis. The findings hold that systems thinking approach could develop an organic structure organization, which would then, activate double loop learning for creating a survival strategy whenever exposed to shocks and disruptions of unprecedented situation. Therefore, this study provides a way for tourism companies to address shortfalls in their contribution to sustainable economic growth within the COVID-19 pandemic; as part of the scope of SDG8.

Based on the contributions highlighted above, this paper also enables us to draw some managerial implications. First, theorizing systems thinking operational design with double loop learning in this study is a starting point for tourism managers to identify new methods for re-designing their workplace to face uncertain stressors and turn them into organisational learning (Bhat et al., 2012). This would imply that tourism managers need to create internal Human Resources Management changes to integrate new cultural norms and practices as part of the performance management systems (Pham et al., 2020). Second, the results show that employees' engagement and readiness to learn within their teams is a cornerstone for enabling knowledge culture. This suggests that person-organization fit concept (Liu, 2018) should be considered by tourism managers as this may enhance employees' motivation and voluntary behaviour (Pham et al., 2020) to capture learning. Third, the principle of systems thinking design of continuous customer demand analysis was found to better prepare the knowledge-base of the tourism organization to facilitate innovative service changes. Thus, it is necessary for tourism managers to provide freedom for employees to have free conversations with tourists (i.e., customers) to explore complex problematic situations. Finally, the research results reported here could help tourism managers become aware of the significance of organic structures, brought about by systems thinking deign, as drivers for competitive advantage creation during a crisis. Thus, building a decentralized organizational structure proves to be vital for tourism organisations during COVID-19 crisis and beyond.

Conclusions and future research directions

In response for calls by the tourism industry for survival strategies during COVID-19 pandemic (Gössling et al., 2021; Hoque et al., 2020; Ranasinghe et al., 2020), this exploratory study has attempted to examine the impact of applying systems thinking approach for service delivery design and enabling "double loop" learning in a leading cruise group company in the Vietnamese tourism sector. The results of the case study demonstrated an interesting dynamic of the cruise company service design based on systems thinking principles and provided a novel conceptualization of organizational learning in tourism companies. The work associated double loop learning capabilities in tourism companies with structural design changes facilitated by the application of systems thinking approach. Therefore, offering new insights on the significance of systems thinking application to knowledge-based structure realization in tourism companies necessary for survival opportunities creation during crisis. As such, the work also provides insights on how tourism companies can maintain sustainable performance and contribute to economic growth within the COVID-19 pandemic. However, despite the several new insights and contributions provides by this paper to tourism research, it has some limitations that can help inform future tourism research. First, the data collection process in this research occurred remotely over Zoom application, so physical observations of the new service delivery were limited due to COVID-19 restrictions. Thus, future research may consider studying the proposed relationships in this research using longitudinal research designs with on-site observations to broaden insights from this research. Second, even though characteristics of cruise ship services are unique (Radic et al., 2020), it would still be valuable to replicate this study in other tourism services such as hotels, resorts, theme parks, camps, and other tourist attractions to validate the results and potentially capture any other dimensions of adaptive capabilities resulting from the systems thinking design. Considering this, a new line of research would be to conduct quantitative studies to test propositions presented in this study, namely:

- P1: Systems thinking design constitutes a mechanism for operationalising double loop learning amidst adversity through enabling an organic structure for the tourism companies.
- P2: Double loop learning emanating from systems thinking design promotes systematic reforms in the tourism companies.
- P3: Double loop learning emanating from systems thinking design promotes creation of problem-based TFTs in tourism companies.
- P4: Double loop learning emanating from systems thinking design promotes service innovation in tourism companies.

Third, although data collected in this research came from various employees and managers at various levels, it was not possible to interview customers. Therefore, future studies may replicate this study while including the customer's perspective. Finally, as the link between service operations design and double loop learning is an integral part of the workplace structure and employees' empowerment (Jaaron & Backhouse, 2017), future research should look at the impact of human resources management theories as moderating conditions to double loop learning in tourism companies.

Disclosure statement

No potential conflict of interest was reported by the authors.

ORCID

Ayham A. M. Jaaron http://orcid.org/0000-0003-4190-0681
Duong Thuy Pham http://orcid.org/0000-0003-2651-1151
Marielyn Espiridion Cogonon http://orcid.org/0000-0003-1238-5967

References

Ali, S., Peters, L. D., Khan, I. U., Ali, W., & Saif, N. (2020). Organizational learningand hotel performance: The role of capabilities' hierarchy. *International Journal of Hospitality Management*, *85*(102349), 102349–102312. https://doi.org/10.1016/j.ijhm.2019.102349

Argyris, C. (1977). Double loop learning in organizations. *Harvard Business Review*, *55*(5), 115–125.

Argyris, C., & Schön, D. (1996). *Organizational learning II: Theory, method and practice*. Addison-Westley.

Attride-Stirling, J. (2001). Thematic networks: An analytic tool for qualitative research. *Qualitative Research*, *1*(3), 385–405. https://doi.org/10.1177/146879410100100307

Bagodi, V., & Mahanty, B. (2013). Double loop learning in the Indian two-wheeler service sector. *The Learning Organization*, *20*(4–5), 264–278. https://doi.org/10.1108/TLO-04-2012-0029

Banki, M. B., Ismail, H. N., & Muhammad, I. B. (2016). Coping with seasonality: A case study of family owned micro tourism businesses in Obudu Mountain Resort in Nigeria. *Tourism Management Perspectives*, *18*, 141–152. https://doi.org/10.1016/j.tmp.2016.01.010

Bayraktaroglu, S., & Kutanis, R. O. (2003). Transforming hotels into learning organisations: A new strategy for going global. *Tourism Management*, *24*(2), 149–154. https://doi.org/10.1016/S0261-5177(02)00061-4

Benbasat, I., Goldstein, D. K., & Mead, M. (1987). The case research strategy in studies of information systems. *MIS Quarterly*, *11*(3), 369–386. https://doi.org/10.2307/248684

Bernsen, P., Segers, M., & Tillema, H. H. (2009). Learning under pressure: Learning strategies, workplace climate, and leadership style in the hospitality industry. *International Journal of Human Resources Development and Management*, *9*(4), 358–373. https://doi.org/10.1504/IJHRDM.2009.025069

Bhat, A. B., Verma, N., Rangnekar, S., & Barua, M. K. (2012). Leadership style and team processes as predictors of organisational learning. *Team Performance Management: An International Journal*, *18*(7/8), 347–369. https://doi.org/10.1108/13527591211281101

Blackman, D., & Ritchie, B. W. (2008). Tourism crisis management and organizational learning. *Journal of Travel & Tourism Marketing*, *23*(2–4), 45–57. https://doi.org/10.1300/J073v23n02_04

Božič, V., & Cvelbar, K. L. (2016). Resources and capabilities driving performance in the hotel industry. *Tourism and Hospitality Management*, *22*(2), 225–246. https://doi.org/10.20867/thm.22.2.8

Braun, V., & Clarke, V. (2006). Using thematic analysis in psychology. *Qualitative Research in Psychology*, *3*(2), 77–101. https://doi.org/10.1191/1478088706qp063oa

Bryman, A., & Bell, E. (2007). *Business research methods*. Oxford University Press.

Burns, T., & Stalker, G. M. (1961). *The management of innovation* (pp. 120–122). London.

Comfort, L. K., Sungu, Y., Johnson, D., & Dunn, M. (2001). Complex systems in crisis: Anticipation and resilience in dynamic environments. *Journal of Contingencies and Crisis Management*, *9*(3), 144–158. https://doi.org/10.1111/1468-5973.00164

Conde Nast Traveller. (2020). *Before and after: How coronavirus has emptied tourist attractions around the world*. Retrieved March 31, 2020, from https://www.cntravellerme.com/before-and-after-photos-tourist-attractions-during-Coronavirus

Dias, A., Silva, G. M., Patuleia, M., & González-Rodríguez, M. R. (2020). Developing sustainable business models: Local knowledge acquisition and tourism lifestyle entrepreneurship. *Journal of Sustainable Tourism*. https://doi.org/10.1080/09669582.2020.1835931

Filho, W. L., Brandli, L. L., Salvia, A. L., Rayman-Bacchus, L., & Platje, J. (2020). COVID-19 and the UN sustainable development goals: Threat to solidarity or an opportunity? *Sustainability, 12*(5343), 1–14.

G20 (Group of Twenty Countries). (2019). *Advancing tourism's contribution to the sustainable development goals (SDGs)*. G20.

Ghaderi, Z., Som, A. P. M. S., & Wang, J. (2014). Organizational learning in tourism crisis management: An experience from Malaysia. *Journal of Travel & Tourism Marketing, 31*(5), 627–648. https://doi.org/10.1080/10548408.2014.883951

Gössling, S., Scott, D., & Hall, C. M. (2021). Pandemics, tourism and global change: A rapid assessment of COVID-19. *Journal of Sustainable Tourism, 29*(1), 1–20. https://doi.org/10.1080/09669582.2020.1758708

Gregory, A. J. (2007). Target setting, lean systems and viable systems: A systems perspective on control and performance measurement. *Journal of the Operational Research Society, 58*(11), 1503–1517. https://doi.org/10.1057/palgrave.jors.2602319

Hannah, S. T., & Lester, P. B. (2009). A multilevel approach to building and leading learning organizations. *The Leadership Quarterly, 20*(1), 34–48. https://doi.org/10.1016/j.leaqua.2008.11.003

Heslinga, J. H., Groote, P., & Vanclay, F. (2017). Using a social-ecological systems perspective to understand tourism and landscape interactions in coastal areas. *Journal of Tourism Futures, 3*(1), 23–38. https://doi.org/10.1108/JTF-10-2015-0047

Hoque, A., Shikha, F. A., Hasanat, M. W., Arif, I., & Hamid, A. B. A. (2020). The effect of Coronavirus (COVID-19) in the tourism industry in China. *Asian Journal of Multidisciplinary Studies, 3*(1), 52–58.

Jaaron, A. A., & Backhouse, C. J. (2014). Service organisations resilience through the application of the vanguard method of systems thinking: A case study approach. *International Journal of Production Research, 52*(7), 2026–2041. https://doi.org/10.1080/00207543.2013.847291

Jaaron, A. A., & Backhouse, C. J. (2017). Operationalising "double-loop" learning in service organisations: A systems approach for creating knowledge. *Systemic Practice and Action Research, 30*(4), 317–337. https://doi.org/10.1007/s11213-016-9397-0

Jackson, M. C., Johnston, N., & Seddon, J. (2008). Evaluating systems thinking in housing. *Journal of the Operational Research Society, 59*(2), 186–197. https://doi.org/10.1057/palgrave.jors.2602521

Jennings, G. (2010). *Tourism research* (2nd ed.). John Wiley & Sons Australia.

Kaushal, V., & Srivastava, S. (2021). Hospitality and tourism industry amid COVID-19 pandemic: Perspectives on challenges and learnings from India. *International Journal of Hospitality Management, 92*, 102707–102709. https://doi.org/10.1016/j.ijhm.2020.102707

Khoshkhoo, M. H. I., & Nadalipour, Z. (2016). Tourism SMEs and organizational learning in a competitive environment: A longitudinal research on organizational learning in travel and tourism agencies located in the city of Ahvaz, Iran. *The Learning Organization, 23*(2–3), 184–200. https://doi.org/10.1108/TLO-07-2015-0043

Kraleva, N. (2011). Learning organizations: Prerequisite for successful tourism organizations. *UTMS Journal of Economics, University of Tourism and Management, Skopje, 2*(1), 77–82.

Kwok, A. O. J. & Koh, S. G. M. (2021). COVID-19 and Extended Reality (XR). *Current Issues in Tourism, 24*(14), 1935–1940. https://doi.org/10.1080/13683500.2020.1798896

Kyburz-Graber, R. (2004). Does case-study methodology lack rigour? The need for quality criteria for sound case-study research, as illustrated by a recent case in secondary and higher education. *Environmental Education Research, 10*(1), 53–65.

Liu, C. H. (2018). Examining social capital, organizational learning and knowledge transfer in cultural and creative industries of practice. *Tourism Management, 64*, 258–270. https://doi.org/10.1016/j.tourman.2017.09.001

Mai, T., & Smith, C. (2015). Addressing the threats to tourism sustainability using systems thinking: A case study of Cat Ba Island, Vietnam. *Journal of Sustainable Tourism, 23*(10), 1504–1528. https://doi.org/10.1080/09669582.2015.1045514

McCracken, G. D. (1988). *The long interview*. Sage Publications.

Minichiello, V., Aroni, R., & Hays, T. N. (2008). *In-depth interviewing: Principles, techniques, analysis*. Pearson Education Australia.

Mustelier-Puig, L. C., Anjum, A., & Ming, X. (2018). Interaction quality and satisfaction: An empirical study of international tourists when buying Shanghai tourist attraction services. *Cogent Business & Management, 5*(1), 1470890. https://doi.org/10.1080/23311975.2018.1470890

Nhamo, G., Dube, K., & Chikodzi, D. (2020). Global Tourism Value Chains, Sustainable Development Goals and COVID-19. In G. Nhamo, K. Dube, & D. Chikodzi (Eds.), *Counting the Cost of COVID-19 on the Global Tourism Industry* (pp. 27–51). Springer. https://doi.org/10.1007/978-3-030-56231-1_2

Nonaka, I., & Takeuchi, K. (1995). *The knowledge creating company*. Oxford University Press.
Nowell, L. S., Norris, J. M., White, D. E., & Moules, N. J. (2017). Thematic analysis: Striving to meet the trustworthiness criteria. *International Journal of Qualitative Methods*, 16(1), 160940691773384–160940691773313. https://doi.org/10.1177/1609406917733847
Patton, M. (2002). *Qualitative research and evaluation methods* (3rd ed.). Sage.
Peric, M., & Djurkin, J. (2014). Systems thinking and alternative business model for responsible tourist destination. *Kybernetes*, 43(3–4), 480–496. https://doi.org/10.1108/K-07-2013-0132
Pham, D. T., & Jaaron, A. A. (2018). Design for mass customisation in higher education: A systems-thinking approach. *Systemic Practice and Action Research*, 31(3), 293–310. https://doi.org/10.1007/s11213-017-9426-7
Quang, T. D., Tran, T. C., Tran, V. H., Nguyen, T. T., & Nguyen, T. T. (2020). Is Vietnam ready to welcome tourists back? Assessing COVID-19's economic impact and the Vietnamese tourism industry's response to the pandemic. *Current Issues in Tourism*. https://doi.org/10.1080/13683500.2020.1860916
Radic, A., Arjona-Fuentes, J. M., Ariza-Montes, A., Han, H., & Law, R. (2020). Job demands–job resources (JD-R) model, work engagement, and well-being of cruise ship employees. *International Journal of Hospitality Management*, 88, 102518. https://doi.org/10.1016/j.ijhm.2020.102518
Ramezan, M. (2011). Intellectual capital and organizational organic structure in knowledge society: How are these concepts related? *International Journal of Information Management*, 31(1), 88–95. https://doi.org/10.1016/j.ijinfomgt.2010.10.004
Ranasinghe, R., Damunupola, A., Wijesundara, S., Karunarathna, C., Nawarathna, D., Gamage, S., Ranaweera, A., & Idroos, A. A. (2020). *Tourism after corona: Impacts of COVID 19 pandemic and way forward for tourism, hotel and mice industry in Sri Lanka*. SSRN. https://ssrn.com/abstract=3587170.
Rao, Y., Yang, M., & Yang, Y. (2018). Knowledge sharing, organizational learning and service innovation in tourism. *Journal of Service Science and Management*, 11(05), 510–526. https://doi.org/10.4236/jssm.2018.115035
Rodriguez-Giron, S., & Vanneste, D. (2019). Social capital at the tourist destination level: Determining the dimensions to assess and improve collective action in tourism. *Tourist Studies*, 19(1), 23–42. https://doi.org/10.1177/1468797618790109
Ropret, M., Jakulin, T. J., & Likar, B. (2014). The systems approach to the improvement of innovation in Slovenian tourism. *Kybernetes*, 43(3–4), 427–444. https://doi.org/10.1108/K-07-2013-0154
Roxas, F. M. Y., Rivera, J. P. R., & Gutierrez, E. L. M. (2020). Framework for creating sustainable tourism using systems thinking. *Current Issues in Tourism*, 23(3), 280–296. https://doi.org/10.1080/13683500.2018.1534805
Seddon, J. (2003). *Freedom from command and control: A better way to make the work work, vanguard education*. Buckingham.
Seddon, J. (2008). *Systems thinking in the public sector*. Triarchy Press.
Senge, P. M. (1990). *The fifth discipline: The art and practice of learning organization*. Century Business.
Shipton, H., Zhou, Q., & Mooi, E. (2013). Is there a global model of learning organizations? An empirical, cross-nation study. *The International Journal of Human Resource Management*, 24(12), 2278–2298. https://doi.org/10.1080/09585192.2013.781431
Sollund, R. (2006). Mechanistic versus organic organizations' impact on immigrant women's work satisfaction and occupational mobility. *Scandinavian Journal of Hospitality and Tourism*, 6(4), 287–307. https://doi.org/10.1080/15022250601003240
Sterman, J. D. (1994). Learning in and about complex systems. *System Dynamics Review*, 10(2–3), 291–330. https://doi.org/10.1002/sdr.4260100214
Stone, M. T., & Nyaupane, G. P. (2018). Protected areas, wildlifebased community tourism and community livelihoods dynamics: Spiraling up and down of community capitals. *Journal of Sustainable Tourism*, 26(2), 307–324. https://doi.org/10.1080/09669582.2017.1349774
Su, D. N., Tra, D. L., Huynh, H. M., Thi Nguyen, H., & O'Mahony, B. (2021). Enhancing resilience in the Covid-19 crisis: Lessons from human resource management practices in Vietnam. *Current Issues in Tourism*. https://doi.org/10.1080/13683500.2020.1863930
Van Mai, T., & Bosch, O. J. H. (2010). *Systems thinking approach as a unique tool for sustainable tourism development: A case study in the cat ba biosphere reserve of Vietnam*. http://journals.isss.org/index.php/proceedings54th/article/viewFile/1457/509
Vietnam Tourism. (2020). *Info for travellers on Covid-19 in Vietnam*. https://vietnam.travel/things-to-do/information-travellers-novel-coronavirus-vietnam
Wiener, N. (1948). *Cybernetics or control and communication in the animal and the machine*. Technology Press.
Yin, R. (2009). *Case study research: Design and methods*. Sage Publications.
Zaragoza-Sáez, P. C., Claver-Cortés, E., Marco- Lajara, B., & Úbeda-García, M. (2020). Corporate social responsibility and strategic knowledge management as mediators between sustainable intangible capital and hotel performance. *Journal of Sustainable Tourism*, https://doi.org/10.1080/09669582.2020.1811289

Responses to vignettes as a methodology to reveal hoteliers' sustainability practices, knowledge and competencies

Cláudia Martins Pantuffi, Janette Brunstein and Mark Edward Walvoord

ABSTRACT
This study analyzes the competencies of hoteliers in handling sustainability dilemmas through the proxy of their responses to vignettes. It uses a practice-based lens to develop a novel methodology to study the reasoning behind sustainability decisions. Vignettes were compiled from stories submitted by hoteliers and tourism specialists that address both social and environmental issues, then validated by university students and researchers. Forty-three hotel professionals from Brazil responded to the six real-world vignettes which asked them to project themselves into different situations with sustainability challenges. Using an interpretive approach of those hoteliers' lived world responses, researchers uncovered what practices they adopted in the hospitality sector. Analysis of the subjects' competencies showed that triggered practices erred more towards hotel interests than to social and environmental ends. These results contribute to understanding the factors that prevent advances in organizational learning processes around sustainability. They also point to the need for a shift in sustainability research towards the lived world practice of professionals, through vignettes or other methodology, and to professional development that directs workers to consider long-term consequences of decisions.

Introduction

In recent years, authors have highlighted the relationship between responsible tourism, stakeholders, and shared value (Camilleri, 2016), calling attention to the mismatch between the theory and practice of sustainability (Font et al., 2012). Barriers to implementing sustainability include employees' knowledge and skills deficits, corporate culture, managerial attitudes, and low employee commitment (Chan et al., 2018). Understanding the learning process and development of competencies in the hospitality industry has become a priority for the sustainability agenda. The pace of research in this area has not advanced as quickly as needed, with 70% of publications in the sector dated between 2013 and 2017 (Font & Lynes, 2018), demonstrating that awareness and relevance of this field are recent developments. Ruhanen and colleagues (2015) argue that this field of research is still maturing in its theoretical and methodological approaches.

Scholarship on sustainability does not often include the hospitality sector as a primary research area (Martinez-Martinez et al., 2019b). When this research does appear, it is only as a theoretical discussion without empirical investigation, as in Mierlo and Beers (2020) discussion of relationships between the concepts of learning and sustainability. Those few empirical studies focus on the linearity of acquiring knowledge, abilities and attitudes using a cognitive perspective, or they focus on a generic list of core competencies (Baum et al., 1997; Dimmock et al., 2003; Chapman & Lovell, 2006; Cheng & Wong, 2015; Bharwani & Talib, 2017; Alberton et al., 2020; Marneros et al., 2020) that do not precisely reflect the hotelier's lived world (Sandberg & Dall'Alba, 2009). These studies reinforce the need for more research on the practices of sustainability and their impacts on the hospitality sector, which in turn contributes to an understanding both in that sector and the entire service industry (Martínez-Martínez et al., 2019a).

This paper fills a gap by focusing on the subject of sustainability practices, the hotelier, to understand their behaviors and enhance their growth in light of socio-environmental demands. The hospitality sector must better understand the hoteliers' reality of sustainability experiences in their lived world, leading to an understanding of how competencies are constructed in specific situations and exposing the factors that foster or prevent advances in this area. The research questions addressed are: (a) What practices emerge from hoteliers when faced with sustainability dilemmas through vignettes? and, (b) What do those practices tell us about hoteliers' learning cycles and competencies in sustainability?

First, a theoretical perspective through which to analyze hoteliers' lived world experiences is proposed, framing their practices as the result of learning cycles that led to competencies. Next, this paper introduces vignette methodology as an important tool to uncover the meaning-making processes and interpretations carried out by participants when faced with real-life sustainability challenges that require decisions or judgments. It is argued that positioning the participants in sustainability events helps to uncover how the hoteliers perceive the reality around them and how their conceptions influence their practices. Results are followed by a discussion of the study's implications on organizational learning processes, giving a new perspective on hospitality training and competency development through practice-based studies.

Using a practice-based lens to understand sustainability learning cycles and competencies

Why is this new perspective necessary to examine professional hoteliers' experiences in sustainability-related problem solving? A practice-based approach to learning focuses on the "real" work in organizations (Geiger, 2009) compared to the traditional, cognitive perspective of learning (Gherardi, 2014). This allows researchers to problematize what *knowing* means in the everyday work of hoteliers dealing with sustainability issues. It uncovers how practitioners activate their explicit and implicit knowledge, carry out daily activities and face dilemmas in their lived worlds. Hoteliers' behaviors are viewed as dynamic processes that result in the generation of new practices, promote the development of competencies in their lived world, shift their theory-in-use or even develop their ability to learn how to learn.

Practices are defined here as the actions of the professional, individual, and collective, that result from the interpretation and resignification of the experience, shared with those involved (Gherardi, 2011) and performed in the sector of hospitality (Sandberg & Dall'Alba, 2009). When reflecting on knowledge revealed by practices, the focus is on the lived world of each subject, including multiple participants (Sandberg & Dall'Alba, 2009; Mierlo & Beers, 2020). In this context, learning occurs both through experience (Gherardi, 2014) and by coping with deviations from normal practices, in their totality, uniqueness and temporality (Sandberg & Tsoukas, 2011).

This practice-based approach also expands the rationalists' perspectives of competencies, allowing interpretation of qualitative data gathered from the lived world of hoteliers. Their practices in handling sustainability challenges are uncovered using vignettes, a projective

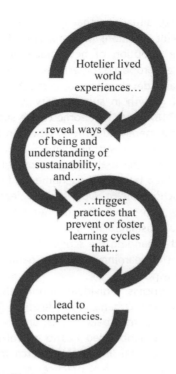

Figure 1. Intertwining perspectives used in this study.
Source: authors, based on literature review

methodology (Nicolini, 2013). The vignettes in this current study were constructed to trigger perceptions, attitudes and practices in the analysis and ultimate action proposed to solve sustainability problems. Subjects' responses portrayed their views of reality, giving researchers clues about how to promote reflection, improve those actions, and facilitate subjects' understanding of concepts (Barter & Renold, 1999; Spalding & Phillips, 2007). Vignettes reveal limits and opportunities in sustainability training while helping identify learning cycles and competencies. Considering this interpretive perspective, and vignettes as a research methodology, it is possible to understand hoteliers' knowledge repertoires, what triggers their actions, and their sustainability theory-in-use.

Figure 1 organizes the framework of the current study used to interpret the sustainability practices in the lived world of hoteliers. This interpretive approach provides an understanding of both barriers to, and possibilities for, sustainability learning and competency development for profound growth in the hospitality sector.

Understanding sustainability practices and learning cycles through hotelier lived world experiences

The present research analyzed how hospitality workers' experiences affected their sustainability-oriented practices. In this interpretive approach, the subject and object of study are inseparably linked in a socio-historical context, and from this context, the tools to build a discourse arise (Sandberg, 2005). Here, the subject of study is the hotelier while the objects of study are both their lived experience and the meaning they attribute to experiences. Studying practices through discourse involves critical reflection, as it promotes continuous distance between the practitioner and the practices (Geiger, 2009).

When individuals are faced with situations that generate incompatibility between real and expected results because of difficult situations or disruption of practices, growth happens. This leads to a review, adaptation or adoption of new practices that can promote performance improvement and achievement of proposed objectives (Argyris & Schön, 1996; Sandberg & Tsoukas, 2011). In turn, learning and development of competencies result, as highlighted in the next section. So far, this arch of growth in sustainability is not happening at the speed and depth needed. Font and Lynes (2018) argue that some of the sustainability practices adopted by the hospitality industry seem to be merely superficial, when, in fact, they need to be rooted in an organizational culture that is focused on sustainability.

Single loop learning refers to this superficial change in practices in quick response to individual factors, like profit, but double loop learning is fundamental for abandonment of obsolete sustainability practices (Argyris & Schön, 1996). Double loop learning involves reflective action, promoting deep learning, quality, and significant changes (Mierlo & Beers, 2020). Double loop learning includes incorporation of sustainability into organizational culture; practices that are more proactive than reactive; and expanding the scope of the dimensions considered in sustainability actions beyond the TBL. This learning promotes paradigmatic change in sustainability beyond the legal and operational aspects.

In the organizational learning process, individuals modify their practices and, consequently, their understanding of the organization. Organizational learning "must become embedded in the images of the organization held in its members' minds, and/or in the epistemological artifacts (the maps, memories, and programs) embedded in the organizational environment" (Argyris & Schön, 1996, p.16). From the international literature, research in sustainable hospitality focuses on TBL (Elkington, 2012), concluding that current practices are ineffective and that greenwashing behavior remains (Font et al., 2012). Sustainability-oriented practices in European hotel chains (Rodriguez-Antón et al., 2012; Prud'Homme & Raymond, 2016) further reveal greenhushing – partial communication of green practices for fear of customer and profit loss (Font et al., 2017). The main questions, from an organization level which then trickles down to hotel staff, seem to be whether sustainability-oriented practices will generate financial returns for the enterprise (Bader, 2005; Claver-Cortés et al., 2007; Aznar et al., 2016; Su & Chen, 2020).

The intertwining of practice with the lived world presupposes engagement in activities and attribution of meaning; and the destabilization of those practices is the only pathway to change. This dynamic evolution makes the relationship between practices and the lived world a challenge for the corporate world and researchers.

Understanding sustainability competencies in the hospitality sector

Developing competencies for sustainability, which originate in a learning process, require a change in organizational values and resignification of work by professionals (Sandberg & Dall'Alba, 2009), since professional competence is framed within a specific means of existing in the world (Sandberg & Pinnington, 2009). However, this has only been minimally studied in the hospitality industry, which means that researchers' attention has not been focused on the analysis and improvement of professionals in this field and, subsequently, on the underlying learning processes. Existing studies generally focus on the managerial skills necessary in that specific sector (Agut & Grau, 2002; Dimmock et al., 2003) and the competencies developed during training (Chapman & Lovell, 2006). Other studies have sought to analyze the specific competencies that become important for professional performance (Baum et al., 1997; Alberton et al., 2020; Marneros et al., 2020), although they lack reflections and research on social and environmental issues or even the analysis of learning processes involved in such dynamics. Bharwani and Talib (2017) review of literature from 1988 to 2015 mapped managerial competencies, but none were related to sustainability. Research on hotel-related competencies also lacks a focus on sustainability, as researchers approach the concept as neither a trend nor a necessity (Teixeira & Morrison, 2004; Reis & Gutierrez, 2008).

Wiek et al. (2011) summarized the literature on sustainability-oriented competencies converging on five key areas, which, when integrated, allow researchers to address sustainability challenges:

- *Systemic Reasoning*: Ability to analyze complex situations considering multiple aspects; involves understanding, verifying, and articulating components.
- *Anticipatory Action*: Ability to analyze situations and facts, comparing them to act preventatively.
- *Normative Behavior*: Ability to insert concepts such as justice, integrity, and ethics into adopted practices; relates to the existence of regulations.
- *Strategic Thinking*: Ability to plan and implement changes and transformations in the organization; requires analysis of the internal and external environment.
- *Interpersonal Skills*: Ability to relate to other individuals, motivating and promoting group collaboration.

These competencies enable better planning, development and application of programs and actions. However, according to Wiek et al. (2011), managing and addressing more complex issues involving sustainability requires business transformation. This change results in an alteration in the way work is understood, as well as its role in society, through reflection and reframing (Sandberg & Dall'Alba, 2009; Sandberg & Pinnington, 2009). Thus, there is not a single competency for sustainability – rather, there are multiple sustainability competencies.

At the organizational level, the sector must move beyond single and even double loop learning into deutero-learning – the process of learning to learn. Individuals working from this perspective are continually developing their abilities to achieve the desired results from the implementation and optimization of new practices and consequent development of competencies. Deutero-learning organizations learn through their professionals – from the discoveries and changes in the theory-in-use and in their relationship with stakeholders. This makes it one of the central points for the development of competencies (Argyris & Schön, 1996; Sandberg & Dall'Alba, 2009; Sandberg & Tsoukas, 2011).

What determines competencies for a professional segment is their lived world (Sandberg & Dall'Alba, 2009), as well as how that group interprets, signifies, and re-signifies the work through its practices. Those practices can be changed by reflection or by the formation of new competencies (Sandberg & Tsoukas, 2011), reinforcing the dynamic nature of practices, learning and new competencies. Thus, for studies that address sustainability skills and knowledge in hotels, it is important to understand how these competencies have or have not been manifested from the analysis of everyday practices, and what can help foster or prevent advancements.

Methods

One way to study practices is through vignettes, the methodology chosen here to capture the learning and competencies developed in context (Gherardi, 2011; Sandberg & Tsoukas, 2011). "Competence is always related to a task or a problem, an object that is socially and discursively constructed and constituted, and, as a consequence, it is also related to individuals' understanding and performance of the particular task" (Ohlsson & Johansson, 2010, p. 242). Understanding the way the hotelier thinks about sustainability problems and responds to events or dilemmas, even in hypothetical situations, helps predict the learning curves and competencies mobilized.

For this reason, vignettes are frequently used to examine judgments and decision-making (Wilks, 2004).

Vignettes for this study were built from stories collected in face-to-face interviews with professionals working in the hotel industry and from university professors teaching undergraduate courses in hospitality in São Paulo, Brazil. The goal of these interviews was to collect stories of lived experiences, so that vignettes originate from real-world situations – a factor that contributes to subjects responding more authentically. Next, stories were only selected in which: the context and problem were clear; they could be generalizable to other hotels; they involved stakeholders; they avoided unusual or exaggerated situations or characters (Barter & Renold, 1999; Hughes & Huby, 2004); and they represented dilemmas, problems or disruptions of social and environmental sustainability. Cultural and territorial dimensions did not appear in any of the collected stories, indicating a possible disregard for these critical axes of sustainability, corroborating previous studies (Bohdanowicz, 2006; Rahman et al., 2012; Rodriguez-Antón et al., 2012; Prud'Homme & Raymond, 2016).

Since qualitative data were collected, vignette validation aligned with qualitative methodologies. The vignettes were tested, prior to use in this study, in two phases with students working on their bachelor's degrees in hospitality at an educational institution in São Paulo, Brazil and who also work professionally in hotels. First, written responses were collected from 10 students in their third year, before holding interviews with each one to ask for any difficulties in carrying out the requested tasks and to note any suggested changes. Second, those updated vignettes were sent virtually to 10 fourth-year students for a virtual validation, since this is how vignettes were to be distributed to test subjects later.

Wason et al. (2002) criteria regarding the validity and reliability of vignettes was applied to the instrument developed in the present investigation: (a) the vignettes are plausible, based on sustainability stories that occur or can occur in the hotel industry, providing proximity to the real world of hoteliers; (b) they provide adequate detail for understanding the context; (c) the same stories were presented to all research participants, increasing internal validity, reliability and ease of replication; and finally (d) vignette wording was edited to best portray real-life situations and to remove politically-charged phrases, to direct respondents' attention to the specific aspects of this research study. Further, participants could analyze vignettes from their point of view, from the perspective of a character or even as a peer of the character (Hughes & Huby, 2004).

The six resulting vignettes were emailed to 115 hotel professionals, selected for their work in hotels and completion of a college education. These hoteliers worked for independent and chain hotels in managerial and operational positions. Enterprise profile and position held were not factors of choice, since sustainability encompasses all enterprises. The email request included a concise introduction to the research, informing the respondents that the stories focused on sustainability and that the intention was to understand their practices through their discursive answers. Demographic and professional data from respondents was also requested.

Responses were considered valid for analysis if the subject answered all six vignettes and if answers expressed the professionals' experiences, practices, and perceptions about sustainability with precise details to capture the competences triggered in the decision-making process. For each vignette, individuals' responses were analyzed by comparing and contrasting meanings of hoteliers' lived world, as revealed in (a) emerging practices in decision-making processes (Hughes & Huby, 2004); (b) type of learning demonstrated (Argyris & Schön, 1996); and (c) the competencies, whether strategic or normative, used by the practices reported (Sandberg & Dall'Alba, 2009). Figure 2 gives an overview of these study methods.

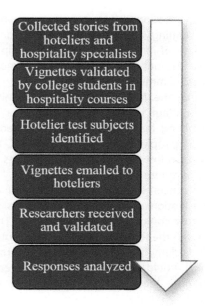

Figure 2. Overview of methods.

Results

Of the 115 hoteliers emailed, 43 returned valid responses. Of those, 24 occupied operational positions (O), and 19 were in managerial positions (M). Respondents represented 14 hotels in Brazil, either independent (I; n = 7) or chain hotels (C; n = 36). The largest number came from the area of lodging. All respondents developed their careers in the southeast region of the country, mainly in São Paulo (33), Rio de Janeiro (6), and Minas Gerais (4). Participants were mostly female, with an average age of 29 years, having graduated 6.5 years prior with a bachelor's or associate degree in hospitality, hotel management or environmental engineering and with an average of 9 years of experience in the sector.

The vignettes, translated into English, and their analyses are presented below, in the same order as in the research instrument, and summarized in Table 1.

Vignette 1

You were hired to participate in the establishment of a resort in the northern region of the country, in a small town with a strong appeal of nature and that still does not have higher education institutions. In this city, there is a predominance of inns. The professionals who work in the hotel sector have a profile that is consistent with this type of facility accommodation. One of your challenges is to assemble the work teams at this resort.
What will your actions and strategies be to overcome the challenge of assembling teams?

This vignette addressed the social perspective of sustainability-related to hiring employees, but only 7 hoteliers out of the 43 participants approached this dimension in their responses. For those 7, their practices focused on the development of the community through partnerships with schools, city hall and competitions, which would facilitate the development of the region and its workforce, indicating that the establishment of the resort might narrow the relationship between the enterprise and the community (Melissen, 2013; Camilleri, 2016). These proposals revealed double loop learning to promote transformation and reflexive processes (Argyris & Schön, 1996).

Some of the 43 responses also mentioned human resource management, indicating competencies in capturing, qualifying, retaining, and monitoring professionals (Bharwani & Talib, 2017). However, there was a predominance of initiatives seeking leadership outside the region in which the resort would be implanted, without any proposal to promote the region, to generate employment or to benefit the local community.

Almost no attempts to balance the interests of the community and the enterprise were observed. For example, one respondent stated: "In the case of a location that lacks qualified workforce, we think about assembling leadership with experienced professionals from another region with the purpose of training people of the region [...]" (MC-19).

Regarding the attraction and retention of professionals, practices were directed toward remuneration strategies and career opportunities.

This vignette also focused on concerns about the environment and the impact of the business, which would require the adoption of practices that address social measures. There were answers that pointed to anticipatory competence (Wiek et al., 2011) that enables the analysis of the impacts potentially caused by the establishment of the hotel enterprise, with possible change in the current theory. This demonstrated double loop learning (Argyris & Schön, 1996). As one respondent exemplified: "I would seek an environmental engineering and sustainability professional so that I could prioritize the maintenance of nature around" (OC −20). However, this concern was rarely mentioned by the hotel professionals.

Vignette 2

You operate in a large hotel's events team located in a capital city with a business profile. Much of the proceeds from the enterprise originate from business tourism. For the first time in this hotel, a large organization from the cosmetics sector, which is nationally recognized for its concern with sustainability, has booked an event that will require the use of conference rooms, bedrooms, coffee breaks and meals. Routine procedures were used for the negotiation. It is noteworthy that the price was attractive to the client, as it was an initial contract to gain loyalty. A few days before the event, the client resumed contact to check on specific details. At this point, several items – that the hotel did not have available – were requested. All items were linked to culture and values related to sustainability, including recycled office supplies, water flow reducers, economical lamps, meals prepared with organic food, and biodegradable products, among others. To meet the customer's demand, there is a need to tailor various hotel practices. There are costs involved in this process, which directly impacts the revenue of the event.

As manager of the events department, how you would manage this situation in terms of a) the client and its needs; b) the revenue from the event; and c) hotel policies?

Vignette 2 addressed the environmental and economic dimensions and demonstrated a conflict situation that involved loyalty related to a new client, meeting its requirements, and the investment that is needed to provide the service, as well as how that affects the expected returns.

Considering the emerging practices in the written reports, responses grouped across five dimensions: (1) short-term perspective; (2) customer service for loyalty development; (3) opportunity to adopt sustainability-oriented practices; (4) reevaluation of policies already adopted by the hotel; and (5) reconciliation of interests between the customer and hotel. It is noteworthy that approaches 3, 4, and 5 indicate double loop learning processes (Argyris & Schön, 1996).

The short-term perspective does not consider customer loyalty and is limited to fulfilling the initial contract or terminating it. The practices that served the customer and engendered its loyalty were related to the costs incurred in meeting those needs, or how the costs are passed on to the contractor. According to one respondent, they were instructed to "assume a posture geared toward sustainability," even if temporary, which is reduced to a discursive change only. This posture can be characterized as a greenwashing solution (Font et al., 2012):

> [...] I would explain to the client that these requests have a cost, and that to serve them, this cost will have to be passed [...] I would inform all my employees of the importance of this event and the practices

they would like to see being used [...] When guests are at the hotel, they can see that the hotel really values their culture, even if it is not the policy that the hotel usually practices in the day-to-day (MC-18).

For some hoteliers, both in operations and management, meeting customer demand was an opportunity to engage in sustainability-oriented practices (Prud'Homme & Raymond, 2016), because it enabled a discussion of the topic with general management. It also engendered an improvement of management practices (Bohdanowicz, 2006).

The practices aimed at reconciling interests, in which the client's needs are met and the hotel becomes more sustainable, would generate, in the perception of hoteliers, the development of green marketing strategies, along with loyalty and attraction of new customers (Bohdanowicz, 2006; Töpke et al., 2011). One participant responded: "I would worry about meeting the demands from the client and learn from them [...] It will be an opportunity for the Hotel to be more sustainable, and it can even be used as social media marketing [...]" (MI −2).

The answers demonstrated the possibility of aligning customer demands with sustainability. But proposals such as "divide investments" – presented by hoteliers who occupy positions both in management and in operations – stand out, because this facilitates the interpretation that, if no client presents this type of demand, requirements of sustainability would not feature in the hotel's future planning.

Above all, it is important to highlight skills of a pragmatic nature, concentrated on the ability to direct the investment in sustainability to the enterprise, via customer loyalty, new business or green marketing. However, none of them expressed a resignification of the work that is capable of significantly boosting sustainability, with the emergence of other types of competencies, designed for purposes other than marketing (Sandberg & Dall'Alba, 2009; Sandberg & Pinnington, 2009). This indicates single loop learning, as the proposals implied shallow changes in the organizational practices and policy.

Vignette 3

Hotel X is undergoing an internal process encouraged by the general manager, which aims to promote awareness and adopt sustainable practices. The leading practices adopted relate to energy and water consumption and selective garbage collection. On his initiative, the hotel manager prepared a proposed project and budget for solar energy deployment. The investment to implement the project was approximately BRL 50,000 [equivalent to USD 9,300]. At the shareholders and board meeting, he presented his proposal in a very motivating way. Participants were not convinced of the initiative and argued that if funding was available, they would invest it in profitable projects, such as expanding event space. After the directors' reaction, the manager was speechless, unable to clearly show his colleagues the studies that have been carried out that demonstrate the projected returns on investment.
Do you agree with the directors? Why?
How would you act if you were the manager who drafted the proposal?
What arguments would you use in favor of the approval of the proposal?

Vignette 3 considered the relationship between economic and environmental dimensions, including the negotiation and convictions of those involved about the importance of investing in sustainability.

When respondents agreed with the position of managers, it was mainly justified by financial issues. Such issues needed better analysis and explanation, since the proposal does not emphasize the benefits to the enterprise. As one participant said: "Not knowing the amount of savings generated, I agree with the directors, because they mainly aim at financial return [...]" (OC-3). Lack of clarity can be characterized as a barrier to sustainability (Prud'Homme & Raymond, 2016).

Some interviewees understood the directors' position but did not agree with it: "I do not agree with the directors, but I understand their point of view, since BRL 50,000 represents too much [...] to invest in a project apparently not so beneficial [...]" (OC-24).

Some responses showed partial agreement with the manager's attitude, indicating an attempt to reconcile interests, since both investments can be considered important and can generate returns. It is noteworthy that the relevance of sustainability is not mentioned, but its return is mentioned. When they showed agreement, the convincing tone of the directors/investors is given by expressions such as: "I would ask for more time" (OC-11); and "I would not give up on the project" (MC-17), pointing out that they considered the topic to be relevant.

The strategies adopted when the interviewees put themselves in the place of the manager proposing the project revealed that the activated competencies would be those aimed at leveraging financial return. They would provide further information; they would make the investment serve as a marketing strategy (Claver-Cortés et al., 2007); and they would consistently point to the financial return in expanding the event space. Sustainability arguments were always present in the background:

> [...] It is necessary to present investment proposals that have a high return capacity – whether financial or not. [...] The proposal for the installation of solar energy system should focus on the issue of saving money spent on energy bills and then on the issue of sustainability and the environment [...] (MC-16).

As much as they totally or partially disagreed with the stance of the directors, it was implied that financial issues and cost savings (Bader, 2005) were prominent in the claims made by hoteliers. The arguments were not directed towards sustainability in its essence, but rather, to the results it can offer, indicating that, when compared to other themes such as planning and investments, sustainability loses its relevance. Hotelier responses revealed neither reflection nor, consequently, learning about competencies related to arguing with the shareholders, which could have made the board of directors more favorable to the solar energy proposal.

Vignette 4

Engaging guests in sustainable practices have become increasingly crucial to the success of such practices, as many of these practices, such as towel changes and energy and water consumption, involve the guests' participation and awareness. Many hotels have replaced standard keys with magnetic cards that enable the electricity, allowing lights, TV, and air conditioning to be activated when inserted into the room's internal device. When the guest is not in the room, the power supply is removed, as the card is not in the device. Even with this measure, guests are reported to be inserting cards into the device that are like those used by the hotel to keep the air conditioner on during their absence, for example.
If you were a manager of a hotel where these events occurred, what would you do?

In Vignette 4, the importance of education, engagement, and awareness of guests in sustainability-oriented practices were highlighted. Hotelier responses confirmed a predominance of passive behavior in dealing with the situation, indicating that the fear of losing the customer predominates. They stated that there is little to do about guest behavior, showing conformity and omission: "Unfortunately, this practice is adopted by many guests [...]" (OC-24).

The practices that emerged in the discourses were directed to clients, not employees. Most respondents described informative initiatives, which hardly promote learning through reflection and consequent competency development, that aim to warn the guests about the need to save energy. In the meantime, they reinforced the difficulties they face while doing so. It is important to consider that for the success of such action, engagement is fundamental, but the attitude of the hoteliers when only informing the clients was more reactive and passive, and less mobilizing, than required: "At no time would I punish the guests [...]. I would put information about the benefits and values about sustainability [...]" (MI-6).

Formative practices, which are more advanced in relation to merely informative practices, were rarely mentioned. Three participants strove to raise awareness and engage guests: "[...] I would invest in awareness-raising campaigns about conscious consumption and would try to engage guests in these campaigns [...]" (MC-15). According to Gössling (2018), educational proposals aimed at guests need to include data regarding the impacts of the hotel and its interrelationship with the community or surrounding environment, increasing the chances of the guest's understanding and participation. This strategy was not apparent in participant responses.

Aiming to maintain customers, the hoteliers' focus was on palliative solutions, operating under the premise that the customer is always right: "[...] We respect the will of the guest; what we can do is put a notice next to the device encouraging and making the customer aware of the economy and its benefits" (OC-24).

In cases of greater initiative, before giving into the appeals and demands of guests, an attempt was made to reconcile the interests of sustainability and guest needs:

> What can be done is for the manager to talk to the client who has this practice and find out a little more about their routine [...] try to figure out the time the customer would return and then, 10 minutes prior to that, turn on the air [...] So the problem would be solved without creating discomfort with the customer (OI-4).

The same can be said of the cases of hoteliers who pointed to practices of control and inhibition of inappropriate guest actions. Although this may immediately have the desired effect, the behavior on the part of the hotel can be characterized as dodging the problem. The practice does not have an educational and lasting impact. There is still a risk of conflict between guest and staff (Hsieh, 2010), as in this example: "[...]When the maid went to clean the room she would check if this was happening and take the key from the stand, informing the reception so that when the guest arrived, they would inform him about the procedure [...]" (OI-2).

Even though hoteliers considered the guest's attitude to be inappropriate, there were no actions that formed a set of educational initiatives aimed at creating a culture oriented towards sustainability and consequent reflexive and learning processes. Their initiatives were done on a reactive and as-needed basis. Secondly, while the case illustrates only one aspect of guest behavior across all hotel experiences (restaurant, play area, etc.), there is little evidence of the development of a sustainable behavior-inducing competence that is strategic and interpersonal (Wiek et al., 2011).

Vignette 5

You have become responsible for a hotel located in region X, characterized by high rates of child prostitution and juveniles with no opportunity to gain professional experience, generating violence in and around the region. For the hotel, the direct consequence has been low occupancy. Upon learning of this situation, you have found that actions should be taken to reverse the situation.
What would these actions be?

In this vignette, the social dimension of sustainability stood out, impacting the occupancy of the hotel and, consequently, financial returns. The hoteliers' solutions addressed different practices. Some solutions revealed their intention to combat and minimize the impacts of the problem in the surroundings of the hotel. Such proposals ranged from actions aimed at developing the community to those of purely welfare. There was a set of responses that included practices that left the social problems of the surroundings completely on the sidelines, such as strategies to improve occupation and pass the problem on to others.

Combative and impact-minimization practices were aimed at identifying the origins of young people and children who might be staying at the hotel; preventing prostitutes from staying in and around the enterprise; conducting information campaigns for guests and staff; and partnering with other hotels in search of solutions and adoption of practices. In essence, they were practices that did not propose any kind of development of those involved, and on the contrary, they encouraged removal, rather than confrontation, of the problem.

Welfare practices would involve guests and the community, but in a way that offered more visibility for the enterprise than effective results for the community. According to Font and Lynes (2018), this may be a strategy that softens the relations between the hotel and community, thus improving its image: "I would look for ways to work with social actions in the region with families and children (raising clothing, food donations, among others) [...]" (MC-9).

Notice these practices involved only marketing and promotion actions to attract customers, without proposing a solution to the surrounding social problems. There were even suggestions to disassociate and exempt the enterprise from any responsibility, directing the solution toward third parties, such as the police: "Unfortunately we cannot fight this kind of 'behavior' of outsiders, but the ideal would be to arrange a meeting with local authorities to increase policing in the region" (OC-16).

Practices that pointed to development proposals included professional qualification projects; sports incentives; and internal training programs, both corrective and preventive: "I would open internal programs to teach and employ young people in the hotel [...]. With this, we would contribute to the development and earn the local community" (MC-7). Some considered partnerships with the community, city hall and schools, to train, develop and employ residents. These examples indicated sustainability-oriented practices that required stakeholders' participation and a broader perspective of action in the search for effective solutions. Those also contributed to business improvement and increased the visibility of the enterprise (Camilleri, 2016; Font & Lynes, 2018).

In a way, hoteliers sought out solutions to the situation, and concern about the occupation was one of the least referenced points. This revealed the importance they gave to the social problem, which is positive, indicating single loop learning (Argyris & Schön, 1996). Many of the practices triggered over time could become corrective or even preventative. However, palliative actions continued to dominate, and the logic of long-term development, the effective action of the hotel in the community, and the establishment of partnerships was not yet the prevailing behavior in the minds of the hoteliers. Among these, normative and strategic competencies were revealed (Wiek et al., 2011).

Vignette 6

Recycling waste separation is a practice adopted by most hotels, and it involves cost, training, and employee participation. In general, the maids are responsible for this collection, as they have appropriate equipment and places to perform the task. However, there is no supervision or manual with guidelines on how to proceed. With the lack of time and a rushed few days, the collection was not done and gradually became an activity that was not conducted correctly, and there was no collaboration with other teams. In order to raise awareness from all employees, the hotel set up mixed teams for the activity, which would be responsible for the task for one week and were staffed by professionals of all levels. The week that the hosting manager was supposed to attend, he informed the project manager that he could not do so, as he had more important things to work on.
How do you rate this manager's actions?
In the position of general manager of this venture, how would you handle this situation?

This vignette considered the environmental dimension and the manager's engagement in sustainability-oriented practices to contribute to the awareness of the team. It revealed a problem with which many hoteliers identified.

The manager's attitude is mostly assessed as negative due to the lack of commitment, engagement and disinterest with this type of project, indicating that his conduct can make room for other employees to do the same. The attitude was characterized as a bad example, and adjectives such as irresponsible, unprofessional, lousy, negative, and inadequate were used to describe it: "The manager's posture is completely irresponsible since the example comes from leadership [...]" (MI-2).

Although the indignation was vehement, the responses of professionals who were empathetic to the manager's behavior were also present. They argued that they did not consider the conduct of the manager as unfavorable, since other tasks may be pressing, as exemplified in one participant's response: "[...] It is understandable that the hosting manager, an operational area [...], has other functions that may even be considered more important [...]" (OC-24).

Regarding the question about the management of the situation by the manager's immediate superior, the interviewees presented four types of practices:

1. *Orientation and awareness practices* were the most cited. These seek to emphasize the importance of the project, and participation is encouraged: "[...] As a general manager, I would discreetly talk to the manager, not to expose him to his team and other employees, but to alert him to the key role of motivating his team to carry out the assigned activities [...]" (MC-9).
2. The *collaborative* actions were directed towards the search for alternatives that guaranteed the presence of the manager, such as reorganization of tasks and substitution in department activities, among others: "I would be available to help him better organize his tasks so that he can dedicate the time planned in the action without disrupting his daily schedule of activities and deadlines [...]" (MC-9).
3. The *formation* practices focused on professional development and were directed towards continuous behavioral change (Prud'Homme & Raymond, 2016): "[...] Quarterly, I would apply reinforcement training, showing the program results and the importance of participation especially by managers, as they become examples for their employees" (OC-23).
4. The *disciplinary and punitive* measures aimed to warn that the behavior was considered inappropriate, as this type of posture can demonstrate a lack of commitment to hotel projects. They warned that this type of practice directs the individual towards the desired behavior but does not promote the incorporation of sustainability as a value (Font & Lynes, 2018), making participation in the project only a way to avoid negative consequences: "[...] In case of a lot of resistance, we would apply warning, conversation, feedback. If those actions do not solve the problem, we follow a resignation process [...]" (OI-3).

It is noteworthy how these formative and collaborative practices were directed towards behavioral changes, contributing to double loop learning (Argyris & Schön, 1996).

When the interviewees put themselves in the supervisor's position, they assumed different positions that varied from the politest to the rudest conduct. They also ranged from the most formative and educational to the merely enforceable, punitive, and disciplinary. In any case, the responses were emphatic about the importance of the managerial role as an exemplar. The triggered competencies identified were systemic and normative (Wiek et al., 2011).

Table 1. Summary of vignette response analysis.

Vignettes	Sustainability-oriented dimensions	Practices	Learning	Competencies
Vignette 1	Social and economic dimensions with community development and job creation	- Professional qualification and / or community development - Recruitment and selection of professionals in the market outside the region - Attraction and retention of professionals	Single loop learning, with evidence of starting double loop	- Anticipatory: analytical capacity of the situation - Interpersonal focused on people management: qualification; adoption of recruitment and retention strategies for professionals

(continued)

Table 1. Continued.

Vignettes	Sustainability-oriented dimensions	Practices	Learning	Competencies
Vignette 2	Economic dimension; predominance of concern with the business	- Meet customer needs without losing sight of the financial return - Meet customer needs and implement sustainability-oriented practices - Compare hotel policy with customer requirements - Reconcile the interests of the enterprise and the client	Single loop learning	- Strategic, but predominantly limited to economic issues. - Normative for analyzing policies and relating them to customer demands
Vignette 3	Economic dimension with struggle between investment and return	- Search for investment information - Conduct a new negotiation with the board - Sustainability research market practices - Highlight sustainability as a differential and attractive for guests	Faulty learning process toward sustainability	- Interpersonal: arguments restricted to trigger sustainability investments in an economic perspective - Strategic: involving planning to articulate managers toward economic sustainability issues
Vignette 4	Directed towards guest maintenance, with sustainability being little considered	- Informational: guest and staff - Control and inhibition of guest action - Meet guests' wishes - Training: guests and staff	Hardly promotes learning because there is no action or reflection that addresses the theme	- Competencies focused on sustainability are not evident in addressing the dilemma - Few strategic and interpersonal competencies, and, if activated, contributed to the analysis of the proposed dilemma
Vignette 5	Social and economic dimensions with search for actions to combat and minimize reality and concern with the hotel's image and occupancy	- Combat and minimize impacts - Local youth development to combat delinquency and child prostitution - Assistance through partnerships - Outsource problem solving	Single loop learning with start of double loop learning when involving stakeholders	- Normative: identified and applied values and rules related to the social dimension of sustainability - Strategic: planned and established partnerships
Vignette 6	Environmental dimension and the relevance of engagement	- Guidance and awareness - Disciplinary and punitive measures - Collaborative measures - Actions of management formation	Double loop learning	- Systemic and normative: context analysis and reinforcement of the sustainability policies and the managerial role

Discussion

Hoteliers' practices seek to increase profit

The results show that, in most cases, hoteliers only considered sustainability when it offered a return to the hotel, either financial (Bader, 2005) or image-enhancing (Jones et al., 2016), to justify the investment. The most frequently emerging practice was the minimization of problems and financial loss while encouraging increased profitability. However, the predominance of this reasoning, and the lack of pro-sustainability behavior that does not put financial interests first, points to the necessity of reflexive learning to engender a shift in current behaviors (Argyris & Schön, 1996). This partly explains the lack of improvement in this area, as the literature has shown (Claver-Cortés et al., 2007; Hsieh, 2010; Camilleri, 2016; Alberton et al., 2020).

Both explicitly and implicitly, hotelier practices were directed towards partnerships, conciliation of interests and involvement of other actors, confirming that sustainability must be better incorporated into organizational and collective practices. Organizational learning was observed, but mostly as single loop (Argyris & Schön, 1996; Table 1). This indicates the need for double loop learning when issues involve stakeholders. The practices that emerged ranged from acceptance and dialogue to punitive and inhibitory measures, alternating between single loop and double loop learning, but without the effective transformation of the context of competency development (Argyris & Schön, 1996).

In this sense, although the practices seek the conciliation of interests between the enterprise and the demands of sustainability, the competencies triggered were more to the service of the hotel industry rather than to the surrounding community and environment (Bohdanowicz, 2006; Grosbois, 2012; Hsieh, 2012). A dominant pragmatic perspective contributes to sustainability becoming a "bargaining chip" and being used as a greenwashing strategy (Font et al., 2012), as was best demonstrated in responses to Vignette 2. The initiatives that prevailed were those that revealed passivity towards problems, punitive or merely inhibiting measures, such as those highlighted in Vignette 6.

However, in Vignettes 1, 4, and 5, there was also a movement towards the establishment of partnerships and involvement of other social actors, such as community, suppliers, guests, and public agencies. This is a necessary behavior for the learning and resolution of sustainability issues, demanding a reflexive action and a shift in current perspectives (Argyris & Schön, 1996). Some practices were directed at turning conflict into opportunity, as noted in Vignettes 2 and 5, possibly indicating innovative actions and a path to deutero-learning. Even so, few responses attempted to establish new dialogues with guests and shareholders or to develop long-term educational actions.

Analysis of vignette responses showed that hoteliers disregard the cultural and territorial dimensions, having instead a segmented view of sustainability that oscillates between uni- and bi-dimensional, rather than the multidimensional perspective that sustainability requires. These less comprehensive competencies won't solve the issues (e.g. the development and preservation of local culture and natural regions).

More specific sustainability competencies, like systemic, anticipatory reasoning, and normative and strategic sustainability measures, were not present, just as they are not in the lived world of hospitality (Sandberg & Pinnington, 2009). Considering that sustainability demands different levels of delivery (Wiek et al., 2011), a new path should be taken to reach the quality of learning that can allow the adaptation and adoption of new practices, aiming to improve performance (Argyris & Schön, 1996; Sandberg & Tsoukas, 2011). The development of competencies that lead to action for sustainability must be developed from deutero-learning. Hoteliers must examine how they learn, since sustainability is a dynamic and comprehensive concept, which involves constant reflection and redefinition of their lived world.

Sustainability practices and competencies must increase

On the one hand, hotelier actions appeared driven by important competencies, such as educational proposals associated with human resources management and environmental assessment of enterprises before their implementation. On the other hand, some actions had weak affinity with environmental development, short-term vision and reach, greenwashing and actions driven only by marketing. Beyond those data, results showed that it is necessary to expand hoteliers' perspectives to territorial and cultural dimensions, neither of which were present in the vignette stories nor emerged from hotelier responses.

If the advancement of hotel sustainability depends on adopted practices and their incorporation into the organizational culture (Font & Lynes, 2018), this study's results have significant theoretical, methodological, and practical contributions.

As a theoretical contribution, this research presented a conceptual lens of analysis, based on an interpretative approach of the intertwining of knowledge, decision-making, and action.

Looking at hoteliers' practices captured their tacit and explicit knowledge and understanding of sustainability from an integrated perspective. The practice-based lens, even if by proxy of vignettes, reveals the dynamics of those processes which contribute to our understanding of what is involved in hoteliers transforming the very structure of meaning and practice. This article advances the discussion beyond a cognitive and rational perspective of learning and competencies (Sandberg & Dall'Alba, 2009), toward a multidimensional view of sustainability in the hospitality sector.

From a methodological point of view, this study introduced vignettes as a qualitative research tool to gather hoteliers' sustainability decision-making processes and practices. Vignettes functioned as a mirror to reality since an advantage of projective techniques is to allow for interpretations "that reflect the interests and concerns of the interviewee and overcome the barriers [...] of rationality and social influences [...] causing, instead, imaginative and unusual associations and hypothetical conjectures ('as if')" (Gherardi, 2014, p.154). This brings researchers closer to the hotelier's lived world experiences.

As a practical implication, results could increase and improve professional development experiences, due to more accurate, precise, and integrative insights regarding hoteliers' thoughts and actions. If there is no development of best practices and competencies over the next few years, leading to a transformation of hoteliers' lived world decisions, sustainability will not significantly advance in the short or medium-term in the hotel sector. Next steps include highlighting the relevance of planning and the adoption of reflexive training based on critical incident analyses, circles of conversations, hoteliers' reflexive diaries, storytelling methodologies and experiences that lead the hoteliers to question and review their ways of being. These could produce more significant results in organizational structure. Hoteliers' development should break negative sustainability habits and build upon their positive practices to advance sustainability. However, these organizational efforts in professional development must be triggered by the industry's political will to tackle sustainability issues.

Conclusions

Hoteliers' practices were extruded from their lived world perspectives by presenting them with sustainability dilemmas through vignettes. Their responses, which were their projected actions in those scenarios, were analyzed using an interpretive approach providing a window into hoteliers' day-to-day work and their understanding of sustainability. Unlike other studies, the intertwining of the hoteliers' knowledge, competencies, practices and lived world experiences were the article's focus, not a specific knowledge, learning process or competency per se. The conceptual lens and methodology presented here can serve other studies on sustainability in tourism, offering insights on learning and competencies for sustainability which is less explored in the tourism literature.

The use of vignettes that present actual sustainability problems in context is shown to be a powerful tool that elicits hotelier's reflection to reveal their beliefs, values, interpretations, and judgments. This helps to reveal the repertories and metaphors that feed their practices and explains the advancements and barriers to the hotel sector's sustainability progress. The results suggest various actions toward expanding the comprehension of sustainability from hoteliers, with subsequent impact on the learning and construction of better competencies in the hotelier's lived world.

There are limitations of this study, which can also become opportunities for further investigations. First, this study focused on the hosting sector and used vignettes as a proxy for making real-time observations of hoteliers' sustainability decision-making. Assumptions were made for honest responses from study subjects. Future studies could capture real-time observations or face-to-face interviews to corroborate these findings. Second, data were collected from a limited geographic area and 14 business hotels. Though southeast Brazil is an important economic and development nexus in South America providing benchmarks for comparative studies, expansion to more and different geographical and cultural regions would contribute to this field of study.

Disclosure statement

No potential conflict of interest was reported by the authors.

ORCID

Cláudia Martins Pantuffi http://orcid.org/0000-0002-2615-0424
Janette Brunstein http://orcid.org/0000-0002-9019-3349
Mark Edward Walvoord http://orcid.org/0000-0002-4003-7532

References

Agut, S., & Grau, R. (2002). Managerial competency needs and training requests: The case of the Spanish tourist industry. *Human Resource Development Quarterly, 13*(1), 31–52. https://doi.org/10.1002/hrdq.1012

Alberton, A., Kieling, A. P., Lyra, F. R., Hoffmann, E. M., Lopez, M. P. V., & Stefano, S. R. (2020). Competencies for sustainability in hotels: Insights from Brazil. *Employee Relations: The International Journal*. ahead-of-print. https://doi.org/10.1108/ER-01-2019-0093

Argyris, C., & Schön, D. A. (1996). *Organizational learning II: Theory, method and practice*. Addison-Wesley.

Aznar, J. P., Sayeras, J. M., Galiana, J., & Rocafort, A. (2016). Sustainability commitment, new competitors' presence, and hotel performance: The hotel industry in Barcelona. *Sustainability, 8*(8), 713–755. https://doi.org/10.3390/su8080755

Bader, E. E. (2005). Sustainable hotel business practices. *Journal of Retail & Leisure Property, 5*(1), 70–77. https://doi.org/10.1057/palgrave.rlp.5090008

Barter, C., & Renold, E. (1999). The use of vignettes in qualitative research. *Social Research Update, 25*, 1–7.

Baum, T., Amoah, V., & Spivack, S. (1997). Policy dimensions of human resource management in the tourism and hospitality industries. *International Journal of Contemporary Hospitality Management, 9*(5/6), 221–229. https://doi.org/10.1108/09596119710172615

Bharwani, S., & Talib, P. (2017). Competencies of hotel general managers: A conceptual framework. *International Journal of Contemporary Hospitality Management, 29*(1), 393–418. https://doi.org/10.1108/IJCHM-09-2015-0448

Bohdanowicz, P. (2006). Environmental awareness and initiatives in the Swedish and Polish hotel industries – survey results. *International Journal of Hospitality Management, 25*(4), 662–682. https://doi.org/10.1016/j.ijhm.2005.06.006

Camilleri, M. (2016). Responsible tourism that creates shared value among stakeholders. *Tourism Planning & Development, 13*(2), 219–235. https://doi.org/10.1080/21568316.2015.1074100

Chan, E. S. W., Okumus, F., & Chan, W. (2018). Barriers to environmental technology adoption in hotels. *Journal of Hospitality & Tourism Research, 42*(5), 829–852. https://doi.org/10.1177/1096348015614959

Chapman, J. A., & Lovell, G. (2006). The competency model of hospitality service: Why it doesn't deliver. *International Journal of Contemporary Hospitality Management, 18*(1), 78–88. https://doi.org/10.1108/09596110610642000

Cheng, S., & Wong, A. (2015). Professionalism: A contemporary interpretation in hospitality industry context. *International Journal of Hospitality Management, 50*, 122–133. https://doi.org/10.1016/j.ijhm.2015.08.002

Claver-Cortés, E., Molina-Azorín, J. F., Pereira-Moliner, J., & López-Gamero, M. D. (2007). Environmental strategies and their impact on hotel performance. *Journal of Sustainable Tourism, 15*(6), 663–679. https://doi.org/10.2167/jost640.0

Dimmock, K., Breen, H., & Walo, M. (2003). Management competencies: An Australian assessment of tourism and hospitality students. *Academy of Management, 9*(1), 12–26.

Elkington, J. (2012). *Sustentabilidade, Canibais com Garfo e Faca*. M. Books do Brasil Editora Ltda.

Font, X., Elgammal, I., & Lamond, I. (2017). Greenhushing: The deliberate under communicating of sustainability practices by tourism businesses. *Journal of Sustainable Tourism, 25*(7), 1007–1023. https://doi.org/10.1080/09669582.2016.1158829

Font, X., & Lynes, J. (2018). Corporate social responsibility in tourism and hospitality. *Journal of Sustainable Tourism, 26*(7), 1027–1042. https://doi.org/10.1080/09669582.2018.1488856

Font, X., Walmsley, A., Cogotti, S., McCombes, L., & Häusler, N. (2012). Corporate social responsibility: The disclosure-performance gap. *Tourism Management, 33*(6), 1544–1553. https://doi.org/10.1016/j.tourman.2012.02.012

Geiger, D. (2009). Revisiting the concept of practice: Toward an argumentative understanding of practicing. *Management Learning, 40*(2), 129–144. https://doi.org/10.1177/1350507608101228

Gherardi, S. (2011). Organizational learning: The sociology of practice. In M. Easterby-Smith & M. A. Lyles (Eds.), *Handbook of organizational learning & knowledge management*. Wiley. 43–65.

Gherardi, S. (2014). Conhecimento situado e ação situada: o que os estudos baseados em prática prometem?. In S Gherardi & A. Strati (Eds.), *Administração e Aprendizagem na Prática*. Elsevier. 3–18.

Gössling, S. (2018). Tourism, tourist learning and sustainability: An exploratory discussion of complexities, problems and opportunities. *Journal of Sustainable Tourism, 26*(2), 292–306. https://doi.org/10.1080/09669582.2017.1349772

Grosbois, D. (2012). Corporate social responsibility reporting by the global hotel industry: Commitment, initiatives and performance. *International Journal of Hospitality Management, 31*(3), 896–905.

Hsieh, E. (2010). Hospitalidade & sustentabilidade. In A. Phillip Jr & D. V. M Ruschmann (Eds.), *Gestão Ambiental e Sustentabilidade no Turismo* (V. 9). Manole. 97–108.

Hsieh, Y. (2012). Hotel companies' environmental policies and practices: A content analysis of their web pages. *International Journal of Contemporary Hospitality Management, 24*(1), 97–121. https://doi.org/10.1108/095961112

Hughes, R., & Huby, M. (2004). The construction and interpretation of vignettes in social research. *Social Work and Social Sciences Review, 11*(1), 36–51. https://doi.org/10.1921/17466105.11.1.36

Jones, P., Hillier, D., & Comfort, D. (2016). Sustainability in the hospitality industry: Some personal reflections on corporate challenges and research agendas. *International Journal of Contemporary Hospitality Management, 28*(1), 36–67. https://doi.org/10.1108/IJCHM-11-2014-0572

Marneros, S., Papageorgiou, G., & Efstathiades, A. (2020). Identifying key success competencies for the hospitality industry: The perspectives of professionals. *Journal of Teaching in Travel & Tourism, 20*(4), 237–261. https://doi.org/10.1080/15313220.2020.1745732

Martinez-Martinez, A., Cegarra-Navarro, J. G., García-Pérez, A., & Wensley, A. (2019b). Knowledge agents as drivers of environmental sustainability and business performance in the hospitality sector. *Tourism Management, 70*, 381–389. https://doi.org/10.1016/j.tourman.2018.08.030

Martínez-Martínez, A., Cegarra-Navarro, J. G., García-Pérez, A., & Moreno-Ponce, A. (2019a). Environmental knowledge strategy: Driving success of the hospitality industry. *Management Research Review, 42*(6), 662–680. https://doi.org/10.1108/MRR-02-2018-0091

Melissen, F. (2013). Sustainable hospitality: A meaningful notion? *Journal of Sustainable Tourism, 21*(6), 810–824. https://doi.org/10.1080/09669582.2012.737797

Mierlo, B. V., & Beers, P. J. (2020). Understanding and governing learning in sustainability transitions: A review. *Environmental Innovation and Societal Transitions, 34*, 255–269. https://doi.org/10.1016/j.eist.2018.08.002

Nicolini, D. (2013). *Practice theory, work, & organization: An introduction*. Oxford University Press.

Ohlsson, J., & Johansson, P. (2010). Interactive research as a strategy for practice-based learning: Designing competence development and professional growth in local school practice. In S. Billett (Eds.), *Learning through practice* (pp. 240–255). Springer.

Prud'Homme, B., & Raymond, L. (2016). Implementation of sustainable development practices in the hospitality industry: A case study of five Canadian hotels. *International Journal of Contemporary Hospitality Management, 28*(3), 609–639. https://doi.org/10.1108/IJCHM-12-2014-0629

Rahman, I., Reynolds, D., & Svaren, S. (2012). How "green" are North American hotels? An exploration of low-cost adoption practices. *International Journal of Hospitality Management, 31*(3), 720–727. https://doi.org/10.1016/j.ijhm.2011.09.008

Reis, G. F., & Gutierrez, A. (2008). Desenvolvimento de competências multifuncionais na hotelaria. *Observatório de Inovação Do Turismo – Revista Acadêmica, 3*(2), 1–24.

Rodriguez-Antón, J. M., Alonso-Almeida, M., Celemin, M. S., & Rubio, L. (2012). Use of different sustainability management systems in the hospitality industry. The case of Spanish Hotels. *Journal of Cleaner Production, 22*(1), 76–84. https://doi.org/10.1016/j.jclepro.2011.09.024

Ruhanen, L., Weiler, B., Moyle, B. D., & Mclennan, C. J. (2015). Trends and patterns in sustainable tourism research: A 25-year bibliometric analysis. *Journal of Sustainable Tourism, 23*(4), 517–535. https://doi.org/10.1080/09669582.2014.978790

Sandberg, J. (2005). How do we justify knowledge produced within interpretive approaches? *Organizational Research Methods, 8*(1), 41–68. https://doi.org/10.1177/1094428104272000

Sandberg, J., & Dall'Alba, G. (2009). Returning to practice anew: A life-world perspective. *Organization Studies, 30*(12), 1349–1368. https://doi.org/10.1177/0170840609349872

Sandberg, J., & Pinnington, A. H. (2009). Professional competence as way of being: An existential ontological perspective. *Journal of Management Studies, 46*(7), 1138–1170. https://doi.org/10.1111/j.1467-6486.2009.00845.x

Sandberg, J., & Tsoukas, H. (2011). Grasping the logic of practice: Theorizing through practical rationality. *Academy of Management Review, 36*(2), 338–360.

Spalding, N. J., & Phillips, T. (2007). Exploring the use of vignettes: From validity to trustworthiness. *Qualitative Health Research, 17*(7), 954–962.

Su, C., & Chen, C. (2020). Does sustainability index matter to the hospitality industry? *Tourism Management, 81*, 104–158. https://doi.org/10.1016/j.tourman.2020.104158

Teixeira, R. M., & Morrison, A. (2004). Desenvolvimento de empresários em empresas de pequeno porte do setor hoteleiro: processo de aprendizagem, competências e redes de relacionamento. *Revista de Administração Contemporânea, 8*(1), 105–128. https://doi.org/10.1590/S1415-65552004000100006

Töpke, D. R., Vidal, M. P., & Soares, R. (2011). Hotelaria sustentável: preocupação com a comunidade local ou diferencial competitivo. *Observatório de Inovação Do Turismo, 6*(3), 1–21.

Wason, K. D., Polonsky, M. J., & Hyman, M. R. (2002). Designing vignette studies in marketing. *Australasian Marketing Journal, 10*(3), 41–58. https://doi.org/10.1016/S1441-3582(02)70157-2

Wiek, A., Withycombe, L., & Redman, C. L. (2011). Key competencies in sustainability: A reference framework for academic program development. *Sustainability Science, 6*(2), 203–218. https://doi.org/10.1007/s11625-011-0132-6

Wilks, T. (2004). The use of vignettes in qualitative research into social works values. *Qualitative Social Work, 3*(1), 78–87. https://doi.org/10.1177/1473325004041133

Index

Page numbers in **bold** refer to tables and those in *italic* refer to figures.

ability-motivation-opportunity (AMO) 58, 60–1
academic literature 6
active networks 98
actor-embedded knowledge and attributes 97
Adams, J. S. 107
Alonso-Almeida, M. D. M. 80
anticipatory action 161
Argyris, C. 139, 142, 143, 151
assessment of common method variance 65–6, **66**

Backhouse, C. J. 141, 150, 151
Bai, X. 22
Bakker, M. 129
Baláz, V. 125
bargaining chip 171
Barney, B. 79
Beers, P. J. 158
Bell, E. 145
Benbasat, I. 144
Bentler, P. M. 23
Besser, T. L. 46
Bharwani, S. 160
Birkinshaw, J. 22
Blackman, D. 139, 143
Bolisani, E. 18
Bontis, N. 17, 28
Boons, F. 37, 49
bootstrapping method 27
Bosworth, G. 44
Bratianu, C. 18
Bredvold, R. 53
Brewer, M. B. 127
Bryman, A. 145
Burns, T. 80
Buys, L. 122, 129

Campbell, P. 129, 130
Castelo Branco, M. 17
Cegarra-Navarro, J. G. 14, 16
Chang, C. H. 14, 21–2
Chang, J. 22
Chen, Y. S. 14, 21–2
Chervany, N. L. 125

Chin, W. W. 21, 27
Chow, W. 22
Chung, L. 19
Claver-Cortés, E. 22
co-creation process 4
codification of manuals 89
Cole, D. H. 131
collaborative actions 169
Comfort, L. K. 140
Committee of Cyclone Recovery Group 81
common method variance (CMV) 8
community-centered strategy 46, 49
community/industry-wide information sharing 92
composite reliability (CR) 24, 46, 66
conservative strategy-making 92–3
control variables 22–3, *23*
corporate social responsibility (CSR): defined 15, 17; first-order reflective constructs 22; role in SIC-PFM link 17–18
Cronbach's α index 24, 66
cultural perspectives and unexpected findings 70–2
culture, role of (Western and local) 62–4, *64*
Czakon, W. 129
Czernek, K. 43, 129

DC barriers 93, **95**
DC enablers 93, **94**
decision-making hierarchy 92
De Groot, J. I. M. 128
Delgado-Verde, M. 14
deutero-learning organizations 161
Dias, A. 3, 7, 142, 151
Dietz, T. 127
Dijkstra, T. K. 23
direct effects 67, **67**
distributive justice 107
Djurkin, J. 140
domestic visitors 148
double loop learning: case study selection and characterization 144–5; COVID-19 response strategy *150*; data collection and analysis 145–6, **147**; defined 139; innovative changes 148–9;

problem-based task force teams 146, 148; service operations design 139; systematic judges and acts 146; tourism crisis management 139; traditional "cause and effects" initiatives 139; *see also* systems thinking
Dumler, M. P. 61
Dumont, J. 58, 59
Du Plessis, M. 129
dynamic capabilities (DCs) 6; barriers of *87*; continuous adaptation 78; data collection 82, **84–5**; definition 77, 79; dynamic service/market environment 78; enablers of *86*; knowledge-based resources 88–6; mutual value creation 97–8; organic structures 78; reliance on external resources 96–7; research site 81; sampling 82, **83**; shared institutional arrangements 97–8; in tourism crisis and disaster environment 79–80; tourism operating context, Australia 81; in tourism organisations 80–1, *88*; validity and trustworthiness 87

Easterby-Smith, M. 4
embeddedness 41
Employee and Customer Social Responsibility (ECSR) 22
employee in-role green performance (EIGP) 58, 60, 69
Engström, T. 17
entrepreneurial communication 49
environmental knowledge 5
environmental performance (EP) 17
Environment and Society Social Responsibility (ESSR) 22
evolutionary theory of firms (ETF) 79
Exact Model Fit 23, **24**
explicit knowledge 105
external process constraints 93–6

Fai Pun, K. 8
Farrell, H. 44
Fields, D. 123, 125
financial capital 89–90
finite mixture-PLS (FIMIX-PLS) 30
Font, X. 18, 123, 128, 131, 160, 168
formation practices 169
formative constructs assessment 25

Garay, L. 18, 123
Ghaderi, Z. 139, 151
GHRM-EIGP relationship 70
GHRM-OCBE relationship 70
Gibson, C. B. 22
Gifford, R. 125, 128
global model assessment 23
government regulation and process 93
Grant, R. 15
Great Barrier Reef Marine Park Authority (GBRMPA) 93
green committees 123
green human resource management (GHRM): AMO framework 59; hospitality industry 58; implications 72; institutional theory 59; issues of 58; research design 64–5; REW and PEM 58
Green Intangible Capital (GIC) 16, 21
green performance management (PEM) 58
green rewards (REW) 58
Gregory, A. J. 140
Group of Twenty Countries (G20) 138
Guba, E. G. 82

Hair, J. F. Jr. 26, 65
Hallak, R. 46
Han, H. 126
Hannah, S. T. 150
Hart, S. L. 14
Henseler, J. 23
Heslinga, J. H. 139
Heterotrait-Monotrait Ratio (HTMT) 24, 46, 67
Hill, R. 111
Hjalager, A. M. 50
Hoang, H. T. 63
Hoarau, H. 38, 43
Hockerts, K. N. 17
Hofstede, G. 58, 63
Holcomb, J. L. 18, 29
Holste, J. S. 123, 125
Hotel Performance (HP) 17
hotel sector, Spain 20–1, *21*
Huang, C. L. 14, 22
Hu, L. T. 23
Hult, G. T. M. 9
human-based resources (internal actors) 90–1
Human Resources Managers (HRM) 20
Huynh, T. L. D. 53

inbound vouchers 148
indirect effects 67, **68**
intellectual capital 16
interactional justice 107
Intergovernmental Platform on Biodiversity and Ecosystem Services (IPBES) 110
internal process restriction 92–3
interpersonal skills 161
Iorio, R. 128

Jaakkola, E. 7, 123
Jaaron, A. A. M. 8, 140, 141, 150, 151
Jabareen, Y. 7, 106–7
Jabbour, C. J. C. 59, 64, 66
Jackson, M. C. 141
Jang, Y. J. 127
Jansen, J. J. 46
Janssen, O. 58, 60, 66
Jiang, K. 60–2
Jiang, Y. 8, 78
justice-as-recognition 108

Kelliher, F. 129, 130
Khoshkhoo, M. H. I. 142
Kim, M. 127

Kim, T. 17, 28
knowledge acquisition 41
knowledge assimilation 41–4, *43*
knowledge-based resources 88–6
knowledge culture 152
knowledge management (KM) 1–2, 121–3; asymmetry in power 104; business decision-making process 3; continuous and unprecedented events 103; destination competitiveness 103; local stakeholders' willingness 104; organisational justice 104, 107–8; *see also* knowledge sharing; local knowledge; organisational learning (OL)
knowledge sharing 105; sustainable tourism development process 108–9
knowledge stock concept 50
knowledge transfer gap 124–6, *126*
Kock, N. 66
Kornilaki, M. 123, 128
Kraleva, N. 143
Kramer, R. 130
Kropp, F. 46
Kung, F. H. 14, 22

latent variable scores 23
Lau, C. M. 63
Lecuyer, L. 108, 110
Lester, P. B. 150
Lima Rodrigues, L. 17
Lincoln, Y. S. 82
Liu, C.-H. S. 130, 143, 151
local knowledge management 103; discrimination of 109; justice-as-recognition 109; knowledge management 39–40; potential and realized phases 40; power asymmetry 110–11; safe space framework 111–13, *112*; and SBMs 39; sustainability issue 106; tacit and explicit 40; TLE-specific mechanisms **40**
local worldviews and knowledge system 110
long-term staff members 89
Lüdeke-Freund, F. 37, 49
Lyles, M. 4
Lynes, J. 160, 168

Maak, T. 124
Mai, T. 140
Mansour, H. E. 80
Martínez-Martínez, A. 14, 16, 123
Maxwell, J. A. 107
Mayer, R. C. 121, 125
McCracken, G. D. 145
McKnight, H.D. 125
McTiernan, C. 7
measured latent marker variable (MLMV) method 8
measurement model assessment 23–5, **25**
mediation analysis 27
Meija-Morelos, J. H. 60
Mierlo, B. V. 158
Mihalic, T. 17
Miller, N. 46
moderation analysis 67–8, *68*, **68**

Molina-Azorín, J. F. 64
Morrison, A. 44
motivating employees 59, 69
mutual value creation 97–8

Nadalipour, Z. 142
Nathai-Balkissoon, M. 8
NemecRudez, H. 17
New Environmental Paradigm (NEP) 127
Ngo, H. Y. 63
Nonaka, I. 6
normative behavior 161
Nunkoo, R. 130
Nyaupane, G. P. 139, 140

Ogbonnaya, C. 62
opez-Gamero, M. D. 14
organisational citizenship behavior for the environment (OCBE) 58–62, 69–70
organisational justice 104, 107–8
organisational learning (OL) 160, 170–1; defined 1–2; ecological and socio-cultural issues 3; inter-organisational collaborations 4; personal protective equipment 3; utilisation of knowledge 4
organisation decision-making process 92
orientation and awareness practices 169

Paille, P. 22, 60, 61, 66
Parisi, C. 17
Parker, L. 19
partial least squares (PLS) path modelling 21, 46
Penrose, E. 79
Peric, M. 140
Perrini, F. 123, 130, 131
person-organization fit 60
Pham, D. T. 140, 143
Pham, N. T. 59, 62, 64, 66
Phillips, P. 23
Pine, R. 23
Pinzone, M. 69
playgrounds of creativity 49
PLS prediction-oriented segmentation (PLS-POS) 30
Podsakoff, P. M. 21
Popoli, P. 17
Porter, B. A. 49
power asymmetry 110–11
practice-based approach to learning: assembling teams 163–4; combative and impact-minimization practices 167; competencies 161; defined 158; events department 164–5; hotelier lived world experiences 159–61; hoteliers' practices, profit increament 170–1; intertwining perspectives *159*; overview of methods *163*; recycling waste separation 168–70; researchers 158; sustainability competencies, hospitality sector 160–1; sustainability practices 171–2; vignettes 162; welfare practices 168

problem-based task force teams 146, 148
pro-environmental knowledge 122, 123

Quang, T. D. 139
Queensland Parks and Wildlife Service (QPWS) 93

Raineri, N. 66
Raisi, H. 105
Ramezan, M. 151
Rao, Y. 143
Rastegar, R. 5, 7, 104, 110
recognition injustice 109
reflective constructs assessment 24
regional tourism organisation (RTO) 92
relational resources (external actors) 91–2
remote leaders 92
Ren, S. 69
Renwick, D. W. S. 58
resource-based view (RBV) 14, 79
Richards, G. 41
Ringle, C. M. 65
Ritchie, B. W. 78, 139, 143
Roberts, N. 25
Rodriguez-Giron, S. 143
Rousseau, D. 130
Roux, D. J. 123, 127, 129
Ruhanen, L. 5, 7, 157
Ruhland, S. K. 127
Russo, A. 123, 130, 131
Ryan, C. 59

SABI-Iberian Balance Sheet Analysis System and Alimarket 20
Saeed, B. B. 58, 62, 69
Schnake, M. 61
Schön, D. 139, 143, 151
Schuitema, G. 128
Seddon, J. 140, 141
Senge, P. M. 142, 143
Sharratt, M. 129
Shepherd, D. A. 82
Shipton, H. 142, 150
single loop learning 160
Skålén, P. 53
slack resources (financial) 89–90
small and medium sized tourism enterprises (SMTEs): environmental behaviour 128–9; managers 121; pro-environmental knowledge, message and medium 129–30; pro-environmental knowledge transfer partnerships 121; sociology and political science 120–1
Smith, C. 140
Smith, S. L. J. 130
Social and Economic Intangible Capital (SEIC) 16, 21
social capital 5, 130–1
Social Exchange Theory 108
Sollund, R. 140
Stahl, G. K. 63
Stalker, G. M. 80

standardised root mean square residual (SRMR) index 23
Steg, L. 126
Stern, P. C. 127
Stone-Geisser Q^2 test 25
Stone, M. T. 139, 140
strategic knowledge management (SKM): economic, social and environmental goals 22; in SIC-PFM link: formulation 18–19; humanistic culture 19; human resource practices 19; intangible assets 18; organisational design and technological platform 19; vision and diagnosis 18
strategic thinking 161
structural equation modelling (SEM) 21, 46
structural model assessment 25–7, **47**
Subramaniam, M. 22
success trap 80
Supanti, D. 130
Surroca, J. 17
sustainable business models (SBMs): elements 37; and TLEs 39
Sustainable Intangible Capital (SIC): assets 15; definition 15, 21; intellectual capital-based view 15; and performance 16–17; resource-based view 15
sustainable knowledge management 4–6
systemic reasoning 161
systems thinking: double loop learning 142–4; and organic structure 141–2; and tourism companies 140–1, **141**

tacit knowledge 6, 105, 111, 121–3, 122
Talib, P. 160
Thatcher, J. 25
tourism companies 140–1, **141**
tourism crisis and disaster environment 79–80
tourism lifestyle entrepreneurs' (TLEs): community spirit 38; financial model 39; ideological concept of sustainability 38; local knowledge management 38; nonfinancial criteria 38; qualitative method 44–5, 48; quantitative method 45–8; supply chain infrastructure 39; theoretical gaps 38; value proposition 39; *see also* local knowledge management
tourism policies and local inclusion 108–9
travel and luggage insurance policies 2
Triple Bottom Line (TBL) 14, 15
2017 Tropical Cyclone (TC) Debbie 78–9
trust: based decisions 124–6, *126*; self-efficacy *126*, 126–8
Tučková, Z. 59, 64, 66
Turker, D. 22
Turner, J. C. 127

Upchurch, R. S. 127
Usoro, A. 129

Valizade, D. 62
Valtonen, A. 41

value-belief-norm (VBN) theory of environmentalism 127
Van der Werff, L. 124, 125, 128
Vanneste, D. 143
Variance Accounted For (VAF)² 27
variance inflation factor (VIF) 25
vignette response analysis 163–9, **169–70**
Vlek, C. 126
Von Krogh, G. 18

Waddock, S. 17
Wäger, M. 79
Wang, C. L. 80
Warner, K. S. 79
Wason, K. D. 162
Weidenfeld, A. 50
Wenger, E. 127
White, A. L. 17
Wiek, A. 161
Williams, A. M. 125
Williams, T. A. 82
Witt, M. A. 63
World Heritage Site (WHS) 109

Xiao, H. 130

Yachin, J. M. 38, 49–51
Yamagishi, T. 128
Yin, R. 144
Youndt, M. A. 22
Yperen, N. W. 58, 60, 66

Zack, M. 18
Zaragoza-Sáez, P. C. 7, 142
Zhang, C. 41, 53
Zhang, Y. 58, 59
Zhao, H. 46
Zhou, M. 107

Milton Keynes UK
Ingram Content Group UK Ltd.
UKHW020641210624
444299UK00004B/11